Crime in England
1550-1800

Crime in England
1550-1800

Edited by

J. S. COCKBURN

PRINCETON UNIVERSITY PRESS
PRINCETON, NEW JERSEY

Copyright © 1977 by J.S. Cockburn

Published by Princeton University Press,
Princeton, New Jersey

Photoset by Red Lion Setters, Holborn
Printed and bound in Great Britain at the
University Printing House, Cambridge

Library of Congress Cataloging in Publication Data
Main entry under title:

Crime in England, 1550-1800.

  Bibliography: p.
  Includes index.
  1. Crime and criminals — England — History —
Addresses, essays, lectures. 2. Criminal justice,
Administration of — England — History — Addresses,
essays, lectures. I. Cockburn, J.S.
HV6943.C74   364'.0942   77-2867
ISBN 0-691-05258-1

Contents

Notes on Contributors

J.H. BAKER is University Lecturer in Law and a Fellow of St Catharine's College, Cambridge. His publications include *An Introduction to English Legal History* (1971) and numerous articles on English law and legal history.

J.M. BEATTIE, Professor of History, University of Toronto, is the author of *The English Court in the Reign of George I* (1967) and of several articles, the most recent dealing with crime and punishment in eighteenth-century England.

J.S. COCKBURN, Associate Professor of History, University of Maryland, is the author of *A History of English Assizes 1558-1714* (1972) and editor of the multi-volume *Calendar of Assize Records*.

T.C. CURTIS, Senior Lecturer in Modern History, Newcastle Polytechnic, has written several articles and an unpublished Manchester University Ph.D. thesis on crime in seventeenth-century England.

G.R.ELTON is Professor of English Constitutional History in the University of Cambridge and a Fellow of Clare College. He has written extensively on Tudor England, most notably in *The Tudor Revolution in Government* (1953), *England under the Tudors* (1955) and *Policy and Police: the enforcement of the Reformation in the age of Thomas Cromwell* (1972).

M.J.INGRAM, a graduate of Oxford, was Junior Research Fellow in History, King's College, Cambridge, from 1971 to 1975. His current interests centre on the work of ecclesiastical courts in early modern England and the English equivalents of *'charivari'*.

L.A. KNAFLA is Associate Professor of History at the University of Calgary. He has published several articles on English legal history and is the author of *Law and Politics in Jacobean England* (1977).

P. LINEBAUGH, Assistant Professor of History, University of Rochester, is a contributor to and editor of *Albion's Fatal Tree: Crime and Society in Eighteenth-Century England* (1975). He is currently revising for publication his Ph.D. thesis on crime and the poor in eighteenth-century London.

A.D.J. MACFARLANE, Senior Research Fellow in History, King's College, Cambridge, and University Lecturer in Social Anthropology, is the author of *The Family life of Ralph Josselin* (1970) and *Witchcraft in Tudor and Stuart England* (1970).

R.W. MALCOLMSON, Associate Professor of History, Queen's University, Kingston, Ontario, is author of *Popular Recreations in English Society 1700-1850* (1973).

P.B. MUNSCHE is a doctoral student at the University of Toronto and is currently writing a general study of the English game laws from the Restoration to 1831.

J.A. SHARPE, a graduate of Oxford, is Lecturer in History at the University of York. He is preparing a study of crime in seventeenth-century Essex.

W.J. SHEEHAN, Assistant Professor of History, Sul Ross State University, Texas, is currently revising for publication his Ph.D. thesis on the London prison system in the eighteenth century.

List of Abbreviations

APC: Acts of the Privy Council of England, 32 vols, ed J.R. Dasent (1890-1907)

Baker, 'Newgate Reports': J.H. Baker, 'Criminal Justice at Newgate 1616-1627: Some Manuscript Reports in the Harvard Law School', *The Irish Jurist*, new ser., VIII (1973), pp.307-22

Beattie, 'Pattern of Crime': J.M. Beattie, 'The Pattern of Crime in England 1660-1800', *Past & Present*, LXII (1974), pp.47-95

Bellamy, *Crime in the Later Middle Ages:* J.G. Bellamy, *Crime and Public Order in England in the Later Middle Ages* (1973)

BL: British Library
  Add.: Additional MS
  Harl.: Harley MS
  Lansd.: Lansdowne MS

Blackstone, *Commentaries:* W. Blackstone, *Commentaries on the Laws of England* (several editions)

CLRO: Corporation of London Record Office
  Ald. Papers: Papers and Reports of the Court of Aldermen 1666-1800
  CLC Jnl: Journal of the City Lands Committee
  Jnl: Journal of the Minutes of the Court of Common Council
  PD.: Printed Documents
  Rep.: Repertories of the Minutes of the Court of Aldermen

Cockburn, *Assizes:* J.S. Cockburn, *A History of English Assizes 1558-1714* (Cambridge 1972)

Coke, *Institutes:* E. Coke, *Institutes of the Laws of England*, 4 pts (1628-1644)

CSPD: Calendar of State Papers Domestic, 91 vols, ed R. Lemon *et al.* (1856-[1964])

CUL: Cambridge University Library

Dalton, *Countrey Justice:* M. Dalton, *The Countrey Justice* (several editions)

Depositions from York Castle: Depositions from the Castle of York, relating to offences committed in the Northern Counties in the Seventeenth Century, ed J. Raine (Surtees Soc. XL, 1861)

Eden, *Principles:* [W. Eden], *Principles of Penal Law* (1771)

ERO: Essex Record Office

Form and Method: A Form and Method of Trial of Commoners (1709 edn)

Hale, *Pleas:* M. Hale, *History of the Pleas of the Crown*, 2 vols (1736)

Hawkins, *Pleas:* W. Hawkins, *Pleas of the Crown* (1771 edn)

HLS: Harvard Law School

HMC: Reports of the Historical Manuscripts Commission (as cited)

Holdsworth, *History:* W.S. Holdsworth, *A History of English Law*, 16 vols (1922-64)

Lambard, *Eirenarcha:* W. Lambarde, *Eirenarcha, or, of the Office of the Justices of Peace* (several editions)

Langbein, *Prosecuting Crime:* J.H. Langbein, *Prosecuting Crime in the Renaissance* (Cambridge, Mass 1974)

MRO: Greater London Record Office, Middlesex Records

Prisons: Subject Series of British Parliamentary Papers on Prisons (Shannon 1969)

PRO: Public Record Office
  ASSI: Assizes
  C: Chancery
  CP: Common Pleas
  E: Exchequer
  KB: King's Bench
  PCOM: Prison Commission
  SC: Special Collections
  SP: State Papers
  STAC: Star Chamber

QS: quarter sessions

Radzinowicz, *History:* L. Radzinowicz, *A History of English Criminal Law and its Administration from 1750*, 4 vols (1948-68)

RO: Record Office

Smith, *De Republica:* T. Smith, *De Republica Anglorum* (1583)

SPCK: Society for Promoting Christian Knowledge

Staunford, *Plees:* W. Staunforde, *Les Plees del Coron* (1574 edn)

Stephen, *History:* J.F. Stephen, *A History of the Criminal Law of England,*
    3 vols (1883)

Thomas, *Religion and Magic:* K.V. Thomas, *Religion and the Decline of
    Magic* (1971)

*Transportation: Subject Series of British Parliamentary Papers on Trans-
    portation and Penal Servitude* (Shannon 1969)

VCH: Victoria County History (as cited)

WRO: Wiltshire Record Office

Unless otherwise stated, the place of publication of works cited in the
footnotes is London. In dating, the year has been taken to begin on 1
January. Quotations have been modernized.

Preface

The decision to bring together these eleven essays on crime and criminal law administration in the early modern period originated in two closely related concerns. First, the desire to promote a dialogue between scholars applying, often independently, a range of different techniques to related historical sources; and second, the need to provide a rational base for the increasing number of students approaching this topic for the first time, as well as for those contemplating further work in a field which has now reached a decisive stage of development.

Despite the illusion of novelty created by the recent flurry of publications on law and order in early modern England, such studies have in fact a surprisingly long tradition. Indeed, this volume might well be viewed as a product of the third wave of interest in historical crime, following as it does the orthodox nineteenth-century treatments of Pike and Stephen and the equally deferential accounts of Holdsworth and Radzinowicz and, much more closely, the pioneer work on legal records which began in the 1960s. Most of the essays collected here reflect, to some extent, this historiographical progression. Many older views are modified or rejected, as are some of the flaws in interpretation which inevitably accompanied the opening-up of hitherto unused manuscript sources. The need to rationalize the historiography of crime is crystallized in the extensive critical bibliography which follows the essays.

A similar concern to provide an authoritative and easily accessible base for further study underlies the inclusion of an account of criminal courts and procedure. In addition to forming an essential background to the individual findings presented here, this chapter, drawn mainly from printed legal sources, serves to isolate another important theme — the increasingly apparent gap between the fact and theory of criminal process. As Professor Elton emphasizes, these procedural uncertainties demand priority treatment. We cannot hope to exploit fully the wealth of court records without a better understanding of the context in which they originated. This is difficult terrain demanding particular expertise, and it is not, perhaps, one into which the uninitiated should be encouraged to venture too boldly. But even allowing for this, the list of topics requiring more or less urgent investigation is almost infinite. Several are isolated in the introduction and many others are implicit in the essays themselves. It is slightly depressing to realize that, despite their apparent diversity, these chapters taken together discuss delinquency in only six English counties and treat in detail only three of a multitude of indictable offences. Substantive law, complex and decisive though it might be in criminal prosecutions, is barely touched upon.

In such a complex and underdeveloped area the value of meaningful communication between the various branches of the historical profession now interested in historical crime can hardly be overestimated. Sociologists cannot afford to ignore those painstaking institutional, procedural and legal inquiries which are slowly establishing the context and limitations of court records. Similarly, in seeking explanations for fluctuations in prosecuted crime or in patterns of acquittal or punishment, legal historians must take into account such unfamiliar socio-economic factors as war, dearth, social structure and class responses. Even in a state of enlightened cooperation, this would be a difficult enough field; for those attempting to work in isolation its complexities may well prove fatal.

This realization finds independent confirmation throughout the volume. While illustrating the variety of questions to be asked and the diversity of techniques available for tackling them, these essays also share other common features. Most importantly, they are, almost without exception, unmarked by the ideological biases which mar both older accounts and some more recent discussions of eighteenth-century criminality. Here manuscript sources have been allowed to speak for themselves, a slightly unfashionable courtesy which has in turn yielded significant results. The discovery that investigations utilizing different techniques may lead to identical conclusions about the reliability of a particular source or the biases of law enforcement agencies tends to confirm the value of empirical inquiry and the validity of the diverse techniques illustrated here.

Finally, one cannot fail to be struck by the caution which pervades this book. To those accustomed to a broad historical canvas, thesis-laden and consistently 'provocative' studies, some of the findings presented here may seem local and conservative to the point of redundancy. Viewed, however, in the context of sensationalism, idealogical bias and uninformed generalization with which this topic has been traditionally associated, a series of essays dealing with essentially practical problems represents a potentially decisive innovation. If this book succeeds only in stimulating a more careful and coordinated approach to the questions facing students of historical crime, it will more than justify the essentially modest ambitions of those who have contributed to it.

J.S.C.

Introduction: Crime and the Historian

G.R. ELTON

Crime and the criminal eternally fascinate; they rather than politics supply the journalist's daily bread, nor is this a particularly modern order of preference. Our popular newspapers fill their pages with crime because that is what sells copies, and even a mildly sensational case fills the court with spectators; the eighteenth century avidly read the *Newgate Calendar* (as sordid a publication as ever was the *Daily Thingummy* or the London *Moon*), gaped at prisoners through bars and attended executions; the sixteenth enjoyed on the stage nothing better than criminals whether contemporary (*Arden of Feversham*) or historical (*Timon of Athens*). Since at least until the eighteenth century the accident of record survival biases the weight of the evidence towards the work of law courts, the people of whom we are most likely to know — at least below the level of the great and powerful — are those that came into conflict with the law. And yet, the present outburst of social history has been slow to turn its attention to crime, leaving that matter still to the kind of writer whose books bear titles like *Olden Days Punishments* or *Highwaymen I have Known*. The dearth of serious studies forces the historian to rely on Sir Leon Radzinowicz's massive *History of English Criminal Law and its Administration from 1750*, for his purposes much too much a lawyer's book, with its deferential attitude to 'the authorities' and its rather uncritical treatment of sources. Perhaps the fact that crime has been little studied owes something to so many lawyers' contempt for the criminal law and its practice, thought to be intellectually undemanding and professionally unrewarding.

Very recently, however, the real historical investigation of the subject would seem at last to have begun.[1] This book explores some of the possible lines. As the frequent signals of doubt, uncertainty and cautious reserve indicate, the essays here assembled are the work of scholars still pioneering in something like a wilderness. They approach crime and the criminal from a concern with social relationships and their effect upon the individual, a worthy and potentially fruitful reason for their studies but also one with hidden dangers, because it is liable to throw back upon the past distinctly present-day preoccupations and concepts. Despite his reliance on some doubtful generalizations of Lawrence Stone's, Mr Sharpe (pp.96-97) sees the difficulties, and his warnings on the point are well taken. However, since these are early days and since some of the snags are at present only dimly discerned, there may be virtue in taking a look — no doubt a look that could be better informed — at the problems facing the historian of crime.

The issues resolve themselves into three: the identification of the subject matter, the machinery used for coping with crime, and the analysis of the criminal material discovered. It is the last that really has attracted the new interest: most of our authors ask questions about the amount of crime committed, the proportions ascribable to different kinds of offences, the people committing crimes (analysed by sex, social standing, age and ultimate fate): crime as a social phenomenon, pursued through time, is the topic of concern. In the present volume only Dr Baker thoroughly attends to the second issue, though several other contributors — and especially Dr Beattie — realize that only a precise knowledge of the machinery can really unlock the meaning of the record. But none of the contributors asks the first and fundamental question, mainly because their acquaintance with modern theory makes them suppose that the answer is obvious.

I

Historians anxious to study crime in the sixteenth, seventeenth and eighteenth centuries must first realize that their subject was not known then by that name. The word was current, but it lacked precise meaning, especially in the law; it rates no entry in Giles Jacob's *Law Dictionary*, an excellent guide. In studying crime we therefore study something like an artificial construct, a compound comprising breaches of the law which at the time of being committed were regarded as diverse and separate. What Jacob knew were felonies and trespasses, the former identifiable by the simple fact that they involved capital punishment. His definitions therefore depended on the identification of penalties, on the possibility of conviction in a court with predictable consequences. This is not the definition present to the writers of these essays who — as a rule tacitly — equate crime with breaches of social norms. A social criterion in place of a legal one has its attractions: it provides a comprehensive category, it turns 'crime' into a tool for analysing social standards and behaviour, and it offers opportunities for moral disapproval. But it does have the disadvantage of using a category unfamiliar to the people studied: it thus introduces occasions for confusion. While most of our contributors confine themselves to offences punishable by the secular law, Mr Sharpe and Dr Ingram reach out to include the work of the archdeacons' courts. Yet it is unwise to throw theft and adultery into one bag because contemporaries did not regard them as of one kind at all: the search for social disapproval as the common element in 'crime' is misdirected from the start when it is assumed that all discoverable offences are descriptive of a single stance. The society in question treated the protection of property and the prevention of illicit sexual relationships very differently, expressing its beliefs by showing respect for the king's courts and contempt for those of the Church. Dr Macfarlane's familiar analysis of witchcraft in Essex stretches the category 'crime' beyond what it can safely bear; the fabric tears, and in that essay we are a long way from the themes studied by the rest.

There is a mildly anachronistic confusion here. It is taken for granted that laws are intended to provide against misdeeds which carry social disapproval. In fact, the law of that age provided against misdeeds thought to be unlawful — contrary to principles at least believed to be eternal and not socially conditioned — and even though, no doubt, that belief at times embodied a measure of self-deception it had consequences: it sometimes led to the prohibition of actions which carried at least partial social approval, such as common immoralities, theft occasioned by hunger, killing in self-defence — approval which could extend so far as biased acquittals of those indubitably guilty in the law. The case of John Ayly cited by Mr Sharpe (p.98), for twenty-three years regularly denounced in the archdeacon's court and yet never effectively punished and in no way socially ostracized, should act as a warning: offenders of his kind cannot be lumped together with vagabonds and thieves of whom authority disposed in short order and with general approval. Treating crime as a social rather than a legal phenomenon further leads the historian to mishandle the problem of enforcement; he can come to see social significance in laws which were applied very haphazardly or even allowed to fall into desuetude. More particularly, it makes impossible a serious study of pardoning, a study which, partly for that reason, no one has yet undertaken for our period; and yet pardoning lies at the heart of the question of enforcement and itself bears heavily upon the question of social attitudes.

The legal criterion, therefore, will distinguish between systems of law as well as systems of courts operating in the realm, producing clearer results. Offences against the law of the Church are not crimes, even though they may constitute disruptive or antisocial activity. In the thinking of the day they were sins — offences against God not man. Sin lacked the strictly criminal element of deliberate and malicious intent against another person's rights which, so far as a principle can be discovered, underlay the common-law definition of the various activities which deserve to be called criminal. It also lacked human enforceability, the appointment of tangible punishment in body or purse, especially as penances imposed ceased to be done. Defamation (one of the archdeacon's main preoccupations) lies on the borderline between sin and crime, as the Star Chamber recognized when it extended its competence over it; its renewed relegation, after 1640, to the spiritual courts left the law of slander in an unsatisfactorily primitive condition, very poorly defined in a few relevant statutes. Defamation was on the point of becoming a crime, so to speak. Strictly, however, the term crime — doubtful though it must remain — should be reserved for offences punishable in the secular courts, though it would be too restrictive to confine it to pleas at the king's suit, a definition applicable only to 'major crimes' — another otherwise uncertain category. In fact, even if we omit sins from the calendar, we still need to make important distinctions because the various types of offence recognized by contemporaries received different treatment, were subject to different processes and ended in different ways, with the result (among other things) that some may be readily studied and some tend to escape historical investigation altogether. All of them, however, still call for investigation not of their occurrence or incidence but of their very nature.

The first category of criminal offences — the real crimes, as it were — comprised treasons and felonies, punishable by death. In the lists of triable misbehaviours found in pardons or charges to juries, murder was usually mentioned separately, but it really constituted a felony at common law. Because these capital crimes pose relatively few problems to the historian, they have been taken for well understood, but some real difficulties remain. Statute often added to and sometimes took away from them, especially in the reign of Henry VIII and in the eighteenth century. That fact is well enough known, but no one seems to have asked why this should have been so and exactly what it meant; it is taken for granted that 'society' was savagely inclined and its rulers sufficiently frightened, for some reason or other, to pile on the felonies. In actual fact, these outbursts of felony-making by Act of Parliament are much less straightforward, especially that of the eighteenth century, and before conclusions are drawn from them they need to be very particularly investigated, without those ready-made assumptions about class interest which bedevil these discussions. The unsolved questions multiply. If the ruling classes really wanted more frightful laws against thieves and robbers, why did they not secure a higher percentage of convictions and why did they suffer — indeed, in the persons of the judges, encourage — contrived acquittals and the substitution of penalties well short of what the law could exact? A good many of those statutory crimes would appear to have been punishable at law anyway: why were arsonists constructively tried under the Waltham Black Act when arson was an ancient common law felony? Why did the new laws add crimes in so piecemeal and specific a fashion — and again crimes which do not look new at all? 15 George II, c. 34, which made stealing from shipwrecks a felony, would seem to have singled out a special case already comprehended in the law concerning larceny; the Act in fact referred to good laws already in existence. Why were so few of those many laws apparently ever applied in court? Legislating about theft could reduce the effectiveness of the common law. Thus it was grand larceny to steal linen and other materials, but when this felony was made statutory by 4 George II, c. 16 strict interpretation reduced the possibility of conviction; an amending Act (18 George II, c.27) explained the need for further legislation on the ground that 'the respective goods and wares, the stealing whereof from the respective places therein mentioned and described is by the said Act intended to be prevented' had not been listed 'with sufficient certainty'. Stealing sheep and cattle was a felony at law; yet Parliament passed the Act 14 George II, c. 6 against sheepstealing, only to find it necessary next year to extend it to cattle, doubts having arisen over the limitation of the statute (15 George II, c. 34). It would seem necessary to look at every one of these statutory felonies — at the way they came into existence and the manner in which they were applied. I suspect that a proper investigation would reveal a story commonplace in eighteenth-century legislation when individuals or very small pressure groups proved regularly able to put their pet projects onto the statute book.[2] If that was the case, there is manifestly a danger in using that statute book to discover general social attitudes or even the attitudes of the often falsely classified upper classes.

Still, the problems of felonies are open to successful investigation; things get worse as one moves down the scale to lesser offences. Trespass started as a genuine form of crime but by the time in question had in the main become a means for resolving the civil disputes of private parties: it should be left out of the count, at least from about the middle of the sixteenth century onwards. Yet the kind of deed which it originally described had not ceased just because the action for trespass had moved into the realm of useful fictions. Breaches of the peace, that mainstay of both quarter sessions and petty sessions, never received proper classification. There is a whole series of illicit acts — let us call them misdemeanours, a term known to the age but never given precise content — which at least in the sixteenth and early seventeenth centuries were largely left to the discretion of magistrates, with very little guidance from law and statute alike; and since subversion short of treason fell into this category (rumour-mongering, for instance, or *scandalum magnatum*, very inadequately legislated for in the reign of Elizabeth) it is evident that any analysis of crime must seriously concern itself with this sort of thing. It is at least possible that the prevalence of offences against property, unsurprisingly discovered in the records of assizes and quarter sessions, springs from the fact that those were the main offences triable there, whereas a good deal of lesser criminal activity (beatings, assaults, various forms of cheating, creation of nuisances) were dealt with in manorial courts, municipal courts, or by single justices acting informally. Summary jurisdiction poses very great problems because it so often left little record and cannot be presumed to have followed a common form. Among all these offences, indictability ought perhaps to offer a good means of distinction, being precise and well understood at the time; unfortunately indictment applied to varieties of offences, and presenting juries included dung-heaps left in streets together with larceny and homicide.

The question may also be raised whether 'crime' should not include offences like fraud, extortion or embezzlement, none of them felonies and ill provided for in the procedural law of the usual commissions (oyer and terminer, and of the peace). Many cases in Star Chamber (incapable of dealing with felonies and treasons) and Chancery involved what would now be called crimes, left out in current studies. Jacob treated fraud as the business of equity, extortion as defined in statutory expositions of the common law and confined to offences by office-holders, and embezzlement as nonexistent. On the other hand, I am inclined to omit *qui tam* actions on the so-called statutes penal or popular.[3] Though they had something of the character of near-criminal legislation and set fines and forfeitures, their purpose was to regulate manufacture and commerce: and if breaches of such regulations are to be accounted criminal the theme loses its last chance of cohesion. Certainly no seventeenth-century lawyer would have understood a single category which comprised both felonies and these kind of statutes. Yet, if they are left out, what do we do about smuggling?

Lastly, we must return to sins punished — or rather, rarely punished with any effect — by the Church courts. Once they have been distinguished in order not to confuse the issue, they must be brought back into the picture because they did concern conduct against which legal action was possible and which did carry potential penalties, however spiritual.

Thus the task — the primary task — of defining the subject matter of a history of crime involves two steps. Firstly, it is necessary to abandon modern categories based on the concepts of social norms, social justice and antisocial behaviour, in order to identify contemporary categories based on legal definition or the absence of it, to analyse the distinctions to be made here, and to resolve their many technical problems (through time, as well). Secondly, one needs to reintroduce those modern concepts in order to discover what possibly criminal activities the strict analysis may have eliminated and whether they should be added to the area of inquiry. Once this is done it is possible to study criminality in the early modern period.

II

The problems of the machinery of repression are, on the face of them, less daunting. Much of it is well known. Dr Baker's chapter in this volume quite admirably delineates the procedural law of trials upon indictment, and the operations of the ecclesiastical courts (where especially cases *ex officio* come within our purview) have been adequately described more than once.[4] As Dr Baker shows, we are much better informed about the trial of felonies than of misdemeanours (even when indictable), but so long as offenders were indicted we know reasonably well how their cases were meant to be handled. Two questions nevertheless remain: how accurately did actual trials follow the rules of process, and what happened to persons accused outside the machinery of indictment and *ex officio* proceedings?

Dr Baker himself raises the question of whether the evidence of cases supports the notion that criminal process at common law was governed by strict rules. This must at present await investigation, though the indications in general are that the answer is yes — with exceptions; we want to learn how serious and frequent those were. As late as the reign of Henry VIII (perhaps later?) juries sometimes behaved in ways contrary to the supposed rules; they could take on tasks proper to prosecution or defence, and they were assuredly not free from pressures and corruptions. A good history of the post-medieval jury, derived from what actually happened, is urgently needed. How careful were the courts of their own principles in interpreting penal (i.e. crime-creating) statutes? They held, we are told, that such acts must be interpreted strictly, that is as applicable only to offences indubitably intended in them. Yet throughout the eighteenth century the judges would appear to have used the notorious Waltham Black Act against alleged criminals whose misdeeds had absolutely nothing to do with the origins or original purposes of the Act: a singular, possibly unique, case of their enlarging the effects of a penal statute which has misled historians into ill-considered views of eighteenth-century Parliaments and supposed class legislation.[5] Real mysteries continue to hang about an important stage in every trial, namely about what happened after the jury's verdict. How did some convicted persons secure the calling up of the case into King's Bench (by *certiorari* or *mandamus*), to have their indictments declared invalid or to plead a pardon? Why did others fail to do so? What part did the judges play in this? How regular was the practice of binding persons acquitted in sureties of good behaviour or for appearance? I am familiar with such things happening in the sixteenth century: did practice change? All these are questions that need to be resolved from a study of actual trials, whereas actual trials can be successfully studied only with a clear understanding of the procedure which ruled what went on: a circular problem not incapable of solution, but at any rate enjoining caution upon the operator.

The biggest procedural problem, at best quarter solved, concerns the initiation of prosecutions: how was it that people found themselves facing a court? The king's courts relied on presentment by jury; the Church courts upon presentment at visitations. Both thus originally thrust the responsibility upon the community and relied on 'common knowledge', not on detection. By our period the situation had certainly altered quite a lot as indictments came increasingly to be drawn on behalf of the crown, with the presenting jury reduced to an opinion on the evidence offered; but that merely raises the question of how offences came to the notice of those responsible for putting bills of indictment before the jury. We need to learn a lot more about how information came to be gathered, processed and introduced. Thanks to Thomas Cromwell, we know a good deal of the manner in which trials for treason originated, but for ordinary felonies we have only a beginning of an understanding, especially as Dr Langbein is inclined to take the words of statutes as describing actual practice.[6] Since we urgently need to comprehend why some people were sucked into the machinery of criminal process while others, who had committed the same offences, were not, we want more searching concentration on that first stage in the process.

For offences outside the strictly criminal machinery, the dark areas of the unknown are larger. Much 'antisocial behaviour' escaped the clutches of indicting juries and archdeacons' visitations, and yet (as we have seen) it needs to be taken into account if a study of crime and criminality is to be complete and balanced. In this respect the studies in the present volume are deficient because they concentrate on a particular layer of the phenomenon — the layer defined by local enforcement in superior courts. By concentrating — as following the obvious evidence rightly leads them to — on assizes, quarter sessions and archdeacons' courts, the investigators miss levels that may be called both higher and lower. On the one hand, they omit the work of the conciliar courts, of the King's Bench itself, and of special commissions of oyer and terminer; on the other they stop short of courts leet. As for the Church, episcopal courts tend to get ignored. Now in some of these omitted regions the regular procedural machinery described applied in theory: special commissions relied on indictment (though one still needs to know something about who the commissioners were), and consistory courts used the same methods as archdeacons', only more so. But what happened in Star Chamber and manors differed in principle; this needs to be allowed for and, where not yet known, clarified. When it comes to summary procedure and arbitration, we have just about everything still to learn. The specific questions asked by students of crime depend for their answers on a really instructed understanding of what went on.

III

That brings us to the real concerns of our contributors who all, in various ways, want to know not what constituted crime or how crimes were dealt with but what crimes predominated and why, who committed crimes and what happened to criminals. All these essays, pursuing such themes from various approaches and in different contexts, stress the uncertainties and insufficiencies of their findings. In particular, it is conceded over and over again that no reliable statistics can be compiled because the evidence does not permit any satisfactory use of quantifying techniques. I must emphasize that I am in no way criticizing the authors for this: on the contrary, they deserve every praise for avoiding spurious certainties and the easy road of ready-made opinions leading to influential but unproven conclusions. All I should like to do here is to identify the source of this lack of positive results and to see whether it is not possible to find at least partial remedies. The exercise seems the more desirable because such conclusions as do get established tend to be somewhat unsurprising. Dr Cockburn (p.57) tells us that homicide was rare and most murderous violence occurred within families. Though it is satisfactory to have the more lurid notions of a people forever battering one another disproved, this remains what one would have expected. Similarly Dr Curtis finds that violence was usually casual and unpremeditated: were we to think that the realm was full of professional hit-men? Dr Cockburn (p.63) also notes that many thefts punished at assizes were commited by vagrants, and his conclusion that 'outsiders' were more likely to be brought to court is supported by Dr Ingram (p.133). Perhaps this really reveals respective attitudes to familiars and strangers, but it would seem as likely that men without possessions or a means of livelihood would do most of the stealing as that people readily blamed their losses on the conventional tramp. Dr Ingram (p.117) seems surprised that men accused of crime could be very bitter about their fate; perhaps this requires no comment. Dr Beattie's careful compilation of statistics leads to the less than surprising conclusion that repression of crime grew more severe as criminal activity increased. Certainly there are other less obvious findings in this volume; in particular Dr Munsche's analysis of poaching most refreshingly departs from the stereotype and revives its subject very satisfactorily. In general, however, the mixture of honestly admitted uncertainty and rather expected answers must raise the question whether the enterprise is bound to remain so inconclusive.

It appears to me that there are two kinds of obstacles to a more formidable attack on the history of crime: the state of the evidence, and some unacknowledged preconceptions with which the task is approached. The first creates the limitations which trouble all our writers, but perhaps these need not be so unyielding. The second inhibits the asking of unprejudiced questions and tends to produce those expected answers.

Of the insufficiencies of the evidence the foremost and least remediable is total absence. As everyone knows, assize and quarter sessions records start late because before the end of the sixteenth century the statutory demand for returns into King's Bench was very poorly obeyed. It is really only from about 1660 that we again get the sort of continuous record which the cessation of the great eyre terminated in the middle of the fourteenth century.[7] The Great Fire of London is likely to have closed the books pretty conclusively on the criminal history of the capital before that date, which — since capitals, being populous, are notoriously interesting in the study of crime — is unfortunate. The records of the ecclesiastical courts, too, do not survive in perfect series, though in this area so far the chief problem has lain in their technical difficulty and illegibility; they call for more urgent exploitation. Losses apart, there is the further difficulty of records never kept. We shall never know much about the inmates of jails, for instance, because few jailers cared to provide us with the evidence. All this needs no labouring: the student of crime works with necessarily very patchy and incomplete materials. One result, as this volume shows, is that the work will concentrate on the eighteenth rather than the seventeenth century, the seventeenth rather than the sixteenth, a commonplace experience in all social history. However, in view of these deficiencies it is a pity that what does exist should not be used more comprehensively. Historians of crime will have to remember that the central government records contain material for them which, while not so immediately the product of criminal activity as are the local records of assizes, sessions, borough courts and manors, can help to narrow the blank areas. I have in mind not only the proceedings of Star Chamber and Requests, but also the records of the Exchequer, the Admiralty and perhaps the Court of Wards in all of which offences against property rights and persons leave some deposit. There may be others. This sort of material is unlikely to improve the opportunities for quantification, but it can still tell us much about breaches of the peace, forcible dispossession, fraud, assault and larceny.

Dr Macfarlane interestingly raises the possibility of yet another source of information when he argues (pp.77-78) that accounts of witchcraft cases in pamphlets show up the inadequacies of the court records. It is probably true that for the spectacular crime, which includes murder, this sort of evidence adds a dimension, but it needs to be used with much scepticism; the history of the 'Elizabethan underworld', for so long too readily written out of the imaginative literature of the day, should stand as a warning. Certainly it is necessary to search chronicles and diaries, though here again the historian will uncover only a very unsystematic collection of cases biased towards the sensational.

There is, in fact, little one can do about missing evidence, except to recognize, as our contributors do, that some questions must remain unanswered while some can be answered only for particular periods and regions. The uncertainties emphasized in these essays come more commonly from the nature of the evidence extant.[8] The most systematic materials are the records of courts, central and local, and it is a characteristic of these that their formality hides as much as it reveals. In a trial for felony, for instance, it is usually easy to discover the court that tried the case, the names and descriptions of accused and victims, the type of crime alleged, the names of the jurors, the fact of conviction or acquittal. We cannot learn from the record the particulars of the crime, the details of what went on in court, or — more surprisingly — quite often whether the sentence was carried out. It is this stifling formality that renders supporting materials so valuable, especially recognizances for appearances, for keeping the peace and for other purposes, such as those which Dr Samaha is at present editing from the Colchester archives. Generally speaking, if investigation is to achieve a reasonable degree of objectivity and completeness, it will be necessary in the first place to concentrate on areas which provide both a more or less continuous record and a variety of unsystematic supporting evidence; and it should be said again that the second will often be found in the Public Record Office rather than the local archive. (I must, however, add what a pleasure it was to find Dr Curtis take one away from ever-present Essex, to the historian the one county equipped with criminals).

Next there is the urgent problem how far we can trust the information provided in the extant records. Dr Cockburn has thrown grave doubts on the accuracy of indictments: he has found strong indications that especially the description of the accused, their status and domicile, could be frequently mis-stated.[9] This is not only a disconcerting but also a somewhat surprising discovery, for there is good evidence (in the 'ancient indictments' and the King's Bench plea rolls) that such mistakes were readily used to get convictions quashed. It is possible that the little people involved in those assize indictments did not know their rights or were overwhelmed by the speed of events, but a good many of those known to have used legal technicalities to escape the consequences of their deeds were insignificant and poor enough. It would appear that among the first tasks to be now performed the critical appraisal of the evidence must stand very high. Before we use these materials to answer questions not of legal but of social history — the social status of alleged criminals, the places whence they came, the relationship between social classes, the attitudes manifested and so forth — we had better be sure that the facts taken from the record can be trusted. Here again recognizances may be more reliable than indictments. At any rate, the discussion initiated by Dr Cockburn needs to be continued.

A peculiar difficulty of this kind is raised by the discovery that so many persons indicted by grand juries got off at their trial. Dr Beattie (pp.175ff.), after describing a system far from considerate to the accused and in which especially trial juries were forced to come to snap decisions, finds that of those brought to trial at eighteenth-century assizes and quarter sessions about a third left the court freed from the threat of rope or transportation. The fact in itself is certainly interesting, but what does it mean? Do we suppose that so large a proportion were falsely accused, or that juries acquitted in the teeth of the evidence, either from compassion or under some kind of pressure? Star Chamber often enough attended to delinquent juries (without being able to reverse the false verdicts rendered); did its abolition free juries for what in law must be called misbehaviour? Most accounts do seem to assume that the savagery of the law was countered by juries' refusal to heed it, but is it certain that presenting juries were more accurate in their findings? The system, after all, rested on the assumption that presentment would inevitably gather in some false allegations; it did not even begin to hold that *billa vera* equalled guilt. Since I am not persuaded that even the indiscriminate savagery of the law has been satisfactorily established — one hears too much of a few bad cases, and tracking back the general statements in the books too often ends up with one of the impassioned parliamentary speeches of certain notoriously unreliable law-reformers of the early nineteenth century — I should like to see the issue of acquittals and convictions tackled without the commonplace preconceptions long enshrined in the literature and sanctified by Radzinowicz.[10] Once again, we need a critical study of sources from the record outwards. This may be pointlessly bland advice from someone who does not know the records in question. I am very willing to be so convicted by any historian who has actually asked such questions of his evidence.

There is, however, one area of possible criminal activity which will escape even the best instructed investigation, however careful of complete coverage and however critical of its sources it may be. What do we do about crime unreported — crime that never reached even the lost records? It is possible to make estimates of offences known but not tried; and though Hext's statement (p.50) that in 1596 these constituted four-fifths of all such occurrences seems astonishingly high, this means only that one's instinctive beliefs need adjustment in the light of the evidence. If his proportion is approximately right over the whole period, one wants to know why so much detected thieving went untroubled and how that society coped with such a prevalence of tolerated criminality. Beyond this lie breaches of the law of which no one told. Experience suggests that there must have been such, and experience (as any policeman will confirm) also says that there is nothing the investigator can do about it. However, Edward Hext's estimate here offers some consolation. If only every fifth known breach got to trial, the chances that beyond this there were still considerable quantities of crime lost to view are not great. Obviously it would be folly to rely on trials only for statistics of crime, but perhaps more could be done, along the lines mapped out by Dr Cockburn, to establish better totals of offences by investigating pre-trial stages. In all these issues — crimes untried and criminals acquitted — one needs to be more continuously aware of the possibilities of false accusations and mere malice than Mr Sharpe, for instance, shows himself to be (pp.107-8). I may misunderstand him, but he seems to be saying that the charges conditioned by the predilections of 'a society attempting to control religious belief and most aspects of sexual morality', while peculiar, were in their own terms truthful. It is as likely that in such a society personal animosities invented accusations of the kind acceptable to the authorities in order to get at a private enemy.

All this amounts to no more than saying that now, with the pioneers half settled in their difficult territory, the time has come to consolidate, and that consolidation calls for a more systematic and more critical analysis of the available sources than has yet been attempted. In this way, the deficiencies of the material will be properly pinpointed but they will also receive such remedy as can be got. The conclusion that the attraction of arriving at substantive answers to the social historian's questions must for the present be resisted, so that ground-clearing operations can be carried out, is also supported by the signs of unconscious, or premature, assumptions which do appear here and there in these essays. This is tricky, even touchy, ground, and I do not mean to be offensive. Yet a brief word should be said. Most of the historians who study this kind of history — history from below — are concerned to redress a balance not only in historiography but also in the fortunes of the men they study. One result is to make them work from preconceptions about class relationships; these essays share certain implicit convictions about the effect of the interests entertained by the possessing classes upon determinations of crime and who shall suffer for it. In consequence the fact that the law protected all property, not only that of the rich, escapes attention, and in consequence we are likely to miss one of the most telling features of the scene, namely that the poorer sort seem to have suffered most at the hands of thieves who yet got tried, convicted and often executed. Dr Beattie (p.182) contributes a peculiar variant of the distorting preconception when he ascribes the relatively lenient treatment of female offenders to the alleged fact that they were regarded as less of a social threat. This allows nothing for an often instinctive chivalry, or if you like embarrassment, which was a common reaction of that day when confronted with women who broke the rules. There are several examples in these papers of answer by jargon — the solemnities of the sociologist overcoming the instructed frivolity of the historian. Crime is no joke, either for the victim or the offender, but nothing is gained by pulling long-worded faces.

It would be utterly unfair to end on such a note. The essays in this volume have much to teach, and if this introductory piece has concentrated on the warnings they contain that is because my assignment constrained me to criticize. Our authors can be trusted to speak for themselves and to deal faithfully with the devil and his advocate. I am sure that they can readily convict me of crass error and possibly of complacency. The latter I repudiate; to the former we are all liable. It is by isolating and correcting error that progress comes, and in the very difficult region of historical inquiry exemplified here the practitioner need not object to having traps and pitfalls pointed out to him, even if some of them turn out to have already been sprung or filled in.

1 *Criminal Courts and Procedure at Common Law 1550-1800*

J. H. BAKER

There are two ways of describing a legal system. The first, favoured by lawyers, is to expound the theoretical conception, the abstract rules revealed by legal authorities. Lawyers are bred on textbooks so written, and it may well be the only practicable way to begin. To the extent that the theory is derived from precedent, it must mirror reality; but the precedent from which such descriptions are derived is of the single kind which makes law, not of the compound kind which makes statistics. The second manner of description, more favoured by sociologists, is based on factual observation. Recorded events are preferred to the theoretical explanations of the lawyer or the commands of the lawgiver. The same distinction governs historical descriptions, in which law flits uncomfortably between intellectual and social history. But it by no means necessarily follows that the two kinds of description must always be in conflict, for anyone who describes a legal system must consider and compare both theory and experience. A true understanding of a legal system, as of chess or cricket, is only to be had from experience of the variety of action and result which can occur within the rules. The rules do not prescribe who will win, and (at least in a legal system) they are not always followed; but they do explain what the participants are up to. The following outline of the processes of criminal justice between 1550 and 1800 has been compiled chiefly from the law books,[1] in an attempt to provide a general background against which details gleaned from original research may be set. Such a brief summary must confine itself not only to generalizations, but also to the main features of a system notable for its eccentricities.

I THE MODES OF PROSECUTION

The prosecution of criminal justice had in a remote past rested with the victim or his kin, but by Tudor times blood-feuds were decidedly outside the law. The drive for retribution had been channelled first into the solemn appeal of felony; and then royal justice, disliking the tendency in the private sector to compromise suits for money, had sought to discourage even judicialized self-help by placing the responsibility for prosecution on the public at large. The frankpledge system and the constabulary, the robbery and murder fines, the hue and cry, the coroner's inquest and, above all, the grand jury, were products of this transfer of responsibility. Each played its part in the sixteenth century, but none of them can be regarded as the primary source of prosecuting energy. Throughout the period under review there was no organized police force, no county prosecuting solicitors, no Director of Public Prosecutions and in most cases no prosecuting counsel; so the detective work, the administrative oversight of prosecutions, the preparation of the case, and the conduct of the trial, did not fall to professional prosecutors. The grand jury was involved in most prosecutions for felony, but we know that the preparatory work had usually been done by the time the case reached the grand jury. It is true that the constable had a police function at a local level, but his lowly office usually ended when he brought an arrested person before a justice of the peace. Was it, then, the justice who managed prosecutions? Plucknett thought the Marian bail and committal statutes had turned the justice into 'something between a detective and a juge d'instruction', a role he filled until the formation of a professional police force in the nineteenth century.[2] This view has recently been persuasively reargued, and it is clear that the justices' duty to see the peace kept included in theory a general supervision of criminal justice, from initial police inquiries down to the trial. Much of the diligent justices' time was spent receiving and investigating complaints, calling witnesses before them and binding them over to appear at trial, examining accused persons and committing them to gaol or releasing them on bail, and attending sessions. In form the justice did not prosecute: he simply coerced the private complainant to do his own prosecuting. What is not clear is whether the initiative remained with the justice to conduct the prosecution at quarter sessions or assizes. Dr Langbein has argued that the justice did indeed 'orchestrate' proceedings at the trial, taking the depositions with him as a kind of policeman's notebook to 'buttress [his] oral performance'.[3] This thesis has been challenged,[4] and it seems more likely that it was the court officers — headed by the clerk of the peace and the clerk of assize — who coordinated prosecution materials once the preliminary investigation was over. It was they who managed the courtroom proceedings by preparing calendars, drawing indictments, arraigning prisoners, calling witnesses and keeping records.

Perhaps it is misleading to seek a single source of prosecuting energy. Certainly we should not expect the same situation in 1700 or 1800 as in 1600. There seems rather to have been a slow shifting of responsibility for preliminary investigation from the populace, as represented first by the victim's kin and then by the grand jury and coroner's jury, to the magistrates, and from them (but beyond our period) to the police force. Of course the old survived alongside the new, and the change was disguised by appearances, disguised perhaps even from contemporaries. As late as 1677 it was said that the grand jury was 'the great and grand spring, or *primum mobile* ... that gives motion to all the other wheels';[5] yet it must by then have been unrealistic to accredit that body with the initiative for the bulk of prosecutions. There is an exact parallel in our own time. The magistrates have taken over the function of the grand jury, and the police have taken over the preliminary work of the magistrates, with the result that the focus is gradually shifting from the formal institution (the 'committal proceedings') to the informal (the 'questioning of suspects' by the police).

As we turn to the mechanics of prosecution, it will be as well to stress that in England it was not for any court to initiate prosecutions, for at common law a court could only resolve disputes brought before it by others.[6] Criminal proceedings were initiated and prosecuted in the name either of a private person or of the king.[7] The type of proceeding depended largely on the difference between felonies and misdemeanours (or trespasses), a distinction which was settled long before 1550. Felony was the more serious and usually carried the death penalty; treason and (according to some writers) murder were higher than felony, but were generally dealt with on the same footing. 'Misdemeanour' is a vague, non-scientific, name for the residuary class. In the case of felony, the private prosecution was by appeal of felony and the Crown prosecution was by indictment. In other cases, prosecutions were either by indictment or information. With the exception of attachment for contempt in the face of the court,[8] and the obsolete procedure of arraignment *sur le mainour*, no other modes of prosecution were countenanced by the common law. And the minimum requirements of the common law were sanctified and protected by chapter 29 of Magna Carta and its progeny, the fourteenth-century statutes of due process.

Appeal of felony
The appeal followed the same pattern as a civil suit. It was commenced by writ or bill, the appellant counted at the bar against the appellee, who pleaded and put himself on trial, and the proceedings were recorded on the plea side of the court. The disadvantages to the appellant were considerable. He had to sue in person and find real pledges of prosecution. If he lost, he might be punished and the appellee had a chance of recovering damages against him; moreover, since the appellee was allowed counsel throughout the proceedings, the possibilities of technical failure were alarming. Even if he won, he had to bear the expense of that which might have been done at the expense of the community. For these reasons the appeal became far less popular than once it had been. By 1550 it was still a regular proceeding, and of sufficient importance (or complexity) for Staunford to give it more

attention than the indictment. Between 1550 and 1650 it very nearly went out of use altogether. The advantage of restitution in the appeal of robbery had been extended to proceedings on indictment in 1529,[9] and it was only the appeal of murder which made much appearance in the later books. The principal surviving advantage of the latter was that it gave the next-of-kin a recourse if the grand jury failed to indict,[10] or the trial jury failed to convict, or the defendant obtained an undeserved pardon. At common law an acquittal either on indictment or appeal barred any further proceedings for the same offence; but by a statute of 1487 it was ordained that acquittal or attaint on indictment was not to bar appeals of murder,[11] and this kept the latter alive during advancing senility and in the face of judicial hostility. As early as 1610, in an appeal which proved 'an angry case, and did very much trouble the Court', Fleming C.J. declared that 'an appeal is in law to be very strictly looked into'.[12] There was a brief revival under Holt C.J., who vigorously defended the appeal as 'a noble prosecution, and a true badge of English liberties'.[13] But the liberty was not often demanded in the eighteenth century, and there are only about a dozen reported cases during the entire century.[14] By 1800 the appeal was as obsolete as any institution can be which has not been formally abolished.

Indictment

In the normal case, where no appeal had been commenced,[15] the prosecution for felony in the king's name could only be by indictment. An indictment was an accusation made by twelve or more laymen sworn to inquire in the king's behalf and recorded before a court of record. The need for an indictment was a constitutional principle of some importance, because it meant that the king and his ministers could not of their own motion put a man on trial for felony. A man could only be tried for his life upon either the appeal of an interested subject or the presentment of at least twelve of his peers. The supporting theory was that as the king had no personal knowledge of his subjects' affairs, he had no ground for proceeding against the subject without a presentment 'of record'.[16] Lord Treasurer Burghley, in a memorable speech in Star Chamber, said that

it was the liberty of the subject of England more than of all other nations that he cannot be molested or imprisoned without indictment. Other nations have an accusation, which is verbal and at the promotion of a party, but this is by the presentment of his neighbours and peers with their oath, and made of record. And this liberty was purchased for the subjects of England with the blood of many people, noble and ignoble, and was the cause of the Barons' War, and it is the noblest accusation that may be.[17]

In his quaint exposition of Magna Carta Burghley evidently gave not a flicker of thought to the appeal, but clearly the nobility of trial by indictment lay in its important consequence: that in matters of life and limb there existed between the Crown and the subject a shield borne by his neighbours. Attempts to remove this shield were hated and short-lived. It had been tried in 1496, when Parliament enabled felonies to be presented by information; but the statute barely outlived Empson and Dudley. Then in 1650 Parliament established a High Court of Justice which could proceed on the mere word of the Attorney-General; this was one of several good reasons for thinking it contrary to the spirit of English justice.[18]

The 'presentment'[19] by twelve could be made in a number of ways. Important in homicide cases — and the only form of communal presentment to have survived in England today — was the finding by an inquest before the coroner upon the view of a dead body that the death had been occasioned by a named person. This operated as an indictment on which the accused could be arraigned for homicide. To conform with constitutional principle it had to be the finding of at least twelve men.[20] Another mode of presentment by twelve was that by the jury in a leet or sheriff's tourn.[21] The most usual body of indictors, however, was the grand jury. At least one grand jury was summoned to appear at every assizes and sessions for the purpose of finding indictments. Each jury was composed of twelve or more substantial freeholders, sworn to present all crimes committed in their county such as were listed in their charge. A majority decision of twelve or more sufficed, and so it became usual to summon an odd number greater than twelve; in later times normally twenty-three.[22] The grand jurors could, as invited, present of their own knowledge, but since they were not omniscient the bulk of their findings were based on draft indictments (called 'bills') prepared by the clerks on behalf of the prosecutors. In considering bills they heard only Crown evidence, since their task was not to convict but to decide whether the Crown had a case to go forward. If they thought there was a case, they found the bill 'true' and endorsed it *'billa vera'*. Some thought this required such a belief in the truth of the accusation that the burden of proof was the same as for a trial jury.[23] Others took it to indicate only that the case was 'meet' or 'fit' to put the accused on trial, which called for a 'strong and pregnant presumption'.[24] Hale required only a prima facie case, made out on a balance of probabilities, though by Blackstone's time a 'thorough persuasion' was needed.[25] Grand juries were at times strongly independent, at others meekly subservient or even superfluous, but it is difficult to assess their work because bills not found true were not supposed to be preserved. When the grand jury was not satisfied, the bill was endorsed with the non-committal word *ignoramus* (or, after 1732, 'not found'). The bill did not then become an indictment, but could be laid before another grand jury later; there was no official reason for preserving or recording it. Even a finding of *billa vera* was not a verdict, and so another indictment could always be found for the same offence; only when a trial tury had given a verdict on one indictment were proceedings on other indictments for the same offence precluded. Sometimes a man was indicted both by the grand jury and by a coroner's jury, and in that case he could be tried upon either or (as was usual at the Old Bailey) upon both together.[26]

The decline of the grand jury began at the beginning of our period, with the introduction of regular pre-trial examination. Eventually the preliminary proceedings before the justices were to supplant it entirely, though until they became indispensable it was necessary to retain both systems. But long before the completion of the process (in 1933 in England), the idea gained ground that the grand jurors' work was 'but matter of course, a ceremony; matter of form',[27] a view strongly resisted by pamphleteers but difficult to dispel in practice. By the end of our period only about one bill in seven was found not true; eighty years later, however, the proportion had dropped to one in twenty-seven.[28] By the latter date it might well have been said that the sifting of prosecutions had passed effectively to the justices; but the statistics show that in 1800 the grand jury still exercised a substantial, if decreasing, parallel responsibility.

Information
Misdemeanours could be, and often were, prosecuted by indictment in the same way as felonies; but the safeguards which the constitution guaranteed the subject in matters of life and death were relaxed in lesser cases to the extent that an alternative was allowed. The alternative was the mere 'information' of an individual, dispensing with the collectivity of a presentment of record and with the oath. Whereas an indictment began (until 1915) 'the jurors for our lord the king on their oath present that ...', an information was recorded with the opening words 'be it remembered that X gives the court here to understand and to be informed that ...'. The principle that felonies could not be prosecuted upon bare information[29] remained inviolate save for the experiments of 1496 and 1650 mentioned above. In non-capital cases, however, prosecution by information was well-established before 1550. The genus included a number of species, some of which were essentially civil and can be distinguished by the kind of process which followed. Criminal informations could be laid either by a common person or by a law officer such as the Attorney-General. The common person could inform either for the Crown, or 'as well for himself as for our lord the king' (the *qui tam* formula). The *qui tam* prosecution was a creature of statute, designed to encourage law enforcement by giving informers a share of the penalty, and the race of 'common informers' to which the procedure gave rise played an interesting if not very worthy part

in the history of economic regulation.[30] The information by a law officer was called an *ex officio* information, and was in daily use in Star Chamber and the conciliar courts. Because it bypassed the grand jury, it was a useful way of commencing unpopular prosecutions and attracted some obloquy.

A private individual could file an information in King's Bench or Star Chamber on behalf of the king, a form of proceeding which had the double attraction that it avoided the grand jury and that the prosecutor did not pay the costs. As a result of alleged misuse in the second half of the seventeenth century, the criminal information came under such odium that in 1691 its legality was seriously challenged in King's Bench. The court, however, thought the matter so clear that it upheld the information without bothering to hear argument in favour.[31] The objection was seen to be, not to informations as such, but to their abuse. That problem was attacked in 1692 by Parliament, which forbade the filing of informations in King's Bench without leave of the court, and also made the prosecutor liable to costs. Thereafter informations were effectively confined to those 'gross and serious misdemeanours which deserve the most public animadversion', such as riot or sedition.[32] The indictment remained the most proper way of initiating any prosecution at common law.[33]

II THE MODES OF TRIAL

Of the two principal types of criminal trial which developed in Europe when human judgment began to replace irrational proofs such as the ordeal, the most widespread was the 'inquisition'.[34] In its usual form, as nurtured by the Laws Civil and Canon, the inquisitorial procedure centred upon an official inquisitor or judge who directed all the proceedings, often in secret, gathered the evidence and gave the judgment. Emphasis was placed on written evidence, and especially on confessions extracted under torture. The second type of trial, more or less peculiar to England, was 'trial by jury'. Under the common-law system, the judge merely presided over a public inquest by twelve ordinary folk sworn to find the truth, before whom the accuser and the accused pleaded to issue and produced their evidence and arguments much as they would in a civil suit. The common-law trial was by personal confrontation, that is, the production of oral evidence in the presence of the accused. Torture, though it was occasionally resorted to behind the scenes, was contrary to English law. Well might constitutional writers from Fortescue to Blackstone praise trial by jury as the palladium of English liberties.[35] Well might Englishmen read into chapter 29 of Magna Carta a fundamental right to jury trial, and inherit an invincible hatred of Romano-Canonical justice. But it is not for historians to indulge in panegyrics or exaggerations. The jury was not available in all criminal cases in England, nor altogether spotless when it was available. Jurymen were at least as liable to prejudice as judges, and more susceptible to intimidation and bribery. If juries freed Sir Nicholas Throckmorton and the Seven Bishops, they also convicted Sir Thomas More and Sir Walter Raleigh. Stephen thought they could be as unjust and tyrannical as Star Chamber.[36] Henry VIII tacitly mocked the Civil Law and torturé when he brought maritime crime within the common law, but evidently it was easier to convict pirates by jury.[37] Nevertheless, the blessings of Magna Carta provided a ready argument when other modes of trial were attacked. The least attractive feature of ecclesiastical inquisition-procedure was the oath *ex officio*, whereby a man might be compelled to accuse (and virtually convict) himself; it was one of the principal reasons for Coke's hostility towards these courts and the High Commission in particular.[38] Coke approved of Star Chamber, but that also proceeded by examination and interrogation in the same vein. The absence of juries in Star Chamber, though not the main grievance, provided a convenient constitutional objection when the court was swept away and its business significantly remitted to 'due punishment and correction by the common law of the land and in the ordinary course of justice'.[39] The pretended High Court of Justice, which was as much an affront to the common law as Star Chamber, brought upon itself the constant objection that the judges decided the facts as well as the law but could not be challenged as if they were jurors.

For all practical purposes, the jury was the only form of criminal trial *at common law* in the period 1550-1800, at least if we regard Star Chamber as outside the common law. Summary 'trial' according to martial law was unconstitutional in time of peace, and (at any rate after the Petition of Right of 1628) even rebels taken in open insurrection were tried for treason at common law.[40] Vestigial survivals of earlier modes of trial, such as infangthief,[41] survived in theory but were not practically significant. Battle, according to Staunford, was 'not so disused that it could not be brought back into use today if the defendant so wished', but it was only waged (as a gesture of bravado) in one or two cases, and no battle was fought in a criminal case in our period. A gauntlet thrown into a startled Court of King's Bench in 1818 provided the occasion for its belated abolition.[42] Yet despite the prevalence of the jury over its precursors, and the resentment of interference with the right to a jury, the legislature had recognized since the fifteenth century that it was too solemn and slow, and perhaps too favourable to defendants, to be allowed without exception in all cases. So, throughout our period, grew a list of novel crimes which, by statute, were triable 'summarily': that is, by magistrates alone. Here, perhaps, England came nearest the inquistion; but there is no need to suppose conscious imitation of other systems,[43] and the idea was never extended to felonies.

Trial by jury

Nearly all lawyers in our period traced the right to trial by jury to chapter 29 of Magna Carta. But the key phrase 'judgment of his peers' was given a restricted exposition. Peers, for this purpose, were of two classes only: temporal lords of Parliament, and commoners. A peer of the realm indicted for treason or felony could only be tried by other peers of the realm, and the form of trial differed somewhat from that of a commoner in that the triers did not take an oath (and so were not 'jurors'), and unanimity was unnecessary so long as there was a majority of at least twelve.[44] The privilege did not extend to misdemeanours. Whereas a lord of Parliament indicted for felony had to pray trial 'by God and my peers', every other subject sought trial 'by God and the country', which meant those men of the county where the indictment was found who were qualified to serve on the jury. The only qualification was that they should be freeholders to the value of 40s. or (in a city or town) owners of 40s. worth of goods.[45] There was no age limit, but women were by custom excluded. The jurors did not have to be 'peers' of the accused in any particular sense; an esquire could be tried by merchants.[46]

The advantages which jury trial were supposed to confer on the accused were principally two. First, since the jurors in giving a general verdict were judges of law as well as fact, they could override strained or unpopular interpretations of the law or of the evidence by government-minded judges.[47] Second, they could mitigate the rigours of the penal system by 'pious perjury' — the merciful use of 'partial verdicts' or false acquittals contrary to the evidence. The precise extent of these advantages is difficult to quantify, but it seems that from the sixteenth to the eighteenth centuries the acquittal-rate (whatever the reasons for acquittal) was between one-quarter and one-half of those indicted. Since the essence of these advantages was that a man's fate rested in the hands not of royal officials but of his neighbours, the theory counted for little if in practice those neighbours were not free to follow their own minds. How free, then, were juries in deciding upon their verdicts?

Once jurors became judges of fact, who adjudicated upon the evidence given in open court rather than on their own private knowledge, it was possible to criticize their verdicts as being against the evidence. The common law enabled a false verdict in a civil suit to be upset by an action of attaint against the jury, and there are statements in the law books that the Crown (but not a convict)[48] could bring attaint in respect of a perverse verdict on indictment. No one seems very sure that such an action was ever brought, but if 'attaint' is used loosely to denote any proceeding against jurors then it was common enough in the century after 1550. Trial judges dissatisfied with acquittals would either fine the jurors instantly, or bind them over to appear in Star Chamber, which took an active interest in misconduct by jurymen. Sir Thomas Smith writes as if such proceedings were rarely pursued to a conclusion, and says that when they were they were accounted very tyrannical; while in 1554 all the judges of England held that trial judges had no power to fine jurors for false verdicts.[49] But the records suggest that both kinds of proceeding were common enough under Elizabeth I and the early Stuarts. The Star-Chamber jurisdiction passed in 1641 to King's Bench, which followed its 'tyrannical' example until it was finally and conclusively decided in 1670 that it was contrary to law to punish jurors for their verdicts.[50] The trial judge could, alternatively, seek to prevent rather than cure by refusing to accept a verdict which had been agreed upon.[51] Some Jacobean judges would even examine the jurors individually to see whether one would give way.[52] This practice ceased at about the same time as the fining. As late as 1680 it was asserted that

> such a slavish fear attends many jurors, that let the court but direct to find guilty, or not guilty ... right or wrong accordingly they will bring in their verdict ... as the court sums up, they find; as if juries were appointed for no other purpose but to echo back what the bench would have done.

From about that time, however, trial judges generally respected the newer principle that the purpose of their address to the jury was not to direct but to 'recapitulate and sum the heads of the evidence', and to state the law in a manner 'hypothetical, not coercive'.[53]

Summary conviction
At common law the judges of superior courts could convict summarily (that is, without indictment or jury) only in respect of offences committed in open court, where knowledge of the offence was conveyed through their own senses. The idea was taken up in statutes which gave justices of the peace the power to punish offences committed in their view out of court; and then (but well before 1550) to punish offences which, though not done in their presence, they discovered by 'examination'.[54] In these latter statutes there was no attempt to disguise the departure from common law; 'examination' was contrasted with 'inquest' and 'presentment' and there was no need for a grand or trial jury. The tendency to confer summary powers on justices accelerated in the seventeenth and eighteenth centuries, and led Blackstone to issue the warning that 'it has of late been so far extended as, if a check be not timely given, to threaten the disuse of our admirable and truly English trial by jury, except only in capital cases'.[55] Blackstone's fears were premature, for they are still voiced today; but they represented a hostile reaction to summary process from the superior courts, which had already erected a wholesome supervisory jurisdiction.

The foundation of the review of summary convictions was the ability to remove records from inferior courts into King's Bench and there to quash the convictions if patent defects were found. The power was there in Elizabeth I's time,[56] but was not commonly used until the later seventeenth century. Its foremost protagonist was Holt C.J., who considered that 'all acts which subject men to new and other trials than those by which they ought to be tried by the common law, being contrary to the rights and liberties of Englishmen as they were settled by Magna Carta, ought to be taken strictly'.[57] King's Bench could not re-examine the merits of the conviction, but could only examine the record to ensure that the proceedings were warranted by law; if the record was good on its face, it was incontrovertible. The main lines of attack were to show that the justices had not pursued the statutory power exactly, or that the accused had not been given an opportunity to attend and defend himself. The latter requirement was a noble piece of judicial law-making attributed to Hale, but not settled till 1703; it did not necessitate the presence of the accused, but only that he should receive a due summons.[58] The principle of 'natural justice' so established has become the foundation of what is now Administrative Law. Some thought the work of King's Bench undermined too far the authority of the justices, and Parliament tried experiments in excluding it.[59] The compromise solution was to provide for an appeal to quarter sessions, often by way of rehearing; this gave the accused a better chance of making his point, and saved the justices' face by keeping the matter within the county; the device was first tried in 1670,[60] and became very common in the next century. Each statute, however, had its own variations, and summary jurisdiction was not homogenized until 1848.[61]

III CRIMINAL JURISDICTION

All criminal jurisdiction in England was in constitutional theory derived from the king, as the fountain of justice and the principal conservator of the peace. Nevertheless, the king could not properly exercise such jurisdiction in person, because he could not be a judge when he was also a party. It had therefore to be delegated. This was done either by grant or by prescription (immemorial usage). As far as the regular courts were concerned, the grant had to be by letters patent conferring either a permanent judicial office in a court of known jurisdiction or a commission to exercise the jurisdiction set out in the patent. The Crown was held to be limited by law (or rather by long usage) in granting commissions, and could not grant a commission which would change the law: for instance, by giving judges power to proceed against notorious offenders without indictment, or to determine minor trespasses.[62] Commissions, restricted in time and space, account for nearly all criminal jurisdiction in the period 1550-1800. The only exceptions worth noticing in a general account are (i) the Court of King's Bench; (ii) those justices of the peace who derived their authority from borough charters or Acts of Parliament; (iii) ecclesiastical courts; and (iv) franchise jurisdictions, such as courts leet. The simple picture was distorted by legislation. Parliament could not only confer or remove jurisdiction in the case of an existing office or institution, but could alter the jurisdiction of those who held or would in the future hold a particular type of commission; it was very sparing, however, in the creation of new criminal tribunals.

Parliament

Parliament had criminal jurisdiction in respect of peers and proceedings by impeachment. Peers were tried either in full Parliament, or by triers presided over by the High Steward; the peer was indicted in the normal way by a grand jury, and the indictment removed by *certiorari* before the High Steward, who received a commission of oyer and terminer to try the one case. Impeachment was not confined to peers, though it was arguable that Magna Carta precluded the trial by peers of a commoner for a capital offence.[63] Between its revival in 1621 and the last instance in 1805 there were over fifty impeachments, two-thirds of them against peers.[64] The House of Commons acted in effect as grand jury, and its presentment (called 'articles') was tried by the House of Lords.

King's Bench

The Court of King's Bench was the only one of the three superior common-law courts in Westminster Hall to possess a criminal jurisdiction, and that it possessed without stint. It was regarded as an eyre in the county where it sat (usually Middlesex), and as such had unlimited jurisdiction to try indictments. It was the only court which could try appeals of felony. It could remove into its purview the record of any inferior criminal court, and quash the conviction or proceed with the trial if it had not taken place. When Star Chamber was abolished in 1641, King's Bench inherited so much of its jurisdiction as was considered worth preserving.[65]

As a court of first instance, it could try indictments found before itself by a grand jury of Middlesex, or informations filed in the Crown Office, or indictments removed by *certiorari* from inferior courts. It was rare throughout our period for indictments to be removed before trial; the *certiorari* was not available as of right, and was generally refused in respect of trials before the superior judges at the Old Bailey or assizes. After removal, the court would either try the case 'at bar' by a jury of the county where it was found, or send the case back to the county to be tried at *nisi prius*: a situation in which the commissioners of *nisi prius* had not only criminal jurisdiction but the power to give judgment. In cases arising in

Middlesex, the trial could take place in term-time at the King's Bench bar before the full court and a Middlesex jury; it was possible for all the judges to address the jury.[66] This seems to have occurred only in cases of some importance, such as criminal informations for offences against public order or morality. The run-of-the-mill Middlesex cases were heard at the Middlesex sessions or the Old Bailey, or (in vacations) by a single King's Bench judge sitting at *nisi prius*.

As a court of review, King's Bench was primarily concerned in the early part of the period with formal defects in indictments and with allowances of pardons. By 1700 the emphasis had shifted to summary convictions and settlement cases. The reason for the decline of the more serious business is that better methods were being developed for reviewing convictions on indictment on their merits, and therefore it became less necessary to poke around for technical flaws.

Assizes

Until their abolition in 1971[67] assizes were for most ordinary purposes the principal criminal courts in the country. Despite their longevity and regularity, assizes were not permanent institutions in the same sense as King's Bench. The assize judges, though most of them were judges of the superior courts, derived all their authority from the commissions which they received ad hoc for each circuit. The country was divided into six circuits,[68] and (save in the extreme north) there were two assizes each year; the first in the Lent and the second in the Long Vacation. Two commissioners, who had to hold the degree of serjeant, were assigned to each circuit. The commission of assize itself, ironically, conferred no criminal jurisdiction because it only empowered the judges to take the 'petty' assizes; these were all obsolete by 1550 save for novel disseisin, which was in decline. But it had become the practice in medieval times, and was enjoined by statute,[69] that the assize commissioners should deliver the gaols on their way. The assize judges therefore received, in addition to their assize commission, the two principal criminal commissions of oyer and terminer and gaol delivery.

The commission of general oyer and terminer[70] was issued to the two assize judges together with the principal justices in the county concerned and commanded them to inquire into, hear and determine all offences committed in the county. The commission of general gaol delivery issued only to the assize judges, with the clerk of assize as associate, and commanded them to deliver the gaols in the county. The jurisdiction conferred by each commission was unlimited in subject matter, but there were procedural distinctions. The commissioners of oyer and terminer could try only indictments found before themselves, because the words 'inquire, hear and determine' were held to be conjunctive. This restriction did not apply to the commissioners of gaol delivery, but they could try only persons already committed to the gaol (including those released on bail).[71] The latter had the additional power to 'deliver by proclamation' all the prisoners against whom no indictments had been found by the end of their session. The combined effect of these commissions was to give the assize judges unlimited criminal jurisdiction within the counties comprised in their circuit and for the duration of that circuit.

In cases of felony, the jurisdiction of assizes overlapped with that of quarter sessions. In practice, however, it was settled custom near the beginning of our period for capital felonies to be reserved to the assize judges. The custom was by no means always observed in the seventeenth century, and it had no legal foundation, but the assertions of Lambard, Dalton and Bacon[72] as to the general rule are borne out by the bulk of records.[73] It may have evolved because the justices had acquired so much minor work by statute that they could not cope and, therefore, almost by default, left serious cases to the assizes. Alternatively, the custom may have been imosed from above, either to secure a more professional or awesome tribunal for capital cases or to emphasize that the justices' role in serious criminal cases was that of prosecutor rather than judge. There are indications of the latter two views in the Marian Bail and committal statutes, which require certification to the justices of gaol delivery (not to the sessions), and in the 'case of difficulty' proviso inserted in commissions of the peace after 1590.[74] The practical consequence was that, for most of the period 1550-1800, the Crown side of assizes was chiefly occupied with murder, robbery, burglary and grand larceny, together with other serious offences such as rape, coining and witchcraft. Of these, it seems that the various forms of theft accounted for about three-quarters of the calendar.[75] Less serious offences, such as petty larceny, were divided between assizes and quarter sessions, presumably as efficiency and convenience demanded.

The assizes were, of course, far more than superior criminal courts. Of their civil jurisdiction, their supervision of the justices and of local government, and of their place in religious and political history, it would be impertinent here to say more than that an excellent full-length study was published in 1972.[76]

Sessions of the peace

Justices of the peace for counties derived their judicial authority from the commissions of the peace, which were issued to most of the knights and principal gentry and lawyers within each county. The medieval form of the commission, after slight revision in 1590, remained in use until 1878. The first *assignavimus* clause appointed the persons named to keep the peace in the county; this conferred no trial jurisdiction, but empowered each individual justice to make inquiries, issue warrants, take informations, record examinations under the Marian statutes and take recognizances to keep the peace. The second *assignavimus* appointed the same persons and any two of them, whereof (*quorum*) one was to be a justice named in the *quorum* sub-clause, to make inquiry concerning all felonies, trespasses and a host of other offences, committed within the county, and to receive indictments and hear and determine the same. This was effectively a commission of oyer and terminer, but the list of offences was archaic and misleading; for instance, murder was not mentioned, and it had been questioned whether it was included in 'felonies'.[77] At the end of this clause was a proviso, that if a case of difficulty should arise they were not to proceed to judgment except in the presence of a judge of either bench or of assize. The third clause, the charge, commanded the justices diligently to apply themselves to the premises; the fourth recited the calling of jurors by the sheriff; and the fifth the appointment of a *custos rotulorum*.

By virtue of the second *assignavimus* the justices held their general sessions of the peace. They were called 'quarter' sessions because they were directed by statute to be held at the four seasons of Michaelmas (week after 29 September), Epiphany, Easter and the translation of St Thomas (week after 7 July).[78] They were supposed to last for three days at least,[79] and to follow the procedure of the common law. At least one of the justices had to be one of those named in the *quorum* sub-clause. In 1550 the justices 'of the quorum' were invariably the legally qualified justices, but soon afterwards the quorum was 'debased' by the insertion of more and more lay justices until in the end only one was omitted for form's sake.[80] This development was associated with the loss of more serious cases to the assizes and the difficulty of assembling justices at sessions. The jurisdiction to try indictable offences was almost coextensive with that of assizes, excluding treason, perjury, forgery and a few other offences. The sessions also made orders touching public works, the poor, wage and price regulation and other matters of local government.[81] If all who were supposed to had attended, there would have been an impressive gathering of three or four hundred people at quarter sessions, including everyone who mattered in the county.

The Webbs showed how different the practice might be from the theory in the seventeenth and eighteenth centuries.[82] There was constant difficulty in some parts in gathering together the quorum of two justices, and quarter sessions sometimes failed to be held for this reason. The constables and other officers were often negligent, and constables' presentments eventually ceased altogether. In many places there was no proper courtroom, and the sessions would proceed in a tavern or adjourn from house to house. We have already seen that serious crime was given up to the assizes; what remained for trial did not occupy more than a few hours, and the local-governmernt work which occupied most of the time could be transacted in private. In some counties there was no chairman of quarter sessions, the justices being free to proceed as they thought fit. If a lawyer was present, he would doubtless rule on points of law, but there was no sanction for this. At Hereford assizes in 1663 Hyde C.J. told the lay justices to abide by the legal rulings of lawyer justices 'and not (as it is commonly practised) put to the vote of many ignorant justices on the bench according to their fancy and opinion'.[83] So long as the record was properly made up there was no appeal; one need not, therefore, suppose that what transpired was always as formal and regular as legal theory required.

In some places quarter sessions were held independently of the county commissions of the peace. The archbishop of York and the bishops of Durham and Ely held sessions within their liberties by statutory authority.[84] Many cities and boroughs held sessions by virtue of their charters, which constituted the mayor and some of the aldermen or jurats as permanent justices, and usually provided for the appointment of a legally-qualified and salaried justice called a 'recorder'. Some boroughs had no jurisdiction in felony, others had; some were concurrent with, some excʻusive of, the county sessions. These permanent sessions were affected neither by the issuing of a new county commission of the peace nor by the demise of the Crown.

In some counties the justices held 'special' sessions between the quarter sessions to prevent delays; Lambard thought they should be held more often,[85] but no doubt they were rare outside the metropolis. What came in the nineteenth century to be called 'petty sessions' were originally called 'private' sessions, because they did not transact public business such as trials on indictment. They were held by virtue of the first *assignavimus*, whereas special sessions were held (like quarter sessions) under the second. They could be used for summary proceedings, but were chiefly for administrative business, such as licensing and poor relief.

Anomalies in London and Middlesex

Long before the establishment of the Central Criminal Court in 1834, the metropolis afforded the most important exception to the general scheme of criminal jurisdiction. There were no assizes for London or Middlesex. The Middlesex sessions, held for most of the period at Hicks' Hall in Clerkenwell,[86] competed in term time with King's Bench. Because of the presence of the latter, Middlesex was relieved from holding sessions quarterly; but, ironically, King's Bench tried so few criminal cases that the county was obliged to hold eight rather than four sessions a year. The liberty of the City of Westminster held distinct sessions, out of term in Westminster Hall. Sessions of the peace for the City of London were held at

Newgate or the Guildhall. The 'Old Bailey' was the popular name for the Justice Hall adjoining Newgate prison, where commissions to deliver that gaol were executed. Newgate was the principal gaol for both Middlesex and London, and so the commissions of gaol delivery gave jurisdiction in both counties and were usually accompanied by separate oyer and terminer commissions for both counties. Until 1785 the Middlesex oyer and terminer could not be executed during term time, because of the presence of King's Bench in the county. The Old Bailey commissions issued to the Lord Mayor and some of the aldermen, the Recorder of London, the Common Serjeant, all the common-law judges and various dignitaries and lay justices. They issued as often as eleven times a year in the earlier part of our period, but towards the end there were eight regular sessions each year. At the Old Baily were also held Admiralty sessions by virtue of special commissions of oyer and terminer to the Lord High Admiral's surrogate and other judges, to try crimes committed outside counties and within the admiralty jurisdiction.

Tourns and leets

The sheriff's tourn and the court leet (which was a species of tourn in private hands) had lost most of their former importance by 1550, their work having been assumed by the justices' sessions.[87] They were never abolished, however, and in some places continued actively. Their common-law jurisdiction was to inquire into and present all felonies, and misdemeanours of a public nature such as affrays and blood-sheds.[88] Since Magna Carta, however, they had been forbidden to proceed further with felonies and their presentments had to be passed to a superior court. In the case of the tourn, the sheriff was supposed to hand in his indictments at quarter sessions; in the case of the leet, the presentment was supposed to be engrossed in a tripartite indenture and delivered to the assize judges.[89] Alternatively, the presentment could be sent to the grand jury for them to find as an indictment.[90] This power to present felonies was probably almost obsolete in our period. But the misdemeanour jurisdiction continued. The presentment of the jury was held to be 'as a gospel' because it could not be traversed; it operated as a summary conviction without trial or even 'examination'.[91] It was an archaic embarrassment, and in 1776 it was held that the conviction could be removed into King's Bench and traversed there, for otherwise the leet would have 'a power superior to that of any other jurisdiction in the kingdom'.[92] The only punishments which could be imposed were fines and amercements, not imprisonment. The most remarkable feature of leets to this day is that, although they are royal courts of record, they can be bought and sold privately with the manors to which they are appendant.

Ecclesiastical courts

Although they did not belong to the common-law scheme of jurisdiction just described, and proceeded in a different tradition without indictments or juries, the courts of the Church exercised a good deal of criminal jurisdiction during our period. They had the severe limitation that they could try only offences not cognizable at common law, but this left a substantial residue. The only capital offence within their purview was heresy, punishable until 1677 with death by fire; a few heretics were burned in our period, but the jurisdiction was not quantitatively significant.[93] More important in practice was the punishment of moral offences in the archidiaconal courts.[94] The sins most commonly dealt with were fornication and other offences against sexual morality; but the list included 'spiritual' defamation, drunkenness, bad language and other manifestations of discordant or dissolute living. The Church courts also, of course, devoted much time to ecclesiastical discipline; to church attendance, recusancy, liturgy, ornament and such like. The usual punishment was penance, the full form of which was performed in church in a white sheet, but which might be varied to suit the crime; a common form was the reading of a public confession. The object was to shame rather than pain the offender, and to edify the congregation. Sometimes, however, the penance was commuted to a money payment, which was tantamount to a fine. The ultimate sanction was excommunication, and so the courts lacked teeth to deal with the irreligious; throughout our period there was a tendency for business other than ecclesiastical discipline to be transferred to the sessions.

IV THE TRIAL FOR FELONY[95]

Most of the persons indicted at the assizes or sessions would already have been in custody, having been committed to gaol to await trial. Anyone could arrest on suspicion of felony, though it was always prudent to seek the aid of a constable or procure a justice's warrant. At the beginning of the period there was some doubt as to the propriety of issuing a warrant to arrest for felony before indictment, because if a justice had no personal knowledge he had no ground to justify an arrest; but by Hale's time at the latest the practice had become commonplace.[96] It was requisite that within three days after any arrest the prisoner be examined before a justice; any detention beyond that period was an actionable false imprisonment.[97] At the examination the accused was accompanied by the person who arrested him and his accusers. If it appeared that a felony had been committed, the justice had no authority to release the accused but was to write down 'the examination of the said prisoner, and information of them that bring him, of the fact and circumstances thereof' for certification to the next gaol delivery. He was then to bind over the complainants to give evidence, and either commit the suspect to gaol by *mittimus* or release him on bail.[98] A single justice was forbidden to grant bail in cases of felony, lest he be tempted by corruption; but two justices, one being of the quorum, could bail for any offence except treason, murder or arson, so long as the guilt was not virtually certain (as where the accused had confessed or been taken red-handed).[99] Suspects who had not been found were indicted upon information given, and process issued against them which could result in outlawry.

From the bail certificates, depositions and gaol calendar, the clerks could prepare a calendar of the prisoners to be tried and a note of those who were bound to prosecute and give evidence. From this material the clerks would busy themselves before the assizes or sessions in drawing bills of indictment. The first business of the court, once the commissions had been publicly read and those due to attend summoned, was to swear and charge the grand jury. The grand jurors' oath was:

> You shall diligently inquire and true presentment make of all such matters and things as shall be given you in charge. The king's majesty's counsel, your fellows', and your own, you shall well and truly observe and keep secret. You shall present no man for envy, hatred, or malice; neither shall you leave any man unpresented for love, fear, favour, or affection, profit, lucre, gain, or any hope thereof; but in all things you shall present the truth, the whole truth, and nothing but the truth. So help you God.

After the charge, the prosecutors and witnesses were called and sworn and sent into the grand-jury room with the bills of indictment. The secrecy enjoined by the oath was generally observed, primarily to protect accusers in the event of an *ignoramus*; but the hearing was occasionally conducted in public at the request of the prosecutor[100] and prosecuting counsel were often admitted at the discretion of the grand jury.[101] The grand jury probably spent as much time on a case as the trial jury, at least in the first half of the period, and they continued their work while trials were taking place in open court, returning at intervals to feed the court with fresh indictments.

Arraignment and plea

As soon as convenient after the indictments were found, the persons indicted were 'arraigned' before the court. The arraignment corresponded to the pleading stage in civil suits, the reading of the indictment being in effect the declaration of the Crown. The prisoner, whom we shall call John Style, was called to the bar and addressed by the clerk: 'John Style, hold up thy hand'. This was not a mere ceremony, but an acknowledgment by the prisoner that he was the person indicted.[102] The clerk then read the indictment, paraphrasing it into English and into the second person: 'Thou art here indicted by the name of John Style, late of London, yeoman, for that thou ...'. It was necessary that the indictment itself be in Latin,[103] but the prisoner was not entitled to have it read in Latin,[104] nor to have a copy of the original, unless he could assign some error in law upon hearing it.[105] This seemingly harsh rule was to prevent trifling exceptions to grammar or form. After reading the indictment, the clerk asked: 'How sayest thou, John Style, art thou guilty of this felony as it is laid in the indictment whereof thou standest indicted or not guilty?' If the prisoner denied the charge he pleaded 'not guilty', to which the clerk replied: 'Culprit, how wilt thou be tried?' The word 'culprit' was not a prejudicial insult, but a corruption of the law-French *'culpable: prist'*, apparently meaning that the Crown was ready to prove the prisoner guilty. This etymology has understandably caused misgivings, because in law no such reply was called for, nor was it entered of record; but no other explanation makes sense.[106]

To the clerk's question the law permitted but one answer: 'By God and the country'. The form was essential, and it was not sufficient to say 'according to the laws of the land' or 'by God and honest men' or 'by twelve men according to the constitutions of the law'.[107] If the prisoner refused to use the required words, this was as much a standing mute as if he had failed to plead.[108] Any prisoner disposed to prevaricate was given due warning of the awful fate of those who stood mute of malice. In cases of high treason, petty larceny and misdemeanour, and in appeals of felony, it was tantamount to a conviction and judgment followed accordingly. In cases of petty treason and felony, the prisoner was adjudged to receive the *peine forte et dure*, whereby he was half-starved and pressed to death. This was perhaps the most barbaric feature of common-law procedure, and resulted from a grisly misunderstanding of a statute of 1275. Babington remarked that the full sentence as described in the year-books was 'so severe, that (I think) never English man as yet (though many were pressed to death) had the heart to execute it according to the letter'; gaolers instead tried to coerce wilful mutes into pleading by tying their thumbs with whipcord.[109] Prisoners chose this penalty in order to protect their dependents from the forfeiture which attended conviction. Pressing continued at least until 1741, but by a statute of 1772 standing mute of malice was made equivalent to conviction in all cases. Inexplicably, there are two cases of standing mute of malice between 1772 and 1800; the prisoners threw away their chance of acquittal for no obvious reason.[110]

Instead of pleading not guilty, the prisoner could plead a 'dilatory' or 'declinatory' plea, such as a plea to the jurisdiction, a plea in abatement for want of addition or some other defect in the indictment, or a plea of sanctuary (virtually obsolete by 1550) or clergy.[111] These were 'dilatory' pleas because, if unsuccessful, the prisoner still had to answer the indictment. In capital cases, however, this was also true of pleas in bar; sentence of death could be given only after a conviction on the general issue. The pleas in bar were three: autrefoits acquit, autrefoits attaint (or convict) and a pardon. Other forms of pleading were forbidden, because a felony could not be confessed and avoided. A third possibility was to demur to the indictment for insufficiency. In civil cases a demurrer amounted to a confession of the facts, and so an unsuccessful demurrer lost the case; Staunford, Hale and Hawkins thought this was also true of a demurrer to an indictment, though Blackstone thought otherwise.[112] Demurrers were rare, because the same advantages were available (without the risks) upon motion in arrest of judgment.

The prisoner who had no defence to make could confess the indictment by pleading 'guilty', which the clerk recorded by writing '*cogn*[*ovit*]' (he confessed) upon it. The court was supposed to ensure that a prisoner did not plead guilty from fear or ignorance, and in cases of doubt to persuade him to plead not guilty.[113] Nevertheless, there is some evidence of 'plea-bargaining'. Lambard condemned the practice of accepting a half-confession, by which a prisoner, protesting his innocence, put himself on the king's mercy in return for a reduced penalty; but the practice continued well into the seventeenth century.[114]

The trial: impanelling the jury

When John Style had pleaded not guilty and put himself on the country, the clerk replied 'God send thee a good deliverance', and wrote on the indictment '*po. se*' (*ponit se super patriam*). The prisoner was then entitled to have any irons or shackles removed, for at common law he was to be free from any duress during his trial.[115] He was also, in appropriate cases, allowed to sit and to have pen and paper; but in the vast majority of cases trials were too rapid to permit of this indulgence. The clerk then arraigned another prisoner on the next indictment, and so on until there were sufficient for the first jury to try. There was no rule that each prisoner should have a distinct jury, and the usual practice until the late seventeenth century was to arraign about half a dozen at a time. Of course, the trials were conducted separately, unless several men were arraigned jointly on the same indictment; but the jurors had to carry each case in their minds until all the trials were over, when they would if necessary retire to consider them all together. When enough prisoners had been arraigned, the jury was impanelled.

The names of those on the sheriff's panel were called, and as they appeared their names were marked with a dot by the clerk. When they had gathered, the clerk informed the prisoners of their right to challenge the jurors as their names were called, and then read out the names again. As each juror stepped forward, the crier reported '*Vous avez* Richard Roe' (or whatever his name was), and Richard Roe was sworn:

> You shall well and truly try and true deliverance make between our sovereign lord the king and the prisoners at the bar whom you shall have in charge, and a true verdict give according to your evidence. So help you God.

The clerk marked his name '*Jur[atus]*' (sworn). When twelve were so marked, the clerk commanded the crier (in law-French): '*Countez*'. The crier then counted them, as the clerk read over for the third time the names marked *Jur'*: '[A.B.] one, [C.D.] two, [E.F.] three ... twelve. Good men and true, stand together and hear your charge'.[116] The crier then made proclamation for evidence against John Style, Style was asked to raise his hand for identification, and he was given into their charge: 'Look upon the prisoner you that be sworn, and hearken to his cause. You shall understand that he is here indicted ... (reciting the indictment in English, in the third person, the plea of not guilty, and the charge to inquire whether he was guilty or not) ... Hear your evidence'. The trial could then commence.

A prisoner in capital cases was entitled at common law to thirty-six 'peremptory' challenges: that is, without cause shown. By statute this had been reduced before 1550 to twenty, though in 1555 prisoners accused of treason were restored to their three dozen.[117] If prisoners exercised their full rights of challenge, it could be time-consuming and might delay the trial, because thirty-two potential jurors were needed to ensure that twelve would be left.[118] If all the prisoners 'severed' their challenges, by taking them in turns, it would become virtually impossible to try them; for, if there were six, a panel of 132 would be needed to exhaust the challenges. This could be a means of achieving separate juries.[119] In practice, however, challenges were rare. Either prisoners did not know the jurors or anything against them, or did not act quickly enough, or were simply too over-awed to understand what the clerk had told them. The Crown could not challenge potential jurors peremptorily, but could require them to 'stand by', which meant that their names were passed over; only when the panel was exhausted were the names called again, and then the Crown would have to show cause or acquiesce. In practice this could give the Crown a greater control over the composition of the jury than the prisoner had; but, like the challenge, it does not seem to have been widely exercised.

The trial: presentation of the case
Throughout the period 1550-1800 prisoners indicted for felony were in law

denied the assistance of counsel in presenting their case unless a point of law arose upon the evidence. The rule did not apply to appeals of felony, nor to misdemeanours, and this made it appear all the more anomalous. St Germain had explained that the judge bore the responsibility for seeing that the proceedings were sufficient in law, to which Staunford added the more realistic (and prophetically true) reason that trials would take too long if men of law were allowed; no-one could better speak about the facts than the prisoner himself. This was a typically medieval view of a trial, as an inquest, an administrative process to collect verdicts; lawyers were concerned wth law, not with disputes about facts. The rule might have disappeared sooner if the possibility of lengthening trials had not been administratively unthinkable. As the King's Bench said in 1602, when refusing counsel to a scrivener indicted for forgery: 'It would be a dangerous precedent, for every prisoner would demand it if it were now allowed'. Two more reasons were put forward in the early seventeenth century. Coke, borrowing from Roman or Scots Law, said that in capital cases the evidence against the prisoner should be so manifest that it could not be contradicted. And Pulton thought that if the party conducted his own defence, 'peradventure his conscience will prick him to utter the truth, or his countenance or gesture will show some tokens thereof, or by his simple speeches somewhat may be drawn from him to bolt out the verity of the cause', which would not happen if counsel did the speaking.[120]

Both Coke and Pulton confused the forensic presentation of the case with what we would regard as evidence. The prisoner was not competent to give evidence on oath, but his speech would serve the same purpose and it was desirable that he should deliver it in person; the prisoner's own account of himself would certainly weigh heavily with the jury. Perhaps the rule led to rough or even good justice in ordinary cases involving intelligent defendants; most prisoners asking for counsel probably hoped for some legal trick to be worked on their behalf rather than for eloquent advocacy. In most cases the Crown did not have counsel either. Perhaps points in the prisoner's favour were fairly taken by the judges or clerks or learned spectators.[121] Contemporaries might well have argued, as we now argue in relation to pre-trial interrogation, that the innocent man has nothing to lose, everything to gain, from telling his story himself. But the denial of counsel seems to have been unfair in Tudor and Stuart state trials, when the Crown was represented by the best advocates of the day.

The relaxation of the rule denying counsel accompanied the establishment of rules of evidence and trial procedure, and the cessation of the practice of questioning the prisoner during the trial. By a statute of 1695 prisoners indicted of treason were given a right to counsel for matters of fact as well as of law,[122] and thereafter the exclusion in felony cases was scarcely supportable. Foster somehow found the rule tolerable, but during the eighteenth century it became normal for counsel to be permitted to conduct the case or to prompt the accused.[123] Perhaps the greatest advantage to the defence, as Pulton had foreseen, was that it shut the mouth of the prisoner; no longer did the jury expect to hear satisfactory explanations from the defendant's own lips, and his counsel could run defences which the accused in person would never have got away with.

The Crown witnesses were called in by the crier, who reported as each one came in : '*Vous avez* Robert Downe' (or whatever his name was), and gave him the oath: 'The evidence you shall give to this jury between our sovereign lord the king and the prisoner at the bar shall be the truth, the whole truth, and nothing but the truth. So help you God'. The witness was then asked what he could say for the king, and was helped along by questions from the judge, the king's counsel (if any were present) and (occasionally) the jurors. In the earlier part of the period there might be a running altercation with the accused as he contradicted statements made against him,[124] but in the seventeenth century it became settled practice to leave the cross-examination until the witness had finished. It was settled at the same time that witnesses should not be asked leading questions during the examination-in-chief, but that greater latitude would be allowed in cross-examination.[125]

When all the Crown witnesses had finished,[126] the accused could call witnesses. There had once been a school of thought that defence witnesses were no more permissible than counsel, because the prosecution case ought to be unanswerable; but we are told that Queen Mary I personally instructed Morgan C.J. that this was an error and that 'whosoever could be brought in favour of the subject should be heard'. Her majesty's view of the matter was not clearly law until the end of the sixteenth century.[127] Even when such witnesses came to be allowed as of course, they were not (until 1695 in treason, 1702 in felony) sworn. Instead they were exhorted to stand in fear of God and tell the truth. Their evidence seems to have been given the same weight as if it had been sworn,[128] though if it turned out more favourable to the Crown an oath was hurriedly administered.[129] The distinction between Crown and defence witnesses was such that a Crown witness might be punished if he gave evidence to acquit the prisoner.[130]

Throughout our period most criminal trials were conducted with great rapidity during very long sittings.[131] It was, indeed, so rare for a case to last more than a few hours that it was not fully settled until the end of the eighteenth century that a criminal court had the power to adjourn a case overnight.[132]

Evidence

In the sixteenth century few recognizable rules of evidence were applied in criminal cases. Staunford, indeed, offers but one laconic remark on the whole subject: 'Anyone may be admitted to give evidence for the king'.[133] If this indicates anything, it is that there was rather a law of witnesses than of evidence. 'The law', said Bacon, 'leaveth both supply of testimony and the discerning and credit of testimony, wholly to the juries' consciences and understandings'.[134] All the evidence was given orally in open court. But, there being no exclusionary rules, hearsay was regularly admitted:[135] the written depositions could be read in evidence even though the deponent was available to give oral testimony,[136] and it was common for the constable and examining justice to give an account of their inquiries and findings. It is doubtful whether the presumption of innocence had been formulated; one writer of James I's time thought a man could be convicted without any Crown witnesses, the indictment being sufficient evidence against him.[137] Nevertheless, without good eye-witness accounts of ordinary criminal trials in the early period it is difficult to say how the system normally operated.

The absence of defence counsel from important criminal trials, and the prevalence of the general issue, hindered the growth of rules of evidence in criminal cases. It seems that the strict common-law rules of evidence first manifested themselves in civil cases, and were extended to criminal trials by analogy in the later seventeenth century. By Hale's time depositions were used only if the deponent were dead or too ill to be produced;[138] and the courts began to entertain frequent objections to other kinds of hearsay evidence. The 'hearsay rule' belongs at the very earliest to the period 1675-1690, and even at the beginning of the eighteenth century Serjeant Hawkins thought hearsay could be used to lead into or augment direct evidence.[139]

By introducing exclusionary rules, the courts were able to use the nascent law of evidence, as in medieval litigation special pleading had been used, to prevent the misleading of jurors. Between the time of Staunford and that of Lord Mansfield the courts reversed their attitude to the role of the jury. Staunford excluded no evidence; its weight was for the jury. But Lord Mansfield believed it was not for courts of law 'to consider how far the minds of men may be capable of resisting temptation, but to take the most anxious care that they shall not be exposed to any temptation at all'.[140]

A recurring problem was raised by the use of accomplices' evidence. The law had long recognized the utility of giving immunity to accomplices who revealed crimes committed by their principals. The medieval technique, called 'approvement', was for the accomplice to confess on arraignment and offer to appeal his confederates; if the court agreed, he received a pardon. It was never abolished, but it went out of use before 1550 because it was extremely dangerous; the court could, in its discretion, sentence the approver on his confession. In its place there developed in the seventeenth century the practice of 'turning king's evidence', whereby an accomplice was promised a pardon in return for evidence against the principal offenders. Hale C.J. had been of the opinion that such a bargain disabled the accomplice from giving evidence,[141] but his highmindedness did not prevail. The accomplice did not acquire a right to a pardon by turning king's evidence, but there was an 'implied confidence' which gave him 'an equitable title to a recommendation for the king's mercy'.[142] By the middle of the eighteenth century the courts had decided that such evidence ought not normally to be admitted without corroboration;[143] had the notion existed a century earlier it would, in Stephen's view, have prevented all the unjust convictions in the state trials of 1678-80.[144]

Verdict and allocutus

When the prisoners in its charge had been tried, the jury was asked to consider its verdicts. In difficult cases the judges summed up the evidence, but in the main the judges simply put the jurors in mind of their duty and left the matter entirely to them. Thus, in a state trial as late as 1661, the Lord Chief Justice was content to say: 'You have heard the evidence, you are to find the matter of fact as it is laid before you, whereof you are the proper judges, and I pray God direct you'.[145] If the jurors wished to retire, they were given into the custody of a jury bailiff, who was sworn to keep them without fire or refreshment and free from outside influence. While the jury was out, more prisoners could be arraigned and tried.

On their return, the jurors were directed to look upon the prisoner and say whether he was guilty or not. The foreman announced the verdict. If it was 'guilty', the clerk asked them to say what property the convict had, so that it could be seized; the usual reply was 'none to our knowledge', because the inquiry would in fact be carried out by the sheriff. The clerk then wrote on the indictment: *cul*[*pabilis*] *ca* [*talla*] *nul* [*la*] ('guilty, no chattels'). If the verdict was 'not guilty', the clerk asked whether the accused had fled, to which a similar answer was customary. The annotation in this case was: *non cul*[*pabilis*] *nec re*[*traxit*], *q*[*uietus*] ('not guilty, did not flee, acquitted'). When the verdicts had all been delivered, the clerk read them out for confirmation: 'Well then, you say that John Style is guilty of the felony in manner and form as he stands indicted, and so say you all?' If none dissented, the prisoner stood convicted. In the case of an acquittal, the prisoner was made to kneel and the judge pronounced him to be discharged on paying his fees.[146] Despite acquittal, he might be bound to good behaviour or even sent to the house of correction if it appeared from the evidence that he had misbehaved. In the case of a conviction, the prisoner was led away by the gaoler. Judgment was not supposed to be given at once, but at the end of the assizes or sessions. The reason was neither to allow the judge time to reflect nor the prisoner to squirm, but to allow time to secure a pardon or prepare a motion in arrest of judgment. By the late eighteenth century, however, the practice had begun of giving judgment immediately upon conviction.[147]

Before judgment was given in cases of treason or felony, there was an indispensable[148] preliminary known as the *allocutus*. The prisoners were brought to the bar, usually in irons, and asked:

> You do remember that before this time you have been severally indicted for several felonies, upon your indictments you have been arraigned and have severally pleaded not guilty and for your trials have severally put yourselves upon God and the country, which country hath found you guilty. Now, what can you say for yourselves why according to law you should not have judgment to suffer death? What sayest thou, John Style?

The convict might take the opportunity of making a necessarily futile speech in mitigation,[149] but the legal purpose of the *allocutus* was to allow the convict to allege anything which would prevent the court from giving judgment: (i) a motion in arrest of judgment, (ii) a prayer of clergy, (iii) a prayer to allow a pardon which had been granted, or (iv) a prayer for respite by a pregnant woman.

Benefit of clergy had been extended by the medieval common law to literate laymen in all cases of murder and felony, but before 1550 statute had limited its availability to the lesser felonies and to first convictions. The statutes limiting clergy were the main reason for the scientific development of the distinctions between murder and manslaughter, robbery and larceny, burglary and housebreaking, and the like; for upon such distinctions a life often depended. The requisite literacy was tested by asking the convict to read a prescribed passage from a psalter, perhaps the first verse of the *Miserere*;[150] this was the 'neck-verse', which the criminal classes presumably learned by rote. The judges could, however, achieve some control over the application of the death penalty to semi-literate convicts, either by helping them or (on the contrary) by selecting passages at random and preventing prompting.[151] Since clergy was available even after judgment, it was possible for a favoured felon to be given a hurried education in gaol so that he could return and recite his verse.[152] If one justification for clergy was that it saved 'useful' persons from the gallows, it might nevertheless be argued that a want of learning made criminal behaviour more rather than less excusable, and in 1706 Parliament extended clergy to the invincibly illiterate by abolishing the reading test.[153] Laymen could claim clergy only once, and to prevent second attempts a statute of 1490 had provided for felonious 'clerks' other than real priests to be burned in the brawn of the left thumb with a 'T' (thief) or an 'M' (manslayer). The burned thumb was not, however, a legal record; it warned the court officers to counterplead the prayer of clergy by producing the record of the previous conviction. So tedious was this procedure that some convicts doubtless had their clergy a second time.[154] Priests were exempt from branding, and in time their exemption (like clergy itself) was extended to the laity. Peers were the first to achieve immunity from the iron, by a statute of 1546, and in the following century it became customary to pardon the branding of persons 'of quality', the court granting respite for the purpose.[155] By the eighteenth century the branding was done so perfunctorily in most cases that it became 'a nice piece of absurd pageantry', and when in 1779 the judges were given power to award fines or whipping instead it went out of use altogether.[156]

Judgment

If the prisoner made no successful motion in arrest of judgment, the crier called for silence, the presiding judge[157] assumed his square cap and judgment was pronounced. It was often preceded by a homily intended for the edification of the convict and the public, but the judgment itself (now called the 'sentence') was in serious cases outside the discretion of the court.

In cases of treason and felony, the judgment was prescribed by law and could not be altered by the judge. In treason, the only judgment permitted for men until the last century was:

> You are to be drawn upon a hurdle to the place of execution, and there you are to be hanged by the neck, and being alive cut down, and your privy-members to be cut off, and your bowels to be taken out of your belly and there burned, you being alive; and your head to be cut off, and your body to be divided into four quarters, and that your head and quarters be disposed of where his majesty shall think fit.

By this horrific standard only, the judgment for women in high and petty treason was more favourable: 'to be burned with fire until you are dead'. This remained law until 1790.[158] The judgment for male petty-traitors was simply to be drawn and hanged. For capital felony (excluding, that is, petty larceny) the judgment was 'to be hanged by your neck until you are dead'. Beyond these fixed details, the judge could not prescribe the manner of execution. When Felton in 1628 confessed the murder of the duke of Buckingham, he asked that his hand might be struck off as a further punishment, but the judges 'answered that it could not be, for in all murders the judgment was the same'. On the same occasion, Sir Francis Ashley, King's Serjeant, remarked in the Common Pleas that he wondered Felton was not sentenced to be hanged in chains; to which Yelverton J. answered that none but the usual sentence could be given.[159] Over a century later, the family of a murdered man asked the court to order a hanging in chains after execution, but the court ruled that it had no power to do so; the executive, however, could and did (throughout the period) order hanging in chains, the body of the deceased convict being at the king's disposal.[160]

Judgments were supposed to be carried out literally, but in fact mercy was often exercised. Traitors might be hanged until dead before the mutilation began; while the terrible punishment for women who killed their husbands or counterfeited coin was usually averted by strangulation at the stake. Technically these *coups de grace* were murder, but they could hardly be punished.[161] Perhaps the most remarkable example of the insistence upon the forms of judgment occured in 1695, when an attainder for treason was reversed (somewhat too late to benefit the accused himself) on the sole ground that the record omitted after the words: *quod interiora extra ventrem trahuntur* ('that his bowels be drawn out of his belly') the necessary words: *et in conspectu eius et ipso vivente comburentur* ('and burned before his sight, he being alive'). It was said that if those words could be omitted, the court might as easily introduce Roman, Jewish or even Turkish judgments.[162]

Very few offences were punished with death at common law, though the commonest offences (homicide and theft) were among them. Parliament added a good many more, and was justly criticized for this by eighteenth-century writers. The criticisms were not usually founded on a humanitarian dislike for the death penalty so much as the observed fact that when over-used it led to excessive leniency in prosecutors, juries, judges and secretaries of state, so that the law was not enforced and criminals escaped scot-free.[163] It has been estimated that the number of convicted felons actually condemned to death, throughout our period, was between 10 and 20 per cent; while the proportion of those condemned who were actually executed probably averaged about one-half, until it dropped to one-third in the later eighteenth century.[164] Clergy and pardons allowed many to escape. Juries showed clemency by finding partial verdicts, such as clergiable larceny instead of burglary, or petty larceny instead of grand larceny. The net effect was that, even in the supposedly savage eighteenth century, only murder and particularly heinous or repeated felonies were punished with death.

The judge had greater discretion to vary punishments for misdemeanours, which were not usually fixed by law. Throughout the period the general practice was to punish petty larceny by whipping, and other misdemeanours by fine. Long terms of imprisonment were rare, since the idea of prison as a reformatory was not taken seriously until the end of the period, while the idea of prison as a punishment would have seemed an absurd expense. Life imprisonment was probably unheard of, the form being 'during the king's pleasure'.[165] The pillory was used for 'exorbitant' misdemeanours, such as sexual offences, seditious utterances and forms of witchcraft. These undefined punishments were in practice administered lightly. The imposition of heavy discretionary punishments, such as the loss of ears or the payment of immense fines, was the primary cause of the downfall of Star Chamber; in the year of its abolition Heath J. promised that King's Bench would not make the same error.[166] In the 1680s, however, King's Bench did fall into Star-Chamber ways. The sentence passed on Titus Oates caused some consternation, and Holt and Pollexfen C.JJ. had the courage to rule it contrary to law; but the House of Lords did not share their view.[167] The provision in the Bill of Rights (1689) against the infliction of excessive fines and cruel and unusual punishments, was clearly directed against these discretionary punishments for misdemeanour; it did not affect judgments fixed by law, however cruel they were.[168]

Reprieve and pardon

If a female convict was quick with child, the judge was bound to respite judgment of death until after delivery; her condition was tried by a jury of matrons, and we learn from Hale that such juries were usually favourable whenever possible.[169] The judge was also bound to respite judgment if the convict appeared to be insane, both because it was no deterrent to punish those of unsound mind and because the convict might, if sane, have moved something in arrest of judgment.[170] In such cases judgment was not given at all for the time being. Besides these cases, judges had a wide discretion to order that a judgment which had been given should not for the time being be executed; this was called a 'reprieve'. This result could be achieved by bribing or persuading the sheriff or under-sheriff to stay execution,[171] but the only circumstance in which a formal reprieve was permissible was where the judge recommended or otherwise expected that the convict should receive a pardon. The judge himself was not competent to pardon; a pardon had to be sealed with the Great Seal on the authority of the secretary of state or the Privy Council. Where a pardon was given because of doubts as to the propriety of the conviction, or on the recommendation of the jury, or because of influence, it was usually 'free' or unconditional. But the majority of pardons were granted on commuting the sentence to a period of exile in the colonies. This practice at first had no legal foundation, and required the convict's consent. It had been considered in Elizabeth's time, was in regular use by 1615,[172] and became common in the course of the seventeenth century. By the eighteenth century it was such common form that trial judges automatically prepared and returned to the secretary of state calendars of those convicted before them, marking those recommended for transportation, or for free pardons; the fortunate were then included in a 'general pardon' for the circuit or session. Over a hundred convicts were spared every year by means of pardons, the majority on condition of transportation for fourteen years. But transportation did not provide the ideal balance between justice and mercy. It was costly to the home community, which received no corresponding benefit; overseas aid was not yet regarded as a social duty. The deterrent effect was small. Although death was supposed to follow if the condition of the pardon were broken by escaping or returning, the authorities were notoriously lenient and usually granted a fresh pardon with a new term of exile.[173] In any case, seven years in America began to lose the terror it had held in James I's time and might even have been a welcome prospect for the down-at-heel. [174] Other, more useful, types of punishment were tried: under Elizabeth I, work on the galleys, and, under James I, foreign military service. In one remarkable case in George II's time a convict agreed to submit to a medical experiment involving the loss of a leg in return for a pardon, though to the credit of the surgeons none would perform it.[175] Finally (in 1779) Parliament introduced, as a regular alternative to transportation, work on the 'hulks' or in a penitential house — the origin of 'hard labour'. Blackstone was enthusiastic about this reform and hoped that thereby 'such a reformation may be effected in the lower classes of mankind ... as may in time supersede the necessity of capital punishment, except for very atrocious crimes'.[176] Thereafter, Parliament increasingly took upon itself to regulate the incidence of transportation and hard labour so that (as in the case of clergy) punishment ceased to represent capricious and tortuous devices for evading the fixed death penalty and came instead to represent something approaching penal policy.

V THE CORRECTION OF ERRORS

It remains to consider the means by which judgments in criminal cases could be questioned in law. The present idea of an appeal did not exist at common law, and the Court of Criminal Appeal had to await the twentieth century. There were only two ways of challenging the validity of a criminal judgment; the formal way was to show some error on the record, the better way was by special verdict or reserved case.

Error on the face of the record

The reversal of judgments for error 'on the face of the record' belonged to King's Bench, whose decisions were in turn reversible by Parliament. Proceedings in error involved making up a complete record of the case in question. Normally, the indictment with its annotations served as the only record, since the minute book which the clerk kept was in law nothing but a private memorandum. The full record was engrossed on parchment. It was written (until 1732) in Latin, and contained a minute and precise recital of the judges' commission, the names of the grand jurors and their finding the indictment, the arraignment, the process against the petty jury, the plea, the verdict, the *allocutus* and the judgment. This record was drawn up and sent into King's Bench by the clerk of the lower court on receipt either of a writ of *certiorari* or a writ of error from King's Bench. Whereas the indictment could be quashed before trial upon *certiorari* alone, a judgment following a trial at common law could be reversed only by writ of error.[177] Hale says that the practice was to sue only a writ of error, though by 1704 there had been a reversion to the older practice of removing the record by *certiorari* and then suing a writ of error *quod coram vobis residet*.[178] The writ of error was not available to quash a conviction where the convict took his clergy, because that was not a judgment,[179] nor to quash summary convictions;[180] in these cases, therefore, the *certiorari* alone was used.

In 'the good old days when barbarous law was tempered by luck'[181] judgments might be reversed for the most trifling slips of form or want of certainty. Thus, in 1595, a murderer escaped because the indictment read that he shot the deceased *'ad sinistram partem cruris sui Anglice* the left thigh', whereas the Latin meant 'the left part of his thigh' without stating which.[182] Instances could be multiplied, and they lead one to suspect that few judgments were immune from reversal. This was the reason why prisoners were not allowed to see their indictments, and it was no doubt the reason for introducing the rule that a writ of error lay only of grace and required the *fiat* of the Attorney-General.[183] It is clear that in some cases errors were allowed only when there was some other reason for quashing the conviction, such as a doubt as to the safety of the verdict.[184] Since these other reasons are rarely mentioned in the reports, the law books are difficult to interpret. The impression given is that, notwithstanding all the checks and safeguards, numerous judgments were reversed for insubstantial reasons from what Barrington termed 'a false compassion'. Hale complained that

> It is grown to be a blemish and inconvenience in the law, and the adminis-
> tration thereof [that] more offenders escape by the over-easy ear given to
> exceptions to indictments, than by their own innocence ... to the shame of
> the government, and to the encouragement of villainy, and to the
> dishonour of God.

As late as 1771, Eden complained that in numberless instances of this kind 'the substance of justice hath been lost in the pursuit of the shadow of mercy'.[185]

The main defect of error, however, was not the punctiliousness of the forms but their emptiness. The merits of the case were irrelevant, because all that mattered was what was (or was not) entered of record. And since no evidence was entered, there could be no argument that the facts proved did not in law support the charge in the indictment. This limitation prevented nearly all substantive questions of law from being raised on a writ of error. Criminal appeals might have had a different history if the bill of exceptions had been allowed in criminal cases; but that hope was extinguished in the case of Sir Harry Vane in 1661.[186]

New trials

In certain situations a trial could be discontinued or set aside and a new jury summoned by a writ of *venire de novo* for a new trial. The only clear case was where the first trial was a nullity, because of misbehaviour or some formal defect. In certain cases, however, a jury might have to be discharged before verdict: for instance, if the defendant was taken ill, or one of the jurors absconded.[187] The practice was then extended to cases where the jurors could not agree,[188] or where the prosecution evidence did not come up to proof.[189] This extension infringed the rule against double jeopardy and was controversial; eventually it became acceptable in the first situation, but not in the second. There was never any attempt to extend the principle, in cases of felony, to the case where a valid but unsafe verdict had been given. In that case, it was too late to discharge the jury and there was no power to order a retrial. Logic demanded the same rule whether the unsafe verdict was for the prisoner or for the Crown. In one situation only did King's Bench relax this rule and grant a new trial: this was where a misdemeanour was tried at bar, or at *nisi prius* from King's Bench, and a conviction appeared unsafe. The first cases, in the middle of the seventeenth century, were all informations for perjury.[190]

Reserved cases

The best method of reviewing points of law arising on the evidence, and by far the most important from the point of view of criminal jurisprudence, was the 'reserved case'. This was not available as of right, but a technique adopted where the trial judge himself had doubts or where an *amicus curiae* had questioned the conviction. The prisoner was simply reprieved until the next assizes, so that the advice of the other judges could be sought in the meantime. If the judges thought the conviction wrong, a pardon was recommended. Discussions of this kind in Serjeants' Inn are reported even before 1550, and they continued until after 1800. By the eighteenth century it had become customary for the trial judge to prepare a written 'case' (a note of the evidence and of the question) for circulation to his brethren.

If legal doubts arose before conviction, it was usual to direct a 'special' verdict, whereby the jurors found the facts in detail and submitted the question of guilt to the court; this obviated the need for a pardon if the defence succeeded. The trial judge would then, if he thought fit, lay the special verdict before the 'twelve judges'.[191] Another method was for the jury to convict generally, subject to the opinion of the twelve judges; in that case a pardon was needed if the conviction was held to be wrong, but the procedure was apparently cheaper.[192] In the event of disagreement among the judges, it was known for a pardon to be recommended even if the majority of judges were against the prisoner.[193] The twelve judges did not always give reasons in public, and sometimes failed to reach any decision at all. Their meetings were purely informal, and were private. They kept no record, save for annotated books of 'cases'. Not until 1848 was the institution formalized, when Parliament erected the Court for Crown Cases Reserved.[194]

Needless to say, none of these courses could be taken upon acquittal, because a verdict of not guilty was final and could not be questioned by the Crown.

2 *The Nature and Incidence of Crime in England 1559-1625: A Preliminary Survey*

J.S. COCKBURN

Crime for our generation has become a commonplace. Conditioned by a bombardment of criminal 'statistics', we tend to regard a soaring crime rate and the attendant debates on law enforcement, capital punishment and gun control as the peculiar monopoly of, and to some extent the natural price for, our modern industrialized society.[1] Viewed in a broader historical perspective, however, our preoccupation with crime appears less novel. Most nineteenth-century Englishmen were convinced that crime was increasing as never before;[2] eighteenth-century commentators were thoroughly alarmed by what they saw as a rising tide of violent criminality;[3] and complaints of the imminent breakdown of law and order punctuated the Middle Ages.[4]

Renaissance Englishmen were no less preoccupied with the prevalence of crime and with fears of lawlessness and disorder. William Lambard, the influential Kent magistrate, echoed the preambles to a dozen sixteenth-century statutes when he lamented in 1582 that 'sin of all sorts swarmeth and ... evildoers go on with all licence and impunity'.[5] English travellers corroborated the opinion of an Italian visitor who declared that in 'no country in the world ... are [there] more robbers and thieves than in England'.[6] In the first miserable decade of the seventeenth century the much-travelled Sir Thomas Chaloner asserted that economic depression 'brings more to the gallows in England in one year than a great part of Europe consumeth in many'.[7] Elsewhere, however, Chaloner had described in graphic terms the dislocation, violence and misery of northern Italy in the 1590s.[8] The crime and violence of sixteenth-century Iberia provides the central theme of the picaresque novel, and has led at least one authority to characterize Golden-Age Spain as an 'otiose and vicious republic'.[9] France, too, under the stress of the subsistence crisis of the late sixteenth century, suffered a general increase in crime and lawlessness.[10] The trends were apparently universal; and Shakespeare's 'take but degree away ...' stands in eloquent testimony to an entire generation of *bons bourgeoises* haunted by the spectre of crime and violent disorder.[11]

Historians have in general accepted this broad impression of a violent and increasingly delinquent society.[12] To replace it with more precise information is difficult. The system by which criminal law was administered in the sixteenth and seventeenth centuries is still imperfectly understood; a majority of criminal court records have been lost or destroyed; and the few that remain are often cryptic and open to various interpretations. As one commentator has recently observed: 'the difficulties of knowing about crime and law enforcement are greater in the sixteenth century than in the thirteenth'.[13]

Nevertheless, a measure of precision is possible. From 1559 onwards criminal records survive in sufficient quantity to allow limited quantification.[14] In addition, there is a substantial vein of collateral material, both printed and manuscript. This, like the court records, must be used with caution; but it suggests at least the gist of contemporary thinking and provides conclusions which can then be tested against data drawn from the criminal records. It is upon a preliminary analysis and correlation of these two sources that this essay is based.

The statistical foundations of this study are the indictments laid at Essex assizes between 1559 and 1603, at Hertfordshire assizes 1573-1625 and at Sussex assizes 1559-1625.[15] It is therefore limited almost entirely to accusations of serious crime and excludes those offences — usually but not always of a minor nature — dealt with at quarter sessions and in the courts of such franchises as the liberties of St Albans and the Cinque Ports. In this sense, then, the data are an incomplete reflection of criminality in these three counties.[16]

The usefulness of assize indictments as sources for the study of crime is also limited by the fact that the information they contain is, of course, categorized according to legal criteria and is presented in a standardized form which reveals almost nothing of the circumstances surrounding the crime or of the motives of the accused. Worse still, there is a strong possibility that in this period even such essential 'facts' of the indictment as the name, residence and occupation of the accused and the nature and date of the crime are rendered unreliable by bureaucratic formalization.[17]

Further weaknesses of indictments as a guide to criminality have been exposed by recent work on eighteenth-century crime, and it is hardly necessary to repeat them in detail here.[18] Given the comparatively inefficient nature of law enforcement, the 'dark figure' of unknown crime must have been very large indeed in the late sixteenth and early seventeenth centuries. Edward Hext, a Somerset magistrate and clerk in Star Chamber, thought in 1596 that 80 per cent of all criminals evaded trial.[19] In the light of modern estimates,[20] his guess is not implausible although there is no way of testing its accuracy. Changes in public or judicial attitudes towards the prosecution of crime over the sixty-seven years under review almost certainly ensure that the discrepancy between actual and indicted crime did not remain constant. In the present state of our knowledge, consideration of these critical variables must be largely conjectural. But the fact that thefts involving an element of breaking, which were running at about 25 per cent of all offences against property up to 1598 when an Act removing such offenders from the protection of benefit of clergy was passed,[21] were, on the evidence of indictments, reduced within a couple of years to 7 per cent of the total suggests the possible impact of such modifications. Jurisdictional changes also affect the reliability of a sample drawn exclusively from the records of one court. Two Acts of 1563, for example, removed coin-clipping from the jurisdiction of the justices of the peace and for the first time empowered them to try cases of buggery;[22] forty years later a Star Chamber ruling limited consideration of forgery to the assize judges.[23] Statistically, such amendments were not significant, and the same can probably be said of changes in the system of judicial administration, variations in the jurisdiction or diligence of local magistrates, for example.[24] Certainly such factors are not in this period the problem they were to become in the eighteenth and nineteenth centuries.[25] Nevertheless, they do emphasize the fact that indictment statistics provide only the most fragile guide to criminality.

The three counties from which the data analysed here are drawn were chosen because of the survival and accessibility of their records.[26] They should not be viewed as a microcosm of the whole of England. Their proximity to London, if nothing else, ensures that the experience of these counties differs to some extent from that of the country at large. They can, however, be meaningfully contrasted. Essex and Sussex were both maritime counties, the one adjoining London to the east, the other lying south of the capital. Essex in the sixteenth century was reckoned one of the most fruitful shires in England.[27] Economically, it was also among the most diverse. Mixed farming predominated in the centre around Chelmsford, the county town; the south and east specialized in dairy produce; wheat, saffron and hops were grown on the open-field lands in the north-west. Despite a profusion of market-towns, only Chelmsford and Colchester were of any size. Colchester was the centre of the Essex woollen industry which, despite signs of depression in the 1560s,[28] continued to thrive throughout this period. Sussex too had its industry. Iron-founding flourished in the Weald for more than a century after 1560.[29] Nevertheless, the county was essentially rural. Unlike Essex, where the coastal areas were thinly settled, most of the population of Sussex was concentrated in the arable parishes along the south coast. There also were the county's ancient ports —

Chichester, Lewes, Rye, Shoreham and Winchelsea — in serious decline in the sixteenth century, and no longer major centres of either trade or population. Hertfordshire, the smallest county of the three, was also predominantly rural. Lying north of London and adjoining Essex to the west, it had, like Essex, numerous small market-towns but only two sizeable centres of population — Hertford, the county town, and the ancient franchise of St Albans.

These geographical and economic factors helped to shape patterns of crime peculiar to each county. But by far the most significant influence on crime in Essex and Hertfordshire was that of London. Essex was the more obviously dominated by the metropolis, both because of its position as London's leading food supplier and through the city merchants and magnates who in the sixteenth century had settled in large numbers in the county. Along the Thames in the built-up and densely populated parishes in the south-west corner of Essex it was virtually impossible, and for most purposes unnecessary, to distinguish the county from the metropolis. The relationship of Hertfordshire to London was more subtle but no less significant. Although the county remained physically distinct, its social and commercial links with the capital were strong. In particular, the county straddled many of the old main roads radiating from London to the north and north-east, and a multitude of Hertfordshire inns and alehouses tapped traffic passing along them.[30] But these arteries also brought to the county the shiftless and vagrant, on their way to or from London, and highwaymen and thieves attracted by the rich pickings on the roads and in the inns and alehouses catering for travellers using them. The capital itself was a magnet for criminals of all types, attracted by its anonymity and unlimited opportunities for profitable dishonesty. By the end of the sixteenth century the overspill of London criminals into the markets and highways of the Home Counties was recognized as a serious problem.[31] Thus both Essex and Hertfordshire suffered and to some extent benefited from their proximity to London. Their crime rates were almost certainly influenced by this urban connection, and although it is impossible to estimate accurately the nature and extent of the relationship it must be borne in mind when comparing them to a county as essentially rural and remote as Sussex in the sixteenth and early seventeenth centuries.

At first glance, the simple totals of indictments for all crimes together suggest that there was little, if any, increase in indicted crime in the sixty-seven years between 1559 and the death of James I in 1625. In Sussex an average of forty-three persons were indicted each year during the decade 1560-69; in the ten years between 1615 and 1625 the annual average was forty-two. In Hertfordshire the average number indicted annually in the decade 1573-82, the first for which records survive, was forty-seven; in the last ten years of the period, 1615-25, an average of fifty-one persons were indicted each year.

Closer analysis, however, reveals that this broad impression is deceptive. Indicted crime in two of the three counties under consideration in fact increased markedly in every decade from 1559 until the end of the sixteenth century. It then began to fall slowly and continued to do so until about 1623, when there are signs of another upward turn continuing into the reign of Charles I. Thus in Sussex an annual average of forty-three suspects indicted in the decade 1560-69 increased to almost fifty-eight in the decade 1580-89, and to sixty-nine between 1590 and 1599; it then fell away to fifty-five in the period 1600-1609 and to forty-three between 1610 and 1619. The limited data from Essex suggest even more clearly the trend during Elizabeth's reign. In that county an annual average of thirty-eight persons indicted in the first decade of the reign increased to seventy-two in the years 1570-79, to eighty-nine between 1580 and 1589 and to 116 in the decade 1590-99. Variations in the Hertfordshire figures, although they point in the same direction, are much less pronounced. The number indicted annually rose from forty-seven between 1580 and 1589 to a peak of fifty-two in the decade 1590-99, and then tapered slowly to fifty-one in 1600-1609 and forty-nine between 1610 and 1619.[32]

Since fluctuations in the number of indictments coming before the courts may well hold clues to the nature of crime in this period, they merit closer examination at a later stage of this paper.[33] For the moment it is sufficient to say that indictment totals apparently support the contemporary notion that crime was increasing during Elizabeth's reign. On the other hand, they suggest that the situation ceased to worsen about 1600 and that the early seventeenth century saw a slow reversal of the dominant upward trend of the preceding forty years.

Any attempt to use population figures to produce rough crime rates for each county is, in the present state of our demographic knowledge, highly speculative. Calculations based on the muster returns for Elizabeth's reign[34] suggest that the population of Essex in the late sixteenth century was approximately 52,000; that of Sussex about 28,000; and that of Hertfordshire a little less than 12,000 persons. Correlation with the indictment data gives a crime rate for Essex of 8 per 10,000 of the population in the 1560s, slightly less than 14:10,000 in the next decade and approximately 20:10,000 by 1600. The Sussex data indicate a relatively static crime rate: 14:10,000 persons between 1569 and 1572; 19:10,000 in 1600-1602; and 16:10,000 between 1622 and 1624. A fairly stable rate is also suggested by the Hertfordshire data: 38:10,0000 in the 1570s; 41:10,000 between 1600 and 1602; 44:10,000 in the period 1621-4. But while the crime rates for Essex and Sussex are broadly similar and not, perhaps, implausible, that for Hertfordshire suggests that all such estimates should be approached with extreme caution. Not only is the Hertfordshire crime rate of between 38 and 44 per 10,000 more than double that for the adjoining and more populous county of Essex, but it is also dramatically higher than the estimated national crime rate (27.3:10,000) in 1921.[35] Other peculiarities in the Hertfordshire data will be noticed later, and the possibility that the county had an exceptionally high incidence of crime, or prosecution, cannot be entirely discounted. At present, however, there is no further evidence to support this hypothesis, and therefore the Hertfordshire figures are perhaps better seen, at least for the moment, as a reminder of the serious limitations of crime rates based on unreliable demographic data.

Although little can be done, then, to establish reliable crime rates for this period, the general indictment totals can be further refined by breaking them down into broad, legally-defined categories. This approach also has limitations since the major legal groupings bring together a complex of offences, many of which may have little in common. Thus 'crimes against the person' encompass such disparate acts as murder, sexual offences and technical assault. Even more confusingly, in this period they also include indictments under the laws against witchcraft. Such charges might allege murder or personal injury by witchcraft or, less frequently, damage to property, usually the bewitching to death of livestock. A detailed analysis of witchcraft indictments lies outside the scope of this essay,[36] and no attempt has been made to differentiate between witchcraft directed against persons and that said to have damaged property. However, two features of the witchcraft statistics presented in Table I (p.55) deserve notice. The data clearly support suggestions that witchcraft accusations declined markedly during the early seventeenth century. Only two of the 546 Sussex indictments surviving from James I's reign allege witchcraft; in Hertford-shire only seventeen of 1018 indictments. In these two counties, therefore, the offence was statistically insignificant after 1603. Even before this date it was never very common. The fourteen witchcraft indictments laid at Sussex assizes between 1559 and 1603 represent less than one per cent of the surviving indictments for all crimes. During the thirty years after 1573 the proportion in Hertfordshire (2.5 per cent) was larger but not significantly so. In Essex, however, the pattern was very different. There the 172 surviving indictments for witchcraft constitute more than 5 per cent of all the indictments laid at assizes between 1559 and 1603. Essex witchcraft was, to put it another way, second only to theft in statistical importance. Further investigation may suggest an explanation for the pattern of witchcraft prosecutions in these counties. All that can be said at present is that, perhaps surprisingly, they appear to have been infrequent in the rural and deeply conservative county of Sussex and most common in Essex, an

Table 1: *Breakdown of indicted crime (persons)*

| | 1559 – 1603 | | | | 1603 – 1625 | |
	Essex	*Herts*	*Sussex*		*Herts*	*Sussex*
Simple larceny	1352	470	654		600	230
Larceny from persons	50	25	26		37	3
Larceny from premises	458	87	332		50	25
Burglary	320	76	267		92	79
Highway robbery	110	53	39		49	9
Property crime total	2290	711	1318		828	346
Homicide	129	24	127		46	55
Infanticide	28	7	27		6	10
Assault	80	22	31		31	42
Rape	26	3	12		5	4
Buggery	8	4	5		1	–
Witchcraft	172	24	14		17	2
Sedition	34	12	15		3	2
Poaching	21	8	66		1	1
Vagrancy	168	55	101		17	7
Other	173	60	205		63	77
Total	3129	930	1921		1018	546

economically diffuse and socially more fluid area lying close to the
metropolis. It hardly need be added that the witchcraft statistics illustrate
again the dangers of advancing general conclusions about crime from the
experience of one county.

We can be sure that witchcraft prosecutions at assizes represent only part
of a complex web of local suspicion and accusations.[37] With indictments
for murder and manslaughter, we are perhaps on safer ground. Mainly
because of the difficulties of concealing a body, indictments for homicide
probably bear a closer relationship to the actual incidence of violent death
than is correspondingly the case with other crimes. Assuming this to have
been so, it seems clear that murder and manslaughter were comparatively
uncommon in this period. Seldom were more than fifteen killings
prosecuted in any one year in the three counties under review, an annual
average of less than 2 per 10,000 population. The number of violent deaths
each year remained fairly constant throughout. But there were some,
apparently significant, differences between the rates in individual counties.
On the evidence of surviving indictments, murder and manslaughter were
least common in Essex, with an annual average during Elizabeth's reign of
0.7 per 10,000 population. In Sussex the rate of indicted homicide
(1.4:10,000) was double that for Essex; while that for Hertfordshire

(1.6:10,000) was higher than both. Attention has already been drawn to possible deficiencies in the demographic data, and we must therefore be cautious about theorizing on the evidence of these calculations. But it is interesting to note that the incidence of murder and manslaughter to some extent bears out the impression of rural violence suggested by the incidence of individual assaults in Sussex.[38] In the light of other idiosyncracies in the Hertfordshire data, it may also be significant that deliberate killing appears to have been proportionately more common in that county.

Overall, however, the pattern of homicide indictments conflicts with the impression conveyed by those contemporary writers who claimed to have detected a trend of growing violence and brutality in sixteenth- and early-seventeenth-century crime.[39] It is of course difficult to reconstruct the circumstances of many killings, even though indictments for homicide are in general more informative than those for most other offences. Some killings clearly were accompanied by inexplicable brutality. For example, in December 1589 two Penhurst labourers attacked a local woman, stabbed her and then slit open her stomach, from which they took an unborn child.[40] Similarly, a Stratford cordwainer, after killing an unidentified woman at Leytonstone in 1560, cut off her arms and legs.[41] In other cases, the motive behind what might at first sight appear to be gratuitous vioence is clear. During the course of a burglary at East Wittering in 1582 one of the thieves was wounded by a servant. His five companions helped the wounded man to escape to Fishbourne, but when it became clear that he would hinder their further flight all five set upon him and beat him to death with their cudgels.[42] Attempts to eliminate incriminating witnesses, to terminate extra-marital pregnancies and to dispose of unwanted children or step-children commonly involved excessive and sometimes protracted brutality.[43] But even in these cases legal form might minimize or conceal altogether the brutal circumstances of a death. At the Hertfordshire summer assizes in 1606 Agnes Dell, an innkeeper's wife, and her son were convicted of killing a boy, Anthony James, whose body had been found in a pond four years earlier.[44] Were it not for two pamphlet accounts of the case we would know nothing of the context of callousness and violence in which the murder had been committed. Anthony's parents had been robbed and murdered by a band of vagrants who had paid the Dells to take the boy and his sister. Shortly afterwards the Dells had murdered the boy and abandoned the girl to die in a wood, having first cut out her tongue. She survived to implicate the couple in what the pamphleteers claimed to be miraculous circumstances.[45] None of this appears on the court records. Similarly, the chance survival of a pamphlet account reveals the violent circumstances in which a Mayfield man murdered his wife in 1595, and that he was convicted on the eye-witness testimony of his five-year-old son.[46] Analysis of the 364 killings known to have been investigated at assizes during this period suggests, however, that the vast majority were not the result of calculated or protracted violence. Rather, they occurred during acts of sudden, unpremeditated aggression and resulted from attacks with a variety of knives and blunt instruments. Fatal quarrels could originate in almost any context — at work, in drink or at play. Five per cent of the deaths analysed followed injuries sustained while playing or arguing about games of various sorts. The circumstances in which Richard Terry, a Throcking tailor, met his death in 1617 during a quiet game of shovelboard with his son and namesake are fairly typical. In the course of the game, young Richard 'found fault with his father for his play'. At this, Richard senior ordered his son to leave the house, and when he refused struck him, causing him to drop his money on the floor. As he bent to pick it up, his father kicked him in the backside, whereupon Richard junior picked up a jug and hurled it at his tormentor. It struck him on the head, inflicting a wound from which he died sixteen days later.[47]

This illustration serves to introduce another prominent feature of homicide in this period — the prevalence of domestic violence.[48] At least 13 per cent of the deaths investigated at assizes involved the killing of one member of a family by, or with the connivance of another: if deaths involving domestic servants are included, the proportion rises to more than 18 per cent. On the evidence of assize indictments, wives were the victims in almost three-quarters of the instances of marital killing. Husbands, several of whom were adjudged insane, apparently favoured blunt instruments or direct physical violence as a means of eliminating family members. Wives, on the other hand, were commonly associated with premeditated murder, often by poison. In at least two instances females followed the notorious example of Alice Arden in hiring professional killers to dispose of unwanted husbands.[49] The motive behind domestic killings is seldom clearly stated. But several were obviously motivated by a desire to regularize or terminate extra-marital liaisons or resulted from violence following the discovery of such relationships.[50] A surprisingly high number of family killings in Essex — ten of the nineteen recorded — involved the murder of sons, daughters or step-children.[51] This feature is virtually absent in the homicide indictments from Sussex and Hertfordshire, as is the killing of servants, another relatively common occurrence in Essex. Although the sample is small, one wonders if these characteristics point to further peculiarities in a locality where the exceptionally high rate of witchcraft prosecutions has already been noticed.[52] A clue to the possible motivation behind at least some killings of this type may lie in the scramble for property and inheritance which underlay the brutal killing of an Essex boy in 1595 by his step-father and brother-in-law.[53]

The murder of unwanted children might be taken to suggest a possible correlation with the incidence of infanticide. Indictments for infanticide were, however, relatively uncommon: only sixty-two survive from the reign of Elizabeth, an average of less than one a year in each county. Table I suggests that indictments for infanticide were even rarer in the early seventeenth century. But the sample is very small and too much reliance should not be placed upon it.

The same must also be said of indictments for sexual crimes. Of 7544 persons indicted, only sixty-eight were charged with sexual offences: fifty with rape, sixteen with buggery and two with sodomy.[54] After 1563 buggery was triable at quarter sessions as well as assizes and this no doubt reduced the number of cases coming before the superior court.[55] Even so, it seems most unlikely that either buggery or sodomy was statistically significant in any part of this period. Rape was probably poorly reported. This fact, coupled with the small size of the sample, makes it virtually impossible to identify any meaningful pattern in the incidence of sexual offences.[56]

One other aspect of violent crime deserves further attention, both for its uniqueness in attracting consistent government attention and because of its peculiar topicality. The dangerous potential of firearms in general and handguns ('pocket dags', as they were commonly known) in particular had been recognized as early as 1541, when their use was prohibited by statute.[57] Over the next seventy-five years a stream of legislation associating firearms with violent crime sought vainly to regulate the one by forbidding the other.[58] 'It is a common thing', asserted the Privy Council while requesting renewed action in 1575, 'for ... thieves to carry pistols whereby they either murder out of hand before they rob, or else put her [majesty's] subjects in such fear that they dare not resist'.[59] The resilience of duelling as a substitute for litigation,[60] and the demands of both national defence and continental war in the years after 1585 increased the potential for armed violence. Military exercises produced their own crop of fatal accidents as rural recruits struggled to master the mysteries of 'arquebus and caliver'.[61] Disorder accompanied bands of pressed men travelling to join their companies,[62] while demobilized and deserting soldiers returning with arms and expertise were widely thought to have introduced a new and unwelcome dimension to violent crime.[63] Black Will and Shakebag, the bungling assassins of *Arden of Feversham* are authentic criminal types — soldiers drifting back from the continent via the Channel ports to an itinerant life of violent crime.[64] Those described by the government in 1596 as 'wandering by the name of soldiers lately come from the wars, who arming themselves with shot and other forbidden weapons ... have not only committed robberies and murders upon her majesty's people in their travel from place to place, but have resisted and murdered diverse constables and others that have come to the rescue'.[65]

A superficial analysis of the homicide indictments provides some support for official claims associating firearms with crime. Approximately 7 per cent of the violent deaths investigated at assizes in this period involved firearms; indeed, almost 16 per cent of the killings tried at Hertfordshire assizes during James I's reign were said to have been committed with guns of various sorts. Most shootings, however, appear to have resulted from ignorance and carelessness rather than malice. Only one of the twenty-five killings attributed to firearms was linked directly to the commission of another felony. Perhaps significantly, it occurred in Hertfordshire and in the course of a highway robbery.[66] A further twelve deaths which did not involve firearms were linked with other crimes. Five of these occurred during robberies and three in the course of poaching affrays. Of the remaining four killings, one took place in the defence of a house against burglars; one involved the murder of a wounded accomplice by a band of thieves; and two the elimination of incriminating witnesses — a girl with whom the murderer had earlier had sexual intercourse, and a maidservant who had been procured by a London painter to rob her mistress.[67] Other crime-related killings may be concealed behind the cryptic wording of homicide indictments; and of course the incidence of such crimes may well have been higher in the metropolis itself.[68] But, by and large, the evidence available at present suggests that fatal violence was not a common feature of provincial crime in this period.

Lesser forms of violence were prosecuted fairly frequently at assizes. Most allegations of non-fatal violence, whatever their expression or motive, were, however, couched as indictments for assault, and since assault indictments tell us almost nothing of the circumstances surrounding an attack it is extremely difficult to categorize them in any useful way. Occasionally, the identity of the victim indicates something of the motive for and nature of an attack. Approximately 16 per cent of the assaults indicted at assizes alleged violence against law enforcement officers, usually constables attempting to make arrests, and less frequently against bailiffs, headboroughs or subsidy collectors. Perhaps too much weight should not be given to the high incidence of assaults on local officers. The probability of such cases finding their way to court was unusually high, both because the government was concerned to discourage emulation and because the officers themselves sought to avoid responsibility for escapes. In most other assault indictments the identity of the victim is of little help in ascertaining the motive behind the attack. This is particularly true of the large number of cases in which an assault, real or fictional, is only one element in a complex of allegations. Most indictments in this category allege assault by two or more persons who are usually accused also of associated offences — illegal assembly, riot, disseisin, unlawful detention of property or other breaches of the peace. Such expressions of group violence constitute a particularly tantalizing problem, not only because they occur relatively frequently, but also because they undoubtedly reflect a wide spectrum of social and economic grievance. Some were by-products of poaching forays, others quite clearly small-scale enclosure riots.[69] On at least one occasion violence sprang out of a trade dispute between a group of Essex fishermen and the corporation of Colchester.[70] Still other riotous assaults occurred in the course of local disputes over tithes or rights of way.[71] Few significant patterns can be isolated. But deep differences in the social and economic make-up of particular localities are perhaps suggested by the fact that in Sussex indictments alleging violence by two or more persons constitute only about 35 per cent of all indictments for assault; in Essex and Hertfordshire instances of group violence constitute almost 70 per cent of the total.

Almost all contemporary complaints that crime was increasing focused upon offences against property. To some extent this merely reflected the obvious fact that trials for theft traditionally dominated criminal court proceedings. Throughout this period the vast majority of indictments laid at assizes were for theft of some sort: of 7544 persons indicted in the three counties under review, 5493 (almost 73 per cent) were accused of larceny, burglary or robbery. For those wishing to moralize or to urge more severe penalties for offences against property, the consistently high proportion of thieves appearing on gaol calendars constituted an undeniably powerful argument.

In seeking to explain this feature, most contemporaries embraced the view that theft was a socio-economic phenomenon. Pamphleteers occasionally noticed that the lower classes did not enjoy a monopoly of theft and violent crime.[72] But rarely did they go on to draw the direct connection between crime and childhood training advanced by the pediatrician John Jones in 1579. Crime in the 1570s was due, he claimed, to 'nothing so much ... as to the manner of bringing up in liberty, void of the fear of God's justice, terror of the Prince's laws, knowledge of themselves, and exercise in youth how to attain lawfully their living and maintenance in age ...'.[73] Privy Councillors, M.P.s and grand jurymen alike regarded thieves, vagrant soldiers, rogues, paupers and the idle as associated, or even indistinguishable categories.[74] Poverty and roguery were cut from the same quarry; ale- and gaming-houses were both resorts for the idle and 'nurseries of naughtiness'; 'the cause of great misdemeanours and outrages'; 'the very stock and stay of our false thieves and vagabonds'.[75] An anonymous pamphleteer in 1595 summed up popular thinking: 'such is the reward of riot; where no regard is had of spending above the course of lawful getting necessity must needs follow; games, wantonness and ease are not continued without excessive cost'.[76] In noting the connection between scarcity and crime and the more permanent dislocating effects of urban life, contemporary writers commonly associated offences against property with those sectors of society thought to have been most affected by the economic and social dislocation of the late sixteenth and early seventeenth centuries — rural labourers driven from the land, unemployed craftsmen, discharged and deserting soldiers.[77] Nor did the more general point that crime may be seen as an indicator of social tensions and instability entirely escape them. 'England had never so much work for a chronicle', mused a commentator on the shooting of a Chancery master in 1616, 'never such turnings, tossings and mutabilities in the lives of men and women and the streams of their fortunes'.[78]

Much of the indictment evidence tends to support those generalizations which sought to explain property crime in socio-economic terms. However, the social classification of criminals in this period poses serious problems. Traditional legal definitions — 'labourer', 'husbandman', 'yeoman' — reflected by this time only the broadest social groupings; court clerks used the terms loosely, and it is not uncommon to find the same man described as a 'labourer' in one indictment and as a craftsman of some sort in another.[79] It is therefore impossible to give statistical definition to contemporary generalizations attributing theft to particular social groups.

On the other hand, individual indictments occasionally confirm the connection between crime and economic misfortune. 'Weavers' occupation is a dead science nowadays', declared a Colchester weaver in 1566. 'We can get no work', said another, 'nor we have no money; and if we should steal we should be hanged, and if we should ask no man would give us; but we will have a remedy one of these days or else we will lose all'.[80]

Less graphic but statistically more persuasive, the indictments of vagrant and deserting soldiers lend support to contemporary allusions to the contribution of this class to criminality in the years after 1589. Lambard attributed the criminal propensities of returning soldiers to bad habits learned abroad and changes in the pattern of conscription: 'now, when not only our gaols are scoured and our highways swept but also the channels of our streets be raked for soldiers, what marvel is it if after their return from the wars they do either lead their lives in begging or end them by hanging'.[81] Successive proclamations issued between 1589 and 1592 insisted that discharged soldiers return to their original settlements and be re-engaged by their former employers.[82] But the passage in 1598 of further legislation declaring vagrant soldiers felons without benefit of clergy[83] and the continued indictment of ex-soldiers at assizes testifies to the intractability of the problem. In Kent soldiers returning from France in 1596 stole books from a parish church.[84] Peter Hatcher, the first deserter to be prosecuted in Sussex, was sentenced to death in 1597 for grand larceny and highway robbery;[85] thereafter, vagrant and deserting soldiers appear regularly in the assize records.[86] A few, like Hatcher, can be identified with violent and apparently premeditated crimes. More often, however, ex-soldiers are associated with the essentially opportunistic petty thefts which were the trademark of vagrant criminals. Two ex-soldiers examined by a Hertfordshire magistrate in 1591 described how, since coming from the Low Countries three months earlier, they had wandered the countryside living on 'the devotion of good people'. Finding a house in North Mimms unattended, they took a cloak lying nearby and departed. Three more examined later in the year had last seen service, again in the Low Countries, a year earlier: they confessed to stealing linen as they passed through Essendon but protested that when arrested they were about to return it.[87] In Kent a soldier who claimed to have been captured by the archduke of Austria was arrested for stealing clothes from a hedge.[88]

At this point it becomes difficult to distinguish thefts committed by returning soldiers from those perpetrated by the vagrant population at large. Vagrant crime is a topic in itself, and although much sixteenth- and early-seventeenth-century vagrant literature has been reprinted[89] very little has been done to test its authenticity. Recent work has tended to minimize vagrant criminality in this period.[90] But it is difficult to dismiss lightly the mass of contemporary evidence associating vagrants with crime, and particularly with crimes against property. Acts of parliament, proclamations, legal writers and private correspondents all agreed that vagrants constituted a menace to public order which was both serious and, at least for much of Elizabeth's reign, increasing.[91] Thomas Harman, a Kent magistrate, wrote of the swarms of vagrants who frequented the Home Counties in the first decade of Elizabeth's reign. His unpretentious account is full of circumstantial information on vagrant criminals and their methods: 'upright men' pilfering stalls and booths at markets and fairs or stealing clothes from hedges or unoccupied houses; 'hookers' plucking clothes and linen through open windows with their hooked staffs; horse-thieves roving the countryside in search of unattended animals.[92] Thirty years later Edward Hext wrote in similar terms of vagrant criminality in Somerset and of the 'wandering soldiers and other stout rogues of England', three or four hundred to a county.[93] Lambard also repeatedly warned his fellow justices against the 'swarms of vagrant and flying beggars who ... infect and stain the earth with pilfery, drunkenness, whoredom, bastardy, murder and infinite like mischiefs'.[94]

Vagrancy as such was not prosecuted at assizes before 1572 when an Act which provided more severe punishments for the offence was passed.[95] Between 1572 and the end of Elizabeth's reign 324 vagrants were indicted under this statute at assizes for Essex, Hertfordshire and Sussex. This figure, we can be sure, bears little relation to vagrant activity in these three counties during this period. Vagrants, particularly vagrant criminals like those already mentioned in connection with the Dell case,[96] were notoriously difficult to apprehend and once clear of the locality, almost impossible to trace. Even if arrested and brought to trial, vagrants can normally be identified as such only when (and only because) they are accused of the crime of vagrancy. Attempts to associate them with other forms of crime are bedevilled by the legal rule which forbade the attribution to a suspect of an illegal occupation, such as vagrancy.[97] All indictments against vagrants had therefore to be framed in non-prejudicial terms and their true occupation concealed, usually by omitting it altogether or by substituting the innocuous description 'labourer'. This is tantalizing, for it frustrates almost all efforts to identify vagrant thieves. Nor is it possible to recognize in indictments the typical vagrant ruses described by Harman and others: characteristically, an indictment for theft reveals almost nothing of the circumstances of the offence.

Pre-trial records, however, indicate quite clearly the prevalence of vagrants and their association with, in particular, opportunistic thieving. Recognizances are particularly useful in that they frequently identify suspects which much greater precision than the associated indictments.[98] For instance, the recognizance accompanying the indictment of Robert Gilham, 'labourer', for stealing clothes from a house at Hatfield in 1593 indicates that he was in fact a vagrant.[99] John Hewson, indicted as a Royston 'labourer' for stealing linen there in 1621 is also revealed by the associated recognizance as a vagrant.[100] Examinations taken by local magistrates indicate even more clearly the presence of vagrant thieves. Francis Bygge of Knebworth in Hertfordshire described how in May 1590 three women stopped at his gate. Two came to the front door to ask for alms while the third made her way to the back of the house to steal clothes which were hanging out to dry. When Bygge later apprehended her, she warned him — in terms strikingly similar to the threats mentioned by Hext — 'that was the hardest he could do, for she had friends would fetch her out of prison'.[101] Three years later a girl described how she had been befriended by two vagrant women. Posing as her mother and grandmother, they had used her to collect drying clothes from gardens in Hertfordshire and on one occasion had pushed her through a window to collect clothes from inside a dwelling. Typically, when indicted all three women were described as 'spinsters of Hitchin'.[102]

These illustrations — which could be multiplied — suggest that vagrant crime, though premeditated in a general sense, was essentially opportunisttic. Vagrants concentrated on isolated or empty dwellings, goods left unattended, solitary or obviously gullible victims. The ease with which stolen goods could be concealed and disposed of was also a decisive consideration. Thus clothes and linen were particularly attractive targets, and it is probably no coincidence that almost one-half of all indicted thieves were accused of stealing such articles. To this extent there was little difference between vagrant thieves and many local criminals. Many thefts seem to have been opportunistic, 'low-risk' ventures perpetrated, typically, by those on the move, whether legitimately or otherwise, or by domestic servants. Asked by a Hertfordshire justice to account for an old cloak, six horseshoes and a goose found in his possession, a Middlesex man confessed that he had taken the cloak from a house in which he had lodged and the horseshoes from an adjoining stable; the goose he had come across while walking. A Hertfordshire man came across a small pig feeding in Cheshunt Wood where he was working as a coalwood cutter. He immediately killed it and carried it to his mother's house, telling her that he had bought it 'to make merry with her'. John Audley, the eleven-year-old servant of a Weston man, stole a purse and 9*s.* which he found on the bed of a fellow servant; he then took to the road and found lodgings in Hitchin where he was arrested.[103] Like the examples involving ex-soldiers and vagrants, these illustrations suggest the existence of a sizeable local population for whom petty pilfering was almost instinctive.[104]

Of course this is not to suggest that all property crime was essentially opportunistic, its nature governed by the availability of easy targets. 'Professional' criminals certainly operated in this area; and although the cryptic nature of the indictment evidence makes it extremely difficult to isolate their activities, some thefts were quite clearly the systematic work of organized gangs. The gang which netted almost £200 in cash as well as plate and other goods from a series of burglaries in Sussex in 1581-2 and beat to death one of their number who had been wounded during a raid were obviously not opportunistic amateurs. Nor were the four men (one of whom went under the alias 'Dick of London') who burgled Cowdray house in 1610 and escaped with fine linen and clothes valued at more than £18.[105]

More generally, at least two types of theft were traditionally associated with 'professionals', operating either singly or in small gangs. Cutpurses and pickpockets haunted most places where crowds were likely to gather — fairs, markets, churches, law courts and even executions 'ordained chiefly for [the] terror and example of evil doers'.[106] They were reputedly organized into an association or mystery; but the ease with which even children could remove valuables in congested surroundings is demonstrated by the case of a small boy who, wanting to buy some cakes, successfully cut the purse of a woman talking with her neighbours outside a church in Kent.[107] Judging by the incidence of indictments for 'stealing from the peson', the market-towns of Hertfordshire in particular were a popular haunt of pickpockets and cutpurses, often working together in small groups of two or three.[108] Writing in 1582, William lord Burghley rejoiced at the recent execution of two notorious Hertfordshire cutpurses, one of whom had earlier been pardoned for a highway robbery.[109] Throughout the period Hertfordshire attracted large numbers of highwaymen, lured by the rich pickings on the main roads out of London. At least one contemporary thought highway robbery the most notorious of English crimes. Unlike other offences against property, which he assumed to be motivated by poverty and necessity, highway robbery was most often perpetrated by young gentlemen seeking an easy living.[110] Although 'gentlemen', some of them clearly working out of London, certainly appear with unusual frequency in indictments for highway robbery, it is difficult to generalize about the nature of this offence on the evidence of judicial records. Some robberies yielded unusually high sums of money or quantities of silver plate, a fact which may indicate the planned assault of a particular traveller. On the other hand, such dramatic successes may represent merely good fortune, perhaps a tiny minority of many chance encounters and fruitless attempts. Similarly, it is impossible to know whether thefts from Hertfordshire inns, usually of pewter utensils or travellers' belongings, represent typically opportunistic pilfering by servants or fellow guests or the systematic work of professional criminals.[111]

In the absence of reliable rates for individual crimes, all attempts to buttress statistically these general remarks on the character of property crime must be extremely tentative. But certain quantitative variations between the three counties under consideration suggest a connection between the availability and nature of targets and the character and, less obviously, the incidence of property crime in particular areas. Highway robbery provides the clearest illustration. In Hertfordshire 7.4 per cent of all those indicted for offences against property during Elizabeth's reign were accused of highway robbery; in Essex the proportion was 4.7 per cent; in Sussex only 2.9 per cent were indicted for this offence. Over the whole period, 1559-1625, 6.6 per cent of those indicted for offences against property in Hertfordshire were accused of highway robbery; in Sussex only 2.8 per cent. This discrepant experience is best explained in terms of variations in the availability of targets, a factor linked in turn to local economic and geographical peculiarities. The principal highways from London to the north and midlands passed through Hertfordshire and the merchants, carriers and drovers using them presented obvious and lucrative targets. Sussex roads, on the other hand, attracted little through-traffic and the pickings on them were proportionately meagre. Thus the great majority of twenty-five highway robberies prosecuted at Sussex assizes between 1559 and 1603 yielded only clothing or personal belongings; only two (8 per cent) netted more than £5 in money. In contrast, only one of twenty-seven highway robberies prosecuted at Hertfordshire assizes in the thirty years after 1573 failed to yield money or silver plate. Eleven (40 per cent) netted sums in excess of £5. These included three robberies of £100 or more, one an astronomical £272 in cash, and cloth valued at £10, taken by an 'esquire', three 'gentlemen' and a 'yeoman' at Amwell in February 1590. Significantly, the only member of the quartet to be brought to trial was arrested in the City of London.[112]

Similar considerations probably dictated the incidence of pick-pockets and cutpurses in these two counties. Again, Hertfordshire seems to have provided the most attractive opportunities. Indictments for stealing from the person, which reflect almost exclusively thefts by stealth, were laid against 4 per cent of those accused of property offences in Hertfordshire between 1573 and 1625. Only 1.7 per cent of the thieves indicted in Sussex between 1559 and 1603 were accused of offences of this type. Conversely, the absence of such targets in Sussex and the scattered nature of settlement in the county probably combined to increase the incidence of thefts from dwelling-houses and other isolated buildings. Forty-two per cent of those indicted for theft in Sussex between 1559 and 1625 were alleged to have broken into such premises, either by day or during the night. Less than 20 per cent of the thieves prosecuted at Hertfordshire assizes were accused of these forms of aggravated larceny.

There are also overall quantitative differences between the two counties. In particular, it seems likely that the incidence of property crime in general was appreciably higher in Hertfordshire than in Sussex. Over the whole period, thieves accounted for almost 79 per cent of all those prosecuted at Hertfordshire assizes, a proportion 12 per cent higher than that for Sussex. Although there are variations in the samples for the two counties after 1603, the data suggest that their experience of property crime differed even more widely in the early seventeenth century. Whereas offences against property in Sussex between 1603 and 1625 declined to just over 62 per cent of the total of indicted crime, in Hertfordshire the proportion increased to over 81 per cent, a difference of almost 20 per cent.

The Essex data suggest that, at least between 1559 and 1603, property crime in that county reflected, though less dramatically, some of the characteristics of both Sussex and Hertfordshire. As a percentage of indicted crime, property offences in Essex (73.1 per cent) were only slightly behind those in Hertfordshire (76.4 per cent). The incidence of indictments for housebreaking and burglary (33.8 per cent) was much higher than in Hertfordshire (22.8 per cent), but considerably less than the figure for Sussex (45.4 per cent). On the other hand, indictments for stealing from the person (2.1 per cent) and highway robbery (4.7 per cent) were proportionately more common than in Sussex (1.9 and 2.9 per cent respectively) but less frequent than in Hertfordshire (3.5 and 7.4 per cent). All this perhaps suggests a more 'typical' county; an area in which targets were more evenly distributed and the character of property crime therefore more balanced than in either of the other two counties.

One series of fluctuations, however, may well have been common to all three counties. On three separate occasions during Elizabeth's reign the statistical data indicate sudden sharp increases in the volume of property offences coming before the courts. After each of these the number of suspects appearing before the courts declined slightly, but without ever returning to pre-crisis levels. The first of these surges occurred over the three years 1572-4; the second between 1585 and 1587; and the last in the period 1596-8. Gaps in the data make it difficult to plot the exact pattern in all three counties; but the trends in Essex, which has the fullest data, can be plotted fairly precisely. In three consecutive years after 1571 the number of persons indicted at assizes for property offences increased by 72, 66 and 103 per cent, respectively, over the annual average for the preceding thirteen years. A second upsurge occurred in 1585 when the number indicted for property crime suddenly increased by 43 per cent over the annual average for the years 1572-84. In 1586 the increase was only 13 per cent, but in 1587 it leaped to 132 per cent over the average for the thirteen years before 1585. Deficiencies in the data again render comparison with Sussex impossible. But in Hertfordshire the number indicted for property offences in 1585 was up 44 per cent over the annual average for the preceding twelve years, while the number indicted in 1587 at the winter assizes alone exceeded the average total for both assizes by 48 per cent. The third and most dramatic increase occurred in 1596. Again its precise dimensions are clouded by gaps in the data. But the only Essex file to survive from 1596 suggests an increase in indicted property crime of approximately 60 per cent over the annual average for the preceding eight years. In the following year, 1597, the increase was 114 per cent, and in 1598 approximately 60 per cent. The trend in Sussex was similar — increases of 76 per cent in 1596, 109 per cent in 1597 and 13 per cent in 1598 — while in Hertfordshire the surviving files point to increases of over 100 per cent in both 1597 and 1598. The years 1596-8 mark an absolute maximum in the volume of indicted property crime during this period. Thereafter, the number of indicted suspects fell slowly and fairly uniformly, although there were minor peaks in 1601 and 1616 and again at the very end of James I's reign.

These extraordinary fluctuations suggest that contemporary commentators were to some extent justified in associating crimes against property with economic conditions. All three of the sudden upsurges in indicted property crime during Elizabeth's reign can be identified with periods in which scarcity and necessity were unusually acute. Indeed, a correlation of indictment levels with trends in the price of foodstuffs strongly suggests that during this period variations in the incidence of theft followed very closely fluctuations in the price of food.

For five years after the bad harvest of 1565, the average price of wheat — a staple in almost all diets — remained stable at between 14s. and 15s. a quarter.[113] In 1571, however, it rose suddenly to almost 17s., increased again in the following year and then in 1573 reached 24s. a quarter, a price exceeded only once since the famine of 1556. Between 1574 and 1584 wheat averaged a little over 19s. a quarter. In 1585, however, the price jumped again to over 26s. and, following a bad harvest, to almost 35s. in 1586, the highest price recorded to that date. Wheat again sold for under 20s. a quarter in four of the seven years between 1587 and 1593 but it would be a hundred and fifty years before it did so again. The harvests of 1594 and 1595 were bad, those of 1596 and 1597 disastrous. Wheat averaged well over 30s. a quarter in 1594 and 1595 and in the following year reached 50s., a price not exceeded until 1630. The Hertfordshire authorities described how the high price of wheat drove up food prices generally;[114] in Essex a rumour that wheat would reach 16s. a bushel provoked talk of a general insurrection;[115] and there were food riots in several parts of the country.[116]

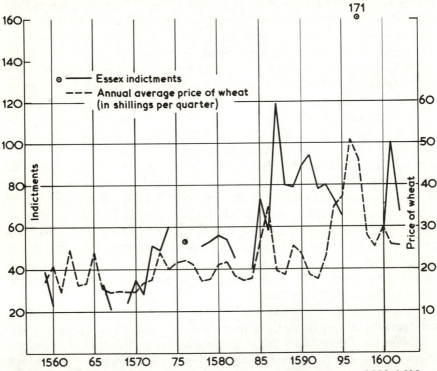

Figure I: Prices and indictments for crimes against property 1559-1600

Figure I above, which matches the rate of indicted property crime in Essex with the annual average price of wheat, indicates the close short-term connection between indictments and prices. The relationship is particularly clear, despite tantalizing gaps in the assize data, between 1596 and 1598 when record prices were followed closely by a massive peak in the level of indictments. Unfortunately, the data for Sussex and Hertfordshire in the sixteenth century are too defective to provide conclusive support for these short-term trends. However, the surviving data from both counties suggest a similar response to suddenly rising prices, at least in the period 1585-87 and during the years of dearth after 1596. There is some suggestion that the impact of scarcity on crime levels in Hertfordshire may have been longer delayed and less acute, features which may be connected in some way with other exceptional characteristics of crime in that county.[117] But the trends are not really clear enough to warrant further speculation.

Over the longer term, also, price trends bear a fairly close relationship to the pattern of property crime. Gaps in the data for all three counties preclude any attempt to assess the impact of the bad harvests of 1560, 1562 and 1565.[118] But after 1569 the trends in prices and indictments seem to be in general harmony. Periods of stable, but higher, prices are accompanied by relatively stable, but elevated, indictment levels, and these plateaus are separated by the sharp and increasingly high peaks echoing the successive crises of the reign. On the evidence of the Hertfordshire data plotted in Figure II below, the connection after 1600 is much less obvious.

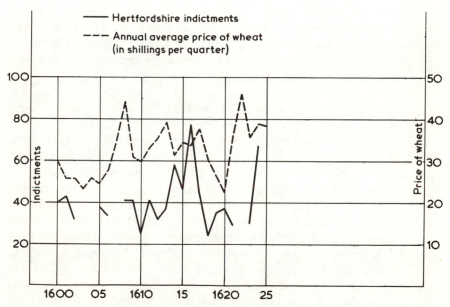

Figure II: Prices and indictments for crimes against property 1600-1625

There is still a general relationship in some years between prices and indictments for property crime. But compared to the precise correlations of the sixteenth century, the response in indictment levels to the bad harvests of 1608 and 1622, when wheat again sold for 45*s*. a quarter, seems both muted and delayed. Moreover, the data for 1616 suggest a sudden rise in property crime which is not readily linked to national trends. A second sudden increase in 1624, however, occurred in a year when after three years of high prices, for the first time since 1596 the price of a 4 lb loaf on the London market reached 6*d*., even though the harvests of this and the preceding year were average.[119]

Obviously much more work needs to be done before a connection between price fluctuations and the incidence of indicted crime can be taken to be established. The Hertfordshire data suggest that, at least in the early seventeenth century, the relationship between prices and property crime may be neither simple nor uniform. Characteristics peculiar to crime or law enforcement in Hertfordshire may have distorted to some extent the statistics from that county. Perhaps the economy of Hertfordshire in the early seventeenth century reflected London trends more closely than those of the country at large. Nor should we forget that other variables — fluctuations in local employment levels, for example — may help to determine the level of crime. These, and other possibilities need systematic investigation, and until this work has been done particular problems will remain. For the moment, however, most of the available evidence suggests a general relationship between the movement of prices and the rate of crimes against property. More specifically, that in the second half of the sixteenth century and, less certainly, in the early seventeenth century theft was to a perceptible degree motivated by economic necessity.

While isolating a number of elements critical to the incidence and character of provincial crime in the late sixteenth and early seventeenth centuries, this examination leaves many questions unanswered. It is therefore as much a preface to and an agenda for future research as a preliminary statement on the nature of crime in this period. Weaknesses in the treatment — a tendency to characterize rather than quantify offences and to identify without defining related factors — stem mainly from the nature and limitations of the available evidence. Phenomena such as vagrancy and military conscription need thorough investigation before any attempt is made to estimate their impact on the level of crime. Worrying uncertainties posed by the Hertfordshire statistics underline the need for more precise demographic data and a clearer picture of the economic and social makeup of the Home Counties in this period. The limitations of the legal records are only too clear; and of course they apply equally to similar material from other counties. Too much should not therefore be expected of work now in progress on the judicial records for Kent and Surrey — the remaining two counties of the Home Circuit. The additional data will, at best, confirm and sharpen the trends suggested here. At worst, they may further complicate an already complex picture, particularly since comparable material for other counties has not survived. Pre-trial records, principally examinations and depositions, hold out the possibility of further qualitative, and perhaps even limited statistical analysis. But the material is scattered and work upon it will be slow. Thus the prospects for a definitive treatment of crime in the period between 1558 and the mid seventeenth century — when judicial records begin to survive in quantity — are not entirely favourable, and it is difficult at this point to avoid the conclusion that the picture which eventually emerges will remain in some respects both unclear and incomplete.

3 *Witchcraft in Tudor and Stuart Essex*

A.D.J. MACFARLANE

'Witchcraft' may be defined as supernatural activity, believed to be the result of power given by the Devil, and causing physical damage, for instance death. The study of this particular offence during the sixteenth and seventeenth centuries has several justifications. Firstly, as we shall see, it was considered important at the time. Secondly, it gives us a unique entry into the mental world of ordinary people living several centuries ago. Thirdly, since it was the concern of several different courts as well as a topic on which people wrote treatises and pamphlets, it provides unusually full material for the historian of crime. Fourthly, since we do not any longer tend to believe in the phenomenon, it poses special problems for those trying to understand the past and provides a test case for the application of anthropological theories to historical data. Finally, it is an excellent illustration of the way in which our knowledge of the past is intimately linked with archival reform.[1] During the last two generations the sources available to the historian of this phenomenon have expanded enormously. This can be illustrated in relation to the English county of Essex. In 1911 Notestein listed some fifteen Essex trials, from literary and pamphlet sources.[2] In 1929 Ewen published 473 Essex indictments for witchcraft from the assize files.[3] He was one of the first to use this source for any topic.[4] The use of further assize records, quarter sessions files, records of the archdeaconry court and other legal records, has now made it possible to locate over 1200 prosecutions and presentments for this offence in Essex during the period 1560-1700.[5] As in so many other fields, a growing interest in a topic has converged with the recovery and rearrangement of classes of data which enable us to look more deeply into the phenomenon.

The first English witchcraft statute was passed in 1542. It was repealed in 1547 along with all the new Henrician statutes, and replaced in March 1563 by a new Act. This Act laid down the death penalty for invoking evil spirits and for using 'witchcraft, enchantment, charm or sorcery, whereby any person shall happen to be killed or destroyed'. Injury of persons or property by witchcraft was punished by imprisonment for one year and four appearances in the pillory for the first offence, and by death for the second. In 1604 this Act was replaced by a more severe one. The invocation of spirits was elaborated; dead bodies were not to be taken out of their graves for witchcraft; injuring a person or his property was now punishable by death for the first offence instead of the second; intending to hurt or destroy people or property was punishable 'although the same be not effected and done'. This Act continued in force until 1736, when it was repealed. It was under these Acts that prosecutions were brought to the secular courts.[6]

Convicted 'witches' were hanged unless the victim was a master or a husband, in which case 'petty treason' had been committed and the guilty person was burned. Witchcraft, because of its secret and almost unprovable nature, was considered a crime apart. For this reason the normal rules of evidence and trial were modified. Suspicion alone was sufficient ground for accusation; it was proper to use children as witnesses; absence from the scene of the crime was no alibi; the victim's character and events occurring many years before and not in the least related to the particular crime were relevant. The 'sufficient proofs', any one of which was strong enough to lead to a conviction for witchcraft, were as follows: accusation by another 'witch'; an unnatural mark on the body of the accused, supposedly caused by the Devil or a familiar;[7] two witnesses to the pact with the Devil or who had seen the accused entertain the small familiars sent by him. One leading contemporary authority, for example, argued that if a person gave a child an apple and the child soon afterwards became ill, as long as there was known malice between them, this was proof enough to be grounds for execution. One of the strongest proofs was the confession of the accused, or a cross-accusation by another proven witch. There was thus considerable stress on the need to extort a confession. Yet confessions played a smaller part in English witchcraft than in Scottish or continental trials because in England the use of judicial torture, allowable in Roman law, was forbidden. Although informal pressures could be brought to bear on the accused and she might be kept awake for night after night or 'swum' to see whether the pure element of water would reject her (and hence show her to be a witch), the rack and the thumbscrew were absent from witchcraft trials in England.

Witchcraft was also an offence under ecclesiastical law, where it had been treated as one form of heresy before the State took cognizance of it. Inquiries concerning witches and 'sorcerers' were made in many of the visitation articles issued by archbishops, bishops and archdeacons during the hundred years following the first Henrician statute. For example, in the diocese of London — within which Essex was situated — Bishop Sandys asked in 1571 for the presentment of 'any that useth sorcery, witchcraft, enchantments, incantations, charms, unlawful prayers or invocations in

Latin'.[8] This was repeated in subsequent years, but there was a growing recognition that the ecclesiastical court only dealt with those offences not covered by the witchcraft statutes. In 1601, for example, reference was made to witchcraft 'punishable by the ecclesiastical laws' and in 1628 the bishop inquired: 'Have you any in your parish which have used any enchantments, sorceries, witchcrafts or incantations, which are not made felony by the statutes of this realm, or any charms; or which do resort to any such for help or counsel?' The penalty in the ecclesiastical court was far lighter than that in the civil courts. If a person admitted the offence, or was unable to bring forward the stipulated number of neighbours to support her denial, then public penance was enjoined, possibly combined with the payment of considerable court fees. The penance usually had to be carried out on a Sunday in the parish church and the accused wore a white sheet and carried a white wand. Having asked the forgiveness of God and of her neighbours, the accused was supposedly reintegrated into village society.

This then was the formal legal background, reflecting current legal processes and ideas concerning the supernatural world.[9] Witchcraft beliefs and accusations occurred throughout most of Europe during this period, and there are numerous studies of the phenomenon. England has been singled out for this study because it has particularly good legal records for the period. Essex was chosen as a sample for several reasons. It is one of the five counties in England which have sixteenth-century assize records and it surpasses the other four in this class in the early commencement of its quarter sessions material. It also has excellent ecclesiastical court records. Furthermore, its records are made easily accessible by the excellent local record office. It is important to stress that although comparison of the Essex cases with those for other counties does suggest that this was one of the areas of densest prosecution, many other counties witnessed witchcraft accusations on a large scale.[10] Part, though not all, of the pre-eminence of this county lies in the fact that more of its records for the crucial period survive. Many counties do not have adequate series of court records of the relevant kind until the middle of the seventeenth century. By that time, even in Essex, witchcraft prosecutions had almost died away. If no Essex documents before 1650 had survived, we would have received the impression that there were two or three famous trials, but we could not have known of the yearly and widespread trials which emerge from the records.

The county of Essex itself is situated to the north-east of London and is approximately forty miles in length and width. It had a population of about 100,000 in 1638, the only date for which we have an estimate. They lived in about 425 villages and seven chartered boroughs. This flat county was still predominantly agricultural, but the late sixteenth century witnessed the growth of an important cloth industry in the north-east of the county. Most of the county, with the major exception of the north-west, had been enclosed before the sixteenth century. Contemporaries thought that Essex ranked with Kent and Suffolk as one of the most advanced and prosperous counties in England during this period. It helped supply London with food and people. Both politically and religiously it had a reputation for radicalism. It was also the locus for numerous witchcraft accusations.

Our first approach to measuring witchcraft is through the formal court records. Some 314 people are known to have been prosecuted under the witchcraft statutes between 1560 and 1680 at Essex assizes and quarter sessions. There were over 500 indictments for witchcraft at assizes alone. One example will show the nature of the prosecutions at assizes. At the Essex winter assizes in 1579, Ellen Smyth of Maldon, spinster, was indicted for bewitching Susan Webbe, then aged about four years. It was alleged that the bewitching occurred on 7 March 1579 and the child died at Maldon on the following day. The presentment was found to be a 'true bill' by the grand jury and the defendant was found guilty and judged according to the statute. It will be seen that such indictments provide information on a number of problems: the place of residence, age, sex and marital position of witch and victim; the duration and nature of the betwitching; and the verdict and sentence of the court. This was one of the 462 indictments surviving for Essex in which a person was accused of injuring or killing people or damaging property. The frequency and importance of witchcraft trials at assizes is well shown if we compare indictments for this offence with those for other crimes. Between 1580 and 1599 an average of five or six people a year were tried at Essex assizes on charges of witchcraft. Over the whole of the period 1560-1680 witchcraft indictments constituted about five per cent of all the criminal proceedings at this court. In the years 1580-89, 118 of the 890 indictments for all offences concerned witchcraft, approximately 13 per cent of all the prosecutions. The trial of witches was second only to the trial of thieves. It was not a peripheral and marginal crime, but of central importance. There were few years when indictments did not occur.[11]

Not all of those accused of this offence were found guilty. On twenty-four occasions the grand jury refused to 'find' the bill of presentment and returned it *ignoramus*.[12] No complete rejections of bills occurred before 1647, but after that date both the total number of bills presented and the number which were accepted by the grand jury as 'true', declined rapidly. There were only thirty-nine presentments between 1647 and 1680, and twenty of these were rejected as *ignoramus*. This seems to reflect a great change in attitude on the part of the minor gentry, of whom grand juries were composed. It seems to have been an important factor in the decline of witchcraft prosecutions in Essex some fifty years before the official repeal of the Witchcraft Act. It is extremely difficult to be sure of what happened to convicted witches. Of the 291 people accused at Essex assizes for witchcraft, 151 were found guilty or the bill of presentment against them was dismissed. Of the remaining 140, 129 were found guilty: seventy-four of these were ordered to be executed, and another fifty-five imprisoned. But even when they were ordered to be executed, it is difficult to be certain of their fate; it has been argued, for example, that 'over the whole period only about ten per cent of those [felons] convicted [at assizes] were actually executed'.[13] This may have been partially balanced by the fact that terrible prison conditions meant that many of those who were theoretically imprisoned were, in fact, condemned to death by 'gaol fever' as it was known. We know from coroners' inquests that at least thirty-six accused witches died of illness in gaol. Probably about one hundred persons died as a result of accusations of witchcraft during this period in Essex.

The other major legal source for the study of witchcraft as an offence is the records of the ecclesiastical courts. Between 1560 and 1680 about 230 men and women from Essex are known to have been presented at the ecclesiastical courts for offences connected with witchcraft and sorcery. Evidence from ecclesiastical cases provides important material on a number of subjects: the efforts to counter the power of a witch and the methods and numbers of witch-doctors or 'cunning folk' as they were known; the characters and motives of suspected witches; and the attitude of the church authorities. Essex was covered by a number of overlapping jurisdictions, the most important being those of the bishop of London and the archdeacons of Essex, Colchester and Middlesex. Nearly all the surviving cases arose out of churchwardens' presentments at the archdeaconry courts. Many of the accused were merely accused of 'witchcraft and sorcery', but there are also twenty-five cases of acting as a 'sorcerer' (cunning folk), thirty-eight for going to 'sorcerers', and twenty-two for defaming a person as a witch.[14] More than half the cases occurred between 1580 and 1592, and there are very few cases after 1620 in any of the ecclesiastical courts. There does not seem to have been any obvious correlation between the nature or quantity of presentments and the personality of the ecclesiastical judges. In the archdeaconry of Colchester, for example, George Withers remained archdeacon from 1570 to 1617, yet there were widespread fluctuations in the number of presentments, the last of which occurred six years before his retirement.

Statistics for a whole county may be reinforced by looking at specific villages. If we select as a sample three parishes near Chelmsford — Hatfield Peverel, Boreham and Little Baddow — we may see how important witchcraft accusations were as a proportion of all crime.[15] Hatfield Peverel, with a total population of about 500, is known to have harboured over the period 1560-90 fifteen suspected witches; another thirty persons were directly involved as husbands or victims of 'witches'. In the neighbouring village of Boreham, about three-quarters of the size of Hatfield Peverel, there were at least four suspected witches. As a proportion of all known offences coming before the quarter sessions and assize courts from these villages during the reign of Elizabeth, accusations of witchcraft were also significant. Thus, in Hatfield Peverel, there were roughly twenty-six assault cases, two murders, one suicide, eleven cases of theft and fourteen cases of witchcraft. It is true that this parish was exceptional, but neighbouring Boreham was less so: here there were five assaults, one murder, twenty thefts and four accusations of witchcraft.

Court records seriously underestimate the amount of formal and informal accusation concerning this crime. Because witchcraft was a subject which made spectacular reading, several pamphlet accounts describing some of the trials were published and these enable us to see what lay behind the formal court records. These descriptions reveal that the records as we see them deal with only a fraction of the evidence that was heard in the court-room. In the case of the indictment concerning Ellen Smyth, the details of which we have given above, the bare bones are filled in by the corresponding pamphlet. We learn that Ellen was the daughter of Alice Chaundeler, previously executed for witchcraft; that Ellen quarrelled with her stepfather over an inheritance and that he subsequently became ill; that she was believed to have a toad familiar which, when burnt, caused pain to its mistress; that her child-victim's mother was driven mad by the sight of another familiar like a black dog; that Ellen's own son described his mother's three spirits called 'great Dicke', 'little Dicke', and 'Willet'; and that the bottles and wool-pack in which they were supposedly kept were discovered when her house was searched.[16] Very little of this appears in the formal record. Another person described in this pamphlet was Margery Stanton of Wimbish. In 1578 she had been found guilty at quarter sessions of bewitching a gelding. The case was later dismissed at the assizes, probably because the owner of the bewitched gelding was not named. From the court record, this would appear to be a mild prosecution, but the chance survival of the pamphlet reveals a web of accusations and beliefs behind this one official indictment. Among those misfortunes which Margery was supposed to have inflicted were: tormenting a man, killing chickens, causing a woman to swell so that she looked pregnant and nearly burst, making cattle give 'gore stinking blood' instead of milk, making a child ill and tormenting another so that it 'fell into such shrieking and staring, wringing and writhing of the body to and fro, that all that saw it were doubtful of the life of it'. Nor did the motives of the witch appear in the formal prosecution. She quarrelled with a man who cut her face; later he grabbed some corn she was carrying and threw it to his chickens, all but one of which promptly died. In another case she 'came often to the house of one John Hopwood of Walden, and had continually her requests. At the last, being denied of a leathern thong, she went her way offended, and the same night his gelding in the stable ... died suddenly'. Among her victims was the vicar of Wimbish's child, the vicar being no other than the renowned William Harrison, who had two years earlier published his *Description of England.*[17]

There are surviving indictments in the assize records concerning eighteen women who are also described in popular pamphlets. In the indictments they are specified as having thirty-one victims. From the pamphlets, however, we learn the names of another fifty-seven victims not mentioned in the formal prosecutions, yet said to be suffering from the witchcraft of these eighteen women.[18] It would thus appear that approximately one in three of those believing themselves to be bewitched went so far as making a formal charge in the courts. It also appears that possibly more than one in four of suspected witches were never brought to court. In four pamphlets, twenty-seven 'witches' are named, but only eighteen appear in the indictments. The study of witchcraft indicates how dangerous it is to use court records even as an index of what went on in court, for the pamphlets are verbatim transcripts of the depositions and examinations in the courts. Yet it is also true that both sources support the literal accuracy of the other. Each source contains information not in the other, but there is very little direct contradiction.

A final way to test the accuracy of the criminal records before we use them is to compare them between themselves, in other words to see the degree of overlap between different courts. This might also contribute to one of the most important problems, the degree to which large numbers of suspected witches were not officially prosecuted. If, for example, the different courts produce entirely discreet and non-overlapping sets of persons accused of this offence, this would tend to suggest that there are considerable numbers of persons who may have never been presented. The 'universe' of suspected persons was very wide and each jurisdiction was able to scoop out large quantities of persons with little overlap. If, on the other hand, the same persons are accused in lower and higher courts, and there was overlap between civil and ecclesiastical jurisdictions, this would tend to suggest that most of those who were strongly suspected of witchcraft have come into our field of vision. A comparison of the records of assize and ecclesiastical courts confirms the view that witchcraft beliefs and prosecutions were far more widespread than any one set of records would indicate. Only about one in fifteen of those accused at assizes appeared at the ecclesiastical courts and approximately one in eighteen of those accused at the ecclesiastical courts appeared elsewhere. We may conclude by guessing that the 500 assize indictments we have constitute less than one-third of the accusations actually made in court, and that these court accusations represented only a very small fraction of the actual suspicions in the Essex countryside at this time. Even if we confine ourselves to the surviving records, however, we find that over 227 villages in Essex at this period are known to have been connected with witchcraft prosecutions in one way or another.

Turning now to an analysis of the records, the distribution of the actual prosecutions may be analysed in various ways.[19] Temporally, the peak of trials at both ecclesiastical and assize courts was in the 1580s and 1590s, with a final outburst in 1645 (see Figure I). The prosecutions died away long before the repeal of the Witchcraft Act in 1736. Although certain years saw peaks, accusations continued year in and year out during Elizabeth's reign. The last case at assizes occurred in 1675.

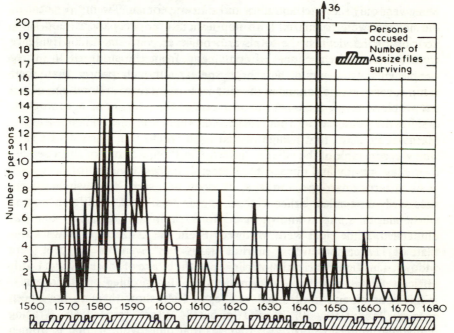

Figure I: Number of persons accused of witchcraft at the Essex Assizes, 1560-1680, and number of Assize files surviving

By geographical area, again, prosecutions were spread all over Essex. They seem to have started in the area around Chelmsford and were, to a certain extent, concentrated in the central and northern strip of the county. The north-eastern Tendring hundred was practically free except for the two most notorious trials, those of 1582 and 1645, when a group of adjoining villages became the centre of prosecutions. All broad attempts to correlate the distribution with economic, social or religious factors have, so far, been unsuccessful. For example, there seems to be no particular relationship to areas of population density, the new draperies, enclosure or forest land.

By sex, it is apparent that witches were usually women. Of 270 suspected witches at the assizes, all but twenty-three were women. Women, also, were slightly more likely to be bewitched; thus, at the same court, indictments stated that 103 males had been bewitched to death, 116 females. Neither in this, nor in the myths and types of injury inflicted, does there seem to have been any marked sexual element in Essex witchcraft. In this respect English witchcraft as a whole differed considerably from that on the Continent.

By occupation and status, it appears that witches were usually from a slightly lower economic level than their accusers. Thus, of fifty husbands of witches whose status is given in the assize records, twenty-three were 'labourers' and four were 'yeoman'; while of forty-five victims whose status was given, only six were labourers and sixteen yeomen. Twenty per cent of the suspects were connected with non-agricultural occupations, and forty per cent of the victims; the totals are, however, very small.[20] Evidence from the pamphlet accounts of trials, and from the study of the three sample villages, suggests that the suspects, although poorer than their victims, were not the poorest in the village. For instance, in Boreham, of the ten people receiving aid from the overseers of the poor, none were witches, despite the presence of four suspected witches in the village. Rather, Margaret Poole of that village, a suspected witch, was married to a man who was constable of the village, and who, in 1566, was one of the assessors of the lay subsidy and himself the sixteenth highest contributor.

As regards marriage and age, it does not seem that witches were necessarily unmarried, either widows or spinsters. Thus, of fifteen women whose marital status is known in the three sample villages, only one was unmarried, while eight were widowed. From the assize records we know that, of 117 persons whose marital status was given, 40 per cent were widows. This figure is clearly interlinked with the age of those involved. It is difficult to get statistical information on this problem, but coroners' inquisitions on five imprisoned witches in 1645 show them to have been aged 40, 'about 50', 70, 70, and 'about 84' years, respectively. Tracing individuals in local records also suggests that older women, that is women over about 50 years of age, were more powerful witches, though it was believed that they tried to impart their witchcraft to their young children.

Detailed analysis of the kinship structure in the three villages has given the negative conclusion that witches were hardly ever related by blood to their victims, though they occasionally confessed to bewitching their husband or relations by marriage. On the other hand, almost all bewitchings occurred within a village and within groups of neighbours. Thus, of 460 cases of bewitching persons or property tried at assizes, only fifty occurred between villages; the rest were within the village. This inter-neighbour bewitching is clearly shown in the pamphlets. In Hatfield Peverel, one witch gave her familiar 'to mother Waterhouse her neighbour', and she in turn 'falling out with another of her neighbours' killed three geese, and 'falling out with another of her neighbours and his wife' killed the husband. In this village it is even beginning to appear that nearly all the accusations took place between the tenants of one manor and not those of another. This manor was composed of a dissolved priory, but there seems to be no general correlation between dissolved monastic foundations and witchcraft tensions. Nor has any connection been found between manors with partible inheritance, or ultimogeniture, and accusations.

Finally, those involved may be analysed to see whether there is any connection between witchcraft suspicions, religious groupings and deviant behaviour of other kinds. The distribution of prosecutions shows no obvious correlation with Puritan centres or with Roman Catholic strongholds. Nor does a detailed study of church attendance and the religious formulae of wills in the three sample villages show any marked relationship between religious attitudes and attitudes to witchcraft. Thus, in Hatfield Peverel, none of the ten women presented between 1584 and 1600 for not attending church were prosecuted as suspected witches. In fact it was recognized by contemporaries that witches might be outwardly godly people; those 'which seemed to be very religious people, and would constantly repair to sermons near them' might be witches.[21] Nor does comparison of those known to be witches and those accused of thefts, suicide, murder, breaking the sabbath, quarrelling, scolding or sexual offences show any clear correlation in the three sample villages. Thus in Boreham, where there were roughly thirteen bastardy cases, six cases of premarital intercourse and seventeen miscellaneous cases of sexual misbehaviour between 1570 and 1600, there is only one possible overlap with a suspected witch. Although witches were thought of as quarrelsome and unpleasant people, they were not usually formally accused of other offences.

One theory for the existence of witchcraft beliefs is that they are, in certain repects, the most satisfactory explanation of misfortune or strange events. If medicine failed to heal and God seemed to turn a deaf ear to prayer, then the individual, it is suggested, could at least busy himself in hunting down the witch and countering her magic, occupations which both took the mind off the grief and held out a partial hope of recovery. So attractive, in fact, was the witchcraft explanation, that some authorities believed that people related almost every injury to a witch. Reginald Scot argued 'that few or none can (nowadays) with patience endure the hand and correction of God. For if any adversity, grief, sickness, loss of children, corn, cattle, or liberty happen unto them, by and by they exclaim upon witches'.[22]

On the other hand, it is quite evident from the three-village study that only a small proportion of the many accidents in an Elizabethan village *were* interpreted as the result of the evil will of a neighbour. In Boreham between 1560 and 1603 witches were accused of killing one child and making one man ill. Even if this was only a small part of the actual suspicions against them, it must have been a tiny proportion of the total illness and 351 known deaths during this period in the village. In the same village, coroners' inquests were held on the bodies of two young men who were squashed to death by a landslide while digging in a sand pit, and on another inhabitant who fell into a stream and drowned. There is no suggestion that they were believed to have been bewitched; the verdict was 'death by misfortune'. Since it seems, therefore, that death or injury could be explained in other ways, we are left with the problem of why certain injuries were ascribed to witches and not others.

To a limited extent the answer lies in the nature of the injury. To begin with, witchcraft explained only individual misfortunes, not general phenomena such as major climatic changes or the burning down of a whole town. Witches were accused in Essex courts of burning down a *particular* barn, nearly blowing down a *particular* house and sinking a *particular* ship. There was also an emphasis on the strangeness of an event: for instance when a huge tree suddenly fell down on a windless day; or when a normally clean woman 'was on a sudden so filled with lice, that they might have been swept off her clothes with a stick', especially when the lice were 'long, and lean and not like other lice'.[23] Again, the amount of pain, physical or emotional, involved and the ability of physicians to deal with it, were partly relevant. Thus witches were, above all, suspected of killing human beings, and those whose deaths were ascribed to witches characteristically languished some time before they died. Of 214 people stated in the assize records to have been bewitched to death where the length of time they were ill is given, only seventeen were said to have died immediately, while seventy were ill for between one and three months.

It is very difficult to know whether certain illnesses were always ascribed to witches, and other types never. It does not seem that the plague was blamed on specific witches; thus in the three sample villages, years of high mortality in the parish registers did not coincide with an increase in supposed deaths by witchcraft. Nor does it seem to have been death at childbirth that was automatically blamed on witches. Of 233 deaths by witchcraft mentioned in the assize records, only seven are known to have been those of infants under three months old. Even children seem to have been less frequently the objects of witches' attacks than mature people: in Hatfield Peverel, nine out of ten of those supposedly bewitched to death were adults. Thus witchcraft was characteristically a relationship between two fully grown people. If, as sometimes was alleged to happen, the witch was unable to bewitch her enemy because of his godly life, she bewitched his children or animals instead.

Some sceptics argued that witchcraft was used as an explanation only where medical knowledge fell short, that physicians themselves blamed witches if they could find no 'natural distemperature of the body'. This seems to have been only partly true, and the conclusion drawn from it, that witchcraft beliefs and accusations declined because of an alleged advance in medical techniques during the seventeenth century, seems even less likely. Such a theory is *not* based on any demonstrable advance in medical knowledge at the village or practical level during this period, nor does it account for the many injuries to animals and property — such as beer and butter — blamed on witches. At a more sophisticated level, both Sir Thomas Browne and William Perkins stressed that, even if an illness was explicable by medical theory, it might still originate in the evil will of another person. Here they were making the distinction between a cause in the mechanistic sense — *how* a certain person was injured — and cause in the purposive sense — *why* this person and not another was injured. When people blamed witches they did it not out of mere ignorance, but because it explained why a certain misfortune had happened to *them*, despite all their precautions; why, for example, their butter did not 'come'.[24] Thus we have an account of a woman who could not have success with her butter; she tried feeding the cows on better food, tried scalding her butter pans, and finally, in desperation, used the old counter-witchcraft charm of sticking in a red-hot horseshoe. The butter came.[25]

A very complex, yet vital, problem is whether people suffered some misfortune and then looked around for a witch, or whether they disliked a person and then blamed subsequent misfortunes on her. There is evidence for both processes, but the more normal form seems to have been for the quarrel to precede the injury, for the suspicion to be present before the accident. The way in which suspicions grew up, intermingling injuries with tensions, is excellently illustrated in the words of George Gifford, writing in 1587:

Some woman doth fall out bitterly with her neighbour; there followeth some great hurt, either that God hath permitted the devil to vex him, or otherwise. There is a suspicion conceived. Within a few years after she is in some jar with another. He is also plagued. This is noted of all. Great fame is spread of the matter. Mother W is a witch. She hath bewitched goodman B. Two hogs which died strangely; or else he is taken lame. Well, mother W doth begin to be very odious and terrible unto many. Her neighbours dare say nothing but yet in their hearts they wish she were hanged. Shortly after another falleth sick and doth pine; he can have no stomach unto his meat; now he can not sleep. The neighbours come to visit him. 'Well neighbour', sayth one, 'do ye not suspect some naughty dealing; did ye never anger mother W?' 'Truly neighbour' (sayth he) 'I have not liked the woman a long time. I can not tell how I should displease her, unless it were this other day, my wife prayed her, and so did I, that she would keep her hens out of my garden. We spake her as fair as we could for our lives. I think verily she hath bewitched me'. Everybody sayth now that mother W is a witch indeed, and hath bewitched the good man E. He cannot eat his meat. It is out of all doubt: for there were [those] which saw a weasel run from her house-ward into his yard even a little before he fell sick. The sick man dieth, and taketh it upon his death that he is bewitched. Then is mother W apprehended, and sent to prison.[26]

This account is amply substantiated in the Essex pamphlets. The gradual growth of feeling over a long period, although no event was ascribed to the witch for several years at a time, and then the way in which more and more disaster was laid at her door, are graphically illustrated. Gifford shows how the whole village community became involved in the gossip and tension. He also shows the process whereby a person cast around in his mind to see who might have bewitched him: in this case he selected a person with whom he felt uneasy and against whom he had offended. Mounting bitterness against an individual could not find an outlet until proof of her witchcraft had been discovered: then she was either forced to confess her guilt and promise amendment of life at the ecclesiastical courts, or removed from the community by imprisonment or death at the assizes. The stress throughout the account is on neither the strangeness nor the painfulness of the injuries, but rather on the social relationship preceding the injury. It would seem, therefore, that the key to understanding Essex prosecutions does not lie primarily in the amount of pain and in explanations of suffering current in Elizabethan villages, but rather in strains between villagers.

Witchcraft prosecutions, we have seen, usually occurred between village neighbours. They almost always arose from quarrels over gifts and loans, when the victim refused the witch some small article, heard her muttering under her breath or threatening him, and subsequently suffered some misfortune. This sequence is particularly well illustrated in the witchcraft pamphlets. The following are some of the motives suggested either by confessing witches or by their accusers in the 1582 assize trial. The witch acted because she was refused the nursing of a child; refused a loan of 'scouring sand'; refused 12*d*. for her sick husband; denied malt at the price she wanted; refused a 'mess of milk'; and denied mutton. If we examine the motives of a single witch, Joan Robinson, we see that her various acts of witchcraft were precipitated by the following acts of her neighbours: she was denied an implement for making hay, the hire of a pasture, the sale of a pig, a cheese, a pig she had been promised and payment for goods 'at her own reckoning'.

Another illustration of the fact that witchcraft was seen as a reply to unneighbourly behaviour is provided by the various counter-activities that were believed to be efficacious against witches. Contemporaries noted that it was those who refused gifts and other neighbourly charity who incurred the wrath of witches. Thus an Elizabethan preacher, Francis Trigge, told his congregation that 'we may see how experience, and the very confessions of witches, agree that the merciful lenders and givers are preserved of God, and unmerciful and covetous Nabals are vexed and troubled of Satan'.[27]

Thus it appears as if it was those who offended against the ideals of a cooperative society by refusing to help their neighbours who found themselves bewitched. The continued force of the old ideals of neighbourliness, as well as the belief that a moral offence would bring physical affliction, is excellently illustrated in the words of an Essex writer in 1656. 'God hath given it as a strict command to all men to relieve the poor', he told his audience, then he quoted from Leviticus:

> Whosoever hearkeneth not to all the commandments of the Lord to do them (whereof relieving the poor is one), the Lord will send several crosses and afflictions and diseases upon them, as followeth in the Chapter ... therefore men should look into the Scriptures, and search what sins bring afflictions from God's hand, and not say presently, what old man or woman was last at my door, that I may hang him or her for a witch; yea, we should rather say, because I did not relieve such a poor body that was lately at my door, but gave him harsh and bitter words, therefore God hath laid his affliction upon me, for God saith, Exod. 22: 23, If thou any way afflict widows, and fatherless, and they at all cry unto me, I will surely hear their cry, and my wrath shall wax hot against thee.[28]

Physical afflictions, he suggested, could be punishment for failure to uphold the social code, and men might well tremble when they heard a neighbour's curse, backed, as it might be, by power from God, or, as they preferred to think, from the Devil.

Cursing was one of the most important methods supposedly employed by witches to injure their victims; often their familiars first appeared when an angry woman cursed or swore revenge on a neighbour. It seems, then, that a sanction which had long been effective in making people live up to social obligations was still felt to be powerful. Thus when Thomas Cooper warned the godly in 1617 to forego indiscriminate charity and especially to be hard on suspected witches, 'to be straight-handed towards them, not to entertain them in our houses, not to relieve them with our morsels', he had to counsel his audience to 'use a Christian courage in all our actions, not to fear their curses, nor seek for their blessings'.[29] It was considered necessary to shun overtures of friendliness on the part of suspected witches, for gifts of food might be the vehicle of witchcraft. In 1579 a witch bewitched two neighbours in gifts of a drink and an apple-pie. Witchcraft beliefs thus provided a mechanism for severing unwanted relationships; a person could be cut off 'because' he or she was a witch. Moreover, since people still felt guilt at such a break with the traditional ideals, witchcraft explained to them their feeling of anxiety — no wonder they were worried since they were in peril of being bewitched, likely to be repaid on the supernatural plane for their lack of charity. Although the outwardly accepted village ethic was still one of mutual aid and intimate neighbourly links, people were constantly forced into situations where they were made to depart from such an ideal. Hence we find people especially sensitive to witchcraft attacks on those occasions when neighbourly sentiments are most openly shown, during festivities such as weddings, or during illness. Suspected witches were often those who went round inquiring about their neighbours' health.

When a person was forced into a situation where he had to break with a neighbour, there must have been considerable difficulties in an Elizabethan village. There was no code to which he could appeal for justification; Christianity still upheld communal values. But through the mechanism of the witchcraft laws, and the informal channels of village opinion, support in a dispute over neighbourly obligations was given to the bewitched person rather than to the witch, who had, in fact, suffered under the older social ideals. Thus it could be argued that the emotion that lay behind witchcraft accusations arose largely from discord within individuals, within people who felt the demands of the old communal values and the power of the old sanctions, while also realizing the practical necessity of cutting down, or re-directing, their relationships. By means of witchcraft prosecutions the older values were undermined or changed while, on the surface, they were still, apparently, subscribed to.

Since some Essex villages seem to have been free from accusations, it is clear that witchcraft was not the necessary or only solution to such a conflict. Nor does it seem probable that disputes were absent before 1560 or suddenly ended in the middle of the seventeenth century. This suggests that alternative methods of settling village tensions were available, both in Elizabethan society and in the periods before and after. This is a huge topic and cannot be treated here. All that can be suggested is that earlier conflict may not have risen to such a pitch since there was a universal standard of behaviour to which appeal could be made, and that during the seventeenth century a new ethic and new institutions, centring on the treatment of poverty and one's obligations to neighbours, emerged and were established.

In Elizabeth's reign we may be witnessing a transitional stage. Such a clash of values could not be settled by most other normal methods of settling disputes. Religious guidance was split, and any comfort given by the ritualization of conflict or the confessional was destroyed at the

Reformation. Various escapes such as suicide, mental breakdown, compulsive work or organization, alcoholism and aggression, physical or verbal, seem to have been limited both in availability and in effectiveness. Thus, tentative as such conclusions must be because of the records, there do seem to have been comparatively low rates of crime, suicide and mental breakdown in the three sample villages. It is even more difficult to decide how useful informal methods of settling disputes between and within villages were — gossip, joking, work and leisure activities, the advice of elders and so on. The only positive evidence is that witchcraft *did* provide many acceptable mechanisms for overcoming uncertainty and anxiety. Physical attack on the witch was encouraged by the popular belief that an effective cure was to draw the witch's blood; a whole detailed set of counter-witchcraft rituals, and myths about the evil doings of witches, gave ample scope for activities and outlet for repressed fears and worries. Probably this all seems very highflown in the context of the historian's usual picture of an Elizabethan village. Perhaps, therefore, I could end by showing the sort of insight into village mentality that witchcraft evidence provides. Not only does it reveal some of the mental concomitants of economic and social change, but it also reveals a much less stable and simple 'popular mentality' than one might expect from the usual local sources.

On the surface, the villagers of Hatfield Peverel were practical, 'rational' farmers and craftsmen. Their seventy-five Elizabethan wills, extensive manor court rolls and criminal and ecclesiastical records show little sign, beyond the witchcraft prosecutions already mentioned, of 'oddness' or tension. Yet, quite by chance, we are enabled to see, through the series of confessions recorded for the assizes of 1566 and 1579, some of their secret fears and thoughts. The result is extraordinary. It immediately becomes clear that overlapping with the ordinary physical world was a sphere inhabited by strange, evil creatures, half-animal, half-demon. A world full of 'power', both good and evil. This cannot be dismissed as a delusion or fantasy of a minority; it appears to have been fully credible to all the villagers, to the examining magistrates, who included Thomas Cole, archdeacon of Essex, and to the presiding judge, Gilbert Gerard, the Queen's Attorney.

Only one example of the beliefs circulating in this village can be quoted here, one of the more extraordinary, but not exceptional. A girl was questioned by the Queen's Attorney and answered that while she was churning butter 'there came to her a thing like a black dog with a face like an ape, a short tail, a chain and silver whistle (to her thinking) about his neck, and a pair of horns on his head, and brought in his mouth the key of the milkhouse door'; the animal demanded some butter from the milkhouse and then departed. When the girl told her aunt of this encounter, she sent for the priest who 'bade her to pray to God, and call on the name of Jesus'.

This manoeuvre caused only a momentary diversion, and the familiar reappeared several times. The Queen's Attorney then turned to Agnes Waterhouse, the suspected witch, and asked her, 'can you make it come before us now? If ye can, we will dispatch you out of prison by and by'. But she replied that she could not call him.

> Then said the Queen's Attorney, 'Agnes Waterhouse, when did thy cat suck of thy blood?' 'Never', said she. 'No?' said he, 'let me see'. And then the gaoler lifted up her kercher on her head, and there was diverse spots in her face and one on her nose. Then said the Queen's Attorney, 'In good faith, Agnes, when did he suck of thy blood last?' 'By my faith, my lord', said she, 'not this fortnight'.[30]

Agnes Waterhouse was duly executed; she was one of the first of a minimum of one hundred Essex inhabitants who were to die, either of prison fever or by execution, on a charge of witchcraft, within the next hundred years.

This study of witchcraft is based on the records of one English county. Further work could be undertaken to supplement the findings of C.L. Ewen on the judicial records of other counties. The other counties within the Home Circuit, which have early assize records, would appear to be best suited for this further work. A detailed survey and analysis of Scottish criminal and kirk sessions records, long overdue, is already under way.[31] A recent study of witchcraft in southern Germany has also shown how rich the material is for a reassessment of this crime on the Continent.[32] Important work on Spanish witchcraft trials is also currently being undertaken.[33] For the period before 1500, there has recently appeared a new survey by Norman Cohn.[34] The magical and religious beliefs which formed the necessary background to the legal prosecutions have now been revealed by Keith Thomas in a work which supplements and expands the brief account above.[35]

It has been stressed throughout this essay that court records are a necessary but not sufficient source for the study of witchcraft as a crime and as a set of beliefs. We cannot begin to study a phenomenon such as witchcraft until we understand how the courts worked and the records were compiled. Yet only a very small part of the phenomenon is revealed in formal court records. Furthermore, in order to study witchcraft, as any other crime, we need to know a great deal about the social, economic and mental worlds within which it occurred. One way of obtaining this insight is through the 'community study' approach adopted in the illustrations drawn from three Essex parishes. This intensive study of particular communities within which witchcraft accusations occurred has recently led to the publication of an almost entirely new interpretation of one of the most researched topics in the whole field of history, the Salem witches.[36] The authors show the way in which all the local records can be blended together to supplement the purely legal ones. They demonstrate that the records of criminal proceedings, used by themselves, produce as distorted a picture of the past as does any other single class of document used in isolation. Criminal records, bulky as they are, constitute only a fraction of the information we have on any set of people in the past. For example, if we take another Essex parish — Earls Colne — in which several witches resided during the sixteenth and seventeenth centuries, the records of assizes, quarter sessions, ecclesiastical and other courts yield only about one-sixth of all the named references to people living in the parish during the Tudor and Stuart period.[37] In terms of gross pages of information about the inhabitants, they represent less than a twentieth of all the sources. Studied in isolation, such records not only give us the tip of the proverbial iceberg, but a tip which is distorted. One of the urgent tasks facing historians is to develop a methodology for setting legal records within the context of other records bearing on the same people. We need to know not only how many committed certain crimes and who they were, but also how many people did *not* commit such crimes.

4 *Crime and Delinquency in an Essex Parish 1600-1640*

J. A. SHARPE

It is, perhaps, inevitable that the most significant type of study produced by the recent growth of interest in the history of crime in pre-industrial England should be that based upon the county and the work of the courts of assize and quarter sessions.[1] Over the last two decades historians have become accustomed to think of English society between the fifteenth and the nineteenth centuries in terms of county units, and the importance placed upon the justice of the peace has generated a concomitant interest in the functioning of quarter sessions. This tendency to view crime, like so many other aspects of English life, on a county basis, has been reinforced by recent work on Tudor and Stuart assizes.[2] Although the activities of the assizes must, for many purposes, be examined in a national context, the judges sat shire by shire to deal with the crimes committed on the circuit they rode, and the indictments for felony, recording the more serious offences, were generally filed by county.

This approach to crime in the period 1550-1800 is both understandable and justified. It is undeniable that England was, in many ways, administered through the machinery of county government. Moreover, the records of assizes and quarter sessions offer obvious attractions to the student of crime. It was in these courts that the graver crimes were dealt with, where the supposed perpetrators of homicide, theft, burglary, rape and witchcraft were brought to trial, and judgment passed upon them. The perspective given upon the crime of this period through the study of cases dealt with by these courts is, therefore, an important one. It is not, however, the only possible approach.

Only the most insensitive student of assize and quarter sessions documents can fail to realize their limitations, and only the most unimaginative can fail to ponder upon the prospects of going beyond them. The details given on an assize or quarter sessions indictment are tantalizingly sparse, and except for those rare cases in which good depositions survive to complement the bare recital of facts upon the indictment, it is impossible to learn much about the persons involved, or to understand the background to court action. This sense of the limitations of the formal records of these courts is rendered more poignant by the constant glimpses that surviving informal documents — letters to the clerk of assize or clerk of the peace, marginal notes on recognizances, petitions about malefactors from individuals or communities — provide of the possible variety of motives and individual case histories that lay behind prosecution. Any reasonably full run of quarter sessions documents should contain evidence of wider dimensions to the criminal than that given on indictments. The Essex records, for example, provide numerous examples of complaints against offenders, often with recommendations for action on the part of the authorities, as in 1657, when the parishioners of Great Horkesley, faced with a violent neighbour, requested the justices 'to tie him up as they use to deal with savage beasts'.[3] Similarly, petitioners could intercede on behalf of malefactors. The inhabitants of Rayne suggested that Joan Bredge, a petty offender, should be released from custody 'for we do hear that there is some hopes that she will become a new creature',[4] and in 1666 the plight of an old woman, allegedly the victim of a malicious prosecution and 'not able to wage law', provoked a sympathetic petition from her neighbours to which a character reference was appended.[5] Such cases as these, together with occasional evidence of prosecutions being settled out of court before formal indictment,[6] reinforce the suspicion that the study of crime in this period would benefit from an attempt to look beyond the formal record of offences in the courts of assize and quarter sessions.

Adequate materials exist to support such a venture, for other courts existed besides the two most familiar to the general historian. Most important were the ecclesiastical courts.[7] These have received a bad press in traditional historiography, with its concentration upon the foredoomed Court of High Commission, the un-English *ex officio* oath and prying apparitors, their significance being further obscured by the emphasis upon the part played in local government by the justices of the peace and quarter sessions. The church courts, however, were vital in enforcing both uniformity to the theology of the Church of England, and conformity to its prescribed moral standards; they were therefore essential agencies in the struggle to secure that totality of religious, moral and social discipline which was the ideal of early-modern English government. In this, the most lowly of the hierarchy of ecclesiastical courts, that of the archdeacon, probably enjoyed a more favourable position than the court of quarter sessions.[8] This tribunal, in common with the other church courts, dealt with cases involving attendance at church, conformity in matters of religion, upkeep of church fabric and furnishings and a number of moral offences, the most frequent of which arose from sexual lapses or from the consumption of alcohol. Unlike both the superior ecclesiastical courts and assizes and quarter sessions, it did so on a very intimate level. The archdeacon's court enjoyed a number of advantages over other institutions. It met locally, each archdeaconry being subdivided into deaneries; it met frequently, about once every three weeks in each deanery in term time; and it was almost certainly cheaper to bring a prosecution there. In many ways the court of the archdeacon was in uniquely close contact with the needs of the community, or at least with that section of the community seeking the enforcement of social discipline.

Another institution whose courts could impinge upon the life of the early-modern Englishman was the manor.[9] Although in decline in many areas, and usually far removed from their medieval powers, the manorial courts could still enjoy some influence, laying down regulations covering the minutiae of everyday life, and enforcing them by fine. The business of a manorial court leet — the removal of dirt from the highway, the repair of hedges and ditches, the prevention of straying by unringed hogs, the occasional assault — may seem far removed from the serious felonies, matters of life and death, tried in the majestic splendour of assizes. Nevertheless, the leet still represented a link in the chain of institutions upon which law and order depended in this period.

The archives of these courts constitute an embarrassment of documentary riches, whose reduction to manageable proportions is difficult on anything except a small scale. Study of the overall impact of these various institutions upon the individual, from which a deeper understanding of the offender and his place in the social framework might be derived, is, for the purposes of the present paper, best carried out by examining cases arising from one parish. This leads, however, to involvement in a developing area of historical interest, the recently instituted work on as total as possible a reconstruction of past communities through an exhaustive exploitation of all surviving sources.[10] Crime, like all historical topics, is just one of a whole spectrum of possibly interrelated subjects, and crime, social control and the enforcement of law and order in the past will become fully comprehensible only when our state of knowledge of village communities in the England of four or five centuries ago passes far beyond its present level. The realization of our ignorance of so much of everyday existence in the past, coupled with an awareness of the archival potentialities for remedying at least part of it, is a great spur to the study of social history. What this paper offers is a reconnaissance into just one area of this ignorance through the medium of crime in the Essex parish of Kelvedon Easterford in the first forty years of the seventeenth century.[11]

Kelvedon Easterford is located on the main road from London through Essex to East Anglia, and lies about midway between the better known towns of Chelmsford and Colchester.[12] It lay on the border of two of the major economic subdivisions of the county.[13] The village was mainly involved in agriculture, and it lay on the edge of the area of mixed farming in the centre of Essex. Good soil, long established enclosed fields, proximity to the innovatory Low Countries and the ever growing stimulus of the London market made this region one of the most advanced agricultural areas in England. Kelvedon also lay on the fringe of the textile-producing belt in the north and north-east of the county, and was one of a number of small centres dependent upon the larger town of Coggeshall. Hence a number of the inhabitants of the parish are described as weavers, combers and clothiers, and although none of this last category made really large fortunes, a few of them, on the evidence of their wills, lived in fairly comfortable circumstances.[14] Further economic variation resulted from the town's location on a main road. The entertainment of travellers between London and the eastern counties was an important service industry, and Kelvedon possessed several substantial inns and a number of brewers and maltings, which provided for the needs of both travellers and local inhabitants.

Until wills and manorial documents relating to landholding are analysed fully the exact nature of the social structure of the parish must remain problematic. Certainly no one family or individual seems to have dominated the parish, possibly a reflection of the complicated manorial situation.[15] Five manors lay partially or wholly within Kelvedon. The most important of these, Felix Hall,[16] was held in this period by Sir Thomas Cecill, a younger son of the earl of Exeter, and later by Sir Thomas Abdy, a London merchant of Yorkshire descent, and member of a family with widespread possessions in Essex. Neither of these lords of the manor seem to have been very active in the affairs of the parish, and were probably not much resident there. Kelvedon's other large manor, Church Hall, was property of the bishop of London. From the late sixteenth century it was leased to the Wakering family, perhaps the most important gentry permanently resident in the parish in this period, and also members of a clan of some importance in the county. In the south of the parish lay Ewell Hall manor, which apparently had no independent rights and was under the jurisdiction of Felix Hall. In the early seventeenth century Ewell Hall was the residence of the Sammes family. Two other manors extended into Kelvedon. Part of Little Coggeshall Hall[17] lay in the east of the parish, while the manor of Kelvedon Hall (despite its name, situated mainly in Great Braxted) included a few fields in the village.

The absence of any dominant landlord or resident justice was compensated for, at least to some extent, by two factors. Firstly, the influence of the church was considerable in the parish. Kelvedon was the administrative base of Witham deanery, part of the archdeaconry of Colchester, which probably accounts for the unusually high number of presentments of inhabitants of the parish in the archdeacon's court.[18]

Morover, Robert Aylett, Ll.D., the archdeacon of Colchester's principal and, from 1622, a justice of the peace, lived at Feering, the next township along the road towards Colchester. Aylett, one of the most important figures in the administration of the eastern half of the county,[19] exercised no small influence over the local machinery of law and order; it is instructive that those conducting the metropolitan visitation of 1636 ascribed the lack of 'any great fault' in the Kelvedon area to Aylett's influence.[20]

Secondly, stability was built into the social structure through the presence of a solid body of minor gentry and yeomen. This group has not yet been subjected to any exhaustive study on a national level,[21] and it is possible that their importance in the life of Tudor and Stuart England has hitherto been underrated. In many parishes these substantial farmers, together with the other lesser property owners, tradesmen and successful artisans, must have formed a sort of informal oligarchy, through which they governed the parish in their capacities of employers, taxpayers, suppliers of credit and local office holders. Several dynasties drawn from this class of middling property owners existed in Kelvedon at this time. The longest established of these, the Marlers, were, in the early seventeenth century, suffering a decline after two centuries of ascendancy in the parish. Simultaneously two families that were to be of some consequence in Kelvedon later in the century, the Cudmores and the Leapingwells, were gaining a foothold in the parish. Beneath the gentry — the Marlers, Cudmores, Sammes, Leaping-wells and the Kelvedon branch of the Wisemans — came the yeomen, men like Anthony Prigmore, a tenant of Church Hall manor who also had interests in the textile trade, and John Yeoman, who held solid estates on both of the large manors.[22] The gentry and yeomen provided an element of permanence and solidity in the parish, compared to which the poor, more given to geographical mobility in that they had less of a stake in the community, and more prone to the impact of the natural hazards and economic downturns of the period, constituted a more unstable force.

The formal embodiment of the social importance of this fixed interest in the community most relevant to the present study was the tendency for its members to hold parish office. Despite the interest in Elizabethan social legislation, which was in many ways to provide a framework for local administration until the early nineteenth century, little attention has been given to those who actually filled the positions of churchwarden, constable and overseer of the poor, and who thus represented government on its lowest, but most necessary, level. Although only fragmentary evidence survives of the identity of those chosen as churchwardens in the parish, and practically none concerning the identity of the overseers, the names of most of the constables of the parish are known from the mid 1620s until 1640.

During this period one constable was chosen annually for each of the main manors, Church Hall and Felix Hall.

The men filling the office of constable in these years were usually recruited from the type of small property owner of middling fortune alluded to above. Most of those chosen at Felix Hall fitted this pattern. Thomas Aylett, constable in 1639, was a member of one of the most widespread gentry families in the county.[23] William Markant, who served as constable in 1629 and 1636, contributed to subsidies throughout the 1620s and was also rated at 15*s.* (an above-average sum) towards ship money. Markant had also served as churchwarden,[24] as had Robert Raven, who followed Markant into office.[25] John Wood, another subsidy-man and contributor to the ship money, constable in 1623, went on to serve the parish as both churchwarden and overseer of the poor.[26] Constables at Church Hall included a similar cross-section of the established members of the parish. John Yeoman, Christopher Yeoman and John Leapingwell were all members of substantial families. John Savell, constable in 1629, was described as a gentleman, and was to serve as churchwarden four years later.[27] Anthony Blackbourne, constable in 1627, came from a large and reasonably prosperous family of small yeomen and artisans.[28] John Clench, chosen in 1632, was one of the earliest representatives in Kelvedon of a family of substantial yeomen that was to produce some of the largest farmers in the parish by the early eighteenth century.[29]

However, despite this evidence of their economic and social standing, it is impossible to label these officers neatly as what contemporaries would have called the 'well affected', and then turn to examine the delinquent elements ranged diametrically against them. Attempting to follow through the biographies of these constables reveals that about half of them had been in trouble with the courts, some of them regularly over a period of years. For example, Nicholas Willowes, constable of Church Hall manor in 1630, probably made his biggest impact on the system of law and order as an offender rather than as an officer. Willowes was presented before the archdeacon in 1609 on charges of fornication with two separate women, while a report that reached the same court two years later that his servant was with child suggests that he was an uncareful employer. He was also presented three times before the archdeacon for keeping disorder in his house on the sabbath, and a few years later was in trouble for refusing to pay a church rate. His further delinquencies included turning dirty water into the street and keeping his pigs penned near the parish sewer.[30] A similar career of minor offences was led by Robert Gosnald, constable at Church Hall in 1626. Gosnald was presented twice before the archdeacon for keeping disorder and drinking in his house on the sabbath, and was once in trouble at quarter sessions for unlicensed victualling. He was, moreover, presented before the leet for subdividing his tenement and taking subtentants, and was one of several men presented at the archdeacon's court for enjoying the apparently well-worn favours of Lydia Banbricke, one of the looser of the women of the parish.[31]

The phenomenon of regular offenders being selected as parish officers raises several questions. The first of these, that of the criteria upon which the choice of such officers depended in practice, as opposed to the recommendations of handbooks, is likely to remain intangible. The limited number of those fitted for service must have placed a curb upon undue discrimination, although it is improbable that this should be the whole explanation. A second problem, or rather set of problems, revolves around the expectations that contemporaries had of the system of law and order. If this system, with its dependence upon amateur officers and mutual neighbourly supervision, was more or less workable in the seventeenth century, it seems obvious that these expectations were different to those current in modern England; the occasional choice of a man who had been in trouble with the courts is just one symptom of these different assumptions. The issue is a complex one, with repercussions that stretch far beyond the present study, although a related problem, that of the definitions of 'crime' and 'the criminal', and our preconceptions about them, must be touched upon.

Most modern thinking about crime is essentially an outcome of nineteenth-century reactions to the novel social problems thought to be inherent in mass industrialization and urbanization.[32] The modern layman still thinks of crime — normally defined in terms of the more dramatic offences, such as crimes of violence, robbery, burglary, theft and prostitution — as typically the prerogative of the urban slum-dweller, and this assumption forms the starting point for the 'conventional wisdom' about crime held by policemen, social workers, judges, journalists and the purveyors of popular fiction. The wider issues involved in the official acceptance of this conventional view of crime in modern Britain again, perhaps fortunately, lie outside the scope of this paper;[33] what must be emphasized is that these preconceptions are of only dubious utility when applied to pre-industrial England.

The central element in this modern outlook on 'crime', that it is essentially an activity carried out by the lowest social groups, breaks down at two main points when applied to the seventeenth century. Firstly, the seventeenth-century equivalents of those social groups which were to form the backbone of public respectability were still given to delinquent behaviour. The gentry were not subjected to the inculcation of a sense of imperial duty, muscular christianity and the public school spirit that was to have such an impact on the governing classes in Victorian England; indeed, in 1600 the English gentleman and aristocrat had barely begun to divest himself of the violent habits of a factious medieval nobility.[34] Given this, it is hardly surprising that the habits of restraint had not yet progressed far among lower social groups, and on the evidence of offenders from Kelvedon, yeomen and artisans were capable of varied illegal activities. The nature of these activities, however, introduces a second consideration, namely how far the types of proscribed behaviour, and the methods by which this behaviour was punished, allows us to postulate the existence of a form of criminality characteristic of the established members of an English seventeenth-century village community.

Returning to the delinquent parish constables, we find that apart from the dramatic exceptions such as Willowes and Gosnald, most of those appearing before the courts did so rarely, perhaps only once, and were usually prosecuted for offences somehow connected with their social position. A number of them were presented for what might be termed economic offences. Anthony Blackbourne was presented before Church Hall leet for breaking the assize of bread,[35] William Gunfield was presented before the archdeacon's court for barbering on the sabbath,[36] William Hitherland for allowing his servants to make a bay on the sabbath,[37] while John Wood was prosecuted by the Maldon borough authorities for selling untreated leather in the town market.[38] The prosecutions of Thomas Turner, John Barker and John Savell for refusing to pay church rates are in themselves evidence that the accused were ratepayers above the poverty line.[39] Presentment at the leet for some types of nuisance offence, as when John Yeoman, surely one of the parish's most respectable inhabitants, was complained against on various occasions for blocking the street with dirty water or dunghills, were unthinkable except in the context of largely self-regulating village communities. The exact nature of this criminality of the 'middling sort' awaits precise definition, as does the social position of its perpetrators, although its main elements will probably be found to consist of nuisance offences, ranging from uncleaned ditches to barratry, violence and economic offences of the type mentioned above. This undercurrent of delinquency represents a different sort of criminality to that reflected in the serious offence tried at assizes, but its existence precludes the formulation of any easy polarity between the lawbreaker and the forces of law and order.

At present, the phenomenon is perhaps best demonstrated by criminal biographies. Osias Johnson provides a good example of the well established parochial nuisance. Johnson, variously described as a yeoman or clothier, came from a family which was, on the evidence of his father's will, of reasonably comfortable means, and he inherited £250 and lands in Kelvedon and Coggeshall. This substance did not prevent him from being a frequent offender, and between 1609 and 1621 he was constantly reported to the courts. His offences included violence, with a presentment for fighting and quarrelling with William Gylson on the sabbath in 1614, and an indictment for assaulting the parish constables in 1619; accusations of fornication with two separate women in 1609 and 1610; refusing to pay church rates, on one occasion 6s.8d. owed the churchwardens after one of his children was buried in the church; standing excommunicate; and obstructing the highway with a dunghill.[40] Johnson, therefore, represents a social type that was probably common to most seventeenth-century English villages, the well-to-do nuisance more or less permanently at odds with the parish authorities. It is, perhaps, significant that when presented for failing to receive the communion at Easter 1614, Johnson should attribute his absence to an unwillingness to leave home resulting from 'some dissension betwixt him and another'.[41]

An even more impressive catalogue of misdeeds can be laid to John Ayly, keeper of 'The Unicorn' inn. Between 1613 and his death in 1636 Ayly was regularly presented at the archdeacon's court. He was reported for not coming to church in 1613, 1614 and 1622, and was presented almost annually in the 1620s for keeping disorder or selling drink on the sabbath. Ayly apparently took part in these activities himself, and it was noted at Felix Hall leet in 1621 that he had been drunk during sermon time on the last three sabbaths, and that 5s. had been distrained from his goods. Ayly was also presented before the archdeacon as a common swearer, although he escaped with a warning after claiming that he had already been summarily fined by a justice; at about the same time he was bound over to answer for unspecified matters at quarter sessions. Sexual transgressions were added to the list; in 1627 came the first reports of his immoral living with his servant, Avis Shepheard, and 'notwithstanding he hath been often admonished by the minister to dismiss her out of his house, he refuseth to do the same'. In 1629 he was allegedly still cohabiting with her, although he had married her off to a youth named Thomas Ungley. The relationship was still causing offence in 1631, when he was reported to be continuing to 'entertain' her. By 1635, however, Ayly had apparently transferred his affections to the wife of John Francis. On denying this accusation, he was ordered to find eleven compurgators to clear his name. It is fitting testimony to Ayly's reputation that he should be asked to provide so many witnesses to his good name when most persons seeking compurgation were instructed to find four or five neighbours for the purpose. What is more remarkable is that Ayly was chosen constable of Felix Hall manor in 1631.[42]

The delinquencies of these more prosperous malefactors are easy to catalogue, and, as has been demonstrated, it is occasionally possible to evolve from the records detailed criminal biographies of their activities. The background to the poor offender is much more elusive. The lives of the more marginal members of society — the vagrant, the migrant worker, the household servant drifting from one year's employment to the next, the cottager on poor relief — are difficult to delineate and will probably remain impenetrable except for the isolated biography culled from a vagrant or petty thief by a magistrate taking an examination. The existence of this rootless population provides one of the biggest problems in early-modern social history; it also created difficulties for the contemporary agencies of law and order. The vagrant has long been familiar to the Tudor and Stuart historian as a criminal stereotype,[43] but the migrant worker, without any stake in the community, and the poor labourer, to whom any place of residence was probably as good, or bad, as another, were equally troublesome. Representatives of this unstable element, a fact of life in the seventeenth century but tantalizingly obscure to the modern historian, impinged continually upon the life of Kelvedon.

A figure that emerges constantly from the army of migrant workers is the pregnant servant girl. Much more needs to be known about the lives of domestic workers in this period, both male and female, but it seems safe to assert that the poor drifting maidservant was especially vulnerable to pregnancy, often as a result of liaisons with her employer. Taking to the road offered a number of advantages to the servant girl with child, and such figures appear frequently in Kelvedon records. In 1608 William Newman was presented for allowing a pregnant maidservant to leave the parish without doing penance,[44] and a year later a certain Merrill was presented for allowing a pregnant servant from Witham to pass through the parish unpunished.[45] Two servants of one of the Wakering family were accused of sexual incontinency that had resulted in pregnancy, the laconic note 'he is gone' by the man's name reminding us that among migrant workers flight in the face of the prospect of a bastard could be attractive to a man.[46] A servant of the tumultuous Osias Johnson, made pregnant by him, had departed for Hatfield Peverel by the time of her presentment.[47] A servant of Nicholas Willowes, it was reported in 1611, 'hath had a child in adultery in Suffolk and never did any penance', and another girl, servant of John Story, was presented for bringing a bastard from Feering to Kelvedon without being punished.[48] These examples, which could be multiplied, illustrate only one area in which social discipline was eroded by the more marginal elements in society.

A related problem, equally damaging to a well-ordered polity, was the vulnerability of the institution of marriage among the very poor, either to straightforward domestic stress or to economic pressures. The impossibility of divorce for the poor must have resulted in many unhappy marriages being dissolved by a simple, if illegal, separation, followed by one or both of the partners taking to the road. It is also probable that many marriages among England's growing masses of dispossessed rural poor were broken by economic necessity, with the husband forced to go to seek work; the impact of poverty must have prevented many of the poor from enjoying what contemporary opinion would have regarded as a normal married life, and many of those that formed the migratory workers and vagrants of early-modern England left spouses many miles and perhaps many years behind them. Individuals of this type were regarded with suspicion as they passed through Kelvedon. Mary Kirby, the wife of a Coggeshall man, was ordered to 'cohabit with her husband as a wife ought to do' when she arrived in the parish in 1611.[49] Similar disquiet was provoked by a certain Adams, who was reported to have left his wife, the couple now dwelling 'he with us and she in Hertfordshire'.[50] Nicholas Abelson, one of the more disorderly members of the parish, with a record of presentment before the archdeacon's court for drink offences, adultery and standing excommunicate, apparently decided to take to the road and in June 1636 was apprehended as a vagrant in Colchester. The borough authorities noted that although he had a wife in Kelvedon, he was now living as man and wife with the wife of Alexander Alcocke of Wisbech.[51] Evidence of this sort reinforces the impression that the very poor were essentially rootless, and in this offered an inherent threat to the tidy and well disciplined society that was the objective of legislators in this period.

The importance of these marginal social groups, and the difficulty involved in finding out very much about their members, becomes obvious when dealing with property offences — theft, burglary and breaking and entering. Twenty-four such offences involving members of the parish are known to have been indicted in the years 1600-1640, and it thus constituted the only category of serious offences frequently committed in the parish. Apart from property offences, felony committed in the parish amounted to one case of manslaughter,[52] and two of infanticide, one committed by the wife of Edward Osbourne in 1621,[53] the other by a Feering girl a few years later.[54] On the level of a parish study, therefore, property offences are the only form of felony recorded often enough to warrant detailed examination, just as the frequency with which they are recorded on a county level has led to their being much used by those engaged in wider studies of crime.[55]

Of the twenty-four property offences, only eleven involved offenders and victims both described as resident in Kelvedon. Eight cases involved persons described as Kelvedon residents who allegedly committed thefts in other locations, all of them within only a few miles of their home parish. Similarly, few of the thieves from outside the parish who allegedly stole in Kelvedon, and who were involved in the remaining five cases, had travelled far, although one of them, a labourer from Little Dunmow, came from the other side of the county.[56] Given that this present study is concerned primarily with Kelvedon inhabitants, these last five cases will be ignored, and attention focused on those who figure in the remaining nineteen indictments.

The offences with which these deal, eleven of them committed against

Kelvedon residents by persons described as Kelvedon residents, and eight committed outside the parish by persons described as Kelvedon residents, involved sixteen accused. Of this total, nine, on the evidence of the sources searched for this study, had no further attachment to the parish than being accused of theft in it. It is, of course, possible that an exhaustive search of all available documentation would reveal that a number of them were, in fact, Kelvedon inhabitants, but this seems unlikely given that their surnames appear to have been unknown in the parish. The most likely conclusion is that these nine thieves enjoyed only tenuous connections with Kelvedon, in many cases that most tenuous of all connections, that they simply committed the crime for which they were accused there. The situation is, of course, obscured by the assize clerks' habit of describing an offender as resident in the parish where the offence was committed. A good example of the confusion that can result from this practice is provided by indictments against Charles Peace, Isaac Spencer and Peter Engyne. This trio was part of a larger group accused of carrying out thefts in the Kelvedon area in 1620, apparently organized and supported by a Little Coggeshall weaver and his wife. All three were described as belonging to Kelvedon and several other parishes — Peace, for example, was variously described as belonging to Kelvedon, Great Braxted, Little Coggeshall and Rivenhall, all of them the location of the offence for which he was being prosecuted.[57] It seems probable that this group, and perhaps all those alleged thieves who cannot be connected to the parish by any evidence other than their indictments, were drawn from the ambulatory population of vagrants, semi-vagrant migrant workers and servants in search of employment.

Those thieves about whom more can be discovered fall into the normal pattern of minor offenders, and were not invariably drawn from the very poorest strata of the parish. Tobias Phillbrick, who apart from theft had also been accused of unlicensed alehouse-keeping and adultery with his wife's serving-woman, had served as a sidesman a few years previously.[58] John Walker, accused of sheep theft in 1617, was described as a butcher,[59] and further evidence of the attractiveness of involvement in sheep stealing for those in the food and distribution trades is provided by Edward Barker, variously described as a victualler or alehouse-keeper, who was accused of receiving stolen sheep in 1600.[60] Robert Collyn, hanged for various sheep thefts in 1617, was also described as a butcher.[61]

Although these men may not have been members of the very poor, and remained resident in the parish for a number of years, it is significant that none of them contributed to the subsidies of the period, which indicates that there were outside the circle of men of some substance whose importance has already been emphasized. At least two of the thieves from Kelvedon, moreover, are known to have belonged to very poor families. Henry Rust, Robert Collyn's accomplice, was an habitual thief who was hanged at the summer assizes 1617 after escaping through benefit of clergy at the previous session of that court; two years earlier his wife, in trouble with the archdeaconry court, had been described as *'pauperissima'*.[62] Similarly, the widowed mother of John Spradborough, a carpenter accused of stealing planks in 1618, had been described as a pauper in the archdeacon's court.[63] Spradborough's offence also provides an insight into the growing tension that must often have preceded court action against a petty offender from within the community. Although his indictment accused him of a specific offence, the relevant gaol calendar notes that he was a regular pilferer of the goods of his accuser, John Lacy.[64]

The established nuisance offender and the poor, more marginal criminal between them constituted a continual irritant to the forces of control, and certain well-defined areas of conflict emerge from court records. The alehouse offered a virtually institutionalized challenge to governmental ambitions for a well-ordered society. The alehouse, and the related problem of drunkenness, was a constant source of *angst* to legislators, moralists, justices and parish officers alike, and the problem was more acute in a parish like Kelvedon, with its legitimate hostelries serving the needs of travellers on the Great Essex road acting as enticements towards illicit emulation, as well as being potential sources of disorder in themselves. The work of licensing sessions, with their recognizances binding victuallers and alehouse-keepers in mutual sureties,[65] points to the existence of a body of legitimate inns in the parish; however, drunkenness, disorder and illicit alehouses were all a major feature of life in Kelvedon.

At the basis of the unease over alehouses lay their tendency to be centres of general disorder. Often this had a flavour of rustic merrymaking far removed from the ideals of sobriety laid down by the church or the statutory insistence that the inn should be no more than a place of simple refreshment and lodging.[66] John Ayly was presented in the archdeacon's court in 1613 'for suffering of a fiddler to play with taber and pipe in his house upon the 9 of May, being the sabbath day, in time of divine service [and] for suffering of ill rule in his house the same time',[67] and six years later it was reported that Ayly's house had been the scene of 'drinking, swearing and singing by diverse of Coggeshall'.[68] The disorders engendered by the alehouse, however, went far beyond innocent peasant gaiety; the alehouse, by encouraging the poor to spend their money and employees to waste their time, offered a serious threat to the bonds of social discipline. It is hardly surprising, therefore, that John Yeoman should witness an indictment against an alehouse-keeper who entertained his servants in an unlicensed alehouse,[69] or that John Ayly's patrons should include young William Sanders, who spent Easter Sunday 1627 in Ayly's house getting drunk on money he had stolen from his father.[70] The alehouse offered a handy means of disposing of stolen goods, and one

Kelvedon alehouse-keeper was indicted for receiving stolen chickens.[71] Violence was often near the surface when drink had been consumed. One night in 1626 Henry Lacy and several companions got drunk, assaulted Thomas Aylett and broke a fishpond.[72] William Lingwood was presented for getting drunk and abusing his step-father on the sabbath,[73] and Robert Wheeler for drunkenness and fighting on his way home from church.[74] The alehouse and drink, therefore, represented a challenge to both personal morality and law and order, and as such represented virtually a rival institution, in social, cultural and recreational terms, to the church.

Opposition to authority sometimes took more dramatic forms than the largely unconsciously-held set of attitudes implicit in recourse to the alehouse. Parish officers can never have operated entirely free from fear of violence or the threat of obstruction, and occasionally this could reach serious proportions. The misdeeds of that arch troublemaker, Osias Johnson, included an assault on the constable;[75] on another occasion the constables were assaulted by a Little Coggeshall man;[76] and in a curious incident in 1621 John Yeoman, then constable, was resisted while attempting to arrest a vagrant.[77] The churchwardens also suffered from some opposition, running, for example, into some predictably harsh comment from the wife of another habitual offender, Nicholas Willowes, when they reproved her for drunkenness and absence from church on the sabbath.[78] Even the minister was not immune from threats of violence when he attempted to enforce the law. When Thomas Hilderslye, then vicar of Kelvedon, presented Jeremy Armin, one of the parish gentry and, interestingly enough, churchwarden at the time, for going to Maldon with his cart on the sabbath, Armin challenged him into the field in the churchyard with his rapier. This display of petulance earned Armin an excommunication.[79]

Such cases were not, however, very common, and should not be elevated into any coherent scheme of resistance to authority. The migrant or vagrant poor might feel an instinctive hostility towards the parish officers, and this would presumably be reciprocated, but personal dislikes obviously affected the relationship between 'police' and the community when the law enforcers were unpaid temporary amateurs drawn from the local populace. A rare insight into the problems inherent in such a situation is provided by the investigations that followed the presentment of Richard Abelson for adultery with the widow Cakebread. One witness deposed that he had heard rumours of the liaison, but denied knowledge of the origins of these tales:

But how or by what means the said fame or report hath arisen or grown he certain knoweth not; only he hath heard that the same was caused or raised by one Henry Remmington, now or late one of the sidesmen of the said parish of Kelvedon, or some others who have been or are ill willers to him the said Abelson.

The same witness went on to say that although the churchwardens and sidesmen were, to the best of his knowledge, honest men, yet 'whether they will present an untruth upon their oaths or no, this deponent knoweth not'. He also deposed that even though he was a poor man living by his day labour, he had neither accepted nor been promised any reward by Abelson other than 'satisfaction for his pains and loss of time in and about his business'.[80] This incident demonstrates many of the problems involved in a minor prosecution: the importance of the good name of the accused, the intrusion of personal factors into the conduct of law enforcement officers, and the difficulties involved in obtaining witnesses when the pressure of time upon them could be heavy. Given the personal nature of the system of justice at its lowest level, it is surprising that there were not more reports of assaults upon parish officers, or of partiality or corruption on their part.

Individual circumstances also preclude the drawing of any general conclusions from evidence of what might have been expected to be the most coherent theme in a discussion of resistance to the forces of control, namely opposition to the official religious ideology. Essex has traditionally been regarded as a Puritan stronghold, but there is little evidence of a consistent, coherent 'Puritan' challenge to the Church of England on the part of the inhabitants of Kelvedon. It is true that a large number of them were presented before the archdeacon for failure to attend church, or to receive the communion at Easter, but this absence seems to have been rarely due to ideological motives. Excuses offered included fear of arrest for debt,[81] immobility caused by a sore leg,[82] and concern at spreading smallpox.[83] Even disorder in church was normally attributable to childish pranks, there being odd instances of services being disturbed 'by vomiting',[84] by laughter and misbehaviour in service time,[85] or by general rudeness and bad conduct on the part of an individual.[86]

The more specific manifestations of disrespect that occurred seem also to have arisen from personal motives. John Ayly, absolved from one of his numerous offences, and apparently incensed at the fees involved in this process, 'swore by God that if he had his money again, he would never be absolved'.[87] Anne Aylward, previously presented as a drunkard and an immoral liver, when brought before the archdeacon for drunkenness on the sabbath, roundly declared that her accusers, the churchwardens, were foresworn.[88] Similarly, it is difficult to see anything very sinister in William Godfrey's attempt to interrupt 'one Hews' while the latter was attempting to perform penance, or Anthony Wheeler's keeping his child unbaptized for a fortnight, in which time it died.[89] Wheeler's explanation that 'it was done of ignorance and not willingly' probably explains many cases apart from his own,[90] and even gentry objections to church policy seem to have arisen from specific grievances or mistakes rather than from an alternative view of ecclesiastical government. The widow Elizabeth Cudmore, an early representative in the parish of what was to become one of Kelvedon's leading gentry families in the second half of the seventeenth century, spent most of the 1630s in dispute with the church over the payment of rates. Her objections, according to her attorney, derived not from any ideological stance, but from a straightforward conviction that she had been unfairly rated.[91]

Such cases demonstrate the difficulties involved in trying to ascertain the nature of popular religious opposition to the Church of England.[92] Too much should not be made of isolated comment on matters theological or random criticisms of local church government. The twin distorting mirrors of over-sensitive governments and historians too given to tidy-mindedness have elevated such scattered evidence into proof of the existence of structured popular attitudes to which might be attached, where appropriate, a suitable label like 'Lollard' or 'Puritan'. Even so, the events of 1640-42, with widespread rioting and demonstrations in Essex, furnish proof of the presence of a popular movement in the county which manifested a violent sensitivity over religious matters. In Kelvedon, as in many other Essex parishes, hostility to the Laudian church broke out in the form of a riot in which the rails around the communion table were torn down.[93] Of the three men indicted for this offence one came from Witham, and another was a fairly obscure resident in Kelvedon. The third was none other than John Ayly, the son of the habitual offender of the past three decades, and himself one of the more disorderly inhabitants of the parish.[94] His involvement in the riot suggests the need for a more stringent examination of popular anti-Laudianism. Not even in the most elastic definition of that much-stretched word can Ayly be described as a Puritan; his attack on the rails probably sprang not from a reasoned disquiet at the implications of Arminianism, but rather from a conviction that they represented an acceptable target for a man who must have born considerable resentment against the intrusions of the Anglican church in its attempts to produce a godly and disciplined society.

There are comparatively few vestiges of mainstream Puritanism. In 1636 Jeremy Aylett, a member of one of the more important gentry families in the parish, complained against being rated towards the costs of railing in the communion table and other innovations, and attempted to cite the churchwardens for exceeding their duty.[95] Nothing as definitely identifiable as reasoned opposition to Laudian policies occurred until February 1640, when Nicholas Brewster, an obscure figure, informed the archdeacon's court that 'he cared not a fart for Bonyman [Kelvedon's vicar] and did swear openly twice by God and told Mr Meighton [presumably a court official] that he was one of Baalam's asses and that your courts (speaking to the judge) were for nothing but cropping of ears and slitting of noses'.[96] Such sentiments obviously marked a bridge between traditional Puritanism and religious radicalism, which was making an impact in the area at about the same time. Reports came in of a conventicle attended by people from Kelvedon and the neighbouring townships of Colchester, Feering, Witham and Hatfield Peverel, in the course of which an infant was baptized and communion held.[97] The background of the Kelvedon inhabitants involved provides a rare insight into the rank and file of an early radical group.

Several of those involved were members of the Barker family. George Barker, who attended with his wife, had been presented for tippling on the sabbath, evidence, perhaps, of a disorderly disposition, and a little after the conventicle was commonly held to be an anabaptist. He was not, however, one of the very poor of the parish, as he was rated at 3s.4d. for ship money.[98] Although little is known about Ursula Baker, also present, more can be discovered concerning her husband John. John was, like George Barker, above the very poorest level of society, being a copyhold tenant of Church Hall manor, where he had served as both constable and aletaster; however, again like George, he had been in trouble in the church courts, for failing to attend church and for refusing to pay a church rate.[99] Anne, wife of Nathaniel Barker, was another woman married to a tenant of Church Hall manor, who was later to serve as aletaster there.[100] The members of the Barker family accused of being at the illegal meeting seem, therefore, to fit into the pattern of established members of the community given to occasional acts of delinquency. Even so, none of them could claim a place among the substantial farmers.

With the other known attenders, Elizabeth the wife of Peter Fuller, and Tobias Phillbrick, we are faced with the disorderly rural poor. Elizabeth Fuller was presented three times for absence from church between 1635 and 1639, and in 1640 was presented for standing excommunicate for six months. She had also been presented for adultery, a failing shared by her husband, who had been presented for this offence with both the wife of Thomas Browne (who himself had allegedly declared an intention not to attend church more than once a month)[101] and the wife of that Tobias Phillbrick present at the conventicle. This last relationship was presumably facilitated by the parties being neighbours, subtenants of Richard Amatt.[102] Phillbrick was either the same Tobias Phillbrick indicted for theft some years previously, or his son.[103] Elizabeth Fuller's activities [104] eventually led to her being indicted at quarter sessions for failure to attend church for three months, being an anabaptist and expressing the opinion that 'the church is a den of thieves and none but rogues come hither',[105] these charges being also levelled against Anne the wife of William Hutley. Fuller, Hutley and their husbands came from the lowest strata of residents in the parish. None of them appear on any list of taxpayers, and the husbands of both Fuller and Hutley were described as labourers. Doubts about the accuracy of a man's 'style' as given in indictments are allayed in the case of Hutley, who was described as a pauper at the archdeacon's court.[106] Hutley, Fuller, Phillbrick, and even the Barkers, who were little more than small husbandmen and artisans, seem to be representative of that body of discontented poor which is currently thought to have provided the membership of the sectarian groups that arose in the aftermath of the Civil Wars.[107]

The intrusion of national affairs as dramatic as those of 1640-42 into what is essentially a parish study provides an attractive point at which to attempt to draw some general conclusions from what has been perforce an anecdotal account of the doings of obscure persons. Firstly, the very fact that a study of crime and delinquency in a seventeenth-century parish should end by describing a group of religious radicals reintroduces the whole problem of the definition of 'crime' in this period. If what might be described as an 'institutional' definition is accepted — a crime is an act which breaks the law and is punishable by a court or by summary action by legally accredited law enforcement agents — it is obvious that crime comprehended different forms of activity in Stuart England to those currently described as criminal. On this definition, crime in Kelvedon covered a variety of behaviour that stretched from the manslaughter and infanticides tried at assizes to the curious affair of the wife of John Harriss, presented before the archdeacon 'for her uncivil and base behaviour in lying down to be tossed in a blanket where she was tossed in such beastly manner as it is shame to speak it'.[108] A society attempting to control religious belief and most aspects of sexual morality through court action will produce a criminality as idiosyncratic as one which lavishes great concern upon the activities of motor-car drivers and the delinquencies of adolescents. Any discussion of crime must take into account the aspirations of the society in which offences occur, and the objectives of the government proscribing and punishing certain forms of conduct.

Moreover, it is incontrovertible that dependence upon local men for law enforcement in the parish gave the whole apparatus of law and order, and the type of crime it encountered, a very different aspect from that with which the modern city dweller is familiar. In drawing general conclusions from the analysis of assize and quarter sessions indictments, it should never be forgotten that the origins of the social tensions upon which these prosecutions were based lay deep in the village community. Presentment at the archdeacon's and manorial courts was often the direct result of parochial indignation or mere gossip. The system depended, ultimately, on a large degree of mutual regulation among neighbours. Court action in this period, even at the assizes, was essentially the outcome of personal decisions by persons offended against rather than the activities of a professional 'police' force.

Governmental ambitions for a disciplined populace and the element of self-regulation combined with the economic and social structure to produce a distinctive type of criminal. Perhaps the most important conclusion to be drawn from this study of offenders in Kelvedon is that crime was not the prerogative of the poor. The antecedents of the post-industrial slum-dwelling criminal existed in what might best be described as the rootless, marginal rural poor.[109] Similarly, it is probable that many examples existed of high-placed equivalents of the modern 'white collar' criminal. [110] Such offenders were frequently prosecuted in Chancery, among them one of Kelvedon's vicars, Alexander Bonyman, accused of a particularly shoddy fraud upon Sir Ralph Wiseman of Rivenhall.[111] But between these two extremes there lay a stratum of offenders drawn from the middle ranks of the community, and a surprisingly high proportion of Kelvedon's husbandmen, artisans and yeomen were prosecuted in one court or another during the forty years under consideration. The 1636 ship-money contributors included fifty-one persons below gentry rank resident in Kelvedon, a sample that arguably excluded the very poor of the village.[112] Of these, twenty-eight had been accused of one or more offences before the courts. These offenders were not usually accused of serious crime, and were often only once in trouble. Even so, on a strict definition, they were criminals. The established, permanent delinquents — men like John Ayly, Osias Johnson and Nicholas Willowes — constituted a persistent under-current of disorder, and provide a distinctive perspective upon crime and social control in the parish. Future research will probably prove that such malefactors formed the basis of a criminal sterotype as distinctive of Tudor and Stuart England as the more publicized vagrant.

Such research will be best directed along the lines of microscopic studies of individual communities, and it is hoped that this paper, despite a tendency to raise issues rather than resolve them, at least illustrates the potentialities of such an approach. Crime is just one of the many aspects of the past that has only recently been afforded serious consideration, several of which would benefit from the methods applied in the present study, with its emphasis upon gleaning as much information as possible about individuals, and then trying to fit them into their social context. Our knowledge of our humbler ancestors will never equal our knowledge of their rulers, for these have left us fuller direct evidence of their motives and opinions. Even so, it is possible to reconstruct much of the lives of the more obscure inhabitants of early-modern England, of which involvement with the criminal courts is but one facet. A research strategy based upon the systematic and exhaustive exploitation of the documentation relating to one community offers considerable rewards to the study of social history, even though it will destroy many comfortably-held preconceptions. It will also involve a great deal of hard work, for the annals of the poor, despite the poet, are neither short nor simple.

APPENDIX

Presentments at the archdeacon's court

Archdeaconry of Colchester act books for the period 1600-1642 (ERO, D/ACA/24-54) were searched for references to Kelvedon inhabitants. These were divided into broad categories, and analysed by quinquennia. The results were as follows:

	1600-1604	1605-1609	1610-1614	1615-1619	1620-1624	1625-1629	1630-1634	1635-1642	
Absence from church	4	39	50	24	12	35	24	36	224
Bridal pregnancy	9	7	8	6	–	–	–	–	30
Sexual incontinency	29	30	43	16	16	16	21	33	204
Ill rule on sabbath	–	3	1	3	22	9	10	4	52
Allowing ill rule on sabbath	6	–	4	3	9	6	6	3	37
Drunkenness	2	5	1	–	–	5	–	–	13
Working on sabbath	4	1	9	2	3	1	5	–	25
Standing excommunicate	11	6	9	3	4	1	9	8	51
Failure to pay rate	2	1	3	1	–	10	14	3	34
Miscellaneous	3	6	31	4	11	7	4	20	86
Quinquennial totals	70	98	159	62	77	90	93	107	756

No clear pattern emerges from the chronological fluctuations in these figures. It is, however, noteworthy that the period of heaviest presentment, 1610-1614, was also marked by heavy mortality during which burials exceeded baptisms for the first time as recorded in the parish register, and that the crisis years comprehended in the decade 1625-1634, which witnessed bad harvests and a depression in the textile industry, had no great impact on the total of presentments. In general, these figures serve to demonstrate two points: firstly, the range of behaviour dealt with by these courts, and especially the emphasis upon sexual offences and church attendance; secondly, the more intimate relationship of the archdeaconry court to the populace, at least in quantitative terms. Compared to the 756 presentments before the archdeacon, only seventy-one inhabitants of the parish were the subjects of presentment, binding-over and indictment at quarter sessions, whose records are almost as complete as those of the Colchester archdeaconry act books. The population of Kelvedon in this period was probably 400-600 souls.

5 Communities and Courts: Law and Disorder in Early-Seventeenth-Century Wiltshire

M. J. INGRAM

According to the first Statute of Westminster, the law was administered that the peace of the land might be maintained in all points, and common right be done to all. The radical Norman Yoke theorists were to challenge the very basis of this doctrine,[1] but even among more conformist thinkers in the early seventeenth century, the principle that the laws of England were beneficent was often accepted only with considerable qualification. Among other sources of doubt was a set of ideas that the operation of the law could be seen, in certain circumstances, as a form of disorder. Some thought that much litigation was essentially vexatious, that the law was exploited as a covert form of violence by a vicious and quarrelsome breed of men who perverted the very instruments of justice for the satisfaction of their contentious passions.[2] It was, moreover, a commonplace ideal that the operation of the law was at best a makeshift for the true exercise of Christian charity, so that even litigation that did not involve abuse could be regarded as a regrettable breach of the harmonious relations which neighbours ought to enjoy, a symbol of disorder. Even Lambard asserted that he did not write 'as though I would not have a justice of the peace to occupy himself ... in pacifying the suits and controversies that do arise amongst his neighbours: yea, rather I wish him to be as well ... a compounder as a commissioner of the peace'; while manuals of godly conduct and the biographies of pious clergy stressed the duty of the Christian minister to reconcile differences and prevent recourse to law.[3] As to criminal prosecutions, the view had long been current that the prescribed penalties for certain offences, notably larcenies, were barbarously excessive; and Rogers was to add only pungency to the argument when he turned the idea of a beneficent law on its head in asserting that it was '*manslaughter* to put any to death for *mere theft*'.[4]

It is difficult to gauge the relevance of these ideas to everyday life, for little is known of the impact of legal proceedings at the local level; and it is this gap in historical knowledge which has stimulated the writing of the present paper. The essay falls into three sections. In the first, a brief attempt will be made to assess the nature and extent of litigation in the early seventeenth century. Building on this foundation, the central section will be concerned with discussing how far certain aspects of the working of the law were socially disruptive; while the concluding pages will deal with mechanisms which arguably helped to limit the tensions arising from the availability of legal process. But in order to reduce the subject to manageable proportions, certain limitations will be imposed. In the first place, virtually all the evidence presented here will relate to the county of Wiltshire. A unit of this size — the shire included some 320 parishes and chapelries and had a population of perhaps 100,000 or more in 1600 — is large enough to be significant, yet sufficiently compact to enable the reader to form from statistics of legal activity some idea of the local density of prosecution;[5] but the typicality or otherwise of this particular area of the country will have to be tested by further research. Secondly, no attempt will be made to take account of forms of prosecution which arose from the regular presentments of juries or officials.[6] With these limitations in mind, let us review the field of early-seventeenth-century litigation.

Prosecutions brought by indictment form the first category. The records of the county quarter sessions exist in an almost unbroken series from 1603, marred only by the fact that *ignoramus* bills were not normally included on the rolls before the eighteenth century.[7] Table I provides an analysis of the indictments filed in the period from 1615 to 1624, and reveals that the annual average of true bills was close to one hundred. Larcenies made up by far the largest group of cases, but a few other felonies and a wide range of common law and statutory misdemeanours also came before the bench. It is unfortunate that no early-seventeenth-century criminal assize records relating to Wiltshire are known to have survived; to judge from the experience of Devonshire, the only county in the Western Circuit for which information exists, the presence of material from this source would have more than doubled the numbers of indictments, adding in particular to the total relating to major felonies.[8]

In this period, recognizances were widely used in proceedings against criminals and other malefactors, and those which were certified to the Wiltshire quarter sessions have survived. Apparently originating mainly in grievances referred to justices by private individuals,[9] the effect of these bonds was to oblige alleged wrongdoers to appear to answer for their actions, to be of good behaviour, to keep the peace or to perform some combination of these conditions. At every sessions, a number of suspects thus bound over were indicted; others had to enter into further recognizances; while the remainder were exonerated — some on simply making an appearance according to their bond, some on undertaking to perform an order, and some after a bill drawn up against them had failed to attain the status of an indictment by being rejected by the grand jury.

Table 1: *Wiltshire Quarter Sessions: analysis of indictments† 1615-24*

	1615	1616	1617	1618	1619	1620	1621	1622	1623	1624
Larceny/compound larceny	23	52	24	35	42	39	36	47	78	48
Vagrancy/incorrigible vagrancy	9	1	3	3	18*	5	5	3	6	6
Assault/false arrest, etc./ rescue										
(a) non-riotous	8	6	22	11	19	22	10	12	10	8
(b) riotous[+]	3	2	2	3	1	2	1	2	4	7
Trespass (lands or goods)										
(a) non-riotous	10	2	4	2	4	5	9	2	3	4
(b) riotous	0	1	1	1	0	0	2	2	1	1
Forcible entry/disseisin	1	1	0	0	0	1	2	0	3	0
Unlawful hunting, etc.**	6	4	3	1	3	1	2	2	8	2
Extortion	5	5	8	5	2	8	0	0	1	7
Barratry/scolding	1	0	2	0	1	6	0	0	0	2
Engrossing/forestalling/ regrating	3	0	0	0	2	0	0	0	0	0
Appenticeship offences	0	3	2	0	2	1	0	2	1	2
Alehouse offences	1	4	2	1	4	3	5	2	4	1
Drunkenness	1	3	3	3	0	2	2	1	1	3
Unlawful cottages/inmates	4	2	2	0	3	8	1	5	3	1
Decayed/obstructed highways/ watercourses, etc.	6	4	4	6	1	3	2	4	1	6
Recusancy	0	0	0	1	0	0	0	0	0	5
Miscellaneous	1	0	7	2	1	2	3	4	5	1
Total	82	90	89	74	103	108	80	88	129	104

†Includes a few inquisitions.

*Includes one indictment of 16 people for leaving off their trades and becoming nightwalkers.

[+]Includes a few cases of riot, rout and public disturbance, and of riotous assault and trespass.

**Some cases involve riotous trespass; and total includes cases of illegal possession/use of handguns, crossbows, nets, greyhounds, etc.

Some exonerations occurred either because the matter at issue was not an indictable offence or on account of defective evidence; but it seems that often, when neither of these factors operated, suspects were dismissed because those who had been wronged had no desire to proceed further.[10] In any event, there were always large numbers of malefactors who were bound over to the sessions but were not indicted. In 1615, for example, there were over 160 such persons; in 1622, over 180, and in 1629, over 240.

Some important classes of legal action may be referred to jointly as 'promoted criminal' prosecutions. The label can be applied with least equivocation to *qui tam* informations on penal statutes, which were prosecuted by an unofficial agent who sued 'as well for the lord the king as for himself'. Before about 1620, the numbers of such actions were considerable. The Exchequer memoranda rolls alone, for example, record over 270 Wiltshire cases for the period 1614-18, mostly concerning the engrossing, forestalling and regrating of corn and other commodities, but occasionally dealing with other matters such as recusancy, the keeping of gaming houses, offences connected with cloth manufacture and breaches of the apprenticeship laws.[11] Again, on the grounds that the distinguishing feature of the jurisdiction of Star Chamber as it had eventually emerged lay in its concern with the maintenance of the king's peace, actions before this court may also be included in the category of promoted criminal causes; although, as will be seen later, the allegations of riot and other illegal activities rehearsed in the bills of complaint of this period often need to be treated with considerable caution.[12] To judge by the surviving body of proceedings, the involvement of Star Chamber with Wiltshire affairs in the early seventeenth century was unspectacular but steady: for the period 1615-24, for example, about ninety suits whose chief venue lay in the county can now be identified.[13]

It is difficult to assess the nature and incidence of civil litigation, for the range of relevant tribunals was very wide. Local courts of common law, in particular, were myriad. The major boroughs of Devizes, Marlborough, Wilton and Salisbury, which together accounted for a significant proportion of the total population of the county,[14] all had courts of civil jurisdiction, but their surviving records are fragmentary and it has not been possible to quantify and analyse their judicial business.[15] Equally difficult to gauge are the activities of manorial courts. A court baron could function not only as a customary court dealing with matters of tenure among the copyholders, but also as a common law tribunal;[16] and some manorial courts were certainly still serving as the forum for civil suits in this period. In the years 1615-19, for example, the court baron of Keevil *cum* Bulkington, to which some fifty-four tenants owed suit in 1618, dealt with an average of three actions *per annum*.[17] It is true that not all manor courts were as active as this; indeed many manors in the dairying country of north-west Wiltshire had been dismembered or had dwindled into insignificance by the early seventeenth century. Yet manorial institutions remained strong in the sheep and corn areas of the county, and it is plain that litigation at this level must not be entirely discounted.[18]

The history of other local courts is obscure. For the pre-civil war period, scarcely any records survive to illustrate the working of the ancient county court;[19] but references to its operation are by no means uncommon in the quarter sessions records, and the institution may still have been doing good business in the recovery of small debts.[20] As to hundred courts, there were living institutions in the hundreds centring on Bradford, Warminster, Calne, Cricklade, Westbury, Amesbury and Mere.[21] A large body of records survives for Mere hundred, which covered five parishes including a small market town; the fact that there were eighty civil suits before the court in the year from Michaelmas 1619 to Michaelmas 1620 indicates that hundredal courts could still enjoy a vigorous life.[22]

Most local courts suffered from the fact that their jurisdiction was restricted to actions worth less than a certain fixed sum, usually 40s., and the progressive decline in the value of money during the sixteenth and early seventeenth centuries was presumably among the factors responsible for the expansion of business in the three great common law courts at Westminster.[23] Of these, the court of Exchequer seems to have been comparatively insignificant.[24] King's Bench was highest in legal status, and had by this period greatly increased its sphere of jurisdiction through the emergence of the writ of *latitat* as the normal means of bringing an action.[25] Unfortunately, the Jacobean plea rolls rarely contain entries of proceedings which took place before the defendant made an appearance to answer to the declaration of his opponent. To judge by the comments of contemporaries, the lacuna is serious, for there were apparently many cases in which no declaration was ever entered, either because the process of the court was unsuccessful in procuring the arrest of the defendant or because the plaintiff for some reason dropped his case.[26] These circumstances need to be taken into account in interpreting the fact that the record of the plea side of King's Bench for the year 1618 deals with the progress of only ninety-four suits which the marginal entries ascribe to Wiltshire.[27] The rolls of the court of Common Pleas are fortunately more comprehensive, and show that this institution was of enormous importance in the early seventeenth century. In Michaelmas Term 1618, for example, over 700 Wiltshire suits were depending at various stages of process.[28]

As to the business of the common law courts, actions of debt easily predominated in all the samples, accounting for 78 per cent of actions in the Common Pleas, 66 per cent in the hundred court of Mere and 44 per cent of identifiable causes in King's Bench; while actions of assumpsit were also important, making up 18 per cent of the known cases in King's Bench, and probably accounting for a large proportion of the suits which in the records of the hundred court of Mere were simply entered as actions of trespass on the case and which comprised 20 per cent of the total business. In the two great Westminster courts, lawsuits for trespass in its various forms were also fairly common. Thus, in the Common Pleas in Michaelmas Term 1618, there were thirty-eight cases of assault before the court (5 per cent of the total business), and about one hundred trespasses in other forms (14 per cent). In King's Bench, actions of trespass, including assault, made up a slightly higher proportion of the known business, while actions of ejectment accounted for a further 7 per cent. Overall, other forms of action were comparatively insignificant, though certain types of suit, such as actions of replevin in the Mere hundred court (4 per cent of the total business) and actions of defamation in King's Bench (5 per cent), were to some extent prominent in the work of particular courts.[29]

Of the courts of equity, Chancery was by far the most important.[30] Professor Jones has estimated that in the last decade of the sixteenth century, at least 500 suits were commenced and made progress each year, but this figure perhaps needs to be doubled if it is to take account of bills of complaint which were entered but went no further. Clearly, this rate of prosecution would seem far less impressive from the perspective of any single county, but certainly not negligible; and it must be borne in mind that the business of Chancery increased considerably during the early seventeenth century.[31]

Finally, mention must be made of the work of the ecclesiastical courts. The Court of High Commission certainly took cognizance of civil actions, but its surviving records are so fragmentary that its local impact cannot be gauged.[32] The major forum for ecclesiastical causes in Wiltshire was the bishop of Salisbury's consistory court, which exercised jurisdiction over some 274 of the 320 parishes and chapelries in the county.[33] Its business was considerable: 158 causes were introduced into the court in 1615, and 161 in 1629.[34] The act books unfortunately fail to specify consistently the nature of the suits; but it is clear from the volumes of depositions and from the surviving court papers that most of the business consisted of actions of defamation, suits for the recovery of tithes and various kinds of testamentary cause.[35] Apart from the work of the bishop's consistory, some suits between parties were also handled by the courts of the two Wiltshire archdeacons, which dealt with a few testamentary actions, and by the courts of the various peculiar jurisdictions.[36]

The survival of court records has been too uneven, and my sampling of what does remain too unsystematic, to make it possible to assess exactly how many lawsuits were begun annually in early-seventeenth-century Wiltshire; but it is plain that the total was very substantial. It may be asked, however, what ranks of society this litigation involved. The evidence on this point is at present unsatisfactory, depending largely on such approximate indications of the status of litigants as are embodied in the court records themselves.[37] Nevertheless, it is at least clear that it would be wrong to suppose that litigation was chiefly confined to those of gentry or noble status. Some courts, it is true, had a more aristocratic clientele than others. Of the chief plaintiffs in the Wiltshire causes begun in Star Chamber in the period 1615-24, slightly more than 60 per cent were nobles or gentry, and most of the remainder were yeomen, with only a few husbandmen, craftsmen and small tradesmen to represent the lower ranks; while the social composition of defendants was similar.[38] In the court of Common Pleas, on the other hand, only 13 per cent of plaintiffs in the suits depending during Michaelmas Term 1618 were designated as gentlemen or noblemen, with clerical plaintiffs making up a further 2 per cent. Among defendants, nobles and gentlemen accounted for about 14 per cent of the total, clerics for 4 per cent. Of non-gentle defendants, by far the most prominent group were those designated 'yeoman', who accounted for over 40 per cent of the grand total, but husbandmen and those professing crafts and trades — some of whom were probably substantial — were both more prominent in numbers than the gentry and aristocracy.[39] The clientele of the church courts, except in tithe suits which were normally begun by clerics or by gentry impropriators, appears to have been drawn largely from the middling ranks of yeomen, husbandmen and craftsmen.[40] The social status of persons involved in felony cases will be examined later;[41] but amongst complainants and defendants in other cases brought by indictment at quarter sessions, and among those bound over for crimes and misdemeanours, the middling ranks were again prominent.[42] In fine, the great mass of early-seventeenth-century litigation, far from affecting only the gentry and nobility, penetrated deep into the society as a whole.

The most obvious conclusion which might be drawn from this survey of legal proceedings is that disagreement and conflict over a variety of issues were common, but were to an impressive extent contained by the rule of law. So judged some contemporaries, and a number of modern historians have taken a similar view, arguing that the multiplication of lawsuits balanced a decline in the incidence and social acceptability of violence, and marked an important step towards a more peaceful and settled society.[43] This assessment has much to recommend it; but my concern here is to explore how far the workings of the law could nevertheless be associated with disorder.

Before examining the effects of legal abuses, it is worth considering whether some of the ordinary features of the operation of the law tended to disrupt relationships in the small-scale communities which made up the fabric of most of early-seventeenth-century Wiltshire society. For the law embodied a paradox. The ideal purpose of legal institutions was to restrain injurious behaviour and to offer just redress for wrongs suffered. Yet in order to fulfil this rôle, the law itself had to utilize force or even violence; and it could therefore feed into an already unstable situation additional sources of tension and conflict.

In the first place, it may be asked whether the harsher legal penalties, notably imprisonment for debt and hanging or flogging for larceny, were popularly seen as excessive, to the extent that the wrongdoer might be ultimately regarded as more sinned against than sinning. Wiltshire sources have, in fact, yielded little evidence that the imprisonment of debtors was popularly regarded as an outrage. There is more reason to think that ambivalent attitudes existed towards criminal punishments, but much depended on the social identity of the sufferer — a point which will be taken up later in the paper.[44]

On the other hand, it is clear that the invocation of the law could arouse a good deal of bitterness and resentment in the accused person and, sometimes, his kinsmen and friends. Important indications that this was so emerge from the study of the examinations of witnesses in ecclesiastical causes. Each party in a suit could administer interrogatories to opposing witnesses, the aim of which was, among other things, to uncover possible sources of bias; and one factor commonly investigated was whether the deponent had been involved in lawsuits with the person against whom he was giving evidence. There are obvious problems involved in assessing the significance of information uncovered in this way. Clearly, the aim of the interrogatory was to discredit the witness as much as possible, and to this end long-dead matters might be raked up. Certainly, the relevance of any particular item of information might be hotly contested, a point best illustrated by considering an issue raised in the case of *Stoneax* v *Blathat*, a defamation cause which came before the bishop of Salisbury's consistory court in 1617. William Pettibone, a prominent witness for the prosecution, was led to admit that Blathat had formerly had his wife arrested for debt; but he claimed that this had taken place long ago, that he was no enemy of Blathat and that he left revenge to God. Two other witnesses, however, deposed that Pettibone had been Blathat's 'deadly enemy' for seven years; and one claimed that he had heard Pettibone say that he would do Blathat any mischief he could.[45] Despite ambiguities of this sort, a reading of many cases leaves the strong impression that recourse to the law could be as powerful in nourishing bad feeling as in allaying it.

These tensions could spill over and affect third parties. The fact that a witness's past life and character might be brought in question in the manner described above probably helped to keep old tensions simmering. More specifically, it is clear that the giving of evidence which necessitated taking the side of one party or another could involve a witness in difficulties. When Alice Francklin gave evidence against Maud Spender in a civil suit, the latter allegedly railed at her and in the ensuing altercation found grounds to sue her for defamation.[46] Sometimes, indeed, tensions might snowball dramatically, a phenomenon illustrated by the case of *Atnoke* v *Hitchcock*, yet another action for defamation in the consistory court. Rebecca Atnoke of Alvediston had been accused by the defendant of sexual immorality, and a substantial section of her small home village became involved in the issue of whether the charge was true or not. One prominent member of the community, indeed, became too deeply implicated, and his advocacy of the accused girl eventually led to his own citation as the defendant in a defamation cause begun by Catherine Hitchcock.[47]

Yet it would be wrong to exaggerate the tensions associated with litigation. There were cases in which it was alleged that recourse to legal action had provoked violence, while individuals sometimes complained that they were unwilling to go to law for fear of reprisals;[48] but the very frequency of lawsuits suggests, *prima facie*, that such terrors were not general. On the assumption that a widespread tendency to resort to violence in the face of legal action would be signalized by a high incidence of recognizances sued out by plaintiffs for their necessary defence against those whom they were attempting to prosecute, a sample of approximately 625 lawsuits of some of the numerically most important types discussed in this paper was collated with the quarter sessions recognizance files.[49] Few connections emerged, a result which I take to indicate that recourse to the law did not normally lead to violence or threats of violence; and this conclusion stands even when account is taken of the fact that the aggression of those subjected to the law's attentions was sometimes displaced from the actual prosecutor onto constables, tithingmen and bailiffs.[50]

But in assessing the significance of these facts, two things need to be borne in mind. In the first place, as I shall argue later, the operation of certain extra-legal mechanisms helped to minimize the *actual* effect of potentially disruptive aspects of the working of the law.[51] Secondly, the existence of a multiplicity of legal institutions made it to some extent possible to use the law itself as a means of covert aggression in response to prosecution. This phenomenon was, however, only part of a wider problem of vexatious prosecution, a subject to which we now turn.

Vexatious prosecution may be defined as the exploitation of legal forms to express aggressive impulses unrelated to the ostensible grounds for action. Such activity, if it existed on any scale, was clearly pernicious, for the law could act in the name of justice with terrifying force, and if unscrupulously perverted could provide an excellent substitute for overt violence; at the least, the victim could be put to trouble and expense.[52] The degree to which the law was open to this kind of manipulation has been to some extent considered by previous writers. In the first place, it has been shown that the numerous penal statutes which regulated various aspects of economic and social life offered scope for vexatious dealing, not only by professional promoters, whose abuses of the law will be discussed later,[53] but also by private individuals, who were responsible for initiating perhaps a third of *qui tam* actions.[54] In the second place, actions in Star Chamber have been discussed by Professor Barnes, who regards many of them as vexatious or near-vexatious because they were designed either as a means of taking revenge on an opponent or to shore up purely civil suits in other courts.[55] The incidence of Star Chamber actions known to have been related to other litigation is indeed arresting: of the ninety Wiltshire suits begun in the period 1615-1624 and for which records survive, forty-nine fall into this category.[56] In interpreting this figure, it has to be borne in mind that some of the offences cognizable in Star Chamber, such as perjury and conspiracy, necessarily often involved other courts of law. But it is striking that a declaration of Lord Keeper Coventry in 1632, which was apparently intended to bar common informers from the court but which Barnes thinks had the effect of temporarily frightening away the common solicitors of causes and vexatious private plaintiffs, resulted in a sudden drop of two-fifths of the volume of bills entered. Barnes concludes that one of the most potent reasons for Star Chamber's attractiveness to litigants was its convenience as a means of mounting flanking attacks on legal opponents; and that the Attorney-General's own suits — a small proportion of the total — 'were by and large alone worthy of the dignity and power of the court'.[57] As to Chancery, Professor Jones's work suggests that in this court also, attempts were often made to prefer trivial and malicious bills. Informal mechanisms operated in the court which were to some extent successful in weeding out vexatious causes, while plaintiffs caught out in patently dishonest machinations might face a whipping, but a persistent residual problem nevertheless remained.[58]

The incidence of vexatious litigation in other legal areas has previously received little attention;[59] the subject is best considered by reviewing broad classes of litigation, rather than the work of individual courts, and we may begin by looking at indictments for felony. An extensive reading of depositions suggests that such prosecutions could only rarely be regarded as vexatious in any simple sense, though examples of malicious dealing can certainly be found. In 1616, for example, a yeoman of Maiden Bradley was prosecuted by a fellow-parishioner for stealing a powder-horn; but he was able to argue convincingly that his accuser had given him the horn some time before, and that the matter had only been raised because the two men were at odds over a land transaction. It is significant that in this, as in almost all other cases of vexatious prosecution for felony which I have been able to identify, the bill was returned *ignoramus*; and it seems likely that, given the draconian penalties to which a convicted felon was subject, the scruples of grand jurymen made it difficult to sustain a charge if there was any suspicion that the prosecutor was acting maliciously.[60]

As is clear from the figures provided earlier, a very large proportion of the total body of litigation comprised suits at common law or in ecclesiastical courts over specific rights and dues: in particular, actions of debt and assumpsit, and tithe and testamentary causes.[61] Inevitably, vexatious cases did occur, some provoking counter-action in quarter sessions, Star Chamber or Chancery;[62] but it is my strong impression that the great majority of such suits were begun in reasonably good faith, probably because the highly specific grounds for action did not easily lend themselves to malicious misrepresentation.[63]

By contrast, the grounds for bringing the various kinds of trespass prosecutions were very elastic. A trespass of land might involve real violence, or consist merely in negligently allowing cattle to graze in another's field or in stepping on a neighbour's property without leave;[64] while merely to place a hand on another person's body, no less than to mount a near-murderous attack, might constitute an assault and battery.[65] Even the fact that some trespasses and assaults were prosecuted by indictment, while the more usual course — to judge from the figures quoted earlier[66] — was to bring civil actions is itself of doubtful significance: comparatively few trespass suits are illuminated by depositions, and in their absence it would be facile to assume that cases prosecuted by criminal procedure were necessarily more serious.[67] Even the addition of a charge of riot on trespass indictments involving more than two accused cannot be assumed to reflect a realistic show of force; and it is probable that, as in Star Chamber, allegations of riot were sometimes included simply to add colour and weight to a prosecution.[68]

The flexibility of trespass prosecutions probably made them useful instruments for vexatious exploitation. A noticeable feature of the quarter sessions records is that indictments for trespass, assault and riot often occur in related groups or in association with other types of prosecution; and this raises suspicions that the court was being used for vexatious legal battles. In the records for the period 1615-24, eleven such groupings are discernible, involving seventeen indictments for simple assault and battery, five indictments for simple trespasses of land, three indictments for riotous trespass and the same number for riotous assault; while associated with them were three indictments for forcible entry or disseisin, two indictments concerning encroachment on or obstruction of highways, an indictment for keeping a subtenant and an indictment for drunkenness. Even though my data on this point are at present imperfect, several of the eleven groupings can be related to prosecutions in one or more courts other than quarter sessions, the additional evidence suggesting that the circumstances underlying the quarter sessions indictments were highly complex, and that the appeal to simple criminal categories, though sometimes technically defensible, was probably disingenuous. For example, one group of five indictments, which spanned the years 1617 and 1618 and involved conflicts among the yeoman and gentry families of Bigges, Tattershall and Pavy, was associated with lawsuits in the bishop's consistory court, Star Chamber, the court of Common Pleas, King's Bench and Chancery.

Inevitably, the record of virtually any single case in this frogspawn mass of litigation gives a misleading impression of the intricacies of the feud, which owed some of its bitterness to religious differences. The leading quarter sessions prosecution, an indictment for riot and trespass, was at first rejected by the grand jury, and precisely how it became a true bill was disputed; and it is significant that although a verdict of guilty was eventually brought in, the justices postponed the imposition of a sentence and recommended that the whole business be referred to arbitration.[69]

Brief mention has already been made of indictments for forcible entry.[70] It is perhaps worth emphasizing that of the eight indictments and inquisitions relating to this offence to be found on the quarter sessions files for the period 1615-24, four are known to have been paralleled by actions in Star Chamber, and at least two were further related to Chancery suits, while one of these was again linked with actions in King's Bench, the Common Pleas and the county court. It may well be that in these cases at least, the indictments were preferred rather because of the facility of obtaining a writ of restitution by this method of proceeding than because any notable violations of the king's peace had occurred.[71]

The circumstances underlying actions of trespass brought by civil procedure are difficult to penetrate, and the vast bulk of the records of the great Westminster courts makes it extremely hard to tease out illuminating cross references. Nevertheless, merely to compare the record of the court of Common Pleas for a single term, Michaelmas 1618, with the quarter sessions rolls reveals several very clear examples of the malicious prosecution of actions of trespass. In 1618, for example, after an order had been made in the manor court of Ogbourne Saint George that horses should not be allowed in the common fields at night until the corn had been removed, Thomas Cookesey and two others were sent to ensure that the ordinance was being observed. On finding some horses belonging to Thomas Coxe, they attempted to impound them, but their owner assaulted the three men, bit off Cookesey's nose and subsequently sued them in the Common Pleas for a trespass.[72]

Such cases are suggestive, but it remains true that in the absence of depositions the underlying circumstances of most trespass prosecutions remain obscure. In the case of church court actions for defamation, however, the situation is slightly better, for a higher proportion are illuminated by the extensive testimony of witnesses. Such causes resembled trespass suits in that the grounds for action were very wide; they could range from serious slanders, which might involve the victim in legal dangers and social inconveniences, to mere abusive expressions like 'whoremaster rogue' and 'whore bitch', ejaculated on the spur of the moment during the course of a quarrel. Over 50 per cent of defamatory utterances alleged in church court prosecutions in early-seventeenth-century Wiltshire were, in fact, very general in form.[73] Somewhat similar were the far less common promoted office causes alleging quarrelling or brawling in churches or churchyards, for the matters of which complaint was made were often trivial.[74] As in the case of trespass prosecutions, causes of these types were sometimes clearly malicious or were related to wider legal battles in other courts.[75] But the depositions also reveal plainly what one can only suspect of trespass prosecutions, that plaintiffs were often the readier to seize upon comparatively trivial wrongs because they were already uncharitably disposed towards the alleged offender. Indeed, the dubious morality of taking such matters to court was often exposed by evidence that the complainants, either by hostile actions or by indulging in invective on their own account, had themselves provoked the defamatory outburst.[76] However, some subtlety is needed to interpret the motives of plaintiffs in such cases. The circumstances which underlay causes often involved quarrels between neighbours — such issues as the beating of a maid, an overhanging ladder or trouble over dogs were typical — which may appear insignificant to modern eyes but which in the context of small-scale communities were evidently capable of arousing strong feelings.[77] My impression is that the subjects of defamatory abuse often found it difficult to distinguish clearly between the anger they felt at being slandered and any feelings of resentment which they already happened to harbour against the defamer. In other words, their recourse to law was unreasonable rather than cynically malicious.

It would therefore seem that most legal actions, especially suits for specific rights, debts and dues, were begun in good faith. But among certain classes of prosecution, cases involving blatant malice are not hard to find, while the business of the courts always included an undercurrent of near-vexatious or unreasonable litigation. But the greyness of the relevant issues probably made it difficult in particular instances for observers to take up a condemnatory attitude, for prosecutors often had a case which was technically good. Certainly, it can be assumed that prosecutions for perjury or conspiracy were only rarely appropriate. Indictments for barratry, an offence which embraced the stirring up of strife between neighbours and the vexatious manipulation of the law, were in theory available only when the culprit vexed many people;[78] while in practice such prosecutions were rare and, when they were not themselves vexatious, often referred to such professional litigants as common informers.[79] As will be seen later, informal mechanisms were the only easily available safeguard against vexatious and near-vexatious prosecutions.[80]

The discussion has so far been confined to the activities of private suitors, but the machinations of professional exploiters of the law formed a more palpable set of abuses. Particularly blatant offenders were common informers, who were often organized in syndicates backed by substantial

Londoners. They did not confine themselves to bringing actions by due course of law and to making compositions by the licence of the courts, but commonly sought to persuade their victims — some of whom were probably guilty of no offence — to hand over cash without legal formality. Scattered prosecutions against informers for practising barratry and extortion occurred throughout the first fifteen years of the reign of James I; but by 1619 the Wiltshire justices had become alarmed that the activities of the racketeers were crippling the corn trade, and with Privy Council support a battery of quarter sessions prosecutions was mounted against a number of local operators. That the rackets were ultimately broken, however, was the result not of action through the courts, but of a shift in official attitudes to the common informer system as it had hitherto operated — a change that produced the Act of 1624 which closed the courts at Westminster against most classes of information. Informers continued to work in Wiltshire after this date, but it is clear that their activities had been severely curtailed.[81]

Although common informers depended on the law for a living, they were theoretically private agents. But officials could also be involved in legal chicanery, and there were occasional complaints against constables, tithingmen and even justices.[82] By far the most prominent group of officials prosecuted for barratry, extortion and other offences, however, were bailiffs. It had long been recognized that the office of bailiff, a key position in the machinery of law,[83] combined the maximum of temptation with the maximum of opportunity to practise abuses, and a long string of Acts had been passed to prevent malpractices. But the very multiplication of statutes bore witness to the difficulties of control, and Michael Dalton's handbook for sheriffs, published in 1623, included a long list of abuses which he thought characteristic of bailiffs and which he felt his readers would be wise to look out for.[84] There are strong indications that in Wiltshire, as in some other counties which have been investigated, Dalton's strictures were warranted.[85] Admittedly, complaints about bailiffs have to be viewed with caution, for the nature of their duties could hardly fail to arouse resentment;[86] but there is considerable evidence that many bailiffs were not simply innocent victims of the unpopularity which comes of doing a distasteful job of work.

Some seventy individuals who were or claimed to be bailiffs are known to have been in trouble, some of them repeatedly, at quarter sessions or in Star Chamber during the sample period 1615-24. This list is substantial as it stands, but on account of the difficulty of identifying under-bailiffs and special bailiffs and because some doubtful connections have been discarded, the total is almost certainly incomplete.[87] Because of the lack of a comprehensive checklist, it is unfortunately impossible to say what proportion of the total body of men who served as bailiffs during the period found themselves called in question; but it is striking that of the seventy-one head bailiffs of hundreds and boroughs whose names can be recovered from the bailiff lists filed on the quarter session rolls — many of whom doubtless left their subordinates to do the really dirty work — as many as one-third were the subject of complaint.[88]

A handful of cases involved allegations of barratry or of the forgery or falsification of legal documents — writ-serving could easily go hand in hand with pettifogging — but the most characteristic offences were extortion and crimes of violence.[89] In the ten-year sample period, quarter-sessions juries found a total of twenty-one indictments for extortion against twenty separate bailiffs, while the presentments of constables and hundred jurors and the records of Star Chamber yield a few more cases.[90] It is clear from the evidence of petitions and informations, however, that the offences actually prosecuted represented only a fraction of those of which complaint was made, and presumably an even smaller proportion of those which were actually committed. A petition from the parish of Brinkworth in 1617, for example, detailed fourteen acts or attempted acts of extortion, involving seven bailiffs and eleven victims; but although most of the alleged offenders were prosecuted at the Michaelmas sessions, none of the particular outrages mentioned in the petition was specified on the indictments.[91] Petitions and other non-indictment materials are also valuable in highlighting certain characteristics of the bailiffs' extortionate activities. In the first place, it is clear that they were often highly organized. The most striking instance concerned a certain Francis Wallys, an attorney of the Common Pleas subsequently debarred from practising, who allegedly gathered together a group of bailiffs, bound to him by oath, whom he called his 'disciples'. The confederacy was said to have purchased large numbers of blank sealed warrants, and to have used them to operate a complex extortion racket in the area around Westbury.[92] Secondly, it is plain that threats and violence on an impressive scale could accompany demands for cash. The Brinkworth petition, for example, described in circumstantial detail how the inhabitants' resistance to extortionate demands was countered by a series of violent acts which culminated when a group of bailiffs 'rode up and down the town with swords drawn', evidently to discourage further recalcitrance. [93] At times, it would seem, bailiffs behaved more like brigands than officers of the law.

In the light of such information, it is not surprising that bailiffs often figured in prosecutions for crimes of violence. On twenty-three occasions in the period 1615-24, bailiffs or their wives were named as defendants in quarter sessions indictments for assault and battery; they were largely responsible for indictments for violent or unjust arrest or imprisonment and for the non-felonious taking of goods and chattels; they were frequently bound over to keep the peace or be of good behaviour; and certain bailiffs were notorious for drunkenness and for ferocious or otherwise illegal behaviour when drunk.[94] Some of the charges of assault and trespass of chattels may well have been vexatiously prosecuted by people lawfully distrained or arrested; but the impression nevertheless remains strong that bailiffs often went about their business with little regard for the niceties of the law.

The evidence of prosecutions shows that bailiffs could not pursue illegal activities completely unchecked, yet it is doubtful how far court action had a strong deterrent effect. Many offences almost certainly went unprosecuted, the culprits were in any case quick to resort to writs of *certiorari*[95] and they could sometimes rely on the complicity of other legal officers, such as gaolers, to get them out of trouble.[96] The basic problems defied solution. On the one hand, because sheriffs served only for a year, they could hardly be expected to maintain a consistent disciplinary policy; their chief concern, in practice, was probably to ensure by a system of bonds that they were saved harmless from the penalties of their subordinates' abuses.[97] On the other hand, the nature of a bailiff's duties were hardly likely to attract the gentlest spirits, or to appeal to men of real substance; and in fact, the indications are that head bailiffs were usually men of only moderate standing, while under-bailiffs and special bailiffs included the shiftless and the desperate. In these circumstances, some degree of corruption and abuse was probably inevitable.

The other potential and actual problems mentioned in this paper, *Part III.* however, could be ameliorated by the actions of local people themselves. In the first place, in situations involving civil suits and to some extent in cases of criminal misdemeanour, there is evidence that arbitration mechanisms were of great importance in limiting bitterness and conflict and helping to restrain those who were too quick to resort to litigation. Mediators could intervene in a dispute and settle it before the matter was taken to law, or could end it after one of the parties had had recourse to legal process but before the multiplication of costs and inconveniences had reinforced the original bitterness. Arbitration could give the wronged party adequate redress, but the relative informality of the procedure made it possible to be flexible, to take all relevant factors into consideration and to persuade the parties at issue to compromise their rights in the interests of harmony.

Previous writers have given prominence to the use of arbitrators by the courts of Chancery and Requests, which frequently commissioned legal officers or local gentry to hear the parties and effect a compromise,[98] but it needs to be stressed that other types of suit were often settled by mediation. Clearly many ecclesiastical causes were ended by concordat, in accordance with the canon law principle that litigants should be given every opportunity for reconciliation;[99] and references to the arbitration of common law actions are not uncommon, although technically the law did not recognize the validity of such settlements. It may well be that those types of action at law which involved complex circumstances and therefore allowed room for give-and-take lent themselves particularly well to arbitration, but it seems that even such suits as pleas of debt in which the facts at issue were relatively straightforward could be settled by compromise.[100] Criminal prosecutions for trespass might also, on occasion, be dealt with by mediation.[101]

There is striking evidence that the mechanisms of arbitration were well developed in early-seventeenth-century Wiltshire and did not wholly depend on judicial initiative. As the basis for further discussion, it is worth giving at length a particularly vivid account of mediation procedures at work. A deponent in the bishop of Salisbury's consistory court described how there had been a dispute between William Beale and Elizabeth Sherer over the possession of a certain pew in the parish church of Brinkworth, and the parties had resorted to legal action:

> but before any sentence passed in the same, John Ayliffe, Esquire ... taking notice of such their differences and controversies, and endeavouring to make a peace between them, called the said Beale and Sherer before him in the church there ... and amongst other speeches tending to the settling of a peace 'twixt them ..., in the presence of divers of the then parishioners there ..., spoke to them as followeth, viz., 'I know not whether either of you have any right in this seat for which you strive ..., but this I know, that I have right to a place ... for a tenement called Jordens and I will rather forgo my right than you shall go on with such unnecessary suits ...'.

This motion was initially unsuccessful, but

> Mr Ayliffe using further means for a peace 'twixt them called Mr Hutchins, the minister there, and Mr John Richman, a chief parishioner, unto him, and by their assistance ... prevailed with them so far as that they were contented to draw lots which of them should sit in the said uppermost seat, and then and there presently lots being made and put into the church book, they ... drew them forth, by which lot the said uppermost seat fell to ... [William Beale].[102]

Other accounts of arbitration mechanisms reveal numerous variations in procedure. Gentlemen and ministers were prominent among mediators, but yeomen and other men of lesser rank sometimes formed a part or the whole of the arbitration panel; on occasion, it would seem, venerable age was regarded as a qualification. In many cases the initiative to go to arbitration came, as in the example quoted, from the intervention of one or more third parties. Such mediators often professed a quasi-moral concern to minimize strife, and were supported by the fact that an individual's reluctance to accept a reasonable settlement could evoke the disapproval of his neighbours — a disapproval which might be publicly expressed in the implementation of the church's rule that those who were in a state of contention should not be admitted to the communion. In some cases, however, one of the disputants himself proposed an arbitrated settlement. In any event, it is clear that frequently the parties were each able to nominate one of the mediators to make sure that their interests were properly represented. There were many variations in the place where the arbitrators met: it might be the church, the parsonage, a manorial court house or the home of one of the arbitrators or of the disputants. As to the method of reaching a settlement, the use of lots seems to have been unusual; the more normal mode of procedure was for the arbitrators to review the circumstances so far as they could establish them — there are instances of the private examination of witnesses — and then proceed to hammer out a practical agreement on a give-and-take basis. The final settlement might involve the making of an apology, the payment of damages or (where a specific right or possession was at issue) a definite adjudication; and there would usually be provision for the payment of outstanding legal costs and for the cessation of court proceedings. If the matter at issue were of any gravity, wise arbitrators would get something in writing. The dispute thus 'ended', the erstwhile enemies might go to the nearest inn or alehouse, perhaps with the mediators, to seal the settlement in drink. On occasion, of course, no solution was achieved, or one of the parties might subsequently fail to honour the bargain; but the overall impression is one of an efficient and realistic system for minimizing conflict.[103]

There is little evidence that these elaborate and well-established arbitration procedures were used in serious criminal cases. There are indications, however, that certain factors operating at a very informal level served to limit recourse to felony prosecutions or to ameliorate their effects, at least in comparatively minor cases of larceny to which most of my evidence relates. But not all types of criminal benefited equally, for these tendencies amounted to a selective bias which worked in favour of local people and against strangers. The situation was not clear-cut, however; cases of the prosecution and punishment of local residents, even for trivial thefts, were by no means unheard of.

The fundamental point is that not all crimes, even when the identity of the culprit was known or strongly suspected, led to rigorous prosecution. In cases of larceny, for example, the victim might content himself with recovering his property, warning the culprit, perhaps going so far as to have him bound over, though without intending that this should lead to further court action.[104] One factor relevant to the decision of whether or not to prefer an indictment was the knowledge that to proceed would cost time, trouble and money.[105] But this consideration presumably applied in all cases, whatever the social identity of the culprit. There are, however, grounds for thinking that certain other factors operated to the particular benefit of local residents.

The Wiltshire records suggest that in cases in which local people were involved, potential prosecutors and other agents were often subjected to pressures to exercise mercy. In one instance, it was said that the fellow-parishioners of an accused man had pleaded with his victim not to prosecute the law lest a death sentence should throw his children on the parish. Richard Downe, having accused Elizabeth Jobson of stealing a pig, was 'earnestly entreated' by her mother to forgive her. When the tithingman of Alvediston 'with other his neighbours' searched the house of Thomas Morris, they found a sack of corn which he had stolen from Thomas Bound; but when Morris entreated 'the searchers to be good unto him and his children or else he should be utterly undone ..., Robert Toomer, tithingman, moved with pity, sought his neighbours that this business might be concealed'. Particularly interesting are cases in which reasons for clemency were generalized into a principle. Thus, a man who was accused of sexually assaulting a girl approached one of the witnesses and begged him to 'use him like a neighbour' and so mitigate his testimony; while in another case, a certain Jacob Woodman explained that although he saw James Ashmead mowing with a stolen scythe, he did not challenge him 'for neighbourhood sake'. There are, moreover, hints that some degree of communal pressure might be deployed to encourage would-be prosecutors to exercise neighbourly tolerance. Thus, when Charles Gunter caused an indictment to be made against two men for taking some money, an intermediary tried to persuade him at least to reduce the charge to cozening, arguing that 'in so doing you shall be well thought of, otherwise some people will speak evil of you'.[106] Pressures like this probably helped to limit recourse to prosecution.

Moreover, the conditions of life in small communities probably helped to shield local people from the strict legal consequences of certain types of illegal behaviour. One factor was the degree to which various modes of acquiring property were actually perceived as theft, or at least regarded as suitable matters for prosecution as larceny. Gleaning was probably widespread, and sanctioned by local custom; but it must have been tempting and easy to progress from picking up stray ears of corn to the surreptitious and technically felonious 'pulling' of sheaves. Examples of this kind of behaviour did occasionally lead to larceny indictments at quarter sessions, but their rarity suggests that many cases of the same kind were passed over.[107] Similarly, the comments of the few people charged with felony for taking wood suggest that this was an equivocal area of behaviour.[108] Local people who were short of necessities thus had at their disposal a number of means of acquiring food or fuel which were unlikely to lead to felony prosecutions. Yet this point should not be stressed too much; some such offences may have been treated as trespasses and punished locally, by stocking or whipping, under the Act 43 Elizabeth I, c.7 or according to manorial ordinances; and, indeed, as we shall see, attitudes to these equivocal areas of behaviour may have been hardening.[109]

Again, if a thief and his victim lived relatively close to one another, the culprit might be able to plead circumstances which could throw doubt on the question of whether he had been guilty of 'flat felony'. Thomas Farmer of Woodborough, for example, when accused of stealing a pig from William Smith, secured an acquittal by claiming that he had found it straying in the street; while Abraham Stockwell was unable to obtain a true bill against a certain Gilbert Kinge for the theft of a sheep, for the latter was able to argue that it had got into his flock by accident. Strangers and outsiders, by definition, could not hope to benefit from such excuses.[110]

If a selective bias did operate in favour of local people, one might hope to find some evidence for it in a detailed analysis of the records of prosecutions. At first sight, however, the study of indictments seems rather to indicate that the idea is irrelevant, for the residential details noted on true bills suggest that in most cases of theft which went for trial, the abode of the alleged criminal and the locus of the crime were identical.[111] From similar evidence, indeed, a student of crime in Elizabethan Essex has concluded that 'almost all' persons charged with theft were neighbours of their victims.[112] As Professor Cockburn has recently shown, however, the data provided by indictments are frequently misleading.[113] One way of arriving at a more accurate picture is to exploit the additional evidence included in the depositions made by the accused, prosecutor and witnesses, and it is fortunate that such documents have survived in considerable quantities among the records of the Wiltshire quarter sessions.[114]

A sample of depositions, consisting of all the papers relating to larcenies and compound larcenies which survive for the years 1616, 1619 and 1623, was selected for detailed study and collated with the appropriate indictments.[115] This body of materials includes examinations and informations relating to 151 accused people.[116] One hundred and seventeen of these individuals, who were together charged with 120 acts of theft, figured on true bill indictments in the quarter sessions files, and will be considered first. Thirteen of them, however, cannot be included in the analysis because the deposition evidence is inadequate.[117] The 104 who remain — and this figure is sufficiently close to one hundred to make it unnecessary to convert raw totals into percentages — may be classified as follows.

Thirty-seven accused, including nine women, may be described as permanent local residents.[118] That is, the members of this group were householders, or the resident close relatives of householders; and they all resided within six miles of their alleged victims. This distance was chosen as a criterion on the assumption that those who lived further apart than this were unlikely, in normal circumstances, to regard each other as neighbours;[119] but most of the accused in fact lived much closer to their victims. Eighteen were actually their fellow-parishioners; the remaining nineteen lived on average about two and three-quarter miles from those from whom they were said to have stolen goods.

Even among this relatively local group, there is little evidence of close relations between prosecutors and prosecuted; and there was certainly a considerable disparity in social status. As far as the economic and social standing of the accused is concerned, the deposition evidence suggests that the information provided on the indictments and summarized in Table 2 was slightly flattering. Of the eight men described as 'husbandman', for example, four were actually day-labourers. Overall, the status of the supposed criminals was fairly low. Those from whom property had been stolen, on the other hand, were on average of markedly better condition; the thirty-two who can be classified with any certainty included the Earl of Hertford, an esquire, six other gentlemen, eight yeomen, two clothiers, two other substantial tradesmen and five husbandmen, the tale being made up by five craftsmen or tradesmen who probably enjoyed only modest resources, a shepherd, and a widow who kept an alehouse. In only a handful of cases is it probable that victim and alleged criminal were of equal status.

Table 2: *'Styles' ascribed in indictments to eighty-three males[+] prosecuted for larceny/compound larceny at Wiltshire Quarter Sessions in 1616, 1619 or 1623*

	Local residents	'Outsiders'	Servants
Gentleman	0	0	0
Cleric	0	0	0
Yeoman	2	0	0
Husbandman	8	7	7
Craftsman/tradesman	9	9	2
Labourer	9	21*	9†
Total	28	37	18

[+]Females are excluded from the analysis because of the small numbers involved and because the common style 'spinster' appears to have had no certain meaning.
　*Includes two 'grooms'.
　†Includes one 'shepherd'.

Forty-seven accused may be classified, in contrast to the first group, as 'outsiders'.[120] In various senses, they were all on the move, and the great majority were apparently strangers in the places where they were charged with theft. A few were probably householders in their own localities, but were on criminal or business expeditions — the choice of epithet depending on how much of their stories is believed — more than six miles from home. William Gasse, for example, claimed to be a butcher from Romsey in Hampshire who had travelled into Wiltshire to buy livestock. But he was taken on suspicion while driving eighteen sheep, allegedly purchased from a chance acquaintance whose name he did not know, through the village of Plaitford two hours before sunrise; and the animals were later claimed by three men from Fordingbridge, fourteen miles from Gasse's home.[121] The social standing of most of the others was more doubtful. They included an itinerant building worker, a few who claimed to be on some specific and lawful errand, servants on the move, people wandering in search of work, a few discharged soldiers and sailors, a number of pedlars and petty chapmen and a residue whose reasons for travel are obscure. More than half were over twenty-five miles from alleged homes; they named London and towns and villages in Wiltshire, Gloucestershire, Somerset, Devon, Cornwall, Buckinghamshire, Middlesex, Essex, Derbyshire and Lancashire 'as their places of origin or last settlement. The additions ascribed to the members of this group on their indictments are summarized in Table II, but it is doubtful whether the majority of them had any significance save as a means of filling the appropriate slot on the record. The fact is that probably many of these 'outsiders' were perceived as vagrants; and the indications are that even those who, like William Gasse, were probably not destitute of substance and habitation were regarded with suspicion by virtue of their itinerancy.

The final category of accused, embracing twenty people of whom two were females,[122] was made up of servants. On the basis of what is known of servants as a class in early-modern England, it may be surmised that two features characterized the members of this group. They were on the whole young — one of the males was, in fact, only fifteen years old;[123] and they were mobile, for servants were noted for their tendency to move from master to master, and from place to place, when their covenants expired. On the other hand, since young people of nearly all ranks of society might go into service, the term 'servant' could embrace individuals from widely differing backgrounds and with radically dissimilar prospects before them;[124] but whether the indictment additions ascribed to the members of the group in any sense accurately reflected such differences is unclear. Some three-quarters of the accused servants were charged with stealing from their masters or mistresses, but in the remaining cases it is unknown what kind of relationship existed between the suspected thieves and their victims. Except that there were no labourers in evidence, the status of those who complained of offences by the members of this group fairly evenly spanned the social scale.

This analysis shows clearly that it is misleading to take the residential information included on indictments at its face value. It suggests that approaching one-half of those indicted for theft at quarter sessions in the sample years were, as itinerants and people operating far from their homes, likely to be regarded as strangers and outsiders by those who prosecuted them. Of the remainder, a considerable proportion were servants, members of the least stable elements in a village population. Only a third or so were permanent residents living within a six-mile radius of the venue of the crime, and half of these did not actually live in the same parish as their victims.

The reasons for supposing that a selective bias worked in favour of local people rest on two lines of investigation.[125] In the first place, it is suggestive that the rate of conviction varied among the three groups. Of the permanent local residents who came to trial, 68 per cent were convicted; of the servants, 88 per cent; while of the 'outsiders', 93 per cent were found guilty. In addition, most of those who suffered death belonged to the last group.[126] An even more interesting line of inquiry is offered by including in the analysis cases in which a complaint of theft was made and depositions were taken, presumably with the intention of framing an indictment, but no true bill was found. It will be recalled that the body of informations and examinations surviving for the three sample years included materials relating to thirty-four suspects whose names did not figure in the relevant indictment files. If we ignore two of these individuals because they were remanded to the assizes,[127] and a further four who figured in particularly obscure depositions,[128] there remain twenty-eight suspected thieves who were apparently exonerated either by a grand jury or before a bill was actually drawn up against them, and who can be confidently assigned to the three categories which have been used already.[129] Table 3 sets out the figures so that the numbers of people in each category who escaped indictment can be compared with those who were committed for trial.

Of the local residents, 67 per cent were indicted; of the servants, 83 per cent; while of the 'outsiders', 89 per cent had to face further process.[130] The indications are, then, that local residents brought into question for theft were as a group least likely to be indicted, and even if they were committed for trial stood the greatest chance of securing an acquittal; while 'outsiders' had the poorest chance of escaping further process once they had been apprehended and brought before a justice, and ran the greatest danger of conviction. Servants perhaps occupied an intermediate position on both counts, though the small numbers in this group produce percentages of doubtful validity.

Table 3: *Pre-trial disposition of 132 persons accused of larceny/compound larceny at Wiltshire Quarter Sessions in 1616, 1619 or 1623*

	Indicted	Not Indicted	Total	% Indicted
Local residents	37	18	55	67
'Outsiders'	47	6	53	89
Servants	20	4	24	83
Total	104	28	132	79

Yet this evidence of a bias in favour of local residents should not convey the impression of a communal arcadia. For on the one hand, the reverse side of the coin of neighbourliness was evidently a measure of xenophobia towards the wandering poor, who not only bore much of the brunt of larceny prosecutions but were also subject to the vagrancy laws. But many of these people cannot be dismissed as wilfully idle vagabonds; they had often, to judge by the evidence of depositions, been squeezed out of a settled life by economic necessity. Probably many of the poor of Wiltshire, especially from about 1615 onwards as the troubles of the cloth industry and a number of bad harvests eroded their livelihood,[131] were forced onto the road and deprived of the benefits of neighbourhood. The case of Anthony Hooper may serve as an example. Born in 1583, he was the son of a Keevil weaver, and before 1620 was himself dwelling there and working at the same trade. Finding himself unemployed, he travelled towards the Vale of the White Horse and for a time found a living there from harvest labour and from work in a woad mill. By October 1620, however, he was again unemployed and set off home; but on his way he stole some clothes from a hedge and was indicted and whipped. In 1623 he was indicted as a vagrant, whipped again and sent to the house of correction; his ultimate fate is unknown.[132]

On the other hand, it is well not to forget that the tendencies which have been considered were not strong enough to save all local people from being subjected to the harsh penalties of the law, even for trivial thefts of foodstuffs. Agnes Slade of Melksham, for example, who was accused of stealing a sheep during the dearth of 1622-3, claimed that she had been tempted to theft by finding the animal caught in a briar; she had stolen it 'for want, and she had not food to relieve her and her child, being almost famished ... for which offence she is sorry and desireth favour'; but she was prosecuted and whipped.[133] A number of factors may have conditioned the prosecution of local residents, apart from such imponderables as the personality make-up of individual victims of theft. For one thing, it is probable that some local people were prosecuted after a series of thefts had eroded the tolerance of their neighbours. At Michaelmas 1620, for example,

Agnes Sawe and Joan Hutchins of Southwick were indicted for stealing two knitches of barley from Jeremy Scott's field. But Scott claimed that they had stolen from him previously; **Henry Whittocke** told how he had met the pair in highly suspicious circumstances on the night that milk was stolen from Edward Pappes earlier in the year; while Edward Jones informed that he had recently caught Hutchins making up a burden of his cut pease. Almost certainly, the decision to take these women to court was influenced by their earlier misdeeds. A more aggravated version of the same situation accounted for the hanging of Nicholas Sedgwick of South Newton, who was not only suspected of various acts of pilfering and theft himself, but had allegedly encouraged others to commit felonies.[134] A more general factor is suggested by Macfarlane's study of witchcraft prosecutions, which indicates that a neighbour who had been reduced to poverty and helplessness might ultimately become an unbearable affront to the consciences of other members of the community.[135] As the economic pressures of the early seventeenth century acted on Wiltshire society, attitudes to the worst victims of change, such as erstwhile sufficient clothworkers who now found it difficult to get a living, may well have hardened, and ideas of neighbourly tolerance come under stress. In the manor court at Keevil, for example, economic strains in 1616 and 1623 were reflected in ordinances which forbade the poor to gather bean stubs in other men's lands on pain of stocking.[136] Whether such orders were consistently observed may be doubted, and neighbourhood ideals were probably difficult to break down; but it is likely that some people, at least, would seize on acts of theft by those less fortunate than themselves as a justification for abandoning a pretence of neighbourly sentiment.[137]

This essay has ranged widely, and its conclusions are necessarily tentative. A striking feature of early-seventeenth-century Wiltshire society was the existence of professional racketeers and extortioners spawned by the machinery of the law. On occasion, their activities could be extremely oppressive and disruptive; at all times they were a social irritant. As regards the impact of the law on people in general, it is clear that litigation was a feature of life among members of the more substantial ranks, while the multiplicity of courts and of types of suit to prosecute therein gave scope for vexatious or unreasonable legal action; but well-established mechanisms of arbitration, drawing some of their strength from ideals of neighbourly harmony, helped to limit and resolve conflict. Attitudes to the penalties for felony were complex. Pressures of various sorts, including ideals of neighbourhood, probably tended to limit recourse to prosecutions for larceny when local residents were involved, while the pursuit of outsiders was less inhibited; but the existence of large and growing numbers of the poor imposed strains on ideals of neighbourliness, and even the patently unfortunate could not rely on favourable treatment.

6 *Quarter Sessions Appearances and their Background: A Seventeenth-Century Regional Study*

T. C. CURTIS

The aim of this essay is essentially modest: to illustrate in a regional context how and why a person came to appear before quarter sessions in the seventeenth century. This will involve discussion of the types of act which contemporaries found unacceptable and the varying steps which were taken to control the people who committed them.[1]

A study of handbooks written for the guidance of justices of the peace in the sixteenth and seventeenth centuries[2] gives the strong impression that early-modern England was infested by a plague of professional and semi-professional criminals: people who wandered the country in pursuit of quick gains by illegal methods. Michael Dalton, for example, wrote of 'infinite swarms of idle vagabonds ... which ... wandered up and down to the great danger and indignity of our nation'. These people were dangerous because they were, 'for the most part, thieves, cut-purses, cozeners or the like'.[3] Their existence was not raised by the writers of such works as a purely academic matter. On the contrary, they gave much advice on how to recognize such persons[4] and urged the justices and their subordinate officers to take positive steps to reduce the number of vagrants.[5] Cheshire — the area with which this study is concerned — did not escape the attentions of this kind of criminal altogether.[6] For the most part, however, the justices were concerned with breaches of the law of a different order.[7] It is obviously impossible to provide a complete description of all the people who came before the courts, or of all their acts; but any understanding of the law enforcement process at this level must begin with a brief sketch of the kind of situation in which the justices and their officers became involved. Perhaps the most satisfactory way to do this is to look at two typical crimes — assault and disturbing the peace — with which law enforcement officers were concerned.[8]

Common assault frequently involved what appears to have been a spontaneous attack by a man, or woman, on his or her neighbours. Such acts seem only rarely to have been carefully premeditated, or the consequences calculated. The motive for such an attack was often equally transient, as an assault by Gregory Hughes and Ralph Anon on William Neald of Tarvin indicates. Neald had been 'at ... Anthony Hodgson's all ... Monday night (being an alehouse) drinking and playing at cards with ... Gregory Hughes ... and Ralph Anon'. Hodgson, the alehouse-keeper, spoke of 'some quarrelling between Gregory Hughes and William Neald'; Gregory, indeed, confessed to striking Neald but said 'that he was much provoked thereunto by ... William Neald'.[9] Not all assaults sprang from such a simplistic base. In other cases there certainly was — as there may have been in Neald's case — a pre-existing source of tension. Frequently this was economic, as the assault by Roger Parsons demonstrates. Parsons, 'coming into the house of John Leigh in Nantwich ... pretending that he came to pay me, this examinate, money that he owed unto me.... After a short space he began to enter into speeches and draw his dagger ... and offered to stab me'.[10] A similar case occurred in 1682 when John Heapes was attacked with great violence by William Swindles, 'and the reason why ... Swindles did so beat and abuse ... John Heapes, this examinate believes, was because ... Heapes asked his money of ... Swindles'.[11]

Violence could also emerge from bitter family quarrels. Again, although it is often difficult to judge from the very limited evidence available, it does not seem that the assaults were the result of premeditation as much as personal passion. The case of the Higginson family illustrates the point:

> Mr Higginson sent [to the constables] ... to come again to his house or his son would kill some of them ... and coming into the house ... [the constable] commanded ... Samuel Higginson to be quiet ... his father offered to thrust [Samuel] forth of the house and Samuel pushed his father back.... Mr Higginson said to [the constable] 'you must be rough with him and take him to the stocks'.[12]

On other occasions this kind of sudden, spontaneous violence broke out in the furtherance of some other crime, rather than during a crude attempt to settle a dispute. An example, again drawn from the records of 1682, may establish the point:

> John Chaddock of Halton, keeper, saith that ... he found Robert Broxon and Thomas Broxon of Runcorn gathering acorns in the park ... and this examinate wished them to go their way and come there no more; and so riding round the park he found [them] ... in the park again. This examinate alighting from his horse to take their bags, they ran away ... this examinate overtaking them, offered to take their bags from them and they both laid hold of him by the hair of the head and pulled him down to the ground and said they would be killed before he should have their acorns...[13]

A further source of sudden violence was personal aggressiveness springing sometimes from drink,[14] sometimes from personal whims or eccentricities. The latter description fits the case of James Livesey, who ran after a boy and when he overtook him 'he did strike him with a staff and did very much abuse [him], being in the highway'. This is not of itself eccentric but a second deponent commented 'that ... Livesey used to quarrel with women and children'.[15]

These few examples perhaps provide sufficient outline and colour for a hasty impression. Violence was localized, sudden, often spontaneous. Immediate causes were often trivial, although backgrounds could be more complex. Physical attack was often the unsophisticated solution to rivalry or personal animosity, or a direct expression of strong feeling. Cases of disturbing the peace into which the law enforcement agencies were drawn were normally of the same kind.

Family quarrels, even when they did not reach the level of violence, could cause problems within the local community. As a justice of the peace reported in 1684:

Forasmuch as it plainly appears ... by the oaths of several credible persons that Alice Hallum, heretofore servant to John Gee of Adlington ... yeoman, is a person of evil behaviour and of lewd conversation and carriage and [causes] great dissension between John Gee ... and his wife ... and further that ... Alice Hallum has confessed ... that she has lately born ... John Gee a bastard man child and that she has been with ... John Gee lately both at Macclesfield ... and ... in his barn.[16]

Drink and personal aggressiveness again had a part to play, even without actual violence, in disturbing the peace. As Humphrey Hulme deposed of Thomas Coppocke, he 'is a very disordered lewd fellow, much given to haunting alehouses and apt to quarrel in his drink'.[17] Sometimes eccentricity was enough. Thus Richard Rylands was 'a person distracted in his senses, wandering about, and disorderly behaving himself, to the great terror of his majesty's subjects, and has been very abusive in his language and actions'.[18]

Thus is illustrated, albeit briefly, the kind of situation in which the law enforcement officers were likely to become involved. This is, however, by no means the whole story. The commission of acts likely to incur disapproval was but the first step to a court appearance. The next lay in coming to the attention of the law enforcement agencies, in such a way that they chose, or were in some way compelled, to begin official action. The problems involved in this situation are complex, but at least some of the ways in which the constables could be involved may be indicated.

First, a person or group could become involved with the law by extreme or recalcitrant personal behaviour, which broke through other forms of control. The operation of unofficial controls such as ridiculing non-conforming community members can occasionally be traced in contemporary documents,[19] and even in modern writers,[20] but, in all its forms, it tends to appear in the quarter sessions records only after its failure. If a number of the cases so far outlined are investigated a little further, the point may become clearer. Roger Parson's assault on John Leigh illustrates the failure of neighbourly intervention to prevent the open flaring of a personal quarrel. It will be remembered that this dispute was left at the stage where violent threats had been made:

> John Leigh and others, seeing ... Roger Parsons offer this abuse, ... offered to hold him ... and persuade him to be quiet, whereupon ... Parsons thrust at ... John Leigh with his dagger ... whereupon ... Leigh did send for the constable. Whereupon this examinate, having a warrant of the peace from Mr Brereton ... to attach the said Parsons and others, did deliver the ... warrant unto the constable ... and charged him by virtue thereof to attach ... Parsons....[21]

Further examination of the Higginson family quarrel will also reveal how personal intransigence could defeat neighbourly control and necessitate official involvement:

> William Williamson, one of the constables of Castle Northwich ... saith that ... William Vernon of Castle Northwich ... called him ... to come to Mr Higginson's house ... to keep the king's peace, for Samuel Higginson of Northwich ... was then in his father's house fighting and quarrelling ... and would not be ruled. This examinant seeming unwilling to go ... Vernon further charged him in the king's name to come and assist him set ... Higginson in the stocks, whereupon this examinate went ... [and] commanded peace in the king's name, which was observed in his sight, and ... Williamson went home again.[22]

In each of the cases so far discussed the behaviour which defeated unofficial control was essentially short term: merely the product of violent passion in a particular situation. This type of behaviour must now be separated from longer term patterns of behaviour which the community found unacceptable but was unable to control. In this context it is irrelevant whether or not the persons involved really behaved in the fashion of which they were accused. The crucial point is that their neighbours thought they did, and required official action.

An example of a fairly generalized problem is seen in the petition from her neighbours which first drew Elizabeth Tushingham to the attention of the Cheshire bench:

Elizabeth Tushingham ... spinster ... hath been a wandering idle person over the country for the space of these twenty years and more, being a woman of very light and incontinent life and a stirrer up of many suits in diverse courts for these fourteen years last past against her father, brother and brother's son without any just cause ... and hath threatened to burn [her nephew's] house and to kill and destroy the cattle.... She being a vile and wilful obstinate woman, the neighbours have often entreated her to live in peaceable sort and honest fashion but could not prevail.... She is also a woman that hath not the fear of God before her eyes [for] she has not come to her parish church this ten or twelve years ... [nor] stands upon any religion, but a very atheist.[23]

However, the complaints against an individual could be a good deal more specific. An example of this kind of case arose in 1611 when the grand jury, on its own initiative, presented two alehouse-keepers: 'William Thomson of Newton [and] John Dennper of Newton ... are persons of evil name and fame and do keep tippling-houses and do entice company at unreasonable times, whereby many servants are diverted from their service and other enormities to the great damage of his majesty's subjects ...'.[24] Alehouse-keepers were perhaps peculiarly liable to generate communal disfavour, and certainly others found themselves in difficulties with the law. Anne Priestnal was one such. She was a widow who lived in Stockport in the early 1680s and kept a drinking-house which may also have housed a brothel. Her activities bitterly offended at least some of her neighbours, who complained of her to the constables, demanding her punishment lest her 'naughty carriage' brought 'a curse ... upon the town'.[25]

Of course these longer term behaviour patterns could also cause problems within the community. This point was made explicitly by two deponents discussing one Mary Mooreton:

This examinate saith upon her oath that she being a door neighbour to the said Mary Mooreton knows ... [that she] is a common drunkard and hath been within this fortnight last past drunk twice of one day. And that when she is drunk she abuses one neighbour or other, calling them whores and thieves.

The second deponent added that 'she knoweth that ... Mary Mooreton is a very troublesome and debased person and sets a great deal of dissension amongst her neighbours ...'.[26] On occasion this kind of troublemaking could take relatively sophisticated forms. An example was revealed in a petition to the justices by fourteen inhabitants of Lostock Gralam, requesting the binding over of John Horton of the same village. The petitioners claimed that he was 'a common barrator, fighter and disturber of the king's majesty's peace ... having heretofore committed many great misdemeanours against divers persons, and especially against Thomas Wilkinson of Lostock Gralam, his neighbour, a man of good, honest and quiet behaviour'. Horton, however, as the petitioners said, had not contented himself with general harassment and physical violence (although he had evidently employed both). 'In former time not long since ... the same John Horton did seek to persuade and induce certain persons to convey any of the neighbours' goods into the house ... of ... Thomas Wilkinson ... to the intent that ... Horton might charge or trouble ... Wilkinson with matter or suspicion of felony'.[27]

Individual recalcitrance was not, however, the only area of behaviour which could set the local community problems which it was unable, within its own resources, to resolve. A second major source of difficulty was the intra-communal quarrel. Frequently, of course, individual recalcitrance was involved in such disputes, but for the purpose of analysis the two may be conveniently separated.

The quarrel between Ralph Calverly and John Edwards is a classic example of the kind of difficulty with which the local community needed outside assistance. Whatever else may have been involved, the occasion of the dispute was a piece of land which contained a hedge and ditch. The quarrel had dragged on over a number of years but was brought to a head late in 1610 when Edwards, with due solemnity, visited Calverly and announced his intention to cut the hedge and clear the ditch. Calverly duly denied all of Edwards's claims. The two men separated and collected their supporters who armed themselves appropriately. The two groups met in the disputed territory. A neighbour intervened to arbitrate and was rebuffed. A few blows were probably struck. Whereupon Edwards, who was one of the high constables of the hundred, demanded the peace in the king's name and the two parties departed to meet again in court.[28]

A high percentage of these long-standing quarrels clearly had an economic basis — often disputes about land[29] — but on occasion they transcended this and became bitterly personal. The dispute between John Stevenson and Elizabeth Orme is a case in point: an argument over land leased by Elizabeth's husband to Stevenson which had led to Stevenson ejecting her from her own holding, or so Elizabeth alleged. However, she went further in her claims than that. In the attack upon her, she claimed, Stevenson was assisted by 'many others with him ... John Stevenson, his sons and daughters and family'. When she procured a warrant against Stevenson, a *supersedeas* was granted. She then asserted that

Stevenson and his family are most wicked, lewd and dissolute persons, sowers of sedition amongst neighbours ... suspected for sundry felonies ...namely for stealing of ... kine now lately, which is not examined but shuffled up as many other misdemeanours of ... John Stevenson and his sons have been by means of their friends.[30]

That at least a part of Elizabeth's case was believed is suggested by the fact that all of the Stevensons were bound over to keep the peace and variously charged with assault, breaking and entering, theft, trespass, malicious damage and riot. For good measure, John Stevenson was also charged with contempt of court.[31] His earlier successes in persuading the authorities of his innocence evidently rebounded with some force.[32]

While other cases with an economic basis could be discussed,[33] it is perhaps more useful now to outline other types of quarrel which ran out of control. Family disputes often came into this category. In October 1610 a Cheshire man petitioned the bench for protection from his mother and step-father. He alleged that they had abused him 'with many evil and contumacious speeches ... and hath attempted most violently both of late and aforetime to assault and molest your petitioner and to seek the destruction of his life and estate'.[34] These family disputes sometimes had tragic overtones. One such was brought to the notice of the justices in January 1611, when John Burgess asked them to bind over William Paul *alias* Winterbottom because he had

> in violent manner and against the laws of God and man taken your petitioner's wife away from his house [and after the constables had brought her back] doth still hold on his ungodly course in seeking all means to cause your petitioner's wife to depart from your petitioner and to return again to him, and hath so wrought his ungodly purpose with her that she is determined to depart quite away from your petitioner and go to him.[35]

Conversely, they could also have their comic side. Thus in January 1610 the justices were confronted with rival petitions, one from the husband and another from his wife, each alleging maltreatment by the other. The nub of the matter, however, was that the husband was petitioning to be released from prison, where the earlier stages of the dispute seem to have landed him, while the wife was attempting to keep him in.[36]

In some cases it simply is not possible to decide what lay behind quarrels. One example will suffice. The constable of Kiddington, Thomas Aldersey, received instructions to collect the poor rate. He attempted to collect a contribution from David Edowe, who refused to pay, saying he would pay him none, but will pay the other constables, and then this deponent replied and said that he was constable, and ... Edowe said 'a knave is constable', and this deponent replied 'there are more knaves than [constables]', and ... Edowe said 'hold thy tongue or I will beat thee soundly'.

After this witty exchange the two men parted but, as is so frequently the case, this argument was only the tip of an iceberg. In fact, as Aldersey himself said, the two men had been in dispute for at least six years; disagreements which had previously involved the collection of the poor rate as well as at least one assault. However, in all of the documentation of the quarrel — which includes a petition from Aldersey's neighbours in his defence, and the comments of a justice[37] — there is no explanation of the causes of the argument.

Perhaps sufficient has been said to illustrate the kind of situation into which the law enforcement agencies were drawn or chose to move. However, to put the matter with greater accuracy it should be said that the official agents were not necessarily the first or the only people to whom problems generated by recalcitrance or inter-neighbourly disputes were put. There is no space here to recount the development of informal arbitration, which has, in any case, been outlined elsewhere;[38] suffice it only to say that, at least as far as Cheshire was concerned, Mr Thomas is unquestionably correct in asserting the existence of an independent arbitration system.[39] One of the problems of using quarter sessions records as a principal source is that, virtually by definition, only failed attempts to arbitrate come to notice. Even so, there is sufficient evidence to indicate this kind of activity.

John Faulkenor had evidently been a source of trouble in his neighbourhood for some time. Eventually his neighbours informed the magistrates that he and his wife were 'persons of evil fame and behaviour' and caused 'dissension and variance in the neighbourhood'. Further, 'they never heard children use such bad language as the ... children [of John Faulkenor] did'. The interesting point, however, is that Faulkenor appeared in court only after the neighbourhood had persuaded the priest to talk to him and, as the clergyman duly deposed, this had failed to achieve its intended end.[40]

The clergy did not, however, have a monopoly of this kind of service. Cheshire also had its wisemen who, for example, tried to resolve difficulties over the identity of thieves — a question which could cause great trouble within the community. Thus in the autumn of 1682 a Cheshire girl accused of theft consulted with one Dr Deane who, for a sixpenny fee, gave a somewhat vague description of the culprit.[41] That his advice was not as specific as some might have desired is suggested by a description of his methods given by an earlier deponent seeking much the same kind of guidance: he 'had looked a little into a book which this deponent thinks had letters or figures of red and black ... colours in it; he told this examinate it was a woman, but would not name her'.[42]

The official law enforcement agencies, then, did not alone attempt to resolve disputes which had run beyond the bounds of the normal control of family or neighbourhood. Moreover, this second method of becoming involved with the authorities was not the last. The individual could also find himself in contact if he chose to make attacks, either verbal or physical, upon members of the official control groups. In this way, for example, Hugh Gandy found himself before the bench in January 1682:

> Richard Fryer, one of the constables of Weaverham ... saith that Hugh Gandy ... assaulted [him] ... and being charged in the king's name to keep the peace ... Hugh Gandy replied he cared neither for king nor constable for he was an officer himself and had as much to do there as ... Richard Fryer, threatening that he would have his life ....[43]

William Reddich behaved in much the same way with much the same result. Two constables discovered Reddich, who had been excommunicated as an adulterer, in Stockport church and, with some difficulty, removed him. Encountering them later in the street, Reddich demanded to know why they had removed him. When he learned, as he surely must have expected, that he had been dealt with as an excommunicate fornicator, he rejoined, '"Callest thou me a fornicator?", calling [the constable] a bastard and a scabby villain in very grievous manner [and saying] that he would be revenged ...'. A court appearance was the consequence.[44]

Some particularly bold characters occasionally aimed their abuse still higher, although the result tended to be the same. In 1684,

> John Brook said he cared neither for Sir John Arderne, [J.P.], nor for this examinate, and further declared and said that Sir John had robbed him ... and that there was never good laws since this king came in, nor would be any whilst he reigned, for setting such men as Arderne in power to rob others ....[45]

Again the bench had the pleasure of dealing with such an unwise character. Resistance occasionally had a more overtly politicaly purpose. After Leftwich Oldfield, J.P., had broken up a Quaker meeting,

> Henry Maddock did ... openly declare and say that if the king had not been more merciful to them, meaning Quakers, than ... Leftwich Oldfield

was, it would have been worse afore now ... further saying that if the king knew how ... Mr Oldfield dealt with them (meaning the Quakers) ... the king would not like well of it ....[46]

The Quakers certainly believed Oldfield to be one of their main enemies in Cheshire,[47] but this kind of resistance could only end, as it did,[48] in yet another court appearance for one of the Friends.

The story behind a quarter sessions appearance has, therefore, now been taken to the point where the offender has found himself firmly entangled with the official agencies and, in some cases, actually in court. However, one important link must still be fitted into the chain. Contact with the authorities did not necessarily involve an actual court appearance. Whether or not this came about depended upon a number of factors which operated in complex interaction, one with another.

Law enforcement agencies certainly exercised preferences and choices as to whether or not they prosecuted a given individual or group. This phenomenon has been noted by other students of local law enforcement, [49] and it was certainly well known to contemporaries.[50] Commonly, indeed almost conventionally, many of the courses chosen by local officials have been attributed to simple negligence or corruption;[51] but, while certainly not wishing to deny the significance of these factors, it is possible to suggest that choices were also decided by other, rather more positive, considerations. It will certainly not be possible to examine all of them here, but the more significant can be outlined.

In the first place, some constables seem to have taken decisions under the influence of politico-religious sympathies. The attack on the Cheshire Quakers in the period 1681-4 provides examples of the exercise of this kind of preference. Middlewich monthly meeting, for instance, was particularly savagely attacked, and two constables and two justices seem to have been especially active. As the Quakers themselves reported,

Leftwich Oldfield came ... and seized upon all the seats in the meeting house, the door and window, and caused them all to be taken away.... And for above half a year Richard Cartwright and Thomas Whitingham, constables, and William Beckitt, the informer, haled them out of their meeting house and kept them out in a cold season, to the hazarding of many of their lives.[52]

These tactics, it may be added, were successful to the point that a meeting which had in November 1681 numbered about one hundred persons[53] had by the end of the year ceased, if only temporarily, to exist.[54]

Conversely, it is likely that a substantial number of constables could be counted as Quaker sympathisers. This is suggested by the fact that the justices found it necessary to indict seventy-three constables in 1682, mainly for neglect of duty.[55] Certainly the Quaker meetings had good contacts among local law officers. Thus, in 1680, the Quarterly Men's Meeting was able to agree that the accounts of Samuel Worral, constable of Frodsham, 'shall be inspected unto and his charges defrayed'.[56]

However, the constables and justices were not always motivated by such relatively high-minded ideals, and other influences upon them need to be examined. Family ties could play a part in influencing their decisions, as one example will demonstrate:

> John Hike of Church Hulme ... saith that having apprehended Randle Furnival the younger of Church Hulme ... by virtue of a warrant of good behaviour for bastardy granted by Sir Robert Leicester ..., Randle Furnival the elder ... who is [his] father (and one of the constables of Church Hulme ...) in contempt of the ... warrant struck it off the table to the ground under his feet and said he would burn it, although this exam- inate charged ... Randle the father (as constable) to assist him in its execu- tion ... whereby ... Randle the son escaped and is since run away....[57]

The constables were subjected to other local ties in addition to those of the family, as John Hollinworth, a constable of Bollin Fee, revealed in his petition to the justices in July 1614. Hollinworth had not prevented the escape of a prisoner, Lawrence Leicester, whom he had arrested on a warrant from Sir Urian Leigh. Although it was not entirely Hollinworth's fault, his enthusiasm for duty seems to have been blunted by the fact that 'Leicester [is] Sir Edmund Trafford's man, [who is] landlord to your petitioner'.[58] Escapes which were engineered, or at least assisted, by powerful local figures such as landlords were not really common by the seventeenth century, but they do reveal the kind of network in which the constables operated.[59]

We are now, therefore, in a position to investigate the kind of choices which the constables and justices made, either for purely personal reasons or for reasons which cannot now be explained. A good place to begin such an examination is the later stages of some cases which have already been partly discussed. The account of Roger Parsons's assault on John Leigh and others had reached the point where the constable had been summoned and requested to execute a warrant against Parsons.[60] However, 'Parsons, seeing the warrant in the constable's hand, snatched the warrant from the constable ... and put it into his pocket, and would not obey it, and said ... in scoffing manner it was but Mr Brereton's warrant and that it would do service for something'. This situation, it might be supposed, would certainly have ensured Parsons an appearance in court. However, 'Parsons did confer with the constable and did read the ... warrant unto him ... and the

... constable told Robert Wright, one other of the persons in the ... warrant, being there, to aid ... Parsons ... and bade him go his way'.[61]

The case of Samuel Higginson eventually ended in much the same way. It will be remembered that Higginson's recalcitrant behaviour had caused the constable to be summoned to him twice.[62] On the second occasion

> Mr Higginson said to this examinate [the constable] 'you must be rough with him and take him to the stocks' ... whereupon this examinate laid hands on ... Samuel Higginson and desired him to be quiet, and ... Samuel spurned him on the left shin ... Peter Worrall ... a neighbour ... laid hands on ... Samuel Higginson to aid this examinate ... to take ... [him] out ... this being done, this examinate released ... Samuel Higginson and did forbear taking him to the stocks at the desire of [his] father and mother....[63]

Not all of the constables' preferences were negative, however. Indeed, in some cases they could be almost distressingly positive, and were all too clearly comprehensible. Thus William Littler, 'constable of Budworth and a seller of ale', came, 'full of drink', to the house of George Golden and 'fell out and quarrelled with some of the company'. On being turned out by Golden's wife, Littler 'threw [her] down several times upon the stones and afterwards pulled [her] by the arm up the town and said he would have her to the stocks'. His wife, it may be noted, evidently had an equally violent disposition for she 'assaulted Richard Shakeshaft ... [pulled] him by the hair of the head, and her husband standing by said, "If my wife had her shoes on, she would beat him"'.[64]

It would be possible to give many further examples of this kind of exercise of preferences,[65] but one more case — this time involving a justice rather than a constable — must suffice. In fact the letter from the justice to the clerk of the peace says all that needs to be said:

> You will find one Davenport, a mason bound to (what he has long wanted) his good behaviour. His is one of the most wicked fellows in [the] country, but since the rule of the bench is not to release one of the good behaviour before the second sessions I need not to say more until the Knutsford sessions. I shall then, God willing, acquaint the court with enough of him to continue him longer, unless I be well assured that he amend his manners in the interim.[66]

Law enforcement agents were not, however, exercising their preferences in a vacuum. They were themselves subject to a series of pressures from both above and below; pressures which had the effect of shaping the kind of decisions which they took. Physical violence against the authorities was one such pressure, as a number of examples may serve to demonstrate:[67]

> Jane Heward ... saith that this examinate, being concerned in a warrant obtained from Kenwrick Eyton, esq., for the searching of one William Meredith's house of Caughall for stolen goods, and being a material witness [was present when] ... one Mary Marsh of Caughall ... spinster, interrupted the constable ... in the search by making such opposition with fighting as the ... warrant was not fully executed....[68]

Although in other cases violence was actually employed,[69] on occasion threats alone were used. After Richard Hamlet, constable of Hunsterson, had apprehended John Turner of Hunsterson with his dogs in a warren belonging to one Mr Venables, and had 'rebuked' him, Turner followed him, 'reviling him with ill language, and since then threatened him ... thereby to terrify him from doing his duty'.[70] It would be misleading to overstress the problem of assault or threatened assault[71] upon law enforcement agents, but they did constitute one dimension of pressure.

More serious, perhaps, was the constant pressure exerted by local opinion. Obviously it would be a complex, and probably controversial, operation to examine and explain in detail how local opinion came to be formed: in the present restricted circumstances it is sufficient merely to demonstrate that opinion in action. The case of Elizabeth Tushingham, already partly outlined,[72] provides one such example. As we have already seen, it was a petition from her neighbours that had originally landed Elizabeth in the lap of authority, but their influence extended further. Elizabeth refused to provide sureties for her future good behaviour, and was subsequently imprisoned. The justice who committed her noted in the margin of his warrant that he thought her 'but a silly creature', but added a cautious rider that all might not be precisely as it seemed since so many persons of good credit were against her.[73] This is a single example of the power of the neighbourly opinion which was institutionalized in the grand jury system,[74] and was deliberately cultivated as a tool of detection.[75]

Equally serious for local law enforcement agents was the pressure which could be applied from above by the central government and its officers. The assize judges were one channel by which the intentions and opinions of the monarchy were carried down to the counties both formally and informally,[76] but, if it considered it necessary, the Privy Council intervened directly and forcefully. Exactly this happened in Cheshire in January 1610. The Council vigorously impugned the integrity of the under-sheriffs, 'whereof there are so many that are bred in nothing but in craft, extortion and corruption'. 'We see so small or rather so bad fruits of accounts of all those things that do depend upon return of honest and sufficient juries ... besides the partiality and corruption in the executions of his majesty's processes ...'. Some of the justices themselves were also open to criticism: those justices who worked energetically 'often meet with hard and envious constructions of those that are not moved with the same zeal and conscience that other men are, who make it a conscience to possess public places and only to attend private things ...'. Finally, the Council instructed their subordinates to take direct steps to suppress unlicensed alehouses and to ensure that the correct fees were collected from the properly licensed outlets.[77]

Thus the bench, the individual justices and the whole range of inferior officers operated and took their decisions in the midst of a complex network of pressures from above and below, and were themselves affected by local loyalties, kinship connections and their own political, religious and purely personal feelings. All of these factors affected what happened to the offender once he found himself involved with the official agencies. However, these were not the only factors: his treatment also depended upon who he was and the crime that had been committed.

A number of examples may help to clarify the significance of the identity, social status and local importance of the offender. Occasionally the wealth and social position of an offender could protect him from the consequences of his actions.[78] Precisely this was alleged in a petition to the justices in April 1610. The petitioners had been presented by the supervisor of the highways for absenting themselves from work on the highways on the appointed day. They maintained that they were there, but the official was not. They added, moreover, that 'the ... supervisor is a man of very lewd behaviour who has heretofore been questioned for felony and has spared divers of the best of the ... chapelry who should have been presented for their default in the amending of the said highway'.[79] Wealth and position, however, were not invariably a source of protection. In a different context, when the authorities were seeking to make examples, wealth and position could be a positive handicap. Thus, when an attempt was being made to discourage recusancy in the 1580s it was Cheshire Catholics of high social standing who were deliberately singled out for punishment.[80]

The significance of the crime need not detain us long. Certain crimes — rape and murder are cases in point — were always likely to be pursued with a fair amount of vigour. Other acts were likely to be treated with more or less severity according not only to their own qualities but also to the circumstances of the time. Thus in October 1682 John Hudson, a Cheadle husbandman, found himself before the bench charged with profaning the sacrament (and subsequently with contempt of court).[81] He had been heard to say that

Mr Beeley, curate of Cheadle ... had given the sacrament to two women ... and that they were no more fit to take the sacrament than Mr

Davenport's sow; for if she could but speak, she knew as much of the sacrament as they did. And further he said, 'What should they go to church to take bread and wine for? For they might take bread and wine at home'.[82]

In a similar fashion, nine months earlier a Cheshire gentleman found himself entangled with the officers of the law for saying that persecution was not necessarily the best way to bring Quakers back into the Church of England.[83] At an earlier or later period such an opinion could certainly have been safely ignored, but in 1682 the bench was about to become involved in a major attack on the Quaker movement in Cheshire and evidently felt that the area was too sensitive for the matter to be disregarded.[84]

We have now sketched the background to an appearance before quarter sessions in the seventeenth century, indicating the kind of behaviour involved and the responses of the authorities according to their personal prejudices and the nature and strength of pressures exerted upon them. Even this outline would not be complete, however, unless some attempt was made to show how the same types of factors continued to influence the behaviour of the bench and juries in dealing with cases which had actually come to trial. Of course the very fact that a much more formal institution, with all its accompanying rules and conventions, was now in operation introduced new factors into the situation; although it is by no means certain that the justices invariably followed theoretical prescriptions for the operation of the legal machinery.[85] However, justices and juries continued to operate in very much the same way, reconciling conflicting pressures or expressing their own prejudices, and in the same types of circumstances, be it recalcitrant individuals or hostile neighbours, as in the preliminary stages of cases. Once again, a series of examples may serve to demonstrate the ways in which the court and its agents went about their business.[86]

We may take as a first illustration the continued pressure of neighbourly opinion upon the justices. It has been shown already how neighbourly opinion could be influential in bringing a case to court, but it continued to play a role at the actual trial. A typical example occurred in April 1680, when Ellen Taylor and Elizabeth Hurstfield were charged with stealing some corn from Daniel Harrison.[87] On the face of it the case was clear enough, with an unambiguous statement by the chief witness, Margaret Kennerly. However, the bench also received a petition from a group of ten neighbours of the Hurstfields, in which they claimed that Margaret Kennerly

In the repute of the county and her own neighbours is a very frivolous idle person and herself, as is reported, guilty of many misdemeanors and one that for hope of gain will not fear to swear to the prejudice of any, and besides, since she took this oath we are credibly informed that she hath reported to do it out of some spite and malice she had to the poor persons ... bound over.

Hurstfield and his family, on the other hand, were 'very careful, painful and industrious in their places without doing prejudice or hurt to any'.[88] It is perfectly plain that, apart from one piece of hearsay evidence, the petitioners had nothing to contribute to the facts of the case; but they still asked that, on the strength of the arguments they presented, the action against Hurstfield and Taylor should be discontinued. Unfortunately, we do not know whether or not they were successful.

Pressure was not always exerted by groups; single individuals could also intervene. Precisely this occurred in the case of Hugh Platt. As the writer of the letter succinctly expressed the matter:

The bearer hereof, Hugh Platt, hath been heretofore bound to the peace to one Thomas Woodson .... This Platt is known, and is reputed, to be a quiet conditioned person and one that would be glad to live in quiet, and was bound not because of any quarrel betwixt him and Woodson but because he favoured [another] who was heretofore bound to the peace to ... Woodson. I pray you [the clerk of the peace] therefore inform the bench hereof and procure his release.[89]

It may have been to meet this kind of situation — amongst others — that the bench evolved the technique of referring cases to the justices of the local hundred, either as individuals or meeting as 'the month's meeting'.[90] Certainly in cases such as those of John Horton of Lostock Gralam and William Thompson and John Dennper of Newton, which were referred to the local men, there was heated local feeling involved.[91]

Another type of pressure which could be exerted was that of the organized religious or political groups. In these cases it is sometimes difficult to decide what is pressure and what are simply defensive movements, although in practice the two may have operated in much the same way. The example of the Quakers may be taken to show the kind of activity which went on. The Quakers, in fact, were as active as possible at every stage of the law enforcement process. We have already noticed their connnection with the constables,[92] but, if necessary, they would also send representatives to the sessions. This was a policy advocated by the yearly meeting in London, partly because of the Friends' distrust of lawyers who had been known to betray them. The purpose of these representatives was to make inquiries of clerks of the ... quarter sessions what Friends are there presented for recusancy or suchlike and to take copies of all such presentments, prosecutions and convictions as they find against any Friends that they may thereby be the better capable and able to take off, prevent and avoid such prosecutions as the truth may point and direct.[93]

This advice was followed in Cheshire, at least from about the middle of 1682.[94] On one level this may appear to be nothing more than the kind of service which might be provided by a lawyer, but that they would go further is illustrated by the advice provided by the yearly meeting in the following year. It was then suggested that 'if any ... who are indicted thereon, that if they have any acquaintance of interest with the grand jury or justices, they improve the same to prevent the grand jury's presentments'.[95] Even after conviction the Quakers did not cease their efforts: in April 1681 the Quarterly Men's meeting 'ordered that Thomas Nimme and Bartholomew Coppock do move the gaoler to release Samuel Ryles, but if he refuse, then to lay his cause before the judge and return an answer to the next meeting; likewise Mary Bartonwood'.[96] It may be argued that the Quakers were only defending themselves from an onslaught which the authorities chose to mount, and in a sense this is true. However, it does not alter the substance of the argument: the Friends were undoubtedly involved, both individually and as a group, in illegal activity and they were employing all the means they possessed to exert pressure to avoid the consequences of that activity.

A major part of the activity of the court therefore — in addition to dealing with the stubborn offender and other problems — lay in reconciling the different pressures exerted. Sometimes the solution bore very little resemblance to the normal processes of the law. It has already been pointed out that early in 1610 the Privy Council demanded the suppression of unlicensed alehouses, and one might suppose that the justices would have taken steps to obey, particularly in view of the tirade to which they had been subjected.[97] However, this was not the case. The problem was that the justices clearly found themselves at the centre of a conflict of interests. Thus while the Privy Council may have desired the closure of unlicensed premises, the constables — and not only in Cheshire[98] — were not enthusiastic about interfering with local drinking habits. The justices therefore took a cautious line. Although they 'did several times confer with the alehouse-keepers in the same [hundreds]', they 'could by no means draw them to any composition according to your lordships' direction in that behalf', and so were compelled to take further action. Thus it was that approximately 1300 individuals found themselves charged with keeping unlicensed alehouses and were all, solemnly, found (or recorded) not guilty.[99]

The case of the alehouse-keepers is the classic example of the politics of compromise triumphing over the letter of the law in Cheshire in the period under review; but it is by no means the only one. On a much smaller scale, the same principle can be seen in action in the case of John Bennet in April 1680. Bennet had been accused of stealing corn from William Rowe. Upon being examined by the mayor of Chester, he confessed. Rowe, for reasons which are unclear, then referred the matter to the Cheshire bench and Bennet, examined by them, said 'he had made such confession ... but it was on the mayor's entreaty and promise [that] he should be no further troubled'.[100]

In this case, as in that of the alehouse-keepers, it is perfectly clear that the justices and juries involved were interested not so much in the invariable application of the law as in the reconciliation of disputes and the minimizing of disturbance. This they attempted to do in a fashion consonant with the pressures upon them and their personal prejudices. It would, of course, be absurd to claim that the law was a matter of indifference to them; but their discretion was wide and the law often flexible. Perhaps the points involved may be clarified if we return to the treatment of the recalcitrant individual.

Bennet, as we have seen, was anything but recalcitrant and had high hopes of avoiding further difficulty: indeed, he was aggrieved when this ambition was not realized. Not everyone, however, was so tactful and it was these people who felt the full weight of the law. An analogous point has been made in the context of lunacy: 'harmless lunatics and idiots continued to be left at liberty as long as they were not considered to be dangerous and caused no social disturbance'.[101] It was those who seemed determined to cause difficulty who found themselves in it, in addition to those, like the Quakers, whom the bench chose to attack.

One such determined individual was Edward Clare, whose case came before the bench in April 1684. The letter from the bench to the master of Nantwich house of correction explained the matter clearly:

Forasmuch as Edward Clare ... being a loose, idle, misordered fellow and being required ... to find sureties for his good behaviour ... but refusing so to do and contemptuously refusing to give any answer ... to such questions as [were] demanded of him touching his behaviour and way of living, we therefore send you herewith the body of the said Edward Clare....[102]

There are several similar cases in the records,[103] but one more must suffice. Samuel Jeffreys, a Northwich butcher, had been involved — according to his neighbours — in several simple frauds. It was not this, however, that was the immediate cause of his imprisonment. Once again, a justice's letter, this time to the gaoler of Chester Castle, explains the matter:

> Forasmuch as Samuel Jeffreys of Northwich, butcher, came before me ... and was then and there accused of several misdemeanours and frauds and likewise has refused to give security to appear at the next general quarter sessions ... these are therefore in his majesty's name strictly to charge and command you ... to receive ... [him] into your custody....[104]

Conversely, the benefits of withdrawing from the fray at the appropriate time were considerable. A letter from Urian Leigh, J.P., to the clerk of the peace establishes the point. There had been a quarrel in his district between two of his acquaintances whom he bound over to appear at quarter sessions: exactly the kind of situation which could lead to charges of disturbing the peace or even assault or theft, if there was any possibility that they might be involved. However, 'afterwards myself with other gentlemen that wished well to both parties did pacify the parties and made them friends, and thereupon released them'.[105] The benefits to the public peace could be equally significant, as Richard Stapleton artlessly revealed. Speaking of previous assaults on himself by George Clayton, he said that he had met Clayton who 'meeting ... Stapleton in the night, did threaten him, saying if he were not bound he would beat him'.[106] On occasion, therefore, the authorities could regard a case as having been resolved to the greater good of the commonwealth, if not, perhaps to the total satisfaction of one of the parties.

The picture that has been drawn is one of some complexity, and deliberately so. Even so, it is not comprehensive and more attention could have been drawn to certain areas; the heinous crime as an act likely to attract the attention of the authorities is an example. Nor can the study be used, except with caution, as a basis for generalizations because of its regional nature. Despite this, however, a number of points do emerge as significant.

First, it should be perfectly plain that no simplistic model will suffice to explain the processes of law enforcement in seventeenth-century England. Second, the machinery of law enforcement did not continuously operate either on behalf of any single class, institution or interest group, or against any such body. The interests of too many groups were involved; too many separate individuals bore responsibility for some stage of the operation; it was too easy to escape the net altogether. Even a group as potentially powerful as the Privy Council had to struggle to enforce its policies, and even then could not hope to do so continually and uniformly.[107] In this context it is important to stress that the dominant role of the law enforcement process in seventeenth-century Cheshire was not, therefore, simple confrontation between the offender and the impersonal might of the State. It was, rather, an intricate chorus of negotiation between all the parties and interests who felt that they had a proper concern in the matter. Third, it is evident that the law, and its precise letter, were not viewed in the depths of the country in quite the way that they would have been in King's Bench or the Inns of Court. Not that the law was regarded anywhere as a simple matter,[108] but that local men regarded it less as an unalterable score and more as a theme upon which they could improvise. Whether or not this meant that the accused received a more or less fair trial at quarter sessions in the seventeenth century than in other courts at an earlier or later date is not a question which can presently be answered;[109] but it did mean that the varieties of treatment and the roads to court were many and varied.

7 *Crime and the Courts in Surrey 1736-1753*

J. M. BEATTIE

In the middle of the eighteenth century, following closely the conclusion of the War of Austrian Succession in 1748, a crime wave of unexampled proportions struck the metropolis of London and its immediate environs.[1] Gaols were suddenly overcrowded and the courts overburdened; and contemporaries in private correspondence and in print complained about the dangers of travelling in and around the capital. Few would have dissented from the shrill prediction of Henry Fielding (whose *Enquiry into the Causes of the late Increase of Robbers* (1751) was inspired by the evidence of the massive increase in crimes against property that he encountered daily as a magistrate) that 'the streets of this town and the roads leading to it will shortly be impassable without the utmost hazard; nor are we threatened with seeing less dangerous gangs of rogues among us, than those which the Italians call Banditti'.[2] Indeed, by 1751 crime in London was so alarming that the House of Commons — responding to an appeal in the King's speech in January — established a committee to consider ways of combatting it, in particular to suggest measures 'for enforcing the execution of the laws and for suppressing ... outrages and violences'.[3]

Within a few months this committee reported more than thirty resolutions dealing with the causes of crime and the problems of law enforcement.[4] Not all were new and few found their way into legislation, for the work of the committee largely fizzled out in the face of opposition from the Lords and a considerable decline of crime after 1753. But their proposals anticipate many of the arguments that were to lie behind the campaigns to reform the criminal law and the system of judicial administration in the second half of the century. The committee's suggestion, for example, that 'it would be reasonable to exchange the punishment of death, which is now inflicted for some sorts of offences, into some other adequate punishments' — a proposal that resulted in a bill (subsequently thrown out by the Lords) to substitute 'confinement and hard labour in his majesty's dockyards' for the death penalty in a number of crimes — reflected a conviction coming to be widely held that the uncritical harshness of the criminal law had distorted the administration of justice and was itself partly to blame for the increase of crime. In general, the committee clearly attributed much of the explosion of ciminality at mid century to the ineffectiveness of the courts, for many of their suggestions were concerned with encouraging prosecutions, speeding up the judicial process and finding more effective ways to punish the guilty.

But how did the courts actually work in the middle of the eighteenth century? How were trials conducted? What proportion of the accused were convicted? How were they punished; in particular how were the capital laws enforced? Were the courts influenced by the level of crime or other extraneous factors? These are the questions that this essay is principally concerned with — at least as far as the largest group of offences is concerned, crimes against property. It rests mainly on data from the courts of quarter sessions and assizes in the county of Surrey between 1736 and 1753. This period has been chosen partly because it is manageable enough to be looked at in some detail in a brief investigation and yet long enough to contain some striking fluctuations in the number of offenders brought before the courts, which make it possible to study the effect of the length of the court calendar on juries' and judges' decisions. And the period has this further advantage, that accounts of the trials in the Surrey assize courts were published in about half of these years. These printed *Proceedings* provide a great deal of evidence about the way the courts functioned and usefully supplement the more official documents — mainly indictments — from which the conviction rates and the patterns of punishment have been derived.[5] The relatively rich documentation and the sharp fluctuations in prosecutions which culminate in a crisis of crime so serious as to stimulate the investigations of the parliamentary committee of 1751 and inaugurate in a sense the long intermittent debate about the criminal law and the administration of justice, make this a useful period in which to study the way the law was in fact applied in the eighteenth century.

In the eighteen years between 1736 and 1753 almost 2000 men and women were accused of crimes against property before the assizes and quarter sessions of the county of Surrey. Just over a third were charged with felonies that were not subject to benefit of clergy and were thus punishable by death (Table I).[6] By 1736 parliament had created a large number of such capital offences. Some were crimes more serious than simple theft because they involved the threat of violence or intrusion into a dwelling house in especially terrifying circumstances. These offences — robbery, burglary and housebreaking during the day under certain conditions — had

Table 1: *Crimes against property, Surrey 1736-53: number committed for trial*

	Urban parishes		Rural parishes		Total		Grand Total
	Male	Female	Male	Female	Male	Female	Total
Capital offences							
Number	342	146	166	27	508	173	681
Percentage	50.2	21.4	24.4	4.0	74.6	25.4	100
Non-capital offences							
Assizes	355	161	169	39	524	200	724
Quarter Sessions	258	155	100	20	358	175	533
Total	613	316	269	59	882	375	1257
Percentage	48.8	25.1	21.4	4.7	70.2	29.8	100
Total	955	462	435	86	1390	548	1938
Percentage	49.3	23.8	22.5	4.4	71.7	28.3	100

been removed from clergy and made capital for all offenders in the sixteenth century and in the eighteenth they remained at the core of the capital code. But by 1736 capital punishment had also been extended to a much wider range of offences that were thought by the men of property in parliament to require the protection of the ultimate deterrent either because the object of the theft was especially valuable or because the offence was especially difficult to prevent or, as often as not, because some members of parliament were persuaded that a particular crime was increasing out of control. Horse-theft and picking pockets had been made capital offences by the Tudors; but it was particularly after 1689 that the regular meeting of parliament afforded M.P.s frequent opportunities to pass harsher laws to combat supposed increases in particular crimes. The gradual enlarging of the capital code by the restriction of clergy seems to have aroused little debate: indeed after the Revolution the criminal law came to be treated as though it were local business, responsive to the interests and fears of private members. By 1736, domestic servants who pilfered from their masters were liable to be hanged, as were shoplifters or men who stole from ships or barges, or from docks or warehouses. In 1741 sheep-stealing became a capital offence and in the next year cattle-theft. The process continued through the century.[7]

This extension of the range of capital punishment obviously greatly increased the numbers of offenders at risk of ending on the gallows and helps to explain why a third of the defendants before the Surrey courts in the years 1736 to 1753 were up on capital charges. The remainder had been accused either of a felony within clergy or of petty larceny. In the case of the former, convicts were still occasionally allowed to plead benefit of clergy and were branded on the thumb and discharged. This was rare, however, by the middle of the century, for the abolition of the literacy test for clergy in 1706[8] had been accompanied by a significant stiffening of the penalties in non-capital felonies. A section of the 1706 Act itself enabled judges to sentence clergied offenders to a period of six months to two years at hard labour in a gaol or workhouse. But more significantly, this was followed in 1718 by an Act[9] that made it possible for the courts to award transportation to America for seven years to those convicted of both clergyable felonies and petty larceny. This did not initiate transportation, for felons had been sent to the colonies by a variety of expedients throughout the seventeenth century.[10] But the courts had not previously been able to award transportation directly. The 1718 Act not only made this possible but applied it to the very largest group of offenders tried in the courts and, increasingly, transportation became the most common consequence of conviction for non-capital property crimes. Even in the case of petty larceny, the courts were disposed by the middle of the century to employ the harsher alternative of transportation to the American colonies.

Apart from this crucial matter of the charges they faced, the offenders brought before the Surrey courts can be distinguished in two other ways, as Table I reveals: most were men (72 per cent); and by far the largest number had been accused of committing offences in the 'urban' parishes in the north-east of the county.[11] Just over two-thirds of the men (69 per cent) and 84 per cent of the women were indicted for crimes in the borough of Southwark and a number of neighbouring parishes along the south bank of the Thames that were, along with Southwark, essentially part of the larger metropolis of London. The remainder were from what I will call 'rural' Surrey — the market towns and rural parishes proper of the county.

Another characteristic of crime against property in Surrey is not revealed in Table I. That is its tendency to fluctuate sharply from one year to another. Perhaps the most persistent fluctuation was seasonal: there were always many more offenders to be tried at the winter assizes in March (which dealt with crimes committed over the winter months) than at the summer assizes in July or August.[12] But apart from this seasonal variation, there was also frequently a sharp difference in annual totals from one year to another. This derives, so it seems to me, from what appears to be the most pervasive reasons behind property crime — want and necessity produced either by unemployment or falling real incomes. This is not to claim that economic conditions explain all aspects of crime — indeed it is more an invitation to further research than a conclusion of it. But it is at least suggestive of the nature of much property crime that there is an apparently close connection between the most striking fluctuations in the number of offenders brought to court and changes in conditions of life and work.

The patterns of fluctuations between 1736 and 1753 in Surrey were different in urban and rural parishes (see Figure 1). This was largely, though

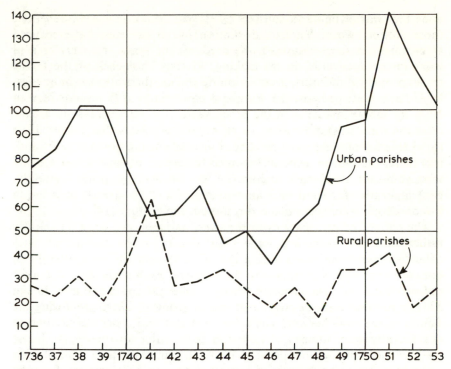

Figure 1: Property offences in urban and rural parishes of Surrey, 1736-53: Total number committed for trial, assizes and quarter sessions.

no doubt not entirely, because the conditions of life and work were different in each and changed in different ways. In general, the number of offenders charged with crimes against property in rural parishes remained relatively stable over the period with the exception of the year 1741 and a modest rise in 1749-51. The urban parishes, on the other hand, are characterized by sharp and significant fluctuations which can be seen to divide into three phases: what appears to be a high and rising level between 1736 and 1739; a period of sharply falling levels with a low point in 1746; and a rapid turn-around after 1748 which rose to the high peaks that got the authorities so concerned in 1751. At least some aspects of this urban pattern seem very clearly to derive from the consequences of the war that began against Spain in 1739, broadened to become part of a European struggle in the following year and ended in 1748. Certainly, the steady decline in the number of accused during the war years seems explainable in part at least by the heavy recruitment of young men into the armed forces and by the enlargement of shipbuilding and other industries tied to the war effort. For large numbers of men and women lived precariously at the best of times on casual and seasonal work in London; many people, as Thomas Firmin said at the end of the seventeenth century, had no employment at all 'or at least none that was certain and constant'.[13] War could only have benefited those seeking work. Though disruptions in trade may have reduced employment in some industries, the needs of the army and navy created work in the dockyards, in sail-making, in those branches of the textile trades providing uniforms, in provisioning and numbers of other industries. Most important, perhaps, the army and navy removed thousands of men from the labour market. On the other hand, the huge increase in arrests after the war seems most likely to reflect the problems that followed the rapid reversal of these wartime conditions: the closing down of jobs and, especially, the sudden demobilization of thousands of sailors and soldiers who would very soon have to compete for the available work. Certainly, contemporaries favoured such an explanation of these trends in crime in London both in this period and throughout the century.[14]

The pattern of prosecutions in the rural parishes of Surrey was clearly rather different. There was some slight decline in the number of rural offenders before the courts during the war and some increase after 1748, but both were modest compared to the swinging levels in the city. The most notable feature of rural property crime is rather the sharp rise in 1740 and 1741, a rise that coincides with a period of stringent dearth following the failure of the 1740 harvest. The price of wheat and other essentials rose dramatically in the summer of 1740 and again, after some recession in the autumn and winter, in the spring of 1741. The unusually high price of food — combined with the shortage of harvest work — was catastrophic for rural labourers' families who lived at the best of times on the slimmest of margins. The privation and hardship of these years was real and widespread; it was noted by contemporaries, and put forward in mitigation of their crimes by numbers of those who found themselves before the courts on charges of theft.[15] It was undoubtedly the depth of rural distress in the winter of 1740-41 that lay behind an apparent increase in the theft of sheep. At least complaints about such an increase, especially in the Home Counties, were received by members of parliament with the result — as happened so often in the eighteenth century — that a committee was appointed to look into it in January 1741 and an Act making sheep-stealing a capital offence received the royal assent two months later.[16] The fact that this committee was also empowered to consider ways of combatting a sharp increase in thefts from orchards and gardens is further evidence of the catastrophic effect on so many in the rural community of the enormous increase in the price of necessities in 1740 and 1741. The return of bountiful harvests after 1741 and the return of prices to their previous levels was accompanied by a similar decline in the number of men and women from rural parishes before the courts for property offences.

Changes in economic circumstances that could fluctuate quickly and with such devastating effect suggest a plausible explanation for the movement in the level of offenders before the Surrey courts in this period. My concern here is not so much to explain these changes in the crime level, however, as merely to note them, for if it was characteristic of property offences to fluctuate sharply from session to session and year to year it is worth asking whether changes in the length of the court calendar (or changes in economic conditions) had any effect on the verdicts of juries or on punishments awarded by judges. We have an opportunity to examine this in these years. The pattern in the county as a whole (and of course the court calendar did not divide the accused into 'rural' and 'urban' categories) was largely determined by the urban parishes, in which almost three-quarters of the offences occurred: that is, a moderately high level in the four years 1736-9 (in which 120 accused came before the courts each year on average); a steady decline during the war to a low point of just over fifty in 1746 and an annual average of eighty-four for the war years as a whole; and a strong and rapid increase after 1748 to a peak of 182 in 1751 and an annual average of 141 in the five years 1749-53. In the course of looking at the way the courts dealt with the 2000 men and women accused of these property offences it is instructive to examine the effects of fluctuations of this magnitude.

Virtually everyone accused of a crime against property in Surrey was committed to the county gaol or house of correction by an examining magistrate to await trial. For most, including all those held on capital charges, this meant trial at assizes.[17] Some minor offenders were bound over in recognizances, but the granting of bail in property cases was uncommon and even those accused of petty larceny and clearly destined for trial at quarter sessions were most often held in gaol.

There was at least one advantage to being tried before the justices in quarter sessions: they met four times a year — or more when business pressed[18] — making a much shorter stay in gaol likely than for those held for trial before the assize court, for whom a lengthy period of pre-trial imprisonment was not uncommon. The winter assizes in Surrey were invariably held in this period in the last two weeks of March and the summer assizes usually in the first two weeks of August. An accused man or woman could thus wait for trial for as long as seven months through the winter.[19] Such a long incarceration under the conditions they had to suffer was in itself a stiff punishment even for many of the guilty; for the innocent, especially for those who were victims of a frivolous or malicious charge, the invariable commitment to gaol to await trial, even if that brought freedom, was cruelly harsh. Judges occasionally recognized this, though there was little that could be done retrospectively to compensate for it. Three men, acquitted of a charge of stealing chickens at the winter assizes in March 1749 who had been in gaol since the previous September, were ordered by the judge to be released immediately instead of waiting to be discharged, as was customary, at the end of the proceedings. They were also excused the usual gaol fees. But that was small comfort for the five and a half months they had spent in gaol.[20] On another occasion a jury made a collection of money for a man they had just acquitted, as though in recognition of the injustice of his having been gaoled for so long on a charge without substance.[21]

Even more cruel in some ways, perhaps, was the fate of those who languished for months in gaol only to find that when their case came on no prosecutor appeared to lay charges and they were simply discharged at the conclusion of the proceedings. On occasion the non-appearance of a prosecutor was proved by affidavit to be due to illness and the unhappy prisoner was returned to gaol to await the next session of the court.[22] But normally when the victim did not appear to press charges the prisoner was discharged. It was not an uncommon situation, for almost 9 per cent of those committed to trial in Surrey on property charges in this period were released because the prosecutor defaulted. This may reflect the failure of examining magistrates to take adequate sureties to compel their attendance. But it is more likely that these prosecutors were willing to risk having their recognizances estreated either because they had had second thoughts about pressing charges or because the accusation was maliciously founded in the first place.

From time to time prisoners were too ill to appear in court and were held over to the next session. And hardly surprisingly, considering the squalid conditions in which prisoners were kept — the Surrey county gaol, the grand jury reported in 1751, was 'greatly out of repair, too small, unwholesome and unsafe for the prisoners'[23] — a number of prisoners did not survive the experience at all. Some of those who are known to have died in gaol took their own lives. But the main cause of death was no doubt the 'gaol fever' that was endemic in eighteenth-century prisons. Outbreaks of this form of typhus were common and frequently deadly and it is likely that 'gaol fever' killed most of the thirty-five men and women who died in the Surrey county gaol between 1736 and 1753 while awaiting trial for property offences. Apart from the virulence of the disease, the ability of prisoners to resist infection was also critically important and it is perhaps not surprising that twenty-five died between 1739 and 1742, the years of dearth, or that ten died during the winter of 1740-41 alone.

A further group of those committed to trial escaped the judgment of the court by turning king's evidence and naming their confederates, helping to apprehend them if they were not already in custody and testifying at their trial.[24] Twenty-four men bought their freedom in this way, all at the assizes and almost all members of gangs charged with robbery or burglary.

The largest number to be discharged before trial, however, were the 215 men and women freed by the grand jury.[25] By the mid eighteenth century, grand juries were on the whole not difficult to convince that charges brought in property cases were reasonable enough to justify a trial: only 11 per cent of the accused were saved from trial by a grand jury verdict. It is of course impossible to know what lay behind these decisions since the jury met *in camera* and there are no records of their discussions. But one can infer from the pattern of verdicts over the period that grand jurors saw in the administration of justice a flexible weapon for the protection of property and that they were as much influenced by the character of the criminal and the circumstances of the times as by the evidence laid before them. As circumstances warranted, they were willing to relax or anxious to stiffen the application of the law. In the four years 1736-9, when the crime level (as reflected at least in the number of accused brought to court) was moderately high, close to 90 per cent of those brought before the grand jury were judged to be worthy of trial. Again, after 1748, when the number of offenders increased rapidly, the grand jury sent more than nine out of ten to face the trial jury. But when the crime level fell off substantially during the war years the Surrey grand juries were clearly more indulgent, more willing to give the accused the benefit of the doubt. Whereas just under 90 per cent of the accused were sent to trial in 1736-39 (when an annual average of 120 came before the courts) and almost 91 per cent in 1749-53 (when the average number of cases rose to 141), during the war years the average number of accused fell to 84 and the level of 'true bill' verdicts by the grand jury also fell, to 82.5 per cent.

Grand juries were also likely to favour women over men, rural offenders over urban and minor (non-capital) offenders over those accused of more serious crimes (Table 2). Their attention to the circumstances of the crime

Table 2: *True bills found by grand jury, Surrey 1736-53 (assizes and quarter sessions)*

	Urban parishes		Rural parishes		Total		Total	
	Male %	Female %	Male %	Female %	Male %	Female %	Urban %	Rural %
Capital offences	90.9	91.6	87.8	69.3	89.8	87.6	91.1	84.9
Non-capital offences	88.2	87.1	80.5	74.5	85.9	85.2	87.8	79.3
Total offences					87.3	85.9	88.9	81.4

and the criminal is nowhere more clearly revealed than in the years 1740-41 when the number of rural offenders increased suddenly. Unlike similar crime waves in the urban parishes, this was met not by increased harshness in the grand jury, but by greater leniency. An unusually large number of these offenders were discharged because the grand jury marked their bills 'not found'. In 1740, for example, 88 per cent of those accused of property crimes in urban parishes were sent to trial by the grand jury while at the same time only 64 per cent of rural offenders were similarly treated. In the following year 72 per cent of those accused in rural parishes were sent to trial, but this is still well below the average level for rural offenders over the whole period — 81 per cent. It seems reasonable to suppose that the grand juries' verdicts in 1740-41 reflect some sympathy for the plight of a rural community suffering from a shortage of food and a steep rise in the price of necessities. The 'facts' of each case were not of course unimportant, but as the jurors assessed the value of the evidence presented before them, the character of the accused (and perhaps of the prosecutor), the circumstances under which the crime was committed, and the general level of crime clearly helped to shape their decisions.

Two hundred and fifteen men and women were discharged by the grand jury. They joined the other 276 who did not come to trial either because their accuser had failed to appear (167), because they had confessed and agreed to impeach their confederates (24), because they had died in custody or were too ill (40) or because they were still at large when the court met (45). Altogether, then, about a quarter of those committed for trial by examining magistrates did not in the end come to court. The remaining 1447 were brought before the petty jury where their fate — for a large number whether they were to live or die — was decided.

The petty or trial jury consisted of twelve men all of whom were supposed to meet a minimum property requirement.[26] The majority of jurors at the Surrey assizes in this period appear to have been tradesmen and craftsmen (tallow chandler, blacksmith, baker, glazier, tailor, bricklayer, shoemaker) with a fair sprinkling of yeomen and farmers and (though the occupational description is no guide to wealth) some who may have been only marginally in the small-property-owning class, fishermen and watermen, for example. [27] In the distant past the chief requirement for petty jurors had been their knowledge of the community in which the crime had occurred and especially knowledge of the accused and prosecutor. Traces of this concept of the jury remained in the eighteenth century,[28] but in practice it had been overtaken, in Surrey at least, by the circumstances in which the courts worked. For at the Surrey assizes the jurors were drawn largely from the neighbourhood not of the crime but of the meeting place of the court: Guildford, Croydon, and especially Kingston-upon-Thames.[29] The assizes were never held in this period in Southwark or the other urban parishes within the metropolis and it was rare for more than one or two jurors to be residents of these parishes where, after all, most of the property crimes in Surrey were committed. In any case, the same jury heard most of the cases throughout an entire court session. Prisoners were arraigned in groups of a dozen or more and one panel of jurors were charged with them;[30] but most often at the Surrey assizes when the first trials were completed substantially the same panel of jurors were given another group in charge. The panels often differed by one or two men; and if the calendar was long enough and four or five juries had to be sworn, the character of the trial jury might change over the course of a four or five-day session. But normally the jury that ended the assize session differed by only a few men from the dozen who had heard the first case.

The property qualification and the limited area from which jurors appear normally to have been drawn combined to narrow the group from which jurors were chosen and the result was that men were called upon with a certain regularity. In the five years 1736-40, for example, eight men served on the trial jury at the assizes in two sessions (out of the ten held in those years) and two men were called on three occasions. Further, though identification is not certain in all cases, it appears that nineteen men who had sat on the trial jury during these years were called on again at least once between 1750 and 1753. It seems likely that a man of some standing in or near an assize town would sit on a trial jury several times during his life and that any one jury would be likely to contain a few men with some previous experience.

From the court's point of view a core of relatively experienced jurors was an advantage, considering the number of cases the jury heard and the pace at which they moved. Take, as an example, the assizes held at Guildford in March 1750. The session began on Thursday, 29 March with the opening of the commission by the judges, Lord Chief Justice Willes and Mr Justice Denison.[31] On Friday morning the grand jury was sworn and by Saturday morning they had found sufficient true bills for the trials to begin. The petty jury sworn on Saturday tried twelve accused that morning and a further five when the court met again at four in the afternoon, following an adjournment for dinner. On Monday morning the same petty jury was sworn, heard thirteen cases before dinner and returned again afterwards to complete the docket by trying the remaining five prisoners. Thirty-five accused had been dealt with in two days. This was a little on the high side for the Surrey assizes in the 1750s, but thirteen to fifteen cases a day was common and of course the court also dealt with numbers of misdemeanours and local administrative matters. This was perhaps a statelier pace than at the Old Bailey, where, as reported in the newspapers at least, twenty to thirty felons were often dealt with in a day.[32] Possibly the Old Bailey kept longer hours. The Surrey assizes began early enough — usually six or seven in the morning — and normally met again after the dinner adjournment at four or five in the afternoon. But this evening session seems rarely to have been very lengthy and occasionally it was not held at all. Nonetheless, even fifteen jury cases a day, especially combined with all the other business before the court, ensured that no time was wasted once a prisoner was actually put to his trial.

Trials began with the complainant telling his story, followed in turn by the witnesses for the Crown who had been bound over to testify by the examining magistrate.[33] The case against the prisoner was unfolded by these witnesses, helped along by the prompting and questioning of the judge. Normally, the prosecution evidence was presented before the prisoner cross-examined witnesses or gave his own side, but few judges seemed to object if a prisoner interrupted to question a witness or to blurt out a denial, and trials often quickly produced a direct confrontation between the prisoner and his accusers.

The impression given by printed accounts of trials, however, is that few prisoners put up a very vigorous defence. Everything was against their doing so in an unfamiliar and overwhelming setting and after a long confinement in which they had no necessary knowledge of the precise charge against them. It was of course especially difficult for those who had confessed to the crime before the examining magistrate, in particular when the magistrate was in court to certify to the authenticity of the confession and that it had been given and read to the accused before he signed it.[34] Examining magistrates were not often in court, but confessions were still introduced with devastating effect by prosecution witnesses. Perhaps even more difficult to surmount was the direct evidence of an accomplice. By the mid eighteenth century such evidence was normally thought to be insufficient in itself to convict, and judges regularly directed not guilty verdicts because the evidence of an accomplice had not been corroborated in court.[35] But the point was still perhaps open to dispute: at least there are cases reported in the printed accounts of the Surrey assizes (though they are not of course official or necessarily complete) that suggest that some judges allowed juries to convict on the unsupported testimony of accomplices.[36]

On occasion juries expressed dissatisfaction with an arrangement that enabled the most culpable of a pair of thieves to escape punishment by offering to confess and convict the other. At the winter assizes of 1738, for example, when Isabella Simms was indicted for burglary in Southwark, the chief witness against her was Margaret Johnson who had been arrested by a constable after trying to pawn two silver spoons. She had confessed before a magistrate and appeared in court to testify how she and Simms had taken a panel of glass out of the back door of the house, slipped the bolt and so got inside. The defendant claimed, however, that Margaret Johnson had been the instigator, that she 'carried me to the prosecutor's house and asked me to be concerned in this robbery she swears against me'. The jury were obviously concerned about this allegation and a juryman asked the judge to inquire into it: 'we want to know which of these were most intimate with the prosecutor's house'. The judge was not interested in that at so late a date. 'That's not material', he told the jury; 'Johnson is evidence and so secures herself.'[37] But a system that allowed confessed thieves to escape punishment produced more general uneasiness, especially in conjunction with the system of rewards, often very large, that the government offered for the apprehension and conviction of robbers.[38] Such inducements encouraged prosecutions undertaken simply for the reward and at their worst even prompted 'thief-takers' to lead young men into crime with the intention of turning them into valuable convicts. Unsavoury cases of this kind were uncovered from time to time; and defendants can be found on occasion claiming that they were victims of such prosecutions.[39] But criticism was inevitably lost in the circumstances that had encouraged such inducements in the first place, particularly the absence of regular police and detective forces which forced the eighteenth-century judicial system to rely on such stratagems. Immunity from prosecution was an especially useful weapon against bands of professional robbers and burglars. As Hawkins said, 'if no accomplices were to be admitted as witnesses, it would be generally impossible to find evidence to convict the greatest offenders',[40] and their cooperation was actively sought by advertisements and after their apprehension.

In the face of the evidence of an accomplice or of their own prior confession or indeed of persuasive evidence from the prosecutor and his witnesses, most prisoners put up only the weakest of defences, if any at all. Many remained silent; others simply denied any knowledge of the facts. Undoubtedly many were overwhelmed by the occasion and by the speed of events and not a few betrayed obvious confusion when, at the conclusion of the prosecution case, the judge asked what they had to say about the evidence brought against them or if they had any questions to put to the Crown witnesses. Some few had the advantage of defence counsel, whose role by the middle of the century was not perhaps as restricted in practice as it was in theory.[41] But counsel must have been beyond the means of most defendants and they were still comparatively rare in ordinary criminal trials at assizes. In their absence, the attitude of the judge was a critical factor.

Judges played the central orchestrating role in most trials. They rarely found it necessary to sum up for the jury, partly because most trials were so brief and so little evidence had been presented that there was no need for such judicial guidance. But, in addition, a judge's opinion of the evidence, of the witnesses and of the prisoner normally emerged very clearly in the course of the trial. And his opinion was immensely influential. A weak defence could be exposed or the value of a character witness entirely undermined by a sarcastic snort from the bench. One woman, found with stolen meat in her lodgings, excused the theft on the grounds that 'she was big with child and longed for the meat'. She also went on to say that 'it would not have done her half so much good if it had been given to her, as if she had stole it'. Whatever the judge made of her independent-mindedness, he was not moved by her appeal to nature, for he reminded her that she had also been accused of stealing a brass mortar and 'desired to know if she had longed for that too'.[42] On another occasion, when a prisoner claimed to have been indicted under the wrong name, the judge, Sir Lawrence Carter, said he would leave that to the jury to decide but for himself he fancied 'that it was so long since you was christened, you have forgot your name'. The prisoner was convicted and sentenced to death. Carter was perhaps more prone than most judges to the sarcastic and damaging retort. At the same session in March 1738, another man on trial for his life, having been arrested at the scene of a burglary, could only say that he had no idea why the stolen goods were found in his possession and brought as his only witness a man who deposed that he had known him for three months and 'knew no ill of him'. 'That's a great proof of his righteousness', Carter retorted. 'I have known him half a day, that's almost as long as you'. And he told another man who said that his friends could not afford to come to court to testify for him, 'if your friends are poor you should have been honest'.[43] So much for the presumption of innocence.

By the same token a judge's massive influence could work in the prisoner's favour and sometimes did. At the same assizes, for example, Carter vigorously cross-examined a man who claimed to have been robbed by a prostitute, exposed the weaknesses in his testimony and undoubtedly encouraged the jury to acquit her.[44] Judicial displeasure in fact fell not infrequently on men who had brought misfortune of this kind upon themselves and judges often went out of their way to undermine the prosecutor's case. Another prostitute escaped in this period because as the case was drawing to a close and after the clearest evidence of her guilt had been presented, the judge noticed that the snuffbox the woman was alleged to have taken was wrongly described in the indictment. He examined the box and announced that it was made not of silver as the indictment charged, but of silver and shell: the woman was acquitted.[45] The sympathy of the bench was also occasionally extended towards prisoners who had been induced to confess by a promise of favour and then prosecuted on the basis of their confession. Many such cases involved servants who had been promised some form of private settlement by their masters after being suspected of pilfering. It seems clear that the extraction of an apology and a promise not to offend again was a regular part of the maintenance of household discipline; for their part, servants would undoubtedly find a confession and apology more palatable than a criminal prosecution, even if their guilt would have been difficult to prove. Judges tended to go hard on masters who extracted a confession in this way and then brought their servant to court. When, for example, Chief Justice Willes was informed by a servant on trial for stealing half a guinea that her master 'promised me, that if I confessed that I robbed him, that he would forgive me', he told her master (Joshua Swainson), after he confirmed the girl's testimony, that:

> No regard is to be had to what you say; for it is the greatest cruelty that can be practised, first to make her a fallacious promise of pardon, then bring her confession as evidence against her. I hope what you have said will have no weight with the jury; for such a man as you ought not to be trusted on any account whatsoever.

It no doubt helped that several of the girl's former employers testified to her honesty and that one asserted that Swainson had 'transported one of his servants already, who was tried in this court'. But the judge's remarks undoubtedly mainly explain her acquittal by the jury.[46]

As a general rule, however, judges were not overly protective of the prisoners on trial before them. In most ordinary cases they were not perhaps overly aggressive, but nor did they display much anxiety to ensure that the prisoner got the benefit of any doubt there might have been in the case against him. Certainly the printed versions of trials at the Surrey assizes in this period do not suggest that prisoners could expect much more from the bench than the opportunity to question witnesses or to produce their own evidence to counter the prosecution's assertions. This 'neutrality' of the bench, if this is the correct way to describe it, clearly worked against the prisoner given the circumstances in which he had been held for trial (the difficulties of arranging for witnesses while in gaol, for example) and the way the trial was conducted. And few prisoners found it possible to mount an effective defence. Their response, in fact, very often took the form not of careful cross-examination but rather of denying the evidence as it was being presented. 'Do you believe that the prisoner at the bar is one of the men [who robbed you?]', the judge asked Joseph Collyer after he had described how two men had stopped him on the highway between Kingston and Tooting in 1738. 'The prisoner I am very sure is one of the men', Collyer replied, 'he had a bargeman's coat on'. At this point the prisoner, William Hoare, shouted out, 'I never wore a bargeman's coat in all my life. I have not wore any other coat than this I have on for these two years, or a year and a half, I am sure.' Collyer went on to assert that he was indeed the man and the trial continued. Hoare did not apparently question him again and never returned to this point of identification.[47]

What passed for cross-examination of the Crown witnesses most often seems to have taken this form, and even this sort of challenge was by no means common. The advantages of having defence counsel are obvious, both for the presentation of a case in court and its organization beforehand. They are clear, for example, in the case of George Ticknell and Thomas Downing who were indicted for two separate burglaries in 1738 on the evidence of an accomplice who testified in court against them. They were represented by counsel who produced a stream of witnesses to give them alibis for the times in question and to testify to their good character. They were acquitted of both charges.[48] The effectiveness of their defence is in striking contrast to most. In general, apart from those few occasions on which a judge intervened on a prisoner's behalf, not many of the accused defended themselves at all skilfully. Acquittals were induced much more by the obvious inadequacy of the prosecution's evidence than by the prisoner's response to it.

Most defendants indeed relied not on exposing the flaws in the prosecution's case but on bringing evidence to their own good character. And this was, indeed, critical information that the trial was intended to produce. It was especially important because the harshness of the criminal law meant that it could only be applied selectively: if every prisoner who was guilty on the evidence of committing a capital offence had actually been hanged, for example, so many would have been executed every year that public acceptance of the law might well have been threatened.[49] The eighteenth-century criminal justice system was designed to achieve a balance of terror, a finely-judged application of the right amount of force and rigour. And the point at which this was perhaps most effectively achieved was at the trial. For both the jury and the judge had large powers of discretion which made it possible for them to temper the law according to circumstances and the nature of the accused. The right of the jury to find a partial verdict and of the judge to reprieve and recommend for pardon were not newly developed in the eighteenth century. But because of the changes in the law over the previous fifty years, they were perhaps more finely tuned and more effectively applied in the middle of the eighteenth century than ever before. On the one hand, the extension of the range of capital punishment had gradually enlarged the umbrella of terror and brought larger numbers under the threat of death; on the other hand, the development of transportation had provided an alternative both to hanging and clergyable discharge, which had been the essential choice open to the courts in felony cases before the punishment of seven years' banishment to America became a possibility. The result was that while in the middle of the eighteenth century a large number of men and women were charged with capital offences, juries were encouraged to find partial verdicts which saved them from hanging because a substantial punishment, transportation, was available as an alternative. And for those found guilty as charged, the judges and ultimately the king (or those who advised him) could select even more to be spared from the gallows. Selection is exactly what took place. Some were selected to be hanged from the large number put at risk; the remainder, and those convicted of simple felonies, were transported, unless they were whipped or imprisoned instead.

The law was applied, and was meant to be applied, selectively, therefore, and with regard to the particular circumstances of the offender, not universally and abstractly. And the discovery of the circumstances of the offender was a crucial part of the business of the trial. Though the trial jury were no longer necessarily members of the community in which the crime had been committed, information about the character of the prosecutor and the prisoner was as critical to their verdicts as it ever had been. Even as the courts became more impersonal, knowledge of the character of the offender remained centrally important and the trial was still designed in the middle of the eighteenth century to elicit it. Hence the importance of character witnesses.

Occasionally such character witnesses were influential enough to win an acquittal, especially when the evidence was not entirely secure or the prosecutor of doubtful character himself. It was, for example, clearly the very favourable testimony of three of her former employers that encouraged the jury to acquit Elizabeth Radford of Croydon when the man for whom she worked as a 'charewoman' prosecuted her for stealing a silver spoon from his house and all she could say in her defence was that she had 'found it'.[50] And the character and reputation of both the prisoners and the prosecutor led to the acquittal of a man and two women accused of stealing rings and money from the house of a woman in Southwark in 1739. The only evidence against the prisoners — elicited by a question from a juror — was that they had been in the house at some point before the rings and money were missed. For their part the prisoners asserted that the house in question was in fact only a room where the prosecutor sold gin and they brought a witness to testify that she was 'a most notorious woman, and one that will swear anything; she has been a base woman all her life'. On the other hand, the witness knew the prisoners to be 'very honest young people and I never knew any harm by any of them'.[51] They were acquitted. Character witnesses, however flattering, did not save many of the accused when the evidence of their guilt was full and apparently certain; but they could be very influential in doubtful cases.

Evidence as to character was perhaps especially helpful in encouraging juries to reach partial verdicts. One significant form of reduced verdict was the finding of someone charged with simple grand larceny (theft of goods of a shilling or over in value) guilty rather of petty larceny (theft of less than a shilling). This did not necessarily affect the sentence the court would award, for petty as well as grand larceny could be punished by transportation for seven years if the judge decided it was warranted. But petty larceny more often led to corporal punishment, a whipping, and the finding of a partial verdict in grand larceny cases often therefore meant the substitution of this short, painful and undoubtedly shaming punishment for transportation — a more attractive alternative presumably, especially for a married man or woman. Good character witnesses seem to have encouraged juries to reach such verdicts. In the case, for example, of Thomas Cunneby and Thomas Hall, two carpenters accused of stealing wood from a lumber yard for which they were in danger of being transported, the prisoners had the support of four men who testified that 'they had employed them as carpenters, and should be very glad to employ them again'. The jury found them guilty to the value of 10*d*. and they were whipped and released.[52]

Even more significant, of course, were partial verdicts in capital cases and by the middle of the eighteenth century such verdicts, by which the prisoner was found not guilty of the original capital charge but convicted of the lesser charge of grand larceny, were very common indeed, especially when the crime was one of the relatively trivial offences that had been made capital in the recent past. In shoplifting cases, or the trial of a servant for stealing goods over the value of 40*s*., or of someone accused of theft to the value of 40*s*. from a ship or a wharf — all of which were among the many forms of larceny removed from clergy since the Revolution — trial juries regularly found partial verdicts. So common indeed by the middle of the century were verdicts of 'guilty to the value of 39*s*.' when 40*s*. was a capital offence, or 'guilty 4*s*. 11*d*.' in the case of shoplifting or theft from a warehouse when 5*s*. marked the lower limit of the capital crime, that it is clear that the character of the prisoner was more likely in these cases to be important in determining who would be selected to be hanged than in encouraging a partial verdict. So few were in fact executed under the capital statues passed since 1689[53] that the disposition of the jury (and of the king, when pardons for those who were convicted were considered) was clearly to lean towards conviction on the lesser charge and thus towards transportation rather than hanging, even when the prisoner's guilt was clear. But some *were* hanged under these statutes: shoplifters and sheep-stealers did go to the gallows in the eighteenth century — to furnish an example to others, or because the individual was thought to be particularly troublesome and incorrigible. Character witnesses were thus not unimportant even in these cases.

But the prisoners most in need of persuasive spokesmen were those charged with what were thought to be the most serious crimes against property — horse-theft, burglary, housebreaking and robbery. Not that character witnesses were likely to prevent a guilty verdict in such cases if the evidence was clear and, in particular, if the prisoner was proved to have used violence or threatened his victims. But good character witnesses could persuade the jury to find a partial verdict, or at least might persuade the judge in the event of a conviction to grant a reprieve and allow the prisoner to appeal for the king's mercy. The crucial evidence concerned his life and habits and his reputation among his neighbours, particularly his more substantial neighbours. Juries and judges were concerned to discover whether the prisoner was a respected member of his community, regularly employed, hard-working, honest and suitably deferential to those in authority, and who was thus likely to have committed a crime out of some misfortune or because he had been misled; or whether, on the other hand, he was a well-known rogue, a troublemaker, an idle and dishonest man, suspected of living by his wits or at any event not settled into an industrious course of life. Evidence as to a prisoner's character could be gathered outside the courtroom, of course, as well as during the trial. Judges undoubtedly received and sought recommendations from local magistrates and others whose judgment they would trust. Mr Justice Gundry told a secretary of state in 1751, for example, that he had left a condemned man for execution because he had pleaded guilty (most unusually) and he, Gundry, had thus been 'shut out from all evidence and circumstances favourable and disfavourable which might have appeared' if the case had gone to trial. Nonetheless, he went on to say, he would have reprieved the man and allowed him to petition for mercy if he had received an application on his behalf from 'persons of worth and reputation and with a favourable account of his character and former manner of life'.[54] Similarly, wider sources of evidence often came into play when a case went before the king, for this stage of the pardoning process provided opportunities for the exercise of patronage and interest and frequently generated appeals on behalf of convicts from the gentry and nobility and other members of the social and political élite, though even when the case was before the king the opinion of a condemned man's less exalted neighbours could be crucially influential.

The fate of most prisoners before the assizes on capital charges was decided, however, by the evidence presented in court. Judges can be found making a special point of inquiring about prisoners' lives. 'What character do the neighbours give of him? Is it that of a sober industrious one, or an indifferent character?' And of another, 'Has Cooper worked at his trade lately? How has he supported himself?'[55] Inevitably, the more respectable the witnesses, the more weight they carried. 'Have you any of the substantial inhabitants of Wandsworth to your character?', Willes asked one man after he had produced eight witnesses whose own characters the judge clearly had some doubt about.[56] But infinitely worse off was the man with no witnesses at all, no one to establish his place within a community, to give him roots. A vagrant could expect little mercy if the case against him seemed at all clear; nor could a man who had given his neighbours trouble, especially if the prosecution had made a point of his bad reputation in developing the case against him. 'I had a violent suspicion of the prisoners, and so had all my neighbours', Mary Sugden told the court in prosecuting William Bray and Jane Owen for breaking into her house and stealing clothes and money. 'Bray and Owen, and Sarah Cecil, lived all in a room together directly opposite to me. I was advised to take them up, and accordingly I took Sarah Cecil, and she confessed the whole affair'. Bray and Owen said nothing in their defence, could find no one to speak for them and were found guilty.[57]

When the prosecution witnesses had been heard and the prisoner had had an opportunity to ask them questions and to call his own witnesses, the jury considered its verdict. The established procedure had long been that the cases of all the prisoners charged to a particular jury were heard in turn and for the jury then to reach verdicts on them all together, relying mainly on their memories.[58] By the 1730s, however, it appears that juries were in fact considering their verdicts at the conclusion of each case. At least that is suggested by a report in December 1738 that at the opening of the sessions at the Old Bailey the Lord Mayor announced:

> that the Court had taken notice of the inconveniences arising from the usual method of trying prisoners there; and that it had been thought improper for the juries to sit so long, and gave their verdicts on so many trials (which have commonly been twelve or more together) depending on the strength of their memories or the assistance of their notes; it was thought more consistent with the justice of the court to alter the method of proceeding, and their seats were accordingly so placed, that they might consult one another, and give their verdicts on each trial immediately; or when any matter of difficulty should arise, they might withdraw to consider thereof.[59]

The Lord Chief Justice gave the new system his approval, for it was, he said, 'agreeable to the constant practice in all other courts'.[60] It seems likely, then, that the jurors in Surrey courts sat together and gave their verdicts at the conclusion of each case. They certainly do not appear to have found it necessary to withdraw very often. After one case that was unusual in virtually every respect in that one gentleman charged another, with whom he was well acquainted, with robbing him on the highway, in that both were represented by counsel who engaged in minute cross-examination of the numerous witnesses summoned on both sides, and in that the trial obviously lasted a long time and the judge found it necessary to sum up, the jury did indeed withdraw for seventeen minutes. The fact that this was noted in the printed account of the trial,[61] and that there are no similar notations in other trials for property crimes in these years suggests that the withdrawal of the jury was as unusual as every aspect of this case.

When the jury considered its verdict, three alternatives were open to it, as we have seen: it could acquit the prisoner; find him guilty as charged; or find a partial verdict, reducing a capital to a non-capital felony or a clergyable felony to petty larceny. How the accused were actually treated before the Surrey courts in these years remains now to be seen.

Just over 1400 men and women were sent to trial for property offences by the grand juries of Surrey between 1736 and 1753. All but thirteen pleaded not guilty and took their trial before the petty jury, 507 charged with capital offences and 920 with grand or petty larceny. Very close to a third of both groups were found not guilty (Table 3) and were discharged at the end of the court session,[62] normally, we must presume, because the evidence was insufficient, though it is clear that good character witnesses occasionally persuaded the jury to acquit a prisoner who would otherwise have been convicted. Acquittals were frequent enough, at any event, to make it clear that though jurymen were men of property in a small way, there was nothing automatic about their verdicts in property cases.

The acquittal rate was very much higher for non-capital crimes at assizes than at quarter sessions (39.1 per cent of those tried as against 28.6 per cent) but this probably dervies more from the fact that quarter sessions dealt with trivial offences — or at least treated the crimes that came before them as trivial — than from any fundamental differences in the attitudes of the juries in those courts. Until 1748 quarter sessions did not in fact deal with many cases of property crime: only three or four a session on average and never more than the most trivial petty larceny. This changed dramatically, however, when the number of offenders increased so suddenly in Surrey after the war. The justices in quarter sessions were then forced to deal with a large number of cases, so many indeed that after December 1752 they found it necessary to hold four adjourned sessions every year in Southwark to deal specifically with larceny cases.[63] Instead of perhaps a dozen cases a year, the court dealt with seventy on average between 1749 and 1753. They were not by any means all petty larcenies, yet until the end of 1752 that is how the court chose to treat them. Quarter sessions had only tried larceny cases in the past when the value of the goods stolen was under a shilling and when the pressure on the gaols forced them to take on more cases — many, indeed most, of which were in fact grand larceny, the theft of goods of 1s. or more — they simply ignored the 'facts' and for several years automatically valued all stolen goods at 10d., even when this produced such patent absurdities as declaring 50s. to be worth 10d., as happened in one indictment. It is as clear a demonstration as one could find of the cavalier way that 'facts' could be

Table 3: *Verdicts of trial jury: Property crime in Surrey, 1736-53*

	No. true Bills	Pleaded guilty	No. to trial	Not guilty		Partial verdict		Guilty		Other or unknown
				No.	%	No.	%	No.	%	
Capital offences	507	–	507	172	33.9	149	29.4	179	35.3	7
Non-capital: assizes	520	6	514	201	39.1	103	20.0	197	38.3	13
Non-capital: quarter sessions	420	7	413	118	28.6	–	–	268	64.9	27
Total	1447	13	1434	491	34.2	252	17.6	644	44.9	47

ignored or bent in eighteenth-century criminal procedure. Not until 1753 were goods assessed in quarter sessions indictments at anything like their real value. This persistent undervaluing of stolen goods possibly explains why juries at quarter sessions were more inclined to convict than those at assizes. That can only be supposition. But it certainly explains other striking differences between the verdicts in non-capital cases in the two courts. It explains, for example, why quarter sessions juries did not find partial verdicts, and thus why almost 65 per cent of the accused before that court were found guilty as charged, while at the assizes 39 per cent were found guilty of grand larceny and another 20 per cent were convicted of petty larceny only.

The behaviour of quarter sessions in these years is particularly curious when one considers the punishments they awarded (Table 4). By this period the invariable punishment at assizes for grand larceny was transportation to America for seven years: 84 per cent of those convicted for a non-capital larceny over the value of 1s. were so sentenced in that court.[64] A partial verdict in these cases thus had some considerable benefits — if we suppose that a public whipping was preferable to being transported — for by far the largest number (in fact more than 85 per cent) of those tried for grand larceny but convicted of petty larceny at the assizes were whipped (Table 4). A few were transported anyway, presumably because the judge did not agree with the jury's assessment of the crime or the criminal; and some were granted a clergyable discharge or imprisoned. But in general, conviction at the assizes for non-capital theft led to transportation if the crime was adjudged to be grand larceny and corporal punishment if the value of the stolen goods was fixed at below a shilling.

Similarly, at quarter sessions for most of this period conviction for petty larceny led to corporal punishment. But when the court began to deal with an increasing number of cases after the war, as often as not conviction for petty larceny brought a sentence of transportation, a punishment authorized under the transportation statute but not previously insisted on in Surrey. Even though quarter sessions persistently treated grand as petty larceny until 1753, they nonetheless began well before that to punish large numbers of those convicted as though they had been guilty of the more serious offence. Before 1750 no one had been transported from quarter sessions; but in the next four years, 1750-53, almost two-thirds of those convicted of petty larceny were sentenced to seven years' banishment in America. In effect, the justices in quarter sessions engaged in a selection of offenders for transportation. Those not so selected continued to be whipped, though some few were imprisoned. At the assizes, on the other hand, juries and judges combined to select from those convicted of grand larceny a group of men and women who were to be whipped and discharged rather than transported. In both cases selection was exactly what was

Table 4: *Sentences in non-capital property cases: Surrey 1736-53*

	No.	Transported 7 years		Whipped		Clergied discharge		Imprisoned		Other or unknown	
		No.	%	No.	%	No.	%	No.	%	No.	%
Assizes: guilty as charged, or pleaded guilty	203	170	83.7	–	–	27	13.3	1	.5	5	2.5
Assizes: partial verdict	103	5	4.9	88	85.4	7	6.8	2	1.9	1	1.0
Assizes: total	306	175	57.2	88	28.8	34	11.1	3	1.0	6	2.0
Quarter sessions	275	122	44.4	106	38.6	–	–	7	2.6	40	14.6

involved: the manipulation of the verdict and selection of the form of punishment that a particular jury and a particular judge thought most appropriate to the crime committed and, even more importantly perhaps, to the prisoner.

An even more ominous selection was made in the assize courts among the 500 men and women on trial for capital offences against property. Almost exactly a third were acquitted by the jury, 35 per cent were found guilty as charged and sentenced to be hanged, and 29 per cent were found guilty not of the capital charge but of simple grand larceny, or, in some few cases, of petty larceny (Table 5). Those against whom partial verdicts were found suffered the punishments normally awarded the lesser crime in the assize courts: transportation for seven years in the vast majority of cases of grand larceny, with an occasional clergyable discharge when transportation was apparently inappropriate; whipping for petty larceny, with, again, occasional insistence from the bench on transportation. Partial verdicts were encouraged, as we have seen, by evidence presented to the jury about the circumstances of the crime and the character of the accused. But the nature of the crime was not, of course, unimportant: indeed, it is clear that juries and judges were most reluctant to see certain crimes punished on the gallows, including most of the trivial offences against property that had been removed from clergy since the Revolution. Not that all who were indicted under these statutes escaped: two sheepstealers and three men convicted of stealing from a shop or warehouse were hanged in Surrey in these years. But juries were generally anxious to reduce the seriousness of the charge in these cases (encouraged, it might be said, by the narrow constructions favoured by judges[65]) and the king was most often ready to grant a pardon to those whom the jury did convict. The extension of capital punishment in the eighteenth century obviously made it possible for the authorities to rid a local community of a man they judged to be particularly dangerous or troublesome; and the extended terror of the gallows may to some extent have strengthened the hand of those who thought themselves threatened by sheepstealers or shoplifters or pilfering servants. But it seems clear that neither juries, nor judges nor the king (or those who advised him on these matters) thought that these laws needed actually to be put into effect very often.

In the case of the more serious offences, however, many more victims were selected to be hanged. In the eighteen years we are dealing with, 179 men and women were convicted of capital offences involving the taking of property. All were sentenced to death, but ninety-two (at least)[66] were pardoned by the king and transported to America for fourteen years — the invariable condition placed on a pardon in this period. Most pardons followed a decision by the judge to reprieve the convict after he pronounced the death sentence — a decision based on his own view of the evidence or of

Table 5: *Sentences in capital property cases: Surrey 1736-53*

	No.	Sentenced to be hanged	Pardoned and transported		Actually hanged		Transported 7 years		Whipped		Clergied discharge		Imprisoned		Other or unknown	
			No.	%	No.	%	No.	%	No.	%	No.	%	No.	%	No.	%
Guilty as charged	179	179	92	51.4	87	48.6										
Partial verdict	149						128	85.9	9	6.0	9	6.0	1	.7	2	1.3

the character of the prisoner; or, as often as not, following an appeal on the prisoner's behalf by those whose opinion the judge would respect — magistrates, jurymen, often the prosecutor himself. The judge's report on the case went to the king for his final decision, but it seems clear that a judge's reprieve was in most cases tantamount to the granting of a pardon. If the judge refused a reprieve, the king could still be petitioned by the condemned man and his friends; the judge's opinion would then be sought and would still be critical, but in these circumstances the support of gentlemen of power and influence often came effectively into play and became extremely valuable.

At least ninety-two of the condemned were pardoned, then, because the judge thought that there were mitigating circumstances in the crime itself or in the character of the prisoner, because the prisoner's respectable neighbours gave him a character, or because the interest of a member of the gentry or nobility was committed on his behalf. The other eighty-seven were hanged. Overwhelmingly they had committed crimes removed from clergy in the sixteenth century because of their seriousness — crimes that threatened life as well as property or that infringed the peace and sanctity of the household: seventy-six of those hanged in Surrey in these years, 87 per cent, had been convicted of burglary, housebreaking and highway robbery. Four others had stolen horses; two were pickpockets; and five, as we have seen, had been convicted under the statutes that had removed clergy from shoplifting and sheepstealing.

The nature of the crime was obviously an important determinant of who was selected to be hanged. But as we have seen, the character of the prisoner was critically important too and it is hardly surprising that many of the robbers and burglars who were hanged appear from the evidence of their trials to have been unable to bring respectable neighbours or powerful friends to speak on their behalf. It was perhaps inevitable that many had lived within the metropolis of London. Not that everyone there was rootless or without influential support. There were settled communities in Southwark and in the urban parishes along the river and magistrates could write on behalf of a convict who was 'allied to a family in the borough of Southwark who have hitherto maintained a fair and unspotted character', and of another, the son of a man who 'although poor hath a good reputation and has sons and daughters married in this borough that are well esteemed'.[67] But without question the close social relationships that still characterized much of rural England and that gave rise to the structures of paternalism and deference which encouraged and were in turn supported by the intervention of those in authority on behalf of members of the community in trouble did not flourish as easily in the crowded and more anonymous urban parishes on the northern edge of Surrey. Most of those who were hanged in Surrey had committed their crimes in these parishes or those immediately adjacent. They were typically like the five Irish members of a gang, taken after apparently committing several highway robberies near Camberwell and tried at the winter assizes in 1738. They brought no character witnesses, made only the most desperate and easily penetrated of defences and in the end were left to be hanged because their crimes were serious, their guilt seemed clear and they had no employer or gentleman, no vicar or magistrate, no well-established neighbours to speak on their behalf. All five were hanged on Kennington Common along with two other Irishmen condemned at the same time. Perhaps the riots in London in 1736 over the employment of Irish labourers in preference to English[68] had made it difficult for these men to get work: they may well have thought themselves forced to take to the highway. Whether that was true, they came in the end to the gallows because they were unable to bring respectable support to their character: indeed, because they had no character at all in the sense required.

Further evidence that the courts were as much concerned to fit the punishment to the prisoner as to the crime is provided by the sharp contrast in their treatment of men and women. It is true that women committed fewer and less serious crimes than men[69] and to some extent this explains why only six of the eighty-seven hanged for property offences were women. But it does not fully explain why women charged with a capital crime were more likely to be acquitted than men, much more likely to be found guilty of a reduced, non-capital, charge and if convicted more likely to be reprieved: why, in general, women were treated much more leniently than men. A total of 43 per cent of the men who came before the trial jury on a capital charge were in the end either hanged or transported for fourteen years; 11 per cent of the women suffered the same penalties. And when granted a partial verdict, women were more likely than men to receive a clergyable discharge or to be whipped or imprisoned briefly rather than being transported for seven years. Similarly, women charged with non-capital larceny at the assizes were more frequently acquitted and punished more lightly than men: 47 per cent of women were found not guilty, 36 per cent of the men; 40 per cent of men were transported to America; 21 per cent of the women. It is true that a number of women were freed because they had committed offences in the company of their husbands and it was widely held that women were not capable of felony in those circumstances because they were 'presumed to have acted under [their] husbands' compulsion'.[70] Several women were in fact acquitted in Surrey for this reason.[71] But such circumstances applied in only a fraction of cases and cannot explain why women were acquitted more freely and punished less severely than men. The most compelling explanation seems clearly that women were seen to be much less dangerous to the community, much less of a threat to authority and social order and that the courts were as much concerned with considerations of this kind as with punishing criminals.

As a result of the trials of the 1441 men and women against whom true bills had been found (or at least of the 1352 whose sentences are known) just over 6 per cent were hanged, close to 40 per cent were transported for seven or fourteen years, 15 per cent were whipped and released. Only a handful were imprisoned (for periods ranging from three months to a year) for it was only when transportation was interrupted by the American Revolution that imprisonment was to become by necessity an important and regular part of the English penal system. About 60 per cent of those tried between 1736 and 1753 were punished, therefore, the remainder were discharged after being acquitted (36 per cent) or being allowed to plead benefit of clergy (3 per cent).

This pattern of verdicts and sentences was not, however, uniform over the whole period. Juries and judges clearly differed in their harshness or indulgence and as a result one session was often very different from the next. One jury, for example, often seemed much more willing than another to find partial verdicts and since the same group of men tried virtually all the cases at each session this could easily produce a distinctive pattern of verdicts. Similarly, judges differed in their sentencing policies when presented with a choice between, say, ordering corporal punishment or allowing a plea of benefit of clergy, or, more crucially, when at the conclusion of the session the opportunity came to reprieve some of those condemned to death. Such differences among juries and judges need to be analysed in detail and at length, and space does not permit that here. But one broad pattern can be examined briefly: that is the tendency for both trial juries and judges, like the grand juries before them, to be more rigorous when crime appeared to be increasing. In the three periods identified earlier as years of moderately high crime (before 1739), of wartime decline, and of post-war increase (after 1749), juries can be shown to have leaned towards a higher conviction rate when crime was high and to have been more favourably disposed towards acquittals when the level appeared to fall; and within the limits that it was possible, judges' sentences varied similarly. At both assizes and quarter sessions the same pattern emerges of a direct relationship between changes in the level of indictments and in the proportion of the accused found guilty by the trial jury. At assizes, for example, a rate of 38 per cent guilty verdicts in 1736-8 fell to 29 per cent during the war years (1744-7) and then rose again to 36 per cent as the number of accused before the court increased after the peace was signed (1749-52).

An even better measure perhaps of the willingness of the courts to convict is to be found in the combined effect of grand jury and petty jury decisions. The verdicts of grand jurors appear to have varied, as we have seen, with fluctuations in the level of crime and since in their more lenient moods they must have thrown out many marginal cases in which the trial jury might well have found a not guilty verdict, the most satisfactory conviction rate is that based on the number of accused brought before the grand jury. If, in addition, we count as a 'conviction' both guilty verdicts and partial verdicts, we can get a more general measurement of the willingness of the courts to convict. On this basis the conviction rate at the Surrey assizes fluctuates from 53 per cent in the pre-war years, to 47 per cent at the low point in the decline of indictments during the war (in the years 1744-7), to 61 per cent in the post-war crisis.

Juries were thus more anxious to convict when crime increased. Judges were also more inclined to hand out stiffer punishments. In deciding whether to grant reprieves to convicts, judges were influenced, as we have seen, by the circumstances of the crime and the character of the accused. But their decisions were also related to the level of crime. Hanging was after all designed to deter would-be offenders and judges were quite prepared to manipulate the level of terror as necessity dictated. If crime increased, the power of the law had to be demonstrated: 'there being great complaints of horse-stealing, which is a crying grievance in that county [Somerset]', a judge reported to the secretary of state in explaining why he had not reprieved a man convicted before him, 'I thought it necessary to make an example'.[72] On the other hand, if crime declined, judges could afford to be magnanimous. It is striking how few were hanged in Surrey when the level of crime fell sharply during the war. Between 1736 and 1739 at least one person was executed following every session of the assize court except one. During the war, however, partial verdicts and judges' reprieves combined to save increasing numbers from the gallows: there were no executions following eight of the eighteen sessions between 1740 and 1748 and no one was hanged at all in Surrey between the spring of 1744 and the spring of 1747.[73] On the other hand, when crime increased again after the war capital punishment was resumed with its old regularity (though because so many were charged the proportion hanged continued to decline) and only two sessions in the five years after 1749 were without their grim conclusion on the gallows at Kennington Common or Guildford.

In choosing among other punishments, judges were similarly inclined to select a stiffer penalty when convictions increased. If transportation was a harsher punishment than whipping or imprisonment for six months to a year, then it is clear that a convicted felon had more chance of being punished lightly (or of being granted a clergyable discharge) during the war than before 1740 or after 1748. As Table 6 shows, 64 per cent and almost

Table 6: *Sentences awarded in Surrey courts for property offences, 1736-9,*
1740-48, 1749-53: Percentage of total sentences

	Hanged	Transported	Whipped	Clergied discharged	Imprisoned
1736-9	16.9	64.0	11.2	6.7	1.1
1740-48	9.8	49.3	31.0	8.8	1.0
1749-53	7.1	66.7	23.7	1.1	2.1

67 per cent of convicted felons were transported in the years 1736-9 and
1749-53, respectively; during the war not quite 50 per cent were sentenced to
seven years in America and judges made much greater use of other options,
especially that of whipping, and they were also then more than usually
inclined to grant clergyable discharges.[74]

In the administration of justice in the mid eighteenth century the courts
clearly obeyed the dictum laid down by Joshua Fitzsimmons in 1751 that it
was not only 'necessary to consider what is the abstract quantum of the
crime, but also the disposition of the offender and the danger to the state of
letting him escape'.[75] The courts were flexibly attuned to the
circumstances of the times and of the prisoner as much as to the nature of
the crime, partly at least because the objectives of the criminal law extended
beyond the mere catching of criminals to supporting the established
foundations of the society. A system of criminal justice in which a judge
could say without embarrassment that though he had serious doubts about
a man's guilt, he had left him to be hanged because of the seriousness of the
crime[76] was not devoted to abstract notions of guilt and innocence, but
rather to dealing with the threat presented by a particular criminal at a
particular time and place. It was a system that had grown out of and was
well adapted to the needs of a rural society in which men were known, in
which the character and disposition of an offender were known in particular
to the respectable members of the community — to gentlemen, clergy,
farmers — and his treatment by the courts could be adjusted in accordance
with their views of his past behaviour. To this extent the criminal law could
be brought to support and sustain the authority of the society's natural
leaders, for when its extended terrors could be tempered by opinion and
influence, the administration of criminal justice could provide powerful
reinforcement to the local authority of those whose opinion mainly counted
and whose interest was mainly effective.[77]

A system of criminal justice that drew its strength and logic from close
social relationships was not, however, so well adapted to the needs of an

urban and commercial society in which these relationships could not flourish so easily. And in urban areas — and particularly in London where large numbers of men and women depended on casual and seasonal work and were so vulnerable to sudden contractions in the supply of jobs or to an oversupply of labour — crime against property was much more common and much more liable to the sudden expansion that so alarmed men in the early 1750s. Although dismay about the failure of the criminal law was not confined to urban society in the second half of the eighteenth century (there was indeed widespread concern about the growth of immorality and social indiscipline), it was perhaps mainly from the enlarging world of manufacturing and commerce that criticism of the law and of the system of judicial administration was increasingly to be heard. The law came to seem not only illogical and horribly cruel but also self-defeating to a society that prized regularity and uniformity and that also suffered most from the growth of crime. It was the failure of the judicial system, indeed what seemed to some its actual encouragement of crime by its excessive harshness and capricious irregularity, that principally stimulated schemes for its reform. The arguments were clarified in the 1760s and after. But the reform movement was perhaps initiated in the early 1750s when London appeared to be engulfed by crime and the House of Commons committee appointed in 1751 began groping towards solutions that would in time create a new faith — a professional police force to guard property and catch criminals; a court system that would try them quickly and impersonally; and a penal system that would not rely on the deterrent power of the death penalty but rather on a range of moderate punishments adjusted to the seriousness of the crime and applied with certainty and uniformity. A society that was coming to see itself confronting a criminal *class* found a system of criminal justice that had been shaped by men who were more likely to think of criminals as members of the community who had gone wrong hopelessly inadequate. The long debate was not seriously joined until the last third of the century, but the reports of the committee of 1751 were an indication of the way the wind was beginning to blow.

8 *Infanticide in the Eighteenth Century*

R. W. MALCOLMSON

On Saturday last was brought to the high gaol for the county of Devon, Mary Light, for that too common and most unnatural crime of murdering her own illegitimate infant. She is about 21 years of age, and lived as servant to one farmer Kerswell at a village near Modbury in this county, where, she says, a young fellow, servant also in the same house, courted her, to whose importunities she yielded, and became pregnant by him. Her condition was suspected by her mother, who charged her strictly with it, but she still denied it, concealing it also from all except her seducer, who, on her acquainting him with it, left her and his service. About five weeks ago she was in bed seized with great pains, and was delivered of a living female child, without the knowledge of two girls who lay in the same room. She gathered up her infant, and got again into bed, wrapping the babe in one corner of the rug, and rising at her wonted hour, went about her household work. Her mistress going into her chamber, found the child stifled.

Northampton Mercury, 8 March 1756

Unwanted pregnancy has always been a matter of serious concern, and numerous societies, and many troubled individuals, have had to cope with the consequences of those conceptions which nobody wanted. Unwed mothers have been reviled and shunned; married women have become demoralized and distracted by the prospect of family responsibilities which were greater than they could bear; and unwanted babies have been abandoned, neglected, maltreated and frequently killed. In recent times unwanted pregnancies have often led to abortion or, in the case of full-term pregnancies, to infant adoptions. Earlier societies, however, were usually less inclined, or less able, to consider such measures. Adoption of completely unrelated children had little appeal in societies which placed great stress on blood lineage. Abortion, although known and sometimes attempted, was dangerous and often unsuccessful, not always an accessible option for a particular individual, and commonly required that a pregnant girl reveal her condition to at least one other person. Usually a mother in early-modern Europe who was determined not to keep an unwanted baby opted for one of two courses of action: either she abandoned her baby in a public place, or she killed her baby — or 'allowed' it to die. A distraught and desperate mother might, with luck, save herself and her reputation but her baby was almost always destined for an early death.[1]

The abandoning of unwanted babies has a long history. In some societies, where new-born babies were left exposed in forests, on hillsides or in open fields, the practice was the virtual equivalent of infanticide. Death was intended and death was almost always achieved; Oedipus survived, but his was an exceptional case. In early-modern Europe, however, it was more usual for abandonment to be chosen as an alternative to outright infanticide, especially in urban areas. By abandoning an unwanted baby the direct responsibility for its survival could be evaded, at least in the mother's own mind, for if the baby were left in a public place there was some reason to imagine that it might be found alive and supported by someone else. Certainly this must have been a common hope of those mothers who left their babies on the porch of a church, in a basket in the marketplace or on the doorstep of a rich man's house. This practice, which seems to have been fairly common, was known in eighteenth-century England as 'dropping'. The newspapers often noticed such abandoned babies: a new-born baby boy left in a hand basket at the steward's door of St Bartholomew's Hospital in September 1729; a baby boy, wrapped in bays, found on a tombstone in St Paul's churchyard, Covent Garden, in November 1729; a new-born boy left in the porch of the parish church in Great Brington, Northamptonshire, in February 1731; a girl about two months old, wrapped in 'a piece of an old yellow blanket', found near the entrance to an alehouse in Daventry in March 1761.[2] 'Dropping' appears to have been particularly prevalent in London: it was claimed, for instance, that during the first half of 1743 a dozen infants were abandoned in the parish of St George's, Hanover Square.[3] The frequency of dropping was a major impetus behind the active movement in favour of a foundling hospital in London, an institution which began its operations, on a modest scale, in 1741.

Foundlings have achieved a modest recognition in the history of European societies. In Catholic countries they were perceived largely through the ideologies and institutional concerns of the Church, the traditional protectress of the weak and the impotent.[4] In England they have appeared periodically in the annals of the poor law and, more memorably, in works of the literary imagination: Fielding's *Tom Jones*, Eppie in George Eliot's *Silas Marner*, and the central character in Oscar Wilde's *The Importance of Being Earnest*. Such recognition attests, perhaps, to the prominence of abandoned infants in everyday experience, but the details of these fictional careers should not be accepted too literally.

For literary convention necessitated a comic structure for most stories of foundlings, and consequently happy endings. In actual experience, however, their fates were usually much different. Some were so weak from exposure and inattention that they died soon after being discovered; and the others, who were put in the hands of uncaring nurses or whose welfare was superintended by a foundling hospital, faced mortality prospects of dismal proportions.

The most direct way of disposing of an unwanted baby was to kill it immediately after its birth. By the eighteenth century the records of European societies are full of references to these personal tragedies. In 1777 Frederick the Great claimed in a letter to Voltaire that there were more executions in Germany for infanticide than for any other crime.[5] Since infanticide was a relatively sensational act, regarded by many as shocking and 'unnatural', and by others as a sad reflection on both the callousness of seducers and the rigours of the criminal law, it received considerable attention and publicity from essayists, social critics, literary figures and the compilers of newspapers. In Germany, where infanticide aroused widespread and intense controversy, it was a major theme in the literature of the *Sturm-und-Drang* period. Between the 1760s and the 1780s dozens of essays, treatises and dramatic writings dealt with infanticide in some form or other; in fact, almost every significant literary figure of the period referred to it at some point in his writings, and a few works, such as H.L. Wagner's *The Child-Murderess* (1775) and Schiller's poem *The Infanticide* (1781), used it as a central literary theme.[6] The Gretchen tragedy in the first part of *Faust* was probably conceived by Goethe during the same period. Although there was no such literary movement in eighteenth-century Britain, some of the implications of infanticide were later developed in Walter Scott's *The Heart of Midlothian* (1818) and George Eliot's *Adam Bede* (1859), both in a historical perspective. Before this, moreover, infanticide had been widely acknowledged in the ephemera of literature, particularly the newspapers, and the subject had attracted the passing notice of several major writers, including John Bunyan, Joseph Addison and Daniel Defoe.

Englishmen tended to look upon infanticide with a combination of fascination and horror. To Joseph Addison the guilty women were 'monsters of inhumanity'; in 1753 the bishop of Worcester spoke of 'the impious barbarity of unnatural parents'.[7] Oliver Heywood, a nonconformist minister in the West Riding of Yorkshire during the Restoration period, diligently reported the circumstances of those women whose crimes had come to his attention.[8] John Bunyan, in condemning 'whoredom', suggested that 'oftentimes it is attended with murder, with the murder of the babe begotten on the defiled bed'.[9] Newspapers were particularly prone to dwell on the lurid details of infanticide: the discoveries of mutilated bodies, the corpses in the Thames, the remains which were turned up by dogs and swine. Some observers gave the impression of an endemic situation. 'Not a sessions passes', claimed Daniel Defoe, 'but we see one or more merciless mothers tried for the murder of their bastard children'; it was said in 1737 that 'such crimes are now become so common that they are heard of almost every day'; a report in 1738 referred to 'the vast numbers of grievous murders of this kind'.[10] Infanticide, thought another writer, '[is] a crime to the scandal of our country, little known but in Great Britain, where more murders of this nature are committed in one year than in all Europe besides in seven'.[11] Thomas Coram, the principal promoter of the London Foundling Hospital, was said to have become committed to the project because of 'the shocking spectacles he had seen of innocent children who had been murdered and thrown upon dunghills'.[12]

A variety of sources allow us to study some aspects of infanticide in eighteenth-century England. The material which we have consulted falls into three main categories: legal records, especially those relating to court trials; newspaper reports, usually of suspected infanticides; and miscellaneous literary sources, such as pamphlets, essays, sermons and personal papers. The relevant medical writings, which focus on the forensic problems associated with infanticide, date mostly from the early nineteenth century.[13] Each type of source has it special limitations. The records of cases brought to trial, for instance, though valuable because of the fullness of their evidence, are not at all numerous. Only the Old Bailey sessions papers, which relate to crime in London and Middlesex, offer a consecutive series of printed trial records, and we have examined these papers for the first forty-five years when they are more or less complete, from 1730 to 1774.[14] The manuscript records of the provincial assize circuits, which are still in the process of being sorted and calendared, provide additional relevant evidence, although only the records of the Northern Circuit include a substantial accumulation of depositions, which is the most useful class of legal documentation for our purposes.[15] Newspaper accounts help to compensate for these limitations in the formal criminal records; however, they much more frequently notice the reputed circumstances of suspected infanticides rather than the actual trial proceedings, and the details which they report, many of which were based on hearsay or rumour rather than close investigation, must be treated with caution and discrimination. As for the literary sources, they are often useful indicators of attitude and outlook, and occasionally they include suggestive analyses of the circumstances underlying infanticide, but many of them lack detail and specificity, and in general they are not sufficiently substantial to be of more than supplementary or illustrative value.

The documentary basis for this essay is a collection of some 350 references to particular instances of infanticide, or suspected infanticide, from the period between the Restoration and the later eighteenth century. Approximately two-thirds of these cases are drawn from the columns of the eighteenth-century provincial press, largely from the period of George II's reign; slightly more than a quarter come from criminal records, of which the Old Bailey sessions papers are the most important; and the remaining cases are taken from a variety of literary sources. About a third of all these cases are stark references to the discovery of a dead (and presumed murdered) baby, to the committal of a woman for suspected infanticide, or to the execution of a woman who had been found guilty by the courts; virtually no information is provided in these instances about the circumstances of the killing or the situation of the mother. The more valuable cases, the other two-thirds, offer varying degrees of detail about the circumstances of the apparent killing and the discovery of the crime, and these are the cases which afford us an opportunity to reconstruct the character, rationale and implications of eighteenth-century infanticide.

One general negative observation can be made about the limitations of our sources: they do not permit any significant degree of quantification. The evidence which exists bears only on reported cases of infanticide or alleged infanticide, not on the actual instances of infanticide, which were almost certainly much more numerous. What is available for study is an unavoidably incomplete collection of infanticide cases; reliable statistics simply cannot be compiled. And this situation continued well into the nineteenth century: as late as 1871 a coroner in Middlesex was pointing out that 'all the statistics which we have of the deaths of newly-born children are very imperfect'.[16] The real incidence of infanticide in eighteenth-century England, then, is unknowable, and the evidence which can be retrieved permits little scope for quantification. All we can say with some degree of certainty is that the actual criminal indictments for infanticide, like other charges of murder, were never very numerous. In Staffordshire the indictments for infanticide (or the concealment of a bastard birth) appear to have averaged slightly less than one per year during the period 1743-1802; they represented approximately 25 per cent of the total indictments for murder and manslaughter in that county.[17] Only sixty-one infanticide cases were tried at the Old Bailey between 1730 and 1774, and in Surrey during the eighteenth century there seem to have been, on average, only three or four trials for infanticide in each decade.[18]

One further matter should be noted before proceeding to the substance of our discussion. Although only a minority of infanticide cases involved an actual criminal conviction, we can safely assume that most instances of suspected infanticide were genuine in the sense that someone was responsible for the baby's death. On a few occasions the wrong person may have been suspected and accused, but when a dead baby was found in a pond, a barn, an outhouse, a box or buried in a garden, there is little reason to doubt that it had probably been murdered, or at the least deliberately not kept alive. If there were a few instances of reputed infanticide in which a baby actually was still-born or accidentally died in the course of delivery, they were almost certainly very much in the minority. Unless, then, the evidence clearly indicates that the mother intended to keep her baby, or that death resulted from misadventure, it seems reasonable to regard the great bulk of suspected infanticides as actual infanticides, and to presume that there was a guilty party somewhere.

In the light of our sources, then, which aspects of infanticide are most clearly revealed? What are the most common characteristics, the 'typical' circumstances, the social regularities about which there can be little debate? First, babies were usually killed by women; men were involved, either as the principal or as an accessory, in only a small minority of cases. Second, a woman who killed a baby was usually the baby's own mother. Third, the great majority of women who were suspected or accused of infanticide were unmarried or, much less frequently, widowed. Documented instances of infanticide within marriage are exceptional. Fourth, women from genteel or middle-class families were seldom accused of infanticide; almost all of the women involved appear to have been from labouring, mechanic or farming backgrounds. Fifth, of the suspected and convicted women whose occupations can be determined, the majority were servant maids or had just retired from being servants. Sixth, almost all recorded infanticides occurred immediately after birth; it was unusual for a baby to be killed more than a few minutes after its birth. And finally, the sex of the baby was an irrelevant consideration in English infanticides, unlike those in some other societies. Boy babies had no better chance of survival than girl babies; the circumstances of the mother provided the rationale for infanticide, not the sex of her infant. These, then, are the basic characteristics of infanticide: they provide a starting point, and a general framework, for a closer analysis.

In eighteenth-century England an unmarried woman who found herself pregnant, and with no foreseeable prospects of a respectable marriage, had good reason, like Hetty Sorrel in *Adam Bede*, to despair of her situation. The social and economic consequences of unwed motherhood were very serious indeed. If a girl was a servant — and a high proportion of young women were — knowledge of her pregnancy would result in immediate dismissal; she would probably receive no character reference, and there would be little chance of her being taken into service again. In all probability she would be virtually stigmatized for life. The employment which might be open to her would be of the most menial and exploitative sort, such as laundering or the sweated dressmaking trades or some other form of casual labour, or it would be socially deviant, such as robbery, begging or prostitution. Moreover, on her small income she might have another mouth to feed, a constant reminder of the cause of her distress. She might be able to get poor relief in the parish where she had a legal settlement, but she would then be officially marked off as a pauper, and in small communities where her situation would be universally known, she would be liable to become an embittered outsider — lonely, probably friendless and treated with condescension by most of her neighbours. If, rather than being a servant, she still lived with her family, she might be disowned, and she would probably fear for the shame which would inevitably tarnish the family's reputation. Moreover, any pregnant spinster would know that, with a bastard child, her chances of marriage were poor. Chastity was valued, in theory if not always in practice, and even men of generous views would have thought poorly of taking for a wife a disgraced and penniless woman, and possibly the extra burden of another man's child. The best that most eighteenth-century women could realistically hope for was a respectable (and perhaps humane) dependence — dependence on a father, a master or a husband — and such dependence was seen as greatly preferable to the hopelessness, the lack of standing and the humiliation which unwed motherhood implied.

Given these various considerations, pregnant spinsters might easily be tempted to conceal their condition. Exactly what went on in their minds, and how they reacted to their situation, is largely a matter of plausible speculation. In almost all cases, though, it is likely that they would have been acting out of fear — fear for the loss of what security and respect they enjoyed, and fear for the hopelessness and disgrace which they envisaged. Some of them may have sought out an abortion; others may have tried to get their lovers to marry them or, at the least, pleaded for material assistance, especially if the man had some wealth. Some pregnancies may have been concealed with the clear and calculated intention of killing the baby at birth — one woman, for instance, who was executed at Canterbury in 1754, 'confessed that she had formed a design to make away with the infant as soon as it should appear';[19] other concealments were probably prompted more by confusion and panic, or perhaps the hope for a fortunate miscarriage, and involved no definite notion of what would be done. Often there must have been simply a dread of facing up to the imminent disgrace, and a desperate hoping that, if the secret were kept, some sort of deliverance would occur. Hetty Sorrel in *Adam Bede* seems to have been in just this state of mind, 'not knowing where to turn for refuge from swift-advancing shame', unable to fix on any course of action which did not lead to certain misery:

After the first on-coming of her great dread ... she had waited and waited, in the blind vague hope that something would happen to set her free from her terror; but she could wait no longer. All the force of her nature had been concentrated on the one effort of concealment, and she had shrunk with irresistible dread from every course that could tend towards a betrayal of her miserable secret. Whenever the thought of writing to Arthur [her seducer] had occurred to her, she had rejected it. He could do nothing for her that would shelter her from discovery and scorn among the relatives and neighbours who once more made all her world, now her airy dream had vanished. Her imagination no longer saw happiness with Arthur, for he could do nothing that would satisfy or soothe her pride. No, something else would happen — something *must* happen — to set her free from this dread.[20]

'In this perplexity', suggested a sympathetic medical observer, 'they are meditating different schemes for concealing the birth of the child; but are wavering between difficulties on all sides, putting the evil hour off, and trusting too much to chance and fortune'.[21] Some women may have been barely conscious of what was happening when labour came — 'their distress of body and mind deprives them of all judgment, and rational conduct; they are delivered by themselves, wherever they happen to retire in their fright and confusion'[22] — and others simply fled after the delivery, leaving the baby behind in a ditch or barn. Infanticide was not always an unambiguously deliberate act; in fact, as often as not it may have been an act of impulse, an uncalculated (though certainly logical) consequence of a successful concealment. But whatever a woman's thinking and emotional state may have been, her main immediate objective before her delivery was concealment, for otherwise her character would certainly be ruined: the hazards of concealment were great, and the anxiety and sense of isolation must have been acute, but the consequence of any revelation would have been almost certain disgrace.

Women who decided to conceal their pregnancies were faced with numerous unavoidable difficulties. Perhaps the most obvious problem was physical appearance: some sort of camouflage had to be attempted. Some women may have altered their postures as a means of disguise, others probably benefited from the loose fit (which could easily be made looser) of the conventional shifts of everyday labour; occasionally sickness, such as dropsy, was pleaded as an excuse. One servant when questioned replied, 'I am only pot-bellied, all our family are pot-bellied — and what a disgrace it is to be pot-bellied'.[23] It is clear, certainly, that many women were entirely successful in concealing their condition, even from close relatives or other maids with whom they shared a room. If suspicions were aroused, a pregnant girl would have to be prepared to deny any charges and persuasively plead her innocence, and hope that much of the suspicion would be effectively disarmed. She would have to be able to cope with any telling physical complaints and avoid showing signs of fatigue. Her working routine would have to be observed as usual and no indication could be given that her normal chores had become a special burden.

The most serious problems occurred during labour and immediately after the delivery. It was not usually possible for a woman to retire to her room for a lengthy labour without attracting inquiries and thus giving herself away. She would have to wait until the delivery was imminent and then carry it out herself as quickly and as quietly as possible. The risk of discovery was probably greatest if the delivery took place indoors in someone else's house (the typical situation for domestic servants), for privacy might be hard to find, especially when rooms were shared, excuses for an absence from work would have to be offered and there could be no unnecessary crying out in pain. During the delivery the woman would have to maintain her faculties and perform the basic functions of a midwife; and afterwards, if she were still intent on concealing her plight, she would be impelled to kill her baby (most commonly by strangulation or suffocation) — for would not the birth have to be concealed just as the pregnancy had been? — before its cries attracted attention. The concealment of a birth tended to follow logically from the circumstances of a successfully concealed pregnancy, and infanticide, though not always consciously intended, was the most immediately available means of concealing a birth. After the birth it would be necessary for the woman to dispose of the body and the after-birth, recompose herself and her clothes, regain some of her physical strength and return to her usual routine before her absence prompted any inconvenient investigations. Moreover, several kinds of tell-tale evidence could give her away unless properly managed: if she were delivered in her own bed the soiled sheets would have to be dealt with, and if the delivery were in a privy the surrounding area would have to be thoroughly cleaned up. If the woman succeeded in all these individual acts, and if no suspicion were aroused during the following few days, her conduct would probably never be discovered.

Obviously there was much that could go wrong during this complicated process of concealment, and luck must have played a large role for many women. 'I had a servant laid in the house last year', wrote the mother of the squire in Shalstone, Buckinghamshire, in 1740, and 'it was by chance she had not murdered her child'.[24] The deception had to be consistently sustained; any weakness of purpose or erosion of will could have resulted in exposure. A long and difficult labour might ruin a girl's plans, as would a chance observer or an inconvenient visitor. The disposal of the baby was particularly awkward for it was usually impossible to get the body very far from the mother's residence. In June 1757 a servant maid in Collingbourne

Ducis, Wiltshire, was discovered by her mistress as she was disposing of the baby in a hole in the brewhouse; she was later found guilty, confessed and was executed.[25] In urban areas the confined conditions of life complicated the tactics of disposal: women commonly resorted to dropping the baby in an outhouse or hiding it in a box. Disposal was sometimes easier in the counryside: the body could be buried, or dropped in a river, pond or well, places of concealment which were not likely to be quickly discovered. A baby discovered, if only recently dead, often meant trouble for the mother since circumstantial inquiries could send the searchers on a general investigation, during which she might be examined for signs of recent childbirth, such as milk in the breasts, and thereby exposed. One case will illustrate the chance character of many such local dramas. In August 1733 at a place north of York a pond dried up and the body of a new-born baby was unexpectedly revealed. A local servant maid was suspected; she was examined 'and on the first search thought innocent', but she unwisely became 'very pert with the women, who thereupon tried another experiment, and found milk in her breast'. She then confessed that the child was hers 'but pretended it was born dead, and that she had laid it by the way-side that it might be the sooner found; but it appearing to the [coroner's] jury that she went from her master's house late one evening, pretending to go to her mother's house, about a mile off, to take a vomit, and by the way bore the child, and went and lay at her mother's that night, and returned to her service early the next morning, without making the least discovery', the woman was committed to York Castle.[26] Cases of this sort, of course — the cases which were reported — are mostly the instances of failure, of apparently guilty women brought to justice; how many women got away with their actions, and thus preserved their characters, we can never know.

The legal basis for trials of infanticide was an Act of 1624 (21 Jas I, c.27) which focused not on the actual killing of a new-born infant — a difficult fact to prove — but rather on the fact of concealment. Recognizing the ease with which the death of an infant could be explained away, the statute permitted a presumption of guilt on the basis of specified circumstantial evidence:

> Whereas many lewd women that have been delivered of bastard children, to avoid their shame and to escape punishment, do secretly bury, or conceal the death of their children, and after if the child be found dead the said women do allege that the said children were born dead; whereas it falleth out sometimes (although hardly it is to be proved) that the said child or children were murdered by the said women their lewd mothers, or by their assent or procurement: For the preventing therefore of this great mischief, be it enacted ... that if any woman ... be delivered of any issue

of the body, male or female, which being born alive, should by the laws of this realm be a bastard, and that she endeavour privately either by drowning or secret burying thereof, or any other way, either by herself or the procuring of others, so to conceal the death thereof, as that it may not come to light, whether it be born alive or not, but be concealed, in every such case the mother so offending shall suffer death as in the case of murder except such mother can make proof by one witness at the least, that the child (whose death was by her intended to be concealed) was born dead.

When a bastard baby was found dead, then, concealment of its birth was to be regarded as evidence of murder; the 'principle of presumption of innocence was not to apply. Even Blackstone thought that this law 'savours pretty strongly of severity'.[27] By the later eighteenth century this severity was being widely acknowledged and frequently criticized, both in England and on the Continent (where similar laws were often found), and a greater sympathy was being shown for the circumstances of those women who were accused of killing their babies.[28] The statute of 1624 was explicitly condemned by several observers, and although attempts to repeal it in 1772-3 were not successful, its removal from the criminal law was finally effected by an Act of 1803 (43 Geo. III, c.58).[29]

While the law on infanticide in the eighteenth century was rigorous in theory, in practice it was seldom enforced. It may have been observed with some strictness during the seventeenth and early eighteenth centuries,[30] but by the reign of George II it seems to have been largely disregarded. In fact, the statute was specifically mentioned in only one of the sixty-one infanticide trials at the Old Bailey between 1730 and 1774.[31] In 1743 the printer of the *Old Bailey Proceedings* was even constrained to add a footnote reminder about the existence of the statute to the report of one trial which resulted in an acquittal: 'Tis thought cases of this kind would not so frequently occur at the Old Bailey, if the law were more generally known'.[32] Although almost all of the women who came to trial were clearly guilty of concealment, forty-six of these sixty-one Old Bailey cases were decided in favour of the defendant.[33] In Staffordshire it seems that not a single indictment for infanticide in the period 1743-1802 resulted in the death sentence (the evidence available includes thirty-nine such indictments).[34] Leniency appears to have been more the norm than the exception. As Blackstone correctly pointed out, 'it has of late years been usual with us in England, upon trials for this offence, to require some sort of presumptive evidence that the child was born alive before the other constrained presumption (that the child whose death is concealed was therefore killed by his parent) is admitted to convict the prisoner'.[35] The proven ineffectiveness of the 1624 statute was seen as a major reason for recommending its repeal: one member of the House of Commons, for instance, argued in 1773 that 'the law is of little use, as the judge, the jury and auditors, notwithstanding the circumstances are plain, often acquit unfortunate women. These acquittals, sir, encourage women who unhappily are in this predicament; and the law, from its severity, is rendered ineffectual'.[36]

It is clear, certainly, that many of the women brought to trial were acquitted very readily. Direct proof of infanticide was hard to obtain and perjury in the interest of the defendant was relatively easy — as Mr Saddletree, the amateur lawyer in *The Heart of Midlothian*, said about the evidence required for Effie Deans's acquittal: 'if we could but find any one to say she had gien the least hint o' her condition, she wad be brought aff wi'a wat finger'.[37] For infanticide the legal process operated with particular tenderness. 'Tho there be 12 or 14 persons summoned to evidence against her from one circumstance or other, yet I believe the fact will not be proved upon her', wrote a Lancashire doctor of a woman charged with (and very likely guilty of) infanticide in 1747, and his prognostication turned out to be correct.[38] In March 1750 four women were tried at Exeter 'for the murder of their bastard children, but the jury (which was a very merciful one) found them not guilty'.[39] Juries were inclined to listen sympathetically to the case of the accused and were often prepared to grasp at the smallest doubts about her guilt. Several kinds of defence were commonly offered in order to gain an acquittal. Many women claimed that the child was still-born[40] — an argument which the Act 21 Jas I, c.27 was intended to disallow — and these claims were frequently accepted. Others argued that they were taken by surprise on the privy, and that that baby suddenly came from them and fell down into the soil. On occasion it was claimed that the baby died accidentally during or immediately after birth, probably because of the lack of proper assistance or the loss of consciousness by the mother. A woman who was executed at Gloucester in April 1755 'positively denied her using any violence to the child, whose death she said was occasioned by a fall and the want of proper care afterwards'.[41] One of the most popular defences, used by some twenty of the women tried at the Old Bailey, involved the presentation of child linen which had allegedly been found among the mother's effects: such evidence of foresight, it was contended, clearly implied that she planned to maintain, not to kill, her baby.

Most of these arguments were very questionable. Still-births, in all likelihood, were relatively more significant in the eighteenth century than they are today (they presently comprise about 1 to 2 per cent of total births); however, in order to give credence to the large number of allegations of still-birth which were put forward by these accused women, it would be necessary to accept the proposition that an extraordinarily high proportion of illegitimate pregnancies in the eighteenth century resulted in still-births, and this is not, in our view, a plausible hypothesis.[42] Those women who claimed to have been delivered by surprise seldom could show, or attempted to show, that they had tried to retrieve the baby from the privy and thus save its life. The argument based on the provision of infant clothing was especially suspect, for such evidence could easily be planted and was inherently inconsistent with the fact of concealment. Daniel Defoe attacked this common plea with particular vigour:

> I wonder so many men of sense, as have been on the jury, have been so often imposed upon by the stale pretence of a scrap or two of child-bed linen being found in the murderer's box, etc. when alas! perhaps it was ne'er put there till after the murder was committed; or if it was, but with a view of saving themselves by that devilish precaution; for so many have been acquitted on that pretence, that 'tis but too common a thing to provide child-bed linen beforehand for a poor innocent babe they are determined to murder.[43]

Suspicion of this sort was voiced by a midwife at the trial of one Mercy Hornby, who was charged with killing her baby on Friday, 15 March 1734. The midwife was asked by the prisoner, 'Did not you take some child-bed linen out of my trunk?'

> Yes, a shirt, a blanket, and a night-cap, a biggin, and a long stay; but these I did not see till Monday [the 18th], and it's much to be feared, that you did not put them there; for indeed I was informed they were borrowed of a neighbour.
> *Court.* That's no evidence — you must not swear what you heard, but only what you know.[44]

Perhaps the most plausible (though not necessarily the most effective) defence was that the baby had died from lack of help, for when a woman was delivered by herself there was undoubtedly a greater chance that the baby might be injured by a fall, or drowned in the natural discharges or unintentionally damaged by an inexpert and rushed delivery in circumstances which, for the mother, were painful and frightening, and about which she was sometimes totally ignorant. The evidence from a few trials is certainly ambiguous but in most cases the mother was clearly 'responsible', in some sense, for the death of her baby, and it is probable that much more often than not she was directly responsible for the killing, either by intent or as an unpremeditated act.

The inadequacies of forensic medicine during the eighteenth century sometimes aided in the acquittal of an accused woman, for though the facts against her might be very strong, and though evidence might be produced which indicated the high probability of a live birth, medical witnesses were normally unable to reject entirely the possibility of a still-birth, and this lack of certainty clearly favoured the cause of the defendant. One form of test was commonly employed in which the infant's lungs, or a portion of the lungs, were placed in water: if the lungs floated it was thought that the child had breathed, whereas if they sunk it was concluded that the child had never lived. This experiment was performed in connection with at least seventeen of the Old Bailey trials, and the lungs were almost always found to float, though the test seldom appears to have carried much weight in favour of a conviction. In fact, in eight of these cases doubt was explicitly raised about the reliability of the lung test — or complicating circumstances were introduced — and several medical witnesses admitted or even emphasized its inconclusiveness. 'I think the experiment (where a person's life is at stake) too slight to be built upon', opined one doctor in 1737; 'I have tried that experiment many a time', said another in 1744, 'but I cannot be downright certain and positive of it'; others looked upon the test as 'not conclusive' and as 'very inconclusive evidence'.[45] 'I did make an experiment on the lungs, which was formerly thought decisive', reported a doctor at one trial in 1771, 'but now that opinion is exploded'.[46] Such hesitance and disagreement on the part of the experts, which was closely noted by judges and juries, offered another convenient ground for 'reasonable doubt' in the interest of the accused.

Although most women killed their new-born infants by themselves, without assistance or support, a minority had accomplices. We have evidence of a few cases in which there was a female accessory to the infanticide, most commonly the mother of the pregnant girl. In March 1775, for example, at Tregoney in Cornwall,

> one Mary Middlecourt and her daughter, who kept the Red Lion in this town, were committed to Launceston gaol, charged with the murder of the daughter's bastard child, and which they are said to have perpetrated by first strangling the infant, and then cutting its throat from ear to ear; after which they buried it in a piece of ground adjoining to the house; but being accidentally overseen by some of their neighbours, they were discovered.[47]

Women outside the family circle were seldom implicated in infanticide cases. It was more common, however, for a man to be involved, almost always the father of the baby: our sources include some two dozen cases of this kind. Two or three such incidents involved fellow servants. It was reported in 1753, for instance, that at a place near Ross in Herefordshire 'a servant maid there had lately delivered herself of a child; and her fellow servant, who was the father of it, buried it in the orchard, where it was found by means of some hounds keeping a prodigious noise near the place'.[48] Four or five cases seem to have involved gentlemen as active participants. At a village near Brill in Buckinghamshire a new-born baby was found buried in July 1733, and 'a maid servant in a neighbouring family of distinction readily owned the child, and charged the gentleman's eldest son both with being the father of it, and that he had prevailed with her to trust him with it, under pretence of carrying it out of the house to a nurse at some distance; upon which the coroner's inquest have brought in the verdict *wilful murder* against the young gentleman, and he has thought proper to leave the country thereupon'.[49] One Anne Loale, at her execution in Northampton in 1759, claimed 'that her master was present when she was delivered ... and that immediately after the birth he took the child from her, stabbed it and put it into the necessary-house'.[50] In four instances of infanticide, incest was suspected or proved, in each case between father and daughter. It was reported, for example, that in 1733 'a carpenter in Ratcliff highway having lain with his own daughter and got her with child, she was delivered by him ..., when he took the infant and killed it, and put it into his bag among his tools and conveyed it away. But he was apprehended and taken in Wapping'.[51] Similarly, in 1766 a tinner in Camborne, Cornwall, 'got his own daughter with child; and when her full time was come, by her father's instigation, they both secreted the birth and death of the child. The father took the infant from her body, tied a cord about its neck and threw the babe into a water tin-shaft'.[52]

Although infanticides were usually detected soon after the delivery (if they were detected at all) — blood was seen on the girl's clothes, signs of weakness and exhaustion aroused suspicion, the baby was discovered in a privy, a midwife's examination forced a confession — there was a handful of cases in which the facts came to light only after considerable delay. In a few instances a buried, submerged or hidden body was accidentally uncovered and inquiries ensued; in others a witness, an accomplice or the girl herself made a confession months or even years after the event.[53] In June 1764, for example, 'a woman at Eversholt near Woburn, in Bedfordshire, having some words with her maid, the latter went to a magistrate and gave information that her mistress murdered her bastard child some years ago; on which she was taken into custody, and likewise the maid, for being privy to the said action'.[54] At Nottingham assizes in August 1759 a gentleman seventy-four years of age was tried 'for the murder of a bastard child about 34 years ago'; he was found guilty, the principal witness against him being his younger brother.[55] One of the most remarkable cases of a delayed discovery — though in this instance the delay was only a fortnight — occurred at Alnwick, Northumberland, in the spring of 1768:

One Ripdeth, who lives at Newton-by-the-Sea, coming to this town to transact some business, and finding a dead child in a pond in the road, he brought it with him: the coroner's inquest sat on the body, and brought in their verdict, wilful murder by persons unknown. Two gentlemen of Alnwick caused the town immediately to be searched to find out its mother, but without success, so that it was entirely dropped. But the most strange part of the story by far is, that Ripdeth came to Alnwick last Wednesday, and related, that he could neither rest day or night, for that the ghosts of the child and its mother constantly attended and buffetted him; that the very night before he left home, they both together pulled him (tho' awake) upon the floor, and beat him very severely, and also added, that if he could but once see the woman, he should know her among ten thousand. Upon this most of the women immediately assembled, who passed before him one by one, many of whom he pronounced innocent, but the mother at last appearing, at first sight he cried aloud, 'This is the murderer'; whereupon she was immediately committed to gaol. Ripdeth is a sober, judicious man.[56]

The majority of the women suspected of infanticide were servant maids — at least thirty-five of the sixty-one Old Bailey cases between 1730 and 1774 clearly involved servants (in one-sixth of these sixty-one cases no occupational identification is possible) — and this predominance of one social group deserves a brief explanation. The most obvious point concerns the relationship between the age and occupational structures. It is now well known that, with a relatively late age of marriage in the seventeenth and eighteenth centuries, a large number of women were employed in service during a significant portion of their potentially child-bearing years; indeed, it may be that at any given time in the eighteenth century as many as half of the unmarried women between the ages of about sixteen and twenty-five were living-in servants — chamber maids, scullery maids, cooks, dairy maids and the like. It is not surprising, then, that they appeared so prominently in infanticide cases. Moreover, it is probable that the circumstances of their lives — the frustrations of physical confinement, the frequent and close contact with men servants, their subordinate and ambiguous relationship with the master and any mature sons he might have — accentuated their vulnerability to seduction and casual affairs. Certainly the guide books for the good behaviour of servants were at some pains to emphasize these hazards. An 'undue familiarity between servants of different sexes in a family, has had fatal and tragical effects', counselled a writer in 1693. 'How often has opportunity and privacy exposed men and maids that live together to the devil's temptations'.[57] Similarly, a guide book of 1743 warned the servant maid that 'if you are in the house of a person of condition where there are many men servants, it requires a great deal of circumspection how to behave. As these fellows live high, and have little to do, they are for the most part very pert and saucy where they dare, and apt to take liberties on the least encouragement'. The author also warned against the lascivious inclinations of some masters and their sons.[58] This theme, of course, was often dwelt on in the popular literature of the eighteenth century, and the history of Pamela Andrews offered to contemporary readers the most vivid representation of the kind of personal circumstances which, in a less melodramatic and embroidered form, must have been often experienced. Pamela herself spoke directly to thousands of servant maids:

> One don't know what arts and stratagems men may devise to gain their vile ends; and so I will think as well as I can of these poor undone creatures, and pity them. For you see, by my sad story, and narrow escapes, what hardships poor maidens go through whose lot it is to go out to service, especially to houses where there is not the fear of God, and good rule kept by the heads of the family.[59]

To say that servant maids were especially liable to unwanted pregnancy does not, of course, necessarily imply that they were uncommonly susceptible to the temptations of infanticide. It seems, however, that the sense of shame and the concern for reputation — the basic components of infanticide's rationale — may have been rather more highly developed among servants than among single women in other employments. A servant's status and security depended very heavily on her 'character', the repute with which she was regarded by her social superiors; and the loss of this character would have been seen by many servants as not simply embarrassing, or inconvenient or humiliating but as completely catastrophic, both socially and economically. And the more she had enjoyed a good character, and been well spoken of by society, the more would a servant girl have been impressed by the disastrous consequences to herself of having her pregnant condition revealed. One girl who had concealed the birth of her baby was said to have been 'a faithful and favourite servant in a family, which she could not leave without a certainty of her situation being discovered; and such a discovery she imagined would be certain *ruin* to her for life'.[60] Unlike some other labouring occupations, such as seasonal farm work, casual street labour in London and cottage industry, domestic servants were under almost constant surveillance for good behaviour, and the favourable character which a girl might have gained often represented a substantial investment of years of conscientious and reliable service, all of which would be threatened by one misfortune. A case tried at the Old Bailey in April 1737 is only one of numerous illustrations of this sort of situation:

one Mary Wilson, a cook maid, was indicted for killing her new-born baby, and during the trial her master outlined some of her previous history:

> Before the prisoner at the bar was taken into my service, we endeavoured to make what inquiry we could into her character. She was recommended to us, as having been a servant to Mr Young, an eminent druggist in Cheapside. I found she had been five years in his service, and that during all that time, she had behaved honestly, soberly, and as became a good servant. On this character I took her into my family, and she continued in my family 13 months, and answered Mr Young's character in every respect. I entrusted her with money for the service of the family, which she always regularly and duly accounted for, and behaved soberly and virtuously, and was a diligent and industrious servant. My health calling me into the country, I left her and a man — a footman, in the house; 'twas during that time that she was seduced by this servant left in the family with her. She having behaved in this manner, gave me less reason of any suspicion that she was with child.[61]

There was, in this case and in many others, much to fear because there was much to lose; shame stood out more boldly against a background of virtuous service. The circumstances of such women were analysed with considerable insight by one of the most able iconoclasts of the eighteenth century, Bernard Mandeville:

> People of substance may sin without being exposed for their stolen pleasure; but servants and the poorer sort of women have seldom an opportunity of concealing a big belly, or at least the consequences of it. It is possible that an unfortunate girl of good parentage may be left destitute, and know no other shift for a livelihood than to become a nursery, or a chambermaid: she may be diligent, faithful and obliging, have abundance of modesty, and, if you will, be religious: she may resist temptations, and preserve her chastity for years together, and yet at last meet with an unhappy moment in which she gives up her honour to a powerful deceiver, who afterwards neglects her. If she proves with child, her sorrows are unspeakable, and she can't be reconciled with the wretchedness of her condition, the fear of shame attacks her so lively, that every thought distracts her. All the family she lives in have a great opinion of her virtue, and her last mistress took her for a saint. How will her enemies, that envied her character, rejoice, how will her relations detest her! The more modest she is now, and the more violently the dread of coming to shame hurries her away, the more wicked and more cruel her resolutions will be, against her self or what she bears.[62]

Eighteenth-century England must have witnessed tens of thousands of bastard births, many of them to servant girls, but it is probable that only a small fraction of these unwanted babies were actually killed. Is it possible to determine why, while many illegitimate babies survived (at least for a while), some were killed, and others abandoned? Were there any distinguishing circumstances in the cases of bastardy which led to infanticide? There is very little evidence which bears directly on these questions but it might be useful to consider some of the conditions which may have been relevant. The choice of infanticide rather than abandonment seems, on the surface, surprising, for the woman who abandoned her baby was less likely to get caught and, even if she were detected, abandonment was not liable to severe punishment. Why, then, did some women assume the large risks of killing their babies when 'dropping' appears to have been an easy option? The answer here may relate to the circumstances which were necessary prerequisites for abandonment. To abandon her baby a mother had to be able to carry the infant some distance from her residence, and she had to be prepared to keep the baby alive until she was ready to move from her place of delivery. And these were two important conditions which many women — particularly servant maids — could not have accepted: they could not risk the baby's cries, which would quickly attract attention, and their circumstances of service would usually not have allowed them the time or the excuse to leave the house at their own pleasure and safely abandon a living baby. For these women, then, if they were intent on concealment, infanticide may have seemed to have been the only appropriate action. 'Dropping', perhaps, was a more common option for women who had not attempted to conceal their pregnancy, or whose attempts had failed.

As for the 'character' of those women who killed their babies, although our considerations are almost entirely speculative, it may be suggested that the more vulnerable women were those who had been particularly respectable, well behaved and reputedly virtuous, and who thus had a good reputation, and probably a relatively secure job, to lose — perhaps a fairly small minority of the female labouring class. In his summing up of the case against Effie Deans in *The Heart of Midlothian*, the king's counsel argued that, 'respecting her previous good character, he was sorry to observe, that it was females who possessed the world's good report, and to whom it was justly valuable, who were most strongly tempted, by shame and fear of the world's censure, to the crime of infanticide'.[63] Women with doubtful reputations, in unsettled circumstances or in casual employments may have envisaged a bastard birth with rather less horror, and consequently have been less motivated to consider concealment at all. As Mandeville argued, though he chose a somewhat extreme case, 'common whores, whom all the world knows to be such, hardly ever destroy their children, nay even those who assist in robberies and murders seldom are guilty of this crime; not because they are less cruel or more virtuous, but because they have lost their modesty to a greater degree, and the fear of shame makes hardly any impression upon them'.[64] It is possible too that, given the heavy demands and burdens of a planned infanticide, it may have been considered more by girls who were relatively determined, resourceful and strong willed, for many women in similar circumstances would not have had sufficient control and toughness to carry out such a difficult task: they would more readily have resigned themselves to their fates. Perhaps, then, the guilty parties included a high proportion of non-fatalistic, non-apathetic women: women who were prepared to take a large risk, and perform a painful act, in order to avoid the derogation of unwed motherhood.

It will be noticed that nothing has been said about infanticide within marriage. Our research, in fact, has turned up fewer than a dozen cases of legitimate babies being killed by their mothers,[65] and in three of these instances the marriage had barely preceded the child's birth. 'It is thought the shame of being delivered too soon after her marriage was the cause of it', reported a newspaper of one such killing.[66] The lack of evidence concerning marital infanticide should not, however, necessarily be seen as a clear indication that it did not exist. Many unwanted babies must have been born to married women — babies who were regarded only as an extra mouth to feed, a distraction from the woman's work, a heavy burden on the domestic economy[67] — and for some of these mothers (and perhaps their husbands as well) the child's death would not have been an unwelcome event. And the causes of such deaths, when they did occur, were not likely to be as closely investigated as those of bastard babies. In a period when forensic medicine was very undeveloped, married women had numerous plausible ways to dispose of their babies if they were determined to do so: a mother could neglect to suckle her infant, which would then die of 'sickliness'; or she could ensure that it was 'overlaid' (smothered while sleeping with the mother), apparently by accident; or she could regret that it had fallen off a table and got a concussion. In all such cases guilt was difficult to prove, for domestic privacy gave some assurance against witnesses, collusion was possible between husband and wife and convincing motives were less easily established than in instances of bastard births. Moreover, accidents and infants' illnesses were common occurrences, accepted hazards of life, and thus were not likely to arouse much suspicion. And little suspicion meant little investigation, and for the social historian little investigation means no solid evidence, only the odd rumour and impressionistic statement. Consequently, we can have no idea of how significant such acts *may* have been. A rationale for marital infanticide can be constructed, and numerous plausible circumstances can be imagined, but since there is virtually no evidence against which such a hypothesis can be tested, any discussion of the issue must remain almost completely speculative.

One final matter. In some societies infanticide has served as an important means of population control, and it might be wondered if this function had any significance in eighteenth-century England. There is little doubt that the farming out of babies to poorly paid and unsupervised nurses often camouflaged a system of virtual infanticide, for many of these nurses clearly understood that an infant's early death would not be much regretted by anyone — by the parents, the community or the local authorities.[68] However, although these practices were fairly prevalent in London, there is little evidence that they were employed to any extent in the rest of the country.[69] As for the direct killing of bastard babies by their mothers, even if our 350-odd cases from this period represent only the tip of the iceberg, and in reality ten or twenty or even forty times this number were actually killed, the effect on aggregate mortality rates would have been negligible, less than that of a severe epidemic lasting for a few weeks. And, as we have said, the importance of marital infanticide is entirely a matter of conjecture. The demographic dimension of infanticide, then, is not open to fruitful investigation. All we can perhaps say is that any significant correlation between infanticide and population control would appear to be unlikely. As J.D. Chambers has argued about pre-industrial Englishmen, 'compared to the natural causes which hovered over them from the moment of birth, death by direct or indirect human agency was of minor significance, a mere eddy on the tide of mortality that swept away the generations'.[70]

In considering the tragic circumstances of infanticide, one is impressed, not only with the brute fact of the snuffing out of a young life, but also with the large burden of private responsibility which was borne by these unwed mothers in situations of almost total isolation. It is just this sort of despairing isolation, the sense of being cut adrift from society, which George Eliot so vividly reconstructs in *Adam Bede*, as Hetty Sorrel wanders uncertainly about the English countryside, at the end, and very briefly, with an infant in her arms. Seldom in these cases were friends or company present to help alleviate the inevitable pain. The women were deprived of consolation and advice, wanting the most basic forms of social solace. Moreover, many of them, at least after the fact, must have been painfully aware of their own immediate responsibility for the baby's death. Unlike those modern women whose abortions are performed by others, with the aid of anaesthetics, in conditions of relative comfort, and whose aborted foetuses are quickly removed from view, eighteenth-century women had to accept full responsibility by themselves, down to the execution of the smallest detail. The concealment, the planning, the delivery, the killing, the disposal of the body, the mopping up: each was usually a solitary act of personal responsibility. The mental scars which these women may have carried with them, especially those who escaped detection or the rigours of the law, are largely a matter of speculation. For those who were punished, though, the suffering was sometimes more visible, as it was with Hetty Sorrel, and as it was with one Mary Mussen, convicted in London in 1757:

> Before she went from Newgate she was almost dead with fear, grief and shame, insomuch that she was obliged to be carried to the cart. In her passage to the fatal tree, she modestly hid her face; when there, behaved with as much Christian fortitude as could be expected. Her body was brought before twelve o'clock to the surgeon's amphitheatre in the Old Bailey, in a country cart; but in what manner otherwise, humanity and decency forbids us to mention.[71]

The extent of and attitudes toward infanticide have varied greatly over the centuries. In many pre-Christian and non-Christian societies infanticide was widely practised as a method of controlling population size, and it was condoned by the value systems of these societies. Infanticide, at least in certain circumstances, was regarded as an appropriate rather than a deviant act, an acceptable and 'rational' way of dealing with unwanted babies.[72] In modern times, of course, unwanted births and unwanted conceptions have been handled in different ways. In industrialized societies facilities for adoption have been established and actively used, and most of these adopted babies have been born out of wedlock. Abortion, which now entails little medical risk, has recently become widely accepted and legally sanctioned as a legitimate means of coping with unwanted pregnancy. As a result of these changes, infanticide — which in principle is hard to distinguish from abortion — is now very uncommon, though the abuse and battering of children, which has sometimes led to death, is very much an immediate social problem. It was in Christian Europe — and most notably during the early modern period — that the disapproval of any physical tampering with pregnancy or birth was particularly severe and the efforts to enforce this prohibition were particularly determined: the authorities of both Church and State were united in their hostility to any sort of interference with the natural course of human generation and were increasingly disposed to take very firm action against the perpetrators of infanticide — more so, it appears, than they had been during the Middle Ages.[73] Religious doctrine and legal pronouncements together offered a vigorous proscription of 'violence' against foetal or newborn life, and the secular courts came to take an active role in the process of punishment. The taboo on infanticide or abortion, then, combined with a strenuous condemnation of 'fallen' women, were especially strong during a period when, given the serious social and economic constraints which women faced, infanticide was still very much an intelligible possible response to unwanted pregnancy. Today, in contrast, infanticide is rare because it is socially inappropriate, for its functions have been superseded by other practices, most notably abortion. For the unwanted babies there has been, perhaps, only moderate change — though adoption is clearly a major innovation — but for their mothers there has been a social transformation of immediate and dramatic relevance to the circumstances of unwelcome pregnancy.

9 *The Game Laws in Wiltshire 1750-1800*

P. B. MUNSCHE

> The time shall come when his more solid sense,
> With nod important, shall the laws dispense;
> A justice with grave justices shall sit,
> He praise their wisdom, they admire his wit.
> No grayhound shall attend the tenant's pace,
> No rusty gun the farmer's chimney grace....
> Poachers shall tremble at his awful name,
> Whom vengeance now o'ertakes for murder'd game.
>
> John Gay, *The Birth of a Squire* (1720)

The game laws of eighteenth-century England are not easily understood.[1] They consisted of a long string of statutes stretching back to the Middle Ages. They were rarely repealed, even when superseded, and, as more than one commentator noted, their wording was often obscure. It was with good reason that Sir Roger de Coverley 'gained universal applause by explaining a passage in the game Act'.[2] But if their meaning was difficult to determine, their intent was not. The purpose of the game laws was to ensure that the hunting of hares, partridges and pheasants[3] was the exclusive privilege of the landed gentry. The legal device employed to achieve this objective was a property qualification. If a person did not possess a certain amount of property, he was forbidden to hunt game, even on his own land. The first such qualification was enacted in 1389. In the aftermath of the Peasants Revolt, Parliament had been alarmed to find that on Sundays and holydays 'when good Christian people be at church' labourers, servants and other members of the lower classes were out hunting game and that 'sometimes under such colour they make their assemblies, conferences and conspiracies for to rise and disobey their allegience'. To prevent these seditious gatherings, the qualification for hunting 'gentlemen's game' was set at 40*s. per annum*. At the beginning of the seventeenth century, the qualification was raised to £10 and after the Restoration there was yet another revision. It was this last qualification Act which was to serve as the cornerstone for the eighteenth-century game laws.[4]

The Game Act of 1671 forbade all persons to hunt game except those who (*a*) had freeholds worth at least £100 a year, (*b*) had leaseholds (for 99 years or longer) worth at least £150 a year, (*c*) were heirs apparent to esquires or persons 'of higher degree', or (*d*) held a royal franchise of park, chase or warren. In addition to increasing the qualification, the Act of 1671 differed from previous qualification statutes in two other important respects. First of all, it did not qualify those with non-landed wealth. Income, however large, from trade, stocks or offices was not in itself sufficient to entitle a person to course a hare or shoot a partridge. This exclusion reflected the Cavalier Parliament's prejudices against 'urban' wealth, but it was to greatly complicate the enforcement of the Act in the following century. Second, the Act of 1671 did not restrict the qualified person's exercise of his privilege to his own land. If he hunted on another's property, he was, of course, subject to the law of trespass, but in 1671 this was not a particularly effective deterrent since the plaintiff in a suit of trespass was denied full costs unless the damages awarded were in excess of 40*s*.[5] For all practical purposes, the qualified sportsman could hunt where he pleased, while the unqualified sportsman could not hunt even on his own land. Thus it was that the game of England became the property, not of the owner of the land on which it was found, but rather of an entire social class, the English country gentlemen.

The problems involved in protecting this newly-acquired property can easily be imagined. Game was to be found not only on the estates of the qualified but also on the commons and farms occupied by those who were not. The penalty of a £5 fine or three months' imprisonment, to which the unqualified were liable if they hunted, was of use only if a witness could be found,[6] and even the corps of gamekeepers which the Act of 1671 authorized country gentlemen to employ could not guarantee that. The answer to this difficulty seemed to lie in preventing unqualified persons from even attempting to hunt — by forbidding them to possess dogs, nets, snares and all other 'engines' used to take game. Gamekeepers were authorized to search for and seize these items and after 1707 possession of them by unqualified persons was subject to the same penalty as hunting itself.[7] Finally, in order to cut off all avenues of escape, possession of killed game by unqualified persons was also prohibited and made punishable by the standard penalty.[8]

Such laws, however, could only be as effective as their enforcement and the responsibility for this rested on the country gentlemen themselves, in their capacities as lords of the manor and as justices of the peace. The basic unit of game law enforcement was the manor, a feudal jurisdiction which was by no means obsolete in the eighteenth century. Most country gentlemen of any substance were lords of at least one manor and it was in this role that they presided over 'the preservation of the game'. For each manor they were allowed to appoint one gamekeeper, who was permitted to hunt game for his master and to search for and seize any guns, dogs or other 'engines' which were kept by unqualified persons within the manor. Searches by gamekeepers were legal even if conducted without a warrant from a justice of the peace.[9] The authority of the J.P. was needed, however, to impose a penalty under the game laws. Until 1671, a minimum of two justices was required but the Game Act halved this, as it similarly reduced the number of witnesses needed for a conviction to one.[10] At the time, this change was more apparent than real, since practically all game cases in the seventeenth century were heard by a jury at quarter sessions, but from the beginning of the eighteenth century persons charged with offences under the game laws were increasingly tried summarily by J.P.s, so that by 1750 few if any suspected offenders appeared at quarter sessions.[11]

For the period covered by this chapter summary trial before a J.P. was the norm. There was, however, another way of proceeding against a poacher; this was by means of a civil suit. Almost all game statutes directed that the fine (if paid) be divided equally between the overseers of the poor of the parish in which the offence was committed and the person who laid the accusing information before the justice. An Act in 1722 gave the informer the choice of either proceeding normally before a J.P. or suing for his portion of the fine 'by action of debt' in any court of record. If he opted for the latter procedure and was successful in his suit, he was entitled to recover not only his half of the fine but also double the costs of the prosecution.[12] The advantage of a civil suit over an ordinary prosecution was obvious: the defendant became liable to a much larger penalty which, if he could not pay it, might confine him to a debtors' prison for a period much longer than the three months which the statute required in this circumstances. But the disadvantage of civil prosecution was equally obvious. The unsuccessful plaintiff had to pay the costs himself and the risk of this greatly limited the popularity of this option among game preservers. Nevertheless, civil prosecution, or the threat of it, could be an important weapon in the hands of country gentlemen determined, and rich enough, to use it.

Such, in outline, was the game law code as it stood in 1750. Its chief characteristic was the distinction between 'qualified' and 'unqualified' persons, a distinction which extended to possessions as well as actions. There was, however, another part of the game laws, one which applied to all persons, qualified or not, and it was on this part that Parliament concentrated from the middle of the eighteenth century until the game laws were completely overhauled in 1831. Indeed, between 1711 and 1831 there were no singificant changes at all in the laws governing unqualified persons; there were no additions to the list of what the unqualified were forbidden to do or possess, nor were the penalties increased. The objective of the game laws — to ensure that the landed gentry were free to pursue the game without competition from the vast majority of the population — remained the same, but Parliament no longer employed the device of the property qualification. Instead it passed laws which limited the actions of all persons, and the penalties imposed were, in most cases, much harsher than those enacted to deter the unqualified from hunting.

The reason for this change in tactics lay in the increasingly commercial character of poaching, a development for which Parliament itself was chiefly responsible. Partridges, pheasants and hares were not only targets for sportsmen; they were culinary delicacies as well, and there was a considerable demand for them in the cities, whose inhabitants were willing to pay for what the law had declared them unqualified to hunt. The demand for game was met by innkeepers, victuallers and poulterers, not all of whom were scrupulous about their sources of supply. Apprehensive that this urban market would encourage violations of the game laws, Parliament made the trade in game illegal. After 1707 every 'higler, chapman, carrier, innkeeper, victualler and alehouse-keeper' was forbidden to buy, sell or possess game under pain of a £5 fine (per head of game) or three months' imprisonment. The ban, however, was widely evaded and in 1755 Parliament was forced to make another attempt, this time forbidding any person, qualified or not, to sell game to anyone, subject to the same penalty.[13] This Act was no more effective than its predecessor in halting the game trade, but it did result in making sellers of game almost completely dependent on poachers for their supply. Poachers had, in effect, been given a lucrative monopoly, the profits from which not only encouraged more persons to violate the game laws but also made it easier for them to pay the fine when they were caught.

As the number and affluence of poachers grew, so did the alarm of country gentlemen, but rather than repeal the monopoly which they had unwittingly given, they attempted to deter poachers with threats of more severe punishment. These new penalties, however, were not intended to apply to all unqualified hunters; it was the destruction of game for the black market which country gentlemen were particularly anxious to stop. A new distinction was therefore created, one between those who hunted at night and those who did not; persons who engaged in the former, it was felt, could have no motive other than a commercial one. Since the late sixteenth century there had been a general prohibition against hunting after dark, and after 1711 this carried the standard penalty under the game laws.[14] In 1770, however, the £5 fine for hunting at night was abolished and replaced by an automatic term of imprisonment ranging from three to six months, in addition to a public whipping.[15] Due to careless phrasing, this Act was widely criticized and three years later was replaced by another which provided for a scale of fines, ranging from £10 to £50 depending on the number of prior convictions. The term of imprisonment if the fine was not paid was kept at three months unless the offender had two or more previous convictions, in which case he might be imprisoned for up to one year (but only after a trial at quarter sessions).[16] There the penalty remained for the rest of the century, but the Night Poaching Acts did not mark the end of Parliament's attempts to deter poachers. In the 1780s one more distinction was grafted onto the game code. It was to prove to be the most lasting of all of them.

In 1784 the newly-formed government of William Pitt introduced a number of new revenue measures, and among them was a tax on hunting. All persons who wished to hunt game were required to take out a certificate on which they had to pay a stamp duty of two guineas. The penalty for hunting without a valid certificate was a fine of £20 or three months' imprisonment.[17] In effect, Parliament set up a new system of qualification, which was to operate independently of the one already in existence. This created a great deal of confusion, but up to a point Pitt's game duty strengthened the old system. The unqualified hunter was now liable to a fine four times the amount imposed previously — indeed, five times, since conviction under the Game Duty Act did not preclude conviction under the regular game laws for the same offence. It was possible, of course, to take out insurance against such an eventuality by purchasing a certificate, but after 1785 the names of all licensed sportsmen were published in the provincial press and few would-be poachers were bold enough to issue such a public challenge. Perhaps more important than the increase in the penalty, however, was the flexibility which this introduced into the old system. The imposition of the heavier fine was not mandatory; it was left to the discretion of the prosecutor whether an offender was to be charged under either, or both, of the qualification systems. It was therefore possible to distinguish in the level of fine between commercial poachers and those who were merely unqualified, without actually having to catch the former hunting at night. This was a point of no small importance, since, as one steward observed to his master, poachers were 'sooner known than detected'.[18] The Game Duty Act, in short, allowed country gentlemen to punish game offences which were 'notorious' as well as those which were proven and that, in a sense, was what they had been searching for since 1389.

No one county in England can be said to be typical of the country as a whole. It was principally due to the survival of an unusually complete set of records that Wiltshire was chosen for this study. Nevertheless, the county has certain characteristics which give an examination of the enforcement of the game laws within its borders wider significance. The economy of Wiltshire in the eighteenth century was not solely agricultural. To the west in the Avon valley, there was a long-established and relatively prosperous cloth industry, providing coarse and fine woollen goods for overseas markets and employment for a considerable number of workers.[19] In addition, Wiltshire contained two distinct types of husbandry. The north-west corner of the county — roughly the area north of a line between Trowbridge and Swindon — was chiefly occupied by small, enclosed dairy farms, worked by their owners and producing cheese and butter. To the south of this line was the 'Chalk country', providing barley, wheat and wool for the market. Here, in contrast to the north-west, most of the land was unenclosed until the beginning of the nineteenth century, and ownership of the land was in the hands, not of many small owner-occupiers, but of a few aristocratic landlords who leased out most of their estates.[20]

Wiltshire, then, was bound to be affected by the two developments which did so much to alter the English countryside after the 1780s: the mechanization of industry and enclosure. The arrival of the spinning jenny in the late 1780s and of the spring loom a few years later was felt not only in cloth towns like Trowbridge, but also on the farms of the small owner-occupier, where income from cottage industry often made the difference between solvency and insolvency. At the same time, the enclosure movement was beginning to transform the landscape of the 'Chalk country'. The bulk of enclosure did not occur until the early nineteenth century, but by 1800 approximately 12 per cent of the common land had been enclosed, and over half of this was accomplished in the last two decades of the century.[21]

Wiltshire appears to have been less affected by the growth in population which the country as a whole experienced in the second half of the eighteenth century. Between 1751 and 1801, the population of England increased by fifty per cent but that of Wiltshire grew by only twenty-one per cent and there are indications that in the 'Chalk country' it actually declined. Behind this moderate growth, however, was a dramatic increase in the numbers of the poor. Between the late 1740s and the mid 1780s, the poor rates rose by 162 per cent and by 1803 they had again more than doubled. Where the per capita contribution to the poor in the late 1740s had been 1.6s., it was 14.2s. in 1803.[22] Even when population growth and inflation are taken into account, there can be no doubt that the ranks of the poor in Wiltshire were swelling at an alarming rate. The reason for this probably lay less in such developments as mechanization or enclosure than in the more traditional problem of inflation. In the second half of the century grain prices doubled. That in itself might have meant prosperity for the countryside, but in the same period farmers were faced with an equally sharp rise in the rents which they had to pay to their landlords. In the 1790s

Wiltshire rents were twice what they had been in the 1760s. Anxious to retain their own prosperous standard of living, farmers attempted to meet these increased charges by holding down wages as well as by other 'economies'. As a result, labourers found it increasingly difficult to pay for the wheaten loaf which was the staple of their diet. As the labourers' standard of living fell, the poor rates inevitably rose, and that in turn provided the farmer with one more reason for not increasing wages.[23] Such was the cruel logic of the age, and it was, sadly, in the condition of its working classes that Wiltshire came closest to being typical of England as a whole.

If Wiltshire was not the promised land for labourers, it nevertheless had its attractions for sportsmen. In the late seventeenth century, John Aubrey had claimed that 'no county of England had greater variety of game' than Wiltshire.[24] While the native sons of other counties would have rejected this boast, Wiltshire was undoubtedly popular with sportsmen, handsomely endowed as it was with covers where game might breed and with open land where it might be pursued. The remnants of the ancient royal forests — Selwood and Chippenham in the west, Savernake, Chute and Clarendon in the east — contained much game, particularly pheasants, and throughout the 'Chalk country' hundreds of partridges could be found sheltering in the stubble left after the harvest. In addition, there were a number of hare warrens — at Bishopstone, Amesbury, Everleigh and West Lavington — which provided sport for the warrens' aristocratic owners and their friends. Coursing, indeed, appears to have been particularly popular with Wiltshire gentlemen; in the 1780s, annual meets were held at which their greyhounds were matched against those from Norfolk.[25] Partridge and pheasant shooting, of course, also had its enthusiasts. Although *battues* on the grand East Anglian scale do not appear to have taken place in Wiltshire in the eighteenth century, a passion for ever larger 'bags' was certainly noticeable in the county after 1750. 'Shooting is become such a trade', observed lord Bruce's steward in 1770, that 'there are but few who have leave [to shoot] that make use of it with any degree of moderation'.[26]

In order to meet this demand for more and more game, landowners engaged in game preservation more intensively than they had in the first half of the century. This did not only — or even necessarily — mean stricter enforcement of the game laws. In the first instance, it meant the concentration of game into certain areas, and thereafter its protection from all hunters except those specifically authorized by the landowner. In some parts of the country, game birds were actually lured into these areas by strategically placed heaps of buckwheat or other types of grain,[27] but of greater importance to the breeding of a large stock of partridges and pheasants was the asylum which the preserves gave from 'vermin', such as rats, hawks, crows, owls and magpies.[28] Shielded from its natural predators, the game population in the woods and warrens of the county flourished, but the very success of game preservation resulted in the creation of a tempting target for poachers and thus in the necessity of expanding the corps of gamekeepers, so that the game could be protected from a more resourceful and tenacious type of predator.

Gamekeepers were appointed by the lords (or ladies) of the manor, a miscellaneous group which in Wiltshire included not only aristocrats like the earl of Pembroke and the marquis of Bath, but also the bishops of Salisbury and Winchester, numerous widows, Oxford and Cambridge colleges and even two almshouses. Not all lords of manors actually appointed gamekeepers and not all gamekeepers actually performed their duties — or were expected to. After 1707 gamekeepers were legally permitted to kill game on the manor for which they had been appointed. Deputation as a gamekeeper, therefore, was a means by which lords of manors might give limited sporting privileges to friends, tenants or other persons they wished to favour. The law frowned on such practices, but they appear to have been widespread in Wiltshire.[29] In addition, gamekeeperships were acquired by lords of the manor themselves in order to extend their sporting rights beyond the limits of their own estates. Thus, in 1773, lord Bruce appointed Francis Dugdale Astley, a neighbouring wealthy landowner, as his gamekeeper for the manor of Collingborne Kingston, and in 1782, the earl of Pembroke was given the deputations to three manors by lord Chedworth.[30] Out of the approximately 250 gamekeepers for Wiltshire manors in the latter part of the eighteenth century, perhaps one-fifth were of this honorary variety. Some may have acted to preserve as well as kill game, but the real burden of guarding the preserves was shouldered by the 200 working gamekeepers.[31]

The gamekeeper's public image in the eighteenth century was a far from complimentary one. Fielding's 'Black George' was a murky amalgam of cowardice and avarice. Many thought that hypocrisy was an even more prominent element in the gamekeeper's character, for it was widely suspected that gamekeepers were among the most active poachers. John Mordant, for instance, advised stewards to keep a particularly 'strict eye' on them since

> many gamekeepers, not only connive at freeholders, tradesmen and unqualified persons poaching in their lord's manors for a half-crown at Christmas, and a jug of ale when they call upon them, but have also the knack of pleasuring market towns ... with game for lucre, by which unjustifiable practice [they] may make near as much *per annum* as their wages.[32]

While some of these charges may have simply been inspired by resentment of the privileges which the gamekeeper enjoyed, it is nevertheless true that he was in an advantageous position to engage in poaching and that he often had a strong financial incentive to do so. Some gamekeepers, of course, were well provided-for by their masters. Robert Mills at Longleat, for instance, received a yearly salary of £40, in addition to livery, a cottage, fuel and medical care. When Robert West, one of Mill's colleagues, retired in 1786, lord Weymouth continued him on full salary until his death ten years later, and after that, provided his widow with a coal allowance.[33] Other gamekeepers, however, were less secure. Salaries of £15 or £20 were not uncommon and out of that they were sometimes required to pay for supplies such as powder and shot, with only a remote prospect of reimbursement by their masters.[34] Charles Bill, lord Ailesbury's steward, concluded that 'the keepers, with all their emoluments, have much ado to make matters meet at the end of the year; and that of all your lordship's servants, their lot is by much the hardest. Their expenses are necessarily great; they certainly have a maintenance, but they can save nothing'.[35]

Suspect as they were, gamekeepers were nevertheless essential to the preservation of the game, since country gentlemen could count on few other persons to inform on poachers. Ideally, they should have been able to rely on their tenants, but the exclusion of the latter from the ranks of the qualified made such cooperation difficult to obtain. Some landowners tried to get around this difficulty — and to save money — by giving gamekeeper's deputations to some of their more 'substantial' tenants, but in this they were hampered by the legal restriction of one gamekeeper to a manor. In addition, many landlords doubted that their tenants had any great enthusiasm for game preservation. These doubts were far from groundless, since farmers did in fact suffer from the rapid growth of the game population during this period. As early as 1757 there were complaints that up to a third of the wheat in fields adjoining hare warrens was 'devoured'.[36] Farmers were also understandably angry at the sight of gentlemen 'riding over their corn fields, breaking their fences, or affrighting their flocks of sheep'. It was in response to the latter complaints that the duke of Queensbury and the earl of Pembroke in the late 1770s set down a code of rules which forbade coursing over the manors adjacent to their warrens before the end of the harvest.[37] Such measures, however, did not answer the farmers' principal complaint, which was 'that we who have bred up a good store of this game, must be wholly denied a little recreation at some of our leisure times, which are not many'.[38] Until they were given some reason to preserve the game, farmers were unlikely to be of much assistance to country gentlemen.

Game preservers in eighteenth-century Wiltshire, then, did not have an easy task. Qualified sportsmen constituted less than 0.5 per cent of the population.[39] Of the unqualified, most had the opportunity to violate the game laws — either as poachers or as receivers of poached game — and little incentive to do otherwise. For the agricultural labourer there was a natural temptation to augment his meagre income by poaching; for the higler, the innkeeper or the coachman, the temptation was equally strong to trade in game on the black market. Farmers, anxious to protect their crops and resentful at being denied a recreation to which they felt entitled, had reason to kill game themselves or at least to cast a blind eye on those who did. Even gamekeepers were perhaps not immune from the lures of the black market. Country gentlemen, however, were not the isolated figures which this description might suggest. Apart from the powers which some of their number exercised as J.P.s, country gentlemen exerted enormous influence as landowners. Clustered around their manor houses were tenants, tradesmen and labourers who, in varying degrees, depended on them for employment, patronage and general prosperity. In a matter as personally important to them as the preservation of the game, country gentlemen were not reluctant to exploit their position.

A landlord's power over his tenants in the eighteenth century was not absolute. Although the trend over the century was toward shorter periods of tenancy, many farmers still held their land under copyhold leases. Even in the case of 'rack rent' farmers, the landlord's influence was always conditioned by the problem of finding an alternative tenant. In matters relating to game, pressure from the landlord generally took two forms. The first was a clause inserted in some leases reserving for the landlord (and his appointees) the exclusive right to kill game on the tenant's land; this was particularly attractive to game preservers in cases where the tenant himself was qualified. Although a comprehensive study of Wiltshire leases has yet to be undertaken, there is some evidence to suggest that such clauses were not common before the 1770s.[40] The other form of pressure used by landowners was simply to demand that their tenants and neighbours respect their wishes in matters relating to game and, in return for this deference, to hold out the prospect of some reward, usually in the form of presents of game. In January 1770, for example, John Neate, a farmer's son, received such a demand from lord Bruce's steward, who had taken note of Neate's frequent coursing on Barton Down:

> His lordship had promised Mr Craven and other gentlemen that the hares should be preserved in that part of the country for hunting, and therefore it is no longer a question between Mr Liddiard and you, but whether his lordship is to have it in his power to oblige his friends ... his lordship says he has always been ready, and still is so, on his part, to show your father any civility as to game or venison, and the only return he can make his lordship ... is not only to forbear destroying, but to preserve the game as far as [is] in his power upon the farm.[41]

Pressure of this kind, however, had its dangers, since the active hostility of a farmer could prove more destructive to the game than an occasional foray into the preserves of his betters. In one case, where a farmer was threatened with prosecution, lord Ailesbury's steward advised his master to drop the matter 'for political reasons — for as he is a qualified man ... he may contrive means to kill every hare and pheasant upon his farm with impunity'.[42] As many eighteenth-century landowners learned, the preservation of game and the preservation of privilege were not always compatible.

While country gentlemen never ceased trying to curb the sporting instincts of their tenants, their primary concern was to protect their game preserves from raids by poachers. A farmer addicted to coursing was a nuisance; poachers, singly or in groups, were a positive threat — one not likely to be removed by the promise of a Christmas basket containing a pheasant or two. 'Those rascals go out ... with arms of some kind', complained lord Bruce's steward in 1765, 'and they know very well. how dangerous it is for any equal number to apprehend 'em, if they should be seen, which makes 'em bold; and nothing but a much superior force would strike any terror into 'em'.[43] Faced with this challenge, game preservers tried to marshal that 'much superior force'. An accurate count of the number of working gamekeepers in Wiltshire is not possible before 1785, but to judge by the Longleat estate accounts, there was a sharp increase in their number after 1750. In 1751 only two gamekeepers were employed by lord Weymouth; a decade later there were five, and the number rose to seven by 1786. Part of this growth was undoubtedly due to the expansion of the estate and the increasingly elaborate nature of an aristocratic sporting establishment. Nevertheless, each new gamekeeper made the task of the poacher that much more difficult, and after 1780 this force was augmented by labourers hired at the rate of 1s. per night 'to watch for poachers' during the hunting season. In the last two decades of the century, almost £260 was expended on 'watchers' for the Longleat estate.[44] How effective they were in deterring poachers it is impossible to know, but it is perhaps significant that during this period the marquis of Bath did not follow the example of landowners in other counties and set up man traps and spring guns in his preserves.[45] Apparently he felt his force was 'superior' enough.

Outside the boundaries of their estates, however, the ability of country gentlemen to command respect for their monopoly on game was less certain. Particularly frustrating to them was the continued operation of the black market in game. In London, in the provincial towns and, indeed, at every turn of the king's highway, game was bought and sold with only scant regard for appearances. More than one Wiltshire gentleman must have found it 'quite shocking at Bath to see at the poulterers at least twenty brace of hares [and] partridges and pheasants without number'.[46] Since few persons other than country gentlemen and their gamekeepers had any interest in ending this illicit trade, game preservers offered rewards to those who would inform on agents of the game trade and their suppliers. They, in fact, made a particular effort to encourage poachers themselves to betray their confederates and customers, offering them not only rewards as high as ten guineas but pardons as well.[47] In 1782 lord Weymouth went so far as to buy one James Price out of the army 'on condition of [his] impeaching a large gang of poachers'.[48] Battling against such enticements, however, was the strong hostility in rural England against any who bore 'the odious name of an informer'. In 1753, for example, it was reported from Marlborough that 'the effigy of one of the inhabitants of that town was hung on a tree and burnt, for informing against several poachers of game'.[49] Several years later, Thomas Bright, a Ramsbury labourer, received a more direct demonstration of the contempt in which informers were held. In January 1767, Bright was caught snaring hares on the Ailesbury estate and in order to escape punishment he informed on a higgler, who was subsequently fined £20 for possessing four hares. According to lord Bruce's steward, Bright

> says now he is very much abused by everybody for 'peaching. That he has a wife and three children and expects another every moment, and that upon applying for relief to Mr Tanner, Mr Jones's bailiff at Axford Farm, who is the [poor law] officer this year, he told him he had done a roguish thing to impeach and would give him no relief, tho' the poor man with tears in his eyes said he had not a bit of bread in the house and did not know where to get any, and he was 50s. in debt to his master ... for rent of his house. He says the people are ready to knock him on the head, not for poaching but for 'peaching.

Powerful as the wrath of the community might be, it was insufficient to deter Thomas Bright. Less than a year later he was back in front of the local J.P. for laying twenty-nine snares, and once again he saved himself by informing on a higgler 'to whom Bright [had] sold a brace of hares at 2s. a piece'.[50] Others too, faced with the prospect of imprisonment, did not scruple at 'peaching.[51] How pervasive the practice was, it is impossible to know, but the clear possibility that it could happen inevitably added another risk to the lives of poachers and their customers, and that, for game preservers at least, was an encouraging development.

Once detected or betrayed, the poacher was usually brought before the local J.P. for trial, but this was not invariably the case. Some poachers simply fled. William Bray, for example, was 'discovered in some night work [and] the penalty being large, he thought fit to decamp towards or to London, leaving his wife and family in St Martin's Marlborough, to whom he has ever since sent subsistence'.[52] In the cases of some others, prosecution was waived in return for the accused man's bond that he would not offend again. In 1776, for instance, four men, caught hunting on the manor of Urchfont, bound themselves in the sum of £100 to the duke of Queensbury not to hunt on his lands in the future.[53] In other cases, however, such a recognizance was deemed insufficient to guarantee a poacher's good behaviour. In 1756, lord Weymouth paid one John Francis 19s. 5½d. for his expenses in searching 'for George Eyres for poaching and having [him] impressed for a soldier'. Since the very detailed Longleat accounts yield no more references of this sort, it seems fair to say that the impressment of poachers was not an everyday occurrence. Nevertheless, during the invasion scare in the autumn of 1779, it was reported that orders had been given to arrest 'all idle young fellows (as well 'prentices, journeymen, lawyers' clerks &c. not qualified) who shall be found with dogs, nets &c.' after the beginning of the hunting season; all persons who handed them over to the nearest recruiting party were to be 'handsomely rewarded ... and [have] their names concealed'.[54] There is no evidence that this was in fact done, but all 'idle young fellows' in the lower classes were vulnerable during a war and some suspected poachers may have suddenly found themselves serving in the armed forces.

Severe as impressment was, it paled beside the landowner's ultimate sanction: unemployment, not only for the poacher himself but for his entire family. In 1767 two men were caught setting snares on the Savernake estate. One of them, 'young Bartholomew', managed to escape, but he left behind a number of relations on whom the wrath of lord Bruce quickly fell. Bartholomew's father (the local sexton, 'now a helpless old fellow with one foot in the grave') and at least three other relatives were threatened with immediate dismissal from their postiions. Bruce even appears to have given orders that they be denied poor relief. Charles Bill, his steward, arguing that it would be 'thought too severe to punish them for the fault of their kinsman', may have managed to get the orders reversed, but the affair did not end there. The bailiff had to promise 'to weed out' the labourers on the estate and pledge that 'the proscribed men' would be kept from re-entering Bruce's employ in the future. Satisfying as such purges may have been to the game preserver, it is doubtful whether they had the desired effect. 'The worst of it is', wrote Charles Bill, 'when a fellow is turned away, he commences [as a] poacher and thief with all his might'.[55] That, in a sense, summarized the weakness of the game preservers' position. Their influence was the product of expectation rather than fear. As long as they could hold out the possibility of some reward, even if it was only a partridge from the first shoot of the season, they had some hope of gaining at least grudging cooperation from their tenants and labourers. 'Condescension' was not a pejorative term in the eighteenth century. But when they exercised their powers of punishment, they cut the bonds of deference and the result was that they endangered the very position they wished to preserve.

On the whole, the measures which country gentlemen took to preserve the game on their estates were preventative rather than punitive. Warnings to tenants, the deployment of gamekeepers and 'watchers' and the resort to recognizances were all meant to deter persons from violating the game laws and thus avoid the necessity of prosecution. The reason for this was, at least in part, financial. Prosecution at the summary level was not necessarily cheap. Clerks' fees at a minimum were 6s. and to this had to be added transport expenses for the informer and the witness. If the accused was imprisoned, there was an additional charge for taking him to the house of correction; if there was a doubtful legal point, a lawyer had to be consulted; and if there was more than one defendant the charges multiplied accordingly. In 1780, the prosecution of just two poachers on the Longleat estate cost £2 9s. 10d.; in 1787, prosecution expenses for the entire estate totalled £37 5s.[56] The extent to which this inhibited the prosecution of poachers depended, of course, on the game preserver's own resources, but in one area of game litigation, the cost of prosecution had a general effect: in civil suits against poachers. The expense of these suits could be very great indeed — one critic charged that they could reach £80 — and was thus beyond the capacity of any but the richest landowners to afford.[57] It was to overcome this difficulty that country gentlemen banded together into 'associations for the preservation of game'.

Game associations first appeared in England in the late 1740s. Their avowed aim was to halt the illicit sale of game and to prosecute poachers. Gentlemen were asked to subscribe to a fund, out of which informers were to be rewarded and prosecutions subsidized — particularly civil prosecutions, which were thought to be more effective than a £5 fine against prosperous game traders and poachers. Unlike Nottinghamshire, Kent and some other counties, Wiltshire did not have a game association at mid-century.[58] It was, however, affected by the activities of a national association, the Society of Noblemen and Gentlemen for the Preservation of Game, which was founded in 1752. This organization concentrated particularly on prosecuting the most prominent violators of the ban on selling game, the London and Westminster poulterers, but it was also active in the provinces. In 1755 at the summer assizes in Salisbury, for example, the Society brought suit against a labourer, Thomas Elkins, for killing a hare and having it in his possession; he was found guilty and the *Salisbury Journal* piously 'hoped it will be a warning to all such unqualified persons'.[59] The national Society, however, led a fitful existence and after the 1750s it was generally left to local associations to bring civil suits against poachers and their customers.

In Wiltshire, this was not done in any continuous or concerted fashion. In 1765, lords Weymouth, Ilchester and Digby joined the duke of Somerset and two other prominent landowners, Henry Hoare and William Beckford, in contributing to a fund 'towards carrying on prosecutions for the preservation of the game', but the arrangement does not seem to have lasted beyond that year. In 1782, another group of Wiltshire game preservers issued a statement warning poachers of their intention to prosecute and offering rewards of two guineas to informers; this association too appears to have been short-lived.[60] Five years later there was yet another attempt. On 13 November 1787, there was a meeting of country gentlemen at *The Antelope Inn* in Salisbury 'to take into consideration the most effectual methods' of preserving the game; it was decided to form an association. Its aims were the usual ones: to prosecute dealers in game and the poachers who supplied them. Members were to contribute from £2 to £20 'in proportion to the number of manors, or extent of property to be protected', and the resulting fund was to finance prosecutions and rewards ranging from two to four guineas. In addition, the association pledged itself to give 'every encouragement to innholders [and] proprietors of stage coaches and wagons, who discourage their coachmen, waggoners, ostlers, horsekeepers and other servants from buying or selling game'. The resolutions of the meeting were duly published, and later that month a Wiltshire J.P., Sir Richard Colt Hoare, noting an information against a poacher in his dairy, added, 'ordered to be prosecuted [by the] Association'.[61] That, however, was the last that was heard of the Wiltshire association. No more meetings were announced and this organization, like those before it, appears to have been quietly abandoned. It is impossible to know how many prosecutions resulted from any of these associations, but considering the high costs of civil suits and the lack of any permanent organization to absorb them, it seems safe to say that the great majority of game cases were tried before local J.P.s.[62]

There were about sixty justices on the Wiltshire bench in the late eighteenth century; aside from a sizeable proportion of clergymen, most were country gentlemen.[63] Singly or in petty sessions, they issued warrants, heard informations and judged the guilt or innocence of those accused of violating the game laws. Unfortunately, records of their activities in this regard are far from complete. In the Wiltshire Record Office almost 450 certificates of conviction under the game laws, dating from 1750 to 1800, have been preserved. When these are compared with the gaol calendars for the period, however, it becomes clear that not all of the conviction certificates have survived. For those imprisoned for game offences in these years, a little less than 30 per cent of the conviction certificates remain.[64] As for those who paid the fine (and thus were not mentioned in the gaol calendars), it is impossible to know for certain what proportion of their conviction certificates have survived, but there is no reason for supposing that it was greater. Assuming, then, that the surviving conviction certificates represent only 30 per cent of the whole, it is probable that there were approximately 1500 convictions for game offences in Wiltshire in the second half of the eighteenth century. The certificates which have survived are not, however, a completely random sample of this total; a large percentage of them originated with a small number of justices. J.P.s were not legally required to report game convictions to the clerk of the peace until 1770 (and even after that, the obligation only extended to violations of the Night Poaching and Game Duty Acts). As might be expected, some J.P.s were more conscientious than others about reporting their convictions, and this seems to have been particularly true of one justice, James Richmond Webb, a country gentleman with an estate near Marlborough. Not only was he responsible for 40 per cent of all the surviving conviction certificates for the last two decades of the century, but a comparison with the gaol calendars indicates that the collection of his conviction certificates is much more complete than is the case for the county as a whole. From Webb's convictions it is possible to form a picture — albeit an imperfect one — of a Wiltshire J.P.'s enforcement of the game laws over a substantial period of time.

We have no way of determining how many persons were brought before Webb between 1780 and 1800 on charges of violating the game laws, but it would appear that approximately 170 of them were convicted by him, an average of 8.5 per year.[65] The surviving certificates provide information about 119 of these cases. Over three-quarters of them involved violations of the laws prohibiting unqualified persons to hunt or possess game; of the remainder, most concerned violations of the Night Poaching Act, with only six persons being convicted under the Game Duty Acts. Not surprisingly, perhaps, a majority of the informers were either gamekeepers or servants of lord Ailesbury, the principal landowner in Webb's district, and in seven out of ten cases the defendant pleaded not guilty to the charge. What is surprising, however, was the ability of those convicted to pay the fine. Over 60 per cent of the defendants were identified as 'labourers'; 13 per cent were 'yeomen'; and the remainder were craftsmen or tradesmen of various descriptions. It would seem fair to conclude from this that a substantial majority were earning less than 2s. a day. Yet, judging by the evidence of the gaol calendars, it appears that three-quarters of those convicted by Webb were able to pay fines which were never less than £5 and sometimes were four times that amount.[66] As lord Bruce's steward noted, 'there is no want of money amongst them'. It is small wonder that country gentlemen and their game associations blamed the black market for the failure of the game laws to deter poachers.[67]

In spite of the black market, however, the number of committals to prison for game offences increased dramatically over the last half of the eighteenth century, as Figure 1 illustrates.[68] The average number of game

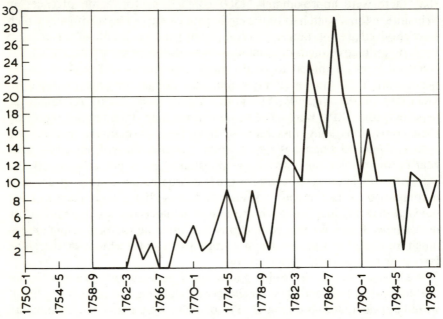

Figure 1: Committals for game offences in Wiltshire 1750-1800 (by season)

committals per year tripled in each decade between 1760 and 1790. This was not repeated in the final decade of the century, but the average in the 1790s was still more than six times what it had been in the 1760s. Part of this increase was due to changes in the law. The Night Poaching Act of 1770 had, in fact, made imprisonment compulsory for those convicted under its provisions. Even after its repeal in 1773, imprisonment was still a likely result of conviction since the fines prescribed by the new Act ranged from two to ten times the standard £5. The Game Duty Act, as has been noted earlier, also increased the cost of getting caught. These legal changes were reflected in the gaol calendars. Approximately half of the committals in the 1770s and 1780s were for offences against these new Acts.[69] The discretionary power of the J.P. could also be used to affect the amount of the fine. Although this power appears to have been most often used to mitigate the penalty (especially in the case of first offenders), there were instances where the poacher was required by the J.P. to pay the costs of the prosecution as well as the fine.[70] These legal devices, however, are only a partial explanation for the increase in committals, since the number of prisoners whose fine was only £5 also grew at an impresssive rate during these years, the yearly average doubling in the 1770s and more than tripling in the following decade.[71] There are at least two factors which might account for this. One was the increase in the number of gamekeepers and 'watchers' after mid-century; it is likely that this resulted in the apprehension of more poachers than would have otherwise been the case. The second factor was that there were more poachers to be apprehended.

There is, of course, no way of knowing for certain whether the actual incidence of game offences was increasing between 1750 and 1800. The 'dark figure' which qualifies any set of criminal statistics[72] is darker than usual in the case of poaching since even the number of convictions can only be estimated. There are, however, some indications that game committals reflected the level of poaching. On the Longleat estate, for instance, expenditure for prosecutions of poachers rose from approximately £23 in the 1770s to £96 in the following decade, and then declined to about half that amount in the 1790s. Even more revealing are the payments to 'watchers' at Longleat. Of the £260 spent on them in the last two decades of the century, over 90 per cent was paid out between 1783 and 1792; thereafter, employment of 'watchers' declined sharply. Payments fell from £20 8s. in 1792 to £7 3s. 6d. in 1793 and then to £1 11s. 10d. in 1794; with the exception of one year (1796), payments stayed at that low level for the rest of the century.[73] The evidence of one estate is not, of course, conclusive proof that poaching in Wiltshire was on the decline in the 1790s, but the correspondence of these figures with the evidence of the gaol calendars is impressive enough to suggest that the trend of game committals was not divorced from that of game offences.

Why there might have been a decline in poaching in Wiltshire at the end of the eighteenth century remains a mystery. Certainly there were strong reasons why this should not have been so. The economic condition of the rural labourer worsened considerably in the 1790s as the average price of wheat rose by almost 40 per cent[74] and as the mechanization of the cloth industry and enclosure began to transform the rural economy. In addition, the ideals of the French Revolution — and the repeal of the French game laws — did not go unnoticed in the countryside. 'Our Gallic neighbours are about to establish the right of farmers and tenants to kill game on their own grounds', announced the *Salisbury Journal* in 1789. 'May our landed interest go and do likewise!'[75] Ironically, it may have been the Revolution — or rather the war which followed in its wake — which provided a respite for game preservers, by removing from the countryside a large body of labourers who might have otherwise occupied themselves by supplying the black market with poached game.

It could only be a respite, however, for by the end of the eighteenth century it was becoming clear that game preservers were engaged in an almost hopeless task. To some extent this had always been the case. Game was too widespread, and the number of persons hostile (or indifferent) to the sporting privileges of country gentlemen were too many for the game laws to have ever been effectively enforced. Indeed, the game laws had actually encouraged the unqualified to kill game by making them the sole suppliers of an expanding and profitable market. In these circumstances, of course, country gentlemen were not powerless. As landowners, they had considerable influence in the rural community, and in their corps of gamekeepers and 'watchers' they commanded the largest law enforcement body in England. As justices of the peace, they also had impressive summary powers and, equally important, the discretionary freedom to apply those powers selectively. In no other endeavour, perhaps, did country gentlemen exhibit the full range of their power and influence as they did in trying to enforce the game laws. It was, however, a demonstration of weakness as well as strength. Had they been less isolated in their efforts to 'preserve the game', recourse to such a variety of incentives and punishments would have been less necessary — or more effective. Yet, to overcome that isolation would have meant sharing 'their' game with farmers and the holders of 'urban' wealth. At the end of the eighteenth century, country gentlemen were still unwilling to do this, but the time was not far off when they would be forced to.[76]

10 *Finding Solace in Eighteenth-Century Newgate*

W. J. SHEEHAN

Of all sufferers ... the fate of the ... prisoner is perhaps the most wretched ... deprived of liberty and rendered totally incapable of relieving himself or doing justice to others ..., shut in prison, there to pine away in want of the absolute necessaries of life ... weighed down with anguish and a load of woe, he meets death with pleasure.

W. Smith, *The State of the Gaols of London* (1776), pp. 1-2

Newgate is a dismal prison ... a place of calamity ... a habitation of misery, a confused chaos ... a bottomless pit of violence, a Tower of Babel where all are speakers and no hearers. There is a mingling of the noble with ignoble, rich with the poor, wise with the ignorant, and the [innocent] with the worst malefactors. It is a grave of gentility, the banishment of courtesy, the poison of honour, the centre of infamy, the quintessence of disparagement, the confusion of wit.

A. Smith, *A Complete History of the Lives and Robberies of the Most Notorious Highway-Men* (1719), I, p.153

As the principal criminal prison for metropolitan London, eighteenth-century Newgate was synonymous with misery, despair, wickedness and death. 'The name of Newgate is a great terror to all', observed a prison officer in 1724, 'from its being a prison for felons ... and the blackest sort of malefactors'; the gaol's sinister reputation was further enhanced by public-spirited citizens who reviled it as a 'tomb for the living', 'the mansion of misery' and even 'Hell itself'.[1] To a great extent this repugnance towards Newgate stemmed from the gaol's squalor and unhealthiness. In warm weather a noisome stench drifted from the prison and permeated the surrounding neighbourhood, forcing local shopkeepers to close their businesses and persuading pedestrians to hold their noses as they passed through the gateway.[2] Physicians flatly refused to enter Newgate and frequently warned that gaol fever, a virulent form of typhus, might spread from the prison and decimate the entire city.[3] Indeed, in

May 1750 this contagion did infect the Old Bailey sessions, killing forty persons, including the Lord Mayor, two judges and several other court officials.[4] In the wake of this disaster, popular revulsion became so intense that in 1767 the City authorities finally razed the ancient prison.[5]

Of course, prisoners in Newgate endured outrageous hardships. Early in the century a series of investigations by the Court of Aldermen and the Common Council, the City's two most powerful governing bodies, revealed that the Newgate officers had grossly mismanaged the gaol and had brutalized, robbed and starved the prisoners.[6] Because of the squalid conditions, there was always sickness in the gaol and it was not unusual for thirty prisoners to perish in a year.[7] Imprisonment in Newgate also had a depressing effect: in 1774 a keeper recalled that he had often observed 'a dejection of spirits among the prisoners ... which had the effect of disease, and many had died broken hearted'.[8] Suffering the vilest sort of *squalor carcercis*, Newgate prisoners welcomed any diversion that would alleviate their suffering. Some of these diversions provided real solace for the prisoners while others, as we shall see, simply added to Newgate's infamous reputation.

Outwardly, Newgate was an unimposing structure. Housed in the ancient gatehouse which spanned the junction of Holborn and Newgate streets near the Old Bailey, the prison stood five stories tall and measured eighty-five by fifty feet. The ancient stone structure dated from the fifteenth century, although it had been completely refurbished after the Great Fire of September 1666. This restoration took almost eight years and cost the City over £10,000, most of which was spent on ornamenting the prison's exterior with Tuscan pilasters, allegorical statues and useless battlements.[9] 'Newgate considered as a prison ... is a structure of more cost and beauty than was necessary', complained one critic in 1734, 'because the gate was erected rather for ornament than use ... and the sumptuousness of the outside but aggravates the misery of the wretches within'.[10]

Newgate's ornate exterior concealed a dismal, warren-like interior that was divided into the 'Common Side' and the 'Master Side'. In turn, each of these sides included various rooms, or 'wards', where the prisoners lived. Newgate was divided into two sides because it was customary for the prisoners to pay the prison-keeper for their lodgings much as if they were staying in an inn or hotel.[11] Affluent prisoners paid as much as £3 6s. 8d. weekly to reside on the Master Side, while all destitute prisoners lodged in the charity wards on the Common Side.[12] The cellar and the north section of the gatehouse together contained nine of Newgate's thirteen common wards, sparsely furnished with hammocks or wooden bunks, cupboards, tables, a fireplace and sometimes a privy. Gross overcrowding often made it necessary for several prisoners to share the same bunk, while those who did not have a bed simply slept on the floor covered with rags and verminous straw, 'huddled like slovenly dogs ... so near the fires that they roasted their asses'.[13] The high prices meant that the Master Side was much smaller, including only five wards, all located in the south section of the gatehouse along with the prison office, the taphouse, several community rooms and the chapel, situated on the uppermost floor.[14]

Adjacent to this south section of the gaol was the Press Yard, a diminutive area which measured only nine by fifty feet and was overshadowed by the keeper's residence and a two-storey building that contained Newgate's most expensive lodgings. Legally, the Press Yard was not part of the prison, but was regarded as part of the keeper's residence.[15] Nevertheless, the keepers did detain prisoners there, providing they were not security risks and could pay exorbitant prices for such luxuries as private rooms, gourmet meals and maid service.[16] In 1717 one prisoner estimated that he had paid enough to rent 'the best house in St James or Piccadilly for several years', but felt that the money was wisely spent because it was 'better to pay the additional cost than to have thieves and villains for your associates and to be perpetually eaten up by insects and vermin' in the other wards.[17] The value of the Press Yard declined considerably after 1726 when the City decided to build new condemned cells there, but the area was still used until 1762 when it was completely destroyed by fire.[18]

Newgate could comfortably accommodate about 150 prisoners at most, but this capacity was rarely observed and the gaol was chronically over-crowded throughout the eighteenth century.[19] The prison records for a typical four-month period in 1735, for example, show that the prison population was never under 275; thirty years later a Newgate keeper told a parliamentary commission that there were always about 250 prisoners in the gaol and that it was necessary for thirty prisoners to occupy a ward measuring only thirty-two by twenty-six feet.[20] This overcrowding became intolerable prior to each sessions when the gaolers from the surrounding metropolitan prisons transferred their serious offenders to Newgate for trial at the Old Bailey. Table 1 illustrates this pre-sessions committal pattern at mid century, while Table 2 shows that it was not unusual for a thousand prisoners to pass through Newgate each year.[21]

Since most persons were committed to Newgate to await trial at the Old Bailey sessions, the length of their imprisonment depended on the court's action. Generally, a prisoner's stay in Newgate lasted from a week to about three months, although there are isolated examples of debtors or State prisoners spending years in prison.[22] Acquitted prisoners had the briefest stay in Newgate because they were discharged *en masse* on the last day of the sessions.[23] On the other hand, the court remanded numerous prisoners back to Newgate pending further action. These remanded prisoners included 'respites' who were appealing their sentences, 'convicts'

Table 1: *Newgate pre-sessions committals 1748-54*

SESSIONS	1748	1749	1750	1751	1752	1753	1754	TOTAL
Jan.	55	103	117	113	118	67	92	665
Feb.	106	128	156	139	124	105	128	886
Apr.	143	123	148	127	134	143	130	948
May	77	85	85	93	73	70	67	550
July	106	167	135	95	108	96	110	817
Sept.	150	190	178	134	148	109	113	1022
Oct.	85	110	69	88	82	123	90	647
Dec.	158	167	139	101	94	113	68	840

sentenced to be transported to the American colonies, 'fines' or lesser offenders who were to be pilloried or otherwise punished and condemned malefactors who were to be hanged at Tyburn. Together with the sundry debtors and State prisoners, these remanded prisoners comprised the more permanent element of Newgate's population and were, of course, most in need of consolation to alleviate the hardships of prison life.

Table 2: *Total Newgate committals 1747-63*

	For sessions		Debtors		
	M	F	M	F	TOTAL
1748-49	641	358	120	28	1147
1749-50	802	306	145	37	1290
1750-51	656	297	165	34	1152
1751-52	593	287	100	26	1006
1752-53	523	282	110	24	939
1753-54	543	329	115	20	1007
1754-55	480	292	109	14	895
1755-56	379	304	134	5	822
1756-57	383	314	124	17	838
1757-58	343	275	118	18	754
1758-59	289	240	104	23	656
1759-60	268	267	108	13	656
1760-61	330	247	95	16	688
1761-62	303	276	85	16	680
1762-63	495	247	91	7	840

These tables were compiled from CLRO, Misc. MSS 185.4, 'Account of Prisoners Committed to Newgate'. This account was presented to the committee considering the destruction of Newgate in 1765 by the keeper, the younger Richard Akerman. In Table 2 the period runs from September to September.

For the most part, life in Newgate was loosely structured and varied little from day to day. The prison day began at 7 a.m. with the loud clanging of a bell and was soon followed by the noisy rattling of keys, locks and leg-irons as the turnkeys unlocked the wards and counted the prisoners. Each prisoner provided his own breakfast before beginning the onerous chores of emptying the chamber pots, carrying water and cleaning the rooms. Following these morning rituals there was little to do until mid-afternoon when the main meal was prepared. Food was usually plentiful on the Master Side where, according to one prison officer, 'the prisoners have every day a very good dinner either roasted or boiled in a decent manner a joint of mutton, veal, lamb or beef'.[24] On the Common Side, however, food was much less abundant and the prisoners had to subsist on the City's meagre ration of bread and water supplemented by charitable donations and the sheriffs' weekly meat supply. 'The food ration on the Common Side', noted one keeper, 'has always been the bare allowance, and would probably be insufficient ... a very poor subsistence, if not for the gifts and help of friends'.[25] In fact, by the end of the century this diet was so inadequate that the keepers were often forced to provide meals out of their own pockets to keep the prisoners from starving.[26]

After lunch the prisoners were again left on their own until about 7 p.m. when dinner was served. Newgate closed at 9 p.m. and the day ended with the turnkeys herding the prisoners back to their wards, 'like drivers with so many Turkish slaves'.[27] All prisoners were supposed to be in bed by 10 p.m. and to maintain strict silence until the following morning but, as we shall see, these quiet hours were rarely enforced and raucous activities continued long into the night.

For centuries the City authorities had formulated regulations to ensure the proper conduct of the Newgate officers but, ironically enough, had never devised adequate ordinances concerning the daily regimen in the gaol.[28] 'From the want of rules and orders, system and method ... with regard to the economy and management of Newgate', complained one sheriff in 1797, 'it has long been felt as a serious grievance by all who have had to contemplate the abuses that have arisen in the gaol'.[29] Fifteen years later, John Addison Newman, a keeper who had served at Newgate for over thirty years, told the City authorities that there was a 'real need for specific, detailed instructions' to regulate daily life in Newgate.[30] Yet, such admonitions notwithstanding, the City did not devise an acceptable set of ordinances until 1816, so that throughout the eighteenth century daily life in Newgate was left to the discretion of the prison staff or, more importantly, to the prisoners themselves who had perfected their own remarkable system of self-government.

Prisoner autonomy had originated at Ludgate, the City's other gate-prison, in the mid fifteenth century and had functioned so smoothly there that in 1633 the Court of Aldermen ordered the Newgate prisoners to establish a similar form of government, 'in much the same manner as at Ludgate'.[31] The prisoners were to hold monthly meetings to discuss their problems and then elect a Steward and wardsmen to deal with any difficulties.[32] We know little of the workings of the Newgate constitution before the late seventeenth century when it becomes obvious that the prison staff callously subverted it for their own benefit. Instead of holding the monthly meetings to elect officers, the keepers simply named four of their favourites, derisively called the 'Partners', who assisted the turnkeys and, too often, brutalized the other prisoners.[33]

The Partners' abuses were especially widespread throughout the 1720s. For example, in 1724 the prisoners complained that these officers had broken into one of the wards and taken the charity money.[34] A few years later the Partners stole the prisoners' meagre bread ration to sell to local merchants and confiscated all gifts from visitors. When a prisoner died, the Partners immediately stripped the corpse and then made the deceased's relatives pay to claim the body for burial. Several prisoners who protested against these outrages were savagely beaten, 'confined in a stinking, wet dungeon ... and loaded with irons'. Such oppressions continued until about 1730 when the City authorities finally curbed the Partners' powers and revived the original Newgate constitution; thereafter, the prisoners managed their own affairs.[35]

There seems little doubt that the workings of the prisoners' government was one of the most notable features of life in Newgate. The elected officers played a major role in enforcing discipline in the gaol by establishing codes of conduct and then sitting as a tribunal to punish those who had violated the rules. In addition, the officers helped the Steward distribute the prisoners' charity funds as well as the rations from the City. In an effort to supplement the prisoners' charity income the officers also collected from each newcomer 'garnish money' which was used to buy candles, coal, soap and other prison supplies.[36] Finally, the officers also named 'swabbers' to supervise the cleaning of the gaol. Since most Newgate prisoners remained in gaol for a fairly short time, there was a considerable turnover among the elected officers; nevertheless, conscientious involvement in prison government must have consumed much of the elected officers' spare time and helped to take their minds off their problems.

For the other prisoners the most frustrating thing about life in Newgate was that they had abundant spare time but few valuable activities with which to fill it. 'In addition to all the other miseries of a gaol', concluded a parliamentary report in 1792, 'innumberable instances might be given to idleness'.[37] Of course the most obvious panacea for the enforced idleness in Newgate was for the City authorities to provide work facilities for the prisoners.[38] In fact, in 1666 Parliament had enacted that all local authorities should make their criminal prisoners do forced labour rather than have them 'living idly and unemployed and becoming debauched ... and instructed in the practices of lewdness and thievery'.[39] As far as the City was concerned, this legislation was ill-timed since Newgate had been badly damaged by the Great Fire. Consequently, it was not until 1684 that a committee was established to implement the provisions of the 1666 Act. This committee viewed the Press Yard in the hope of constructing a workhouse there but rightly concluded that the area was too small.[40] Besides, overcrowding and prisoner transiency also mitigated against any widespread labour in Newgate.[41] Because of these problems, there was no organized prison labour in the gaol until the early nineteenth century, although some prisoners did busy themselves with such handicrafts as leatherworking, woodcarving and tailoring.[42]

The religious services provided by the City to comfort the prisoners and, hopefully, to reform them were also of questionable value. There had been a full-time chaplain, or Ordinary as he was popularly known, at Newgate since the early seventeenth century and it was his duty to read prayers daily, attend all condemned prisoners and preach on Sundays, holidays and once during the week.[43] Attendance at religious services was supposedly compulsory, but since the tiny chapel was unable to accommodate the entire prison congregation, the prisoners were permitted to miss services provided they stayed in their wards and did not create a disturbance.[44] Prisoners who disrupted chapel services were to be ironed, put in solitary confinement and deprived of their food ration.[45] By and large, however, these punishments were rarely enforced and the prisoners tended to be scandalously irreverent during the religious services. They wandered about the gaol and caused so much noise that the Ordinaries had to shout their sermons.[46] In September 1716 the Ordinary protested that several prisoners 'were eating and drinking on the communion table and that it is now broken'.[47] A decade later another chaplain recalled that the prisoners often sauntered through the chapel during services and relieved themselves in a corner so that 'there is always an evil smell'.[48] Such misconduct was common throughout the century and in 1814 prompted one Ordinary to describe himself as nothing but a drillmaster or 'fugleman' because he constantly had to warn disorderly prisoners 'who were continuously laughing, yawning, coughing ... and teasing the other prisoners'. The embittered cleric concluded that 'it would take ten turnkeys to maintain any order in the prison's chapel services'.[49]

Chapel services at Newgate took on an almost carnival-like atmosphere when the Ordinaries preached to the condemned prisoners on the day before their execution. The unfortunate prisoners sat in front of their black-shrouded caskets, while the turnkeys stationed themselves at the chapel entrance where they sold tickets to curiosity seekers wishing to view the morbid spectacle.[50] 'For a full two months we have been hindered from going to chapel', grumbled the prisoners in December 1724, 'because the keepers ... make a show of the condemned prisoners in the chapel by which they raise great sums of money'.[51] Five years later another petition protested that 'several hundred strangers and sightseers' paid to see the condemned malefactors and that the turnkeys made 'over twenty pounds a day' from selling tickets to this 'sideshow'.[52] Although the Court of Aldermen forbade this custom in 1735, it was soon revived and continued into the nineteenth century.[53] In 1750 Horace Walpole wrote that over 3000 people had paid to view a notorious highwayman on the day before his execution;[54] as late as 1814 the Newgate officers estimated that they made almost £300 each year from spectators' fees.[55]

Since outsiders were permitted to come and go at Newgate virtually at will, visitors thronged into the gaol to comfort the prisoners and to supply them with food, money, drink and other necessities. 'A true friend', philosophized one prisoner, 'is one who visits you in prison and labours to help you out, spends more money than sighs and is sorry for your misfortune'.[56] The prisoners' families were the most frequent visitors to Newgate and they often caused pitiable scenes at closing time. 'It was a most pathetic sight', recalled one gaoler, 'to see wives and children ... so distressed at parting'.[57] In 1765 a visiting clergyman recalled how one pregnant wife visited her husband daily 'to supply him with sufficient food and when they were together they rarely talked, but she simply sat at his side; throwing her arms around his neck, they would shed mutual and sympathetic floods of tears'.[58] Rather than be separated from their families, prisoners often tried to conceal their spouses and children in the gaol. In 1815 one prison officer frankly admitted that although he was constantly vigilant for prisoners who tried to hide their families 'many wives do manage to stay overnight'.[59]

On the other hand, affluent prisoners did not have to conceal their families in Newgate but merely paid a fee to have them reside in the gaol. For example, in 1717 William Pitt, the keeper, regretfully informed several prisoners that although he wished to have all their wives in the gaol, there simply was not enough room.[60] However, a few of the wives did move into the gaol eventually and in April 1717 a certain George Flint made an easy escape with his wife's connivance.[61] A decade later a frequent visitor to Newgate was surprised to find that several prisoners on the Master Side had rented a ward for their families.[62] Major John Bernardi had probably the most famous family in eighteenth-century Newgate: he married in the gaol and eventually raised three children in the Press Yard.[63] By 1809 it cost 1s. per night to have a prisoner's family in the gaol.[64]

There were no nursery facilities in Newgate so children had to stay in the wards with the other prisoners. To their credit, the prison staff had recognized the undesirability of this arrangement and removed the children to a local parish workhouse or foundling home. In 1743, however, the wardens of Christchurch parish objected to the increasing number of Newgate children on the parish rolls.[65] The Court of Aldermen heard these objections and then ordered that the parish should be compensated for their trouble and that, in future, only nursing children should be allowed in Newgate and that they should be removed as soon as possible.[66] But despite this order Newgate continued to house a considerable number of children. 'We have a vast deal of difficulty with children', complained one keeper in 1811, 'to know how to dispose of them'.[67] It goes without saying that Newgate was certainly no place for children to grow up for, as one prisoner put it, 'they are quickly debauched'.[68]

In addition to their families, prisoners in Newgate were allowed to keep pets. In 1717 the prisoners actually staged a badger-baiting in the Press Yard and 'caused a great deal of noise and bustle' which so excited the dogs that one of the prisoners was bitten.[69] The City authorities finally prohibited the keeping of dogs in the gaol in 1792 and forbade 'pigs, pigeons and poultry' in 1814.[70]

Literacy was not high in Newgate but a few prisoners did find some comfort in reading. They were especially anxious to keep abreast of current news and paid the turnkeys to deliver the daily papers; some keepers even encouraged this newspaper reading by placing a literate prisoner in each ward to read to the others.[71] Law books were also popular reading and prisoners pored over these volumes in order to prepare their defences, often with the assistance of law students preparing for the bar.[72] There was also considerable inspirational reading, particularly among the condemned prisoners who spent their final hours seeking solace from Scripture and other religious works provided by the City and the Society for Promoting Christian Knowledge.[73] 'Prison was the best school that I ever went to', proclaimed one prisoner, because 'I read the Bible constantly ... and my soul was delighted ... experiencing a spiritual rejuvenation ... and a return to Christian teaching'.[74] But spiritual reading did not always work such a reformation. For example, in April 1680 the City bought two Bibles for the prisoners but had to purchase another pair a few months later and have them chained down because the originals had been stolen.[75] In 1717 a newcomer to the Press Yard was amazed to find that his colleagues were quite cultured, well-educated and read the classics; indeed, it was customary for these prisoners to end the day with a poetry reading.[76] Not all reading material in Newgate was as edifying as Scripture or the classics: in September 1719 the Ordinary complained that a prisoner had completely disrupted chapel services when he circulated a bawdy pamphlet concealed in his hat.[77] The most ambitious effort to increase reading in Newgate occurred in 1760 when Alexander Cruden, an eccentric dissenting preacher, gained permission to establish a school in one of the gaol's vacant wards. Cruden's school flourished briefly but attendance soon declined and he reluctantly decided to discontinue the classes.[78]

Writing materials were available in Newgate so that the prisoners spent part of their time writing letters or petitioning various governmental authorities. Illiterate prisoners frequently hired better educated colleagues to do their writing; the prisoners' friends or the prison staff delivered this correspondence.[79] Newgate had always been a popular subject for Jacobean pamphleteers and this tradition continued into the eighteenth century as several prisoners wrote pamphlets describing conditions in the gaol.[80] In 1729 Major John Bernardi published his autobiography from Newgate and some modern literary critics contend that Daniel Defoe may have written one pamphlet during his brief imprisonment in the Press Yard.[81] The volume of Newgate pamphlets increased considerably by the end of the century and included the prison's most prolific author in the Reverend William Dodd who wrote several pamphlets and a lengthy narrative poem prior to his execution in 1777.[82] At least two Newgate prisoners engaged in serious scholarship: a certain Judge Jenkins wrote a lengthy treatise on common law in the late seventeenth century, while in 1750 Usher Gahagan published several translations of Roman literature.[83]

In the final analysis, however, the most famous literature from eighteenth-century Newgate were the many autobiographies of condemned prisoners. Condemned malefactors recognized the morbid fascination crime held for the popular imagination and often attempted to make a final, dying profit from this appeal.[84] As soon as a condemned prisoner learned the day of his execution, he immediatly turned his final hours to writing his autobiography which would be sold at Tyburn.[85] Often the unfortunate prisoner would seek the help of other prisoners or of the Ordinary of Newgate.[86] This gallows literature had such an enormous appeal that the authentic autobiographies often had to compete with gross forgeries and even the Ordinary's account of the dying man's last hours and final confession.[87] Eventually, the Ordinary's accounts gained the greatest appeal and became one of the most profitable perquisites of that office.[88] Undoubtedly, the most opportunistic of the Newgate Ordinaries was John Villette (1774-99) who not only authored a considerable number of these accounts, but also edited many of the earlier accounts into a four-volume collection entitled *The Malefactors' Register; Or the Annals of Newgate*, published in 1776.[89]

Because Newgate was so small, there was virtually no place for any worthwhile recreation, although the prisoners did use their ingenuity to get some exercise. Early in the century they converted a large room on the second floor into a sort of gymnasium where they jogged and did calisthenics until overcrowding made this impracticable.[90] In addition, prisoners sometimes went up on the prison roof for air and exercise but even this was discontinued by mid century for security reasons and because the prisoners pelted neighbouring buildings with debris.[91] For a price, prisoners could stroll about the Press Yard and some even tried to organize games in the tiny area. 'The prisoners were playing skittles', recalled one newcomer to the Press Yard, 'where there was scarce room to set up the pins'. Another prisoner preferred solitary exercise and arose early early morning to walk a measured course around the Press Yard, 'much as if he had travelled to Hampstead'.[92] But after the completion of the new condemned cells in 1728, the Press Yard became useless because the new building encroached on the small space, cutting off air and filling it with 'ill-smells and dismal noises ... all very offensive'.[93] Of course, the lack of exercise facilities had a debilitating effect on the prisoners' health and morale. 'There should be room for games ... and exercise', warned a physician who visited Newgate regularly late in the century, 'or spirits sink and the body turns to flab'.[94]

All of the diversions we have discussed thus far made confinement in Newgate endurable to some extent, but it would be mistaken to think that they were the primary sources of solace for the prisoners. Instead, like so many other despondent inhabitants of Georgian London, the prisoners turned to excessive drinking in hope of forgetting their troubles. Among the Newgate prisoners, an observer noted in 1725, 'drunkenness is mistaken for intrepidity ... and great fear is overcome by greater drinking'.[95] Throughout the eighteenth century, then, the Newgate taphouse was the centre of prison life where the prisoners could get drunk night after night, or pass their time gaming, smoking or merely conversing.

The Newgate taphouse had always been a perquisite of the keeper's office.[96] In turn, the keeper appointed a full-time tapster who expanded the enterprise into a sort of general store selling coal, candles, soap, tobacco and whatever else was marketable in prison. Usually a turnkey or his wife managed the taphouse, although prisoners sometimes held the post.[97] During the eighteenth century there was increasing criticism of this trade in beer and spirits, but the Newgate keepers were able to devise some disingenuous arguments to justify their role as publicans.[98] In 1730 William Pitt argued that the taphouse played a vital role in the prison's security because the tapsters could overhear conversations in the taphouse 'where escapes were often contrived ... but the turnkeys' wives being constantly there do often prevent their villainous designs by giving timely notice to their husbands'.[99] The keepers also contended that drinking had medicinal value and in 1787 one keeper even suggested that drunkenness improved prison discipline because 'when the prisoners are drunk, they tended to be docile and quite free from rioting'.[100] It would also seem that the £400 annual profit from the taphouse was an important reason for the keeper to encourage insobriety.[101]

Since dishonest publicans were a common nuisance in eighteenth-century London, it is not surprising to find that the Newgate tapsters often resorted to unscrupulous frauds to increase their profits. The City records contain numerous petitions from Newgate prisoners complaining that the tapsters served short measures, diluted the beer or charged exorbitant prices.[102] In 1724, for instance, the tapster refused to allow visitors to bring beer into the gaol; four years later the keeper moved the prisoners out of two wards and converted them into additional taprooms; and in 1729 the prisoners complained that the beer was 'fresh and new without coming to its natural perfection', while the prison spirits were 'intolerable and not half-measure'.[103] The City authorities took harsh action against the Newgate tapster in 1756 after the prisoners had protested that they were forced to pay exorbitant prices for watered-down beer which tasted like 'hog-wash'. When the sheriffs paid a surprise visit to the gaol and confronted the keeper with the prisoners' complaints, he defended the tapster and 'vociferously swore and damned ... stinking and blasting and affirming' that the Newgate beer was as good as any in the City. However, when the sheriffs sampled the beer they agreed with the prisoners and ordered the gaoler and the tapster to compensate the prisoners and promise never to serve such poor quality beer again.[104]

Harrassed by such petty frauds, it is no wonder that many prisoners refused to buy from the prison taphouse and had their friends bring them beer and spirits. It was common to see visitors enter Newgate with several bottles and even kegs under their arms.[105] In 1737 a turnkey recalled that one prisoner had a local public house deliver his beer in a nine-gallon cask.[106] Twenty years earlier Captain James Forster, a prisoner in the Press Yard, had accumulated such a fine assortment of French wines that he was often visited by the keeper, William Pitt. In the end, however, this relationship turned out disastrously for Pitt when Forster made an easy escape after the keeper had got drunk and Forster had sent a turnkey into the cellar for another bottle of wine.[107] Probably the most enterprising attempt to undermine the taphouse came from Joseph Woolan and his wife in 1730. The Woolans first appear in the Newgate records in November 1720 complaining about the diluted beer and high prices in the prison taphouse.[108] The City authorities took no action on their complaint and nothing more was heard from them until 1730 when they converted a derelict ward into their own taphouse and undersold the prison tapster.[109] Business thrived for a while until the keeper demanded that the sheriffs close the Woolans' taphouse and their location was taken over by the prison tapster. Another ingenious effort to supply the prisoners with cheap spirits was made in 1737 when several prisoners set up a still in their ward and distilled a 'new type of liquor, called two-penny'.[110] Again, the keeper's complaints forced the sheriffs to dismantle the still. By the end of the century the Newgate prisoners had organized a sort of co-operative to supply their drinking needs.[111] In each ward the prisoners appointed one of their own number to purchase beer, wine and spirits from local public houses in large quantities to be sold among the prisoners of the particular ward. In March 1788 one of the sheriffs visited Newgate and found 'several kegs of gin', a large supply of wine and numerous casks of beer in one of the wards.

Tippling in Newgate was not confined solely to the prisoners. In 1717 a witness recorded that 'towards evening visitors began to flock in to take a bottle ... and comfort the distressed inhabitants of the place'; among this group were an alderman's son, several wealthy merchants and a local vicar 'all enjoying considerable drink ... and screaming out of the windows for the turnkeys to bring more bottles'.[112] Later that same year a contingent of Jacobite prisoners who had received a royal pardon held a party to celebrate their good fortune and they and their friends got 'drunk for joy'.[113] In 1725 one observer objected that the visitors to Newgate consumed 'seas of beer'; and two years later two prisoners used the riotous drinking in the taphouse to cover the noise they made as they tore a hole in the prison roof and escaped.[114] A prison officer complained in 1737 that visitors often became quite hostile when he tried to close the taphouse and that there was often 'great disorder ... which he feared would prove fatal to the keeper and his servants'.[115] Early in the nineteenth century, one keeper admitted that the visitors often became so drunk and boisterous that the only way he could tell them from the prisoners was to keep the latter in irons.[116]

Drunkenness was so widespread in Newgate by the latter half of the century that the prisoners actually organized a drinking society called the 'Free and Easy Club'.[117] They devised a farcical set of by-laws which proclaimed that the society had been formed to 'promote tumult and disorder' and held regular drinking bouts or 'hops'; the prisoners sold tickets, brought in vast quantities of beer and sometimes even provided music.[118] One keeper counted over 150 revellers at such a party not long before the drinking society was prohibited in 1808.[119] 'No visitors shall be permitted within the prison', ordered the City authorities, 'to dance or be present at any Free and Easy Club or other meeting of persons assembled for the purpose of tippling, singing songs or gaming'.[120]

By and large the tippling in Newgate was convivial and good-humoured but a few prisoners did become violently drunk. On at least two occasions drunken prisoners murdered prison officers; one prisoner later confessed that 'he had no antipathy against the turnkey, and did not know what he did, as being drunk'.[121] In 1756 a certain Thomas Gresham died from injuries sustained in a fight which began in the taphouse but, remarkably enough, the City records contain no other references to such drunken brawls.[122] There are also a few isolated examples of drunken prisoners trying to make mass escapes, but these were unsuccessful.[123] Finally, visitors sometimes complained that they had been robbed or molested by drunken prisoners.[124]

At times the riotous drinking in Newgate became a public nuisance. Pedestrians were often scandalized by the obscenities shouted at them from the prison grates, especially from foul-mouthed women prisoners who 'behaved like a troop of hell-cats ... having no place to divert themselves but at the grate joining the foot passage ... where they swear at passers-by'.[125] Neighbours complained that the loud noise from the taphouse kept them awake all night.[126] In addition, anyone passing near the prison had to be on guard because the prisoners enjoyed urinating out of the windows or dousing unsuspecting cirizens with excrement and dirty water from their chamber pots.[127]

The City authorities had long recognized the unfortunate effects of drunkenness in Newgate, but their efforts to halt these excesses were futile.[128] In 1633 the Court of Aldermen had ordered that only beer could be sold in the gaol but the trade in spirits still flourished.[129] During the eighteenth century a series of statutes aided the City's temperance campaign in Newgate. A 1750 Act prohibited the sale or use of all spirits in the gaols and thirty-five years later the prisons lost their licences to sell beer, wine or ale.[130] According to these statutes, only beer was permitted in the gaols and it had to be brought in by friends; anyone caught smuggling spirits into prison could be prosecuted. Unfortunately, this impressive legislation was laxly enforced at Newgate and the prisoners were able to buy whatever they wanted to drink. 'We cannot restrain them', declared a keeper in 1787, 'and their friends bring in [liquor] in great quantities'.[131] Clearly, drunkenness was the primary source of solace for Newgate prisoners who, as one sheriff put it, perceived a certain 'infamy in living and dying drunk'.[132]

Drunkenness and carousing naturally encouraged other vices at Newgate. Tobacco and pipes were available in the taphouse so that the prison's poorly ventilated wards were choked with evil-smelling smoke. Early in the century one prisoner wrote that the gaol reeked of 'mundungus tobacco' and made him sick to his stomach.[133] The clouds of tobacco smoke were so thick in the taphouse that the prisoners were compelled to compare the drinking room with 'Hell itself'.[134] In November 1763 the Ordinary of Newgate complained that the smoke was so stifling in the chapel that he was unable to hold services.[135] There is also some evidence which suggests that the prisoners' careless smoking may have caused several fires at Newgate.[136] The City authorities had made numerous attempts to prohibit smoking in the prison, but all these efforts were unsuccessful and tobacco continued to be a vital part of Newgate life.[137] Ironically enough, some physicians argued that smoking was helpful because the tobacco smoke tended to counteract the ever-present prison stench which was thought to transmit gaol fever.[138]

Gambling was also widespread in Newgate. In 1717 a prison officer observed that the prisoners in the Press Yard spent most of their time at cards, dice or other games.[139] Visitors to the gaol often noted that the condemned prisoners spent their final hours gambling.[140] In 1784 the sheriffs personally tried to stop all gaming in Newgate and ordered the keeper to confiscate all cards, dice, cribbage boards and 'other instruments of gaming'.[141] A decade later another sheriff recommended that there should be 'no cursing, swearing or obscene language, neither any cards, dice, dominoes, Bumble Puppy, What's Clock or any other game ... played and no betting shall take place ... whatsoever'.[142] Despite these enjoinders, gambling still flourished in Newgate, forcing one keeper to admit dejectedly that 'there is no way to stop them from gaming'.[143]

Illicit sex offered a pleasurable diversion from the rigours of Newgate and enhanced the gaol's notorious reputation. In order to prevent sexual promiscuity, the sexes at Newgate had always been separated and were to come together only during religious services.[144] At the same time, the prison officers were charged to scrutinize all female visitors. In 1617 the Lord Mayor ordered that no female could be alone with a male prisoner 'but only his wife, daughter, sister or niece'.[145] Twenty-five years later the prison officers were warned to enforce this separation rigidly or face harsh recriminations.[146]

Such restrictions notwithstanding, overcrowding and the physical shortcomings of the prison made effective separation impossible so that the sexes intermingled freely. According to a 1643 report presented to the Aldermen, one prisoner had 'eight or nine children by one woman' in Newgate and has recently 'taken another'.[147] During the early decades of the eighteenth century the Newgate turnkeys charged 6d. to allow male prisoners to enter the female chambers.[148] Indeed, in 1702 a group from the Society for Promoting Christian Knowledge visited the gaol several times and was scandalized to see the female prisoners openly soliciting in hope of becoming pregnant so that they could 'plead their belly' and be pardoned by the justices at sessions.[149] In 1766 a visiting cleric was shocked to enter a condemned cell and find the condemned malefactor engaged in 'wanton intercourse' with a female prisoner.[150] Even the chapel was sometimes the scene of the prisoners' sexual misconduct. In October 1720 the Ordinary complained that he had often seen the prisoners misbehave in 'an indecent manner' during divine services; almost a century later another cleric complained that worship was always disrupted when the women entered the chapel because the men made a 'dreadful row by all sorts of lewd hallooing and whooping'.[151] As late as 1818 a member of Parliament visiting the gaol saw 'the grossest scenes in daylight'.[152]

Such debaucheries, of course, meant a profit for the Newgate staff. Early in the century one prisoner observed that it was 'common practice' for whores to pay the officers to enter the gaol.[153] In fact, during the years 1700-1707 William Robinson, the deputy-keeper, virtually transformed the gaol into a brothel. The City authorities learned in July 1702 that Robinson permitted 'lewd women and common strumpets ... to constantly lay there all night'. Moreover, whores were admitted to the condemned cells where they drank all night and 'wished that God would damn King William and Parliament'. When several investigations confirmed these allegations the keeper, James Fell, vowed to halt the excesses and later assured the City officials that Robinson and his cohorts had reformed and were now 'so sensible of their former wickedness ... that they now take the sacrament frequently'.[154]

As it turned out, however, Robinson's rehabilitation was short-lived and in 1707 he was again in business.[155] In July the Aldermen visited Newgate and discovered that Robinson permitted male and female felons to spend all night together for 12*d*. or 'just visit' for half that price. Once again the gaol was swarming with whores and 'these lewd women caused much disturbance because of their drinking and boisterousness at night'. Moreover, Robinson encouraged the prostitutes to bring in stolen goods and actually made the gaol a clearing house for contraband items. When confronted by the City officials, Robinson pleaded his innocence and argued that all these women were, in fact, prisoners' wives. But this story collapsed when several prisoners testified that one 'Polly Pope' must have been a bigamist since Robinson permitted her to spend the night with several prisoners. Robinson lost his post but the whoring continued at Newgate.

When a large number of Jacobites were confined in Newgate in 1717 whores flocked to the gaol. 'The greatest and nicest ladies', remarked one prisoner, 'were very numerous and liberal with their favours'.[156] Eventually most of these Jacobites received a royal pardon but one prisoner's sexual misadventures nearly cost him his freedom when the wardens of a local parish demanded that he be excluded from a pardon because he 'had got a wench with child'.[157] Fearing that the mother and child would end up on the parish, the wardens demanded that the prisoner provide subsistence money for them before being released. In 1729 Thomas Bambridge, the infamous warden of the Fleet Prison, was gaoled in Newgate for murdering several prisoners and was frequently visited by whores before he persuaded the prison tapster, Anne Jones, to move in with him as 'his mistress ... although he quickly dropped her when he was discharged'.[158]

It appears that after 1730 the officers did less procuring, but illicit sex was still available for any prisoner who was willing to pay. As late as the nineteenth century objections were raised concerning the debaucheries in Newgate. In February 1810 one prisoner testified before an Aldermanic committee that he had frequently seen the turnkeys collect a shilling from the 'common women' so that they could remain overnight.[159] Newgate is 'much like a bagnio' concluded another prisoner, while a frequent visitor noted in 1818 that 'the depravity of the Metropolitan prison is proverbial ... since every man is visited by a woman ... for the purposes of general prostitution'.[160]

Undoubtedly the ultimate source of solace in Newgate was money. Wealthy prisoners paid to make their imprisonment tolerable in the Master Side or Press Yard where they enjoyed fine meals, choice wines and other amenities. 'Those offenders who have the means of purchasing the comforts of life', observed one sheriff in 1797, 'scarcely felt ... the horrors of prison or the inconvenience arising from confinement ... finding it so exceedingly ameliorated and softened down by the indulgences which are granted from money'.[161] On the other hand, indigent prisoners in the Common Side were unable to buy a comfortable life. Surrounded by squalor and apprehensive of their future, they tried to forget their troubles in sex, drunkenness and gaming, activities which only confirmed Newgate's notorious reputation.

11 *The Ordinary of Newgate and His* Account

P. LINEBAUGH

The eleventh plate of Hogarth's series, 'Industry and Idleness', depicts the hanging of Tom Idle.[1] A vast crowd is arranged in the shape of a bowl: on one side scores of figures are perched in galleries erected for the hanging, and on the other are soldiers on horseback, their lances held high. In a vast sweep between these extremes, the London throng has turned out for the hanging. Butchers, coal-heavers, bakers, tailors, wounded veterans, gin-sellers, barrow-women, pickpockets and apprentices, infants and the old have come to drink, to fight, to jostle for a place to watch the hanging. Tom Idle leans against his coffin in the tumbril, his face ashen, mumbling from a book marked 'Wesley'. Off to one side his mother weeps. The hangman nonchalantly smokes his pipe atop the gallows. All the rest (save two) either have their attention fixed upon the coming scene at the 'triple tree' or have been temporarily diverted from it by drink, laughter, a punch in the face, by an accident, a theft or a fall. In this immense throng only two people face us.

Powerfully implanted in the front and centre, clothed in old rags, with a face that looks to have seen some of the stormiest winds of human existence and supporting a baby on her strong right arm, is a woman shouting to us to read (and to buy) 'The Last Dying Speech of Tom Idle'. The only other figure in the picture to face us is the Ordinary of Newgate, safely ensconced in a distant hackney coach. Though they are separated by the crowd, the artist's perspective places both in the middle of the picture, the diminutive Ordinary just above the compelling woman in the foreground. Weak and strong, far and near, quiet and loud, the two figures are yet united by the picture's design, united in being alone of the numerous crowd to face us, and united in that these were the only constant commentators at London hangings.

Each, we know, has a version of Tom Idle's history and crimes to tell us. One perhaps will produce ballads and stories; the other bombastic 'awful examples'. One will be remembered below decks, in gin-shops, at the work-bench and under hedges; the other by schoolmasters, vicars and magistrates. However, though their voices might be different, they spoke from the same text. That which the street-seller hawked the Ordinary wrote for each hanging. It was called *The Ordinary of Newgate, His Account of the Behaviour, Confession, and Dying Words of the Malefactors who were Executed at Tyburn.* Those *Accounts* have in part survived and they remain, as they were in Hogarth's day, the principal source of knowledge of hangings and the men and women who were thus 'launched into eternity'. A reading of the *Accounts* must attend to the ambivalent circumstances giving rise to them, an ambivalence that Hogarth has represented for us.

In libraries in England and North America we have been able to locate 237 different *Accounts*, most dating from the first sixty years of the eighteenth century.[2] They record the hangings and biographies of fifty-eight women and 1129 men. Compared to the total of those who in any given year found themselves in trouble with the law, it is not a large number. Nevertheless, these 1187 people do provide us with a 'sample' of the London population that may be as interesting to the social historian as a sample from ducal families or Members of Parliament may be to the demographic or political historian. The *Accounts* have usually been dismissed as eighteenth-century ephemera, with little interest for students of literature and of doubtful value to the historian. A commentator on English rogue literature considered that they 'fall below the dignified historian's horizon line'.[3] A careful student of Henry Fielding says that they are characterized by 'brevity, fabrication, circumstantial realism, luridness and moral pretentiousness'.[4] Dorothy George is less categorical, though guarded, when she writes that the *Accounts* are 'a mine of information on manners and contemporary opinion'.[5] Here we may briefly describe the form of the *Account*, the office of the Ordinary of Newgate, the eighteenth-century objections and attacks upon the *Accounts*, and then argue that much of their contents, especially the biographies of the condemned, can be verified from external sources and that therefore, if carefully used, the *Accounts* can provide an important source of knowledge on many aspects of eighteenth-century English history.

The external form of the *Account* underwent several changes in the century. They were published as folio broadsheets until 1712 when they were enlarged to six folio pages. During the 1720s the type size was reduced and a third column was added, thus enlarging the copy appearing in each. In 1734 the *Account* was again transformed: after that date it was published in sixteen or twenty-eight quarto pages and instead of selling for 2*d.* or 3*d.* it now sold for 4*d.* or 6*d.* From little more than a broadside, it changed over twenty years to become a small pamphlet, a change that reflected both its consolidation as a specific genre and its acceptance by the City officials. At the beginning of the century the Court of Aldermen regarded it as one of the 'undue practices' of the Ordinary. By 1774 the Ordinary was able to write that he had 'at the instance and desire of the public, with permission of the late right honourable Lord Mayor and worthy Aldermen of this city, undertaken to make the behaviour, confession and dying words of such culprits as suffer the execution of the law within my precinct known to the world'.[6]

Despite changes in its size, format and layout, the internal form of the *Account* remained largely unchanged through the century. Usually it contained five sections. The first described the basic facts of the trial — its date, the magistrates present, the members of the two juries and a summary of the proceedings. The second part cited the Biblical texts from which the Ordinary preached to the condemned and provided a synopsis of his sermons. The third and most valuable part of the *Account* contained descriptions of the life and crimes of each of the malefactors condemned to death. The fourth part of the *Account*, a miscellaneous but rich section, contained various items — sometimes a narrative purporting to come from the hand of the condemned, sometimes copies of letters sent to the condemned, sometimes a brief essay on some topic (smuggling or the robbing of country merchants) that the Ordinary (or his printer) thought appropriate. Finally, the *Account* contained a section entitled 'At the Place of Execution' in which was recounted the events of the hanging itself — the condition of the malefactors, the psalms sung or attempts to escape.

The author of this *Account*, the Ordinary of Newgate, was the prison chaplain. Appointed by the Court of Aldermen of the City of London, he held office during good behaviour.[7] He was always a clergyman of the Established Church. During the eighteenth century eleven men filled the office. John Allen held it at the opening of the century but was dismissed for extortion and 'undue practices'.[8] In June 1700 he was replaced by Roger Wykes who served for only a few months before being replaced by Paul Lorraine. One of the most enterprising of eighteenth-century Ordinaries, Lorraine sought to expand the publishing possibilities of his position by printing his sermons, translating compendia of funeral rites, working up biographies of famous malefactors and establishing the *Account* as a periodical and semi-official publication.[9] It was probably these activities and the criticism they provoked from Augustan writers (for there was little else to distinguish him from other Ordinaries) that secured Lorraine a place in the *Dictionary of National Biography*. Lorraine died in 1719 and was replaced by Thomas Purney. Born in Kent in 1695, Purney attended the Merchant Tailors' School and went up to Cambridge in 1711. In 1718 he took Holy Orders and was able to acquire the living at Newgate gaol through the intervention of the bishop of Peterborough. Having published a couple of volumes of pastoral poetry and a 'Heroical-Comical Poem', it is as 'a forgotten poet' that he has been remembered. Amidst illness and other difficulties, he held office until 1727 when he resigned in favour of James Guthrie.[10] Guthrie served longer than any other eighteenth-century Ordinary: if we include the years when Purney was usually in the country leaving the care of Newgate to Guthrie, he served in the office for twenty-one years (1725-46). As we learn from his petition to the Court of Aldermen in 1734, when his behaviour in office was under investigation, Guthrie had formerly held the curacy of Coleman Street and had once been a schoolteacher of Latin. In 1746 the Court found him 'rendered incapable ... by age and other infirmities',[11] and dismissed him on an annual pension of £40. Samuel Rossell, for twenty years the curate of St Giles, Cripplegate, was then appointed Ordinary but he died within a year.[12] John Taylor was elected to the position in 1747 from a field of five candidates, and he officiated for ten years.[13] In 1755 Stephen Roe became Ordinary. His tenure, which lasted until 1764, was distinguished by little except his implacable opposition to the London Methodists and the fact that Goldsmith parodied him.[14] Following Roe's death, John Moore became Ordinary. He held the office for five years, 1764-9, and was followed by John Wood who served between 1769 and 1774. From then until the end of the century John Villette served as Ordinary of Newgate.[15]

Taken together, they were not a particularly memorable group of men. One was a disappointed poet, another a former schoolteacher, one was too fond of drink, a fourth probably senile. None were distinguished and all to some degree had to suffer not only the various tribulations inherent in the position but also the wit, barbs, sarcasm and laughter of more fortunate and gifted men. For all their sham, mediocrity, false posturing and painful attempts to join the witty and allusive world of the eighteenth-century literati, we must nevertheless pay closer attention to the Ordinaries' work as a whole if we are to understand the circumstances that produced the *Account.*

In general the Ordinary's duty was to 'read prayers, preach and instruct the prisoners'. On several occasions, due to neglect or absence, the Court of Aldermen had to issue orders defining the Ordinary's duties more precisely. Thus in 1746 with the translation of Samuel Rossell to the office which under Guthrie before him had suffered from continual abuse, the Court ordered that the Ordinary was to read prayers twice on Sundays and once on all other days of the week, that he was to administer the sacrament once a month and that he was to preach sermons twice a week, on Wednesdays and Sundays.[16] As ecclesiastical livings went in eighteenth-century London, that of the Ordinary of Newgate, while not especially lucrative, nevertheless possessed opportunities beyond its salary and usual gifts, and for that reason there were usually two or three contestants for the vacant office.[17]

Income from the office of Ordinary, like that of most offices in the eighteenth century, was irregular in both form and payment. Complaints and petitions from the Ordinaries for payment of salary in arrears were common.[18] However, the £35 salary from the City constituted only a small part of the Ordinary's income. Besides enjoying the interest on various bequests, the Ordinary had a house on Newgate Street 'clear of the land tax'. The City also granted him two, three or four 'freedoms' to the City each year and these could usually be sold for about £25 apiece. John Howard estimated the total income of the Ordinary at £180 but this sum cannot stand as even a rough guide to the real magnitude of his income.[19] Several Ordinaries exploited the position by publishing various religious guides. Lorraine did this. Samuel Rossell published *The Prisoner's Director* and *The Clergyman's Companion in Visiting the Gaols*. Better money and a bigger market could be had from the publication of individual 'Lives' of notorious malefactors or by cooperating with those who organized their publication. We can have very little idea of the exact extent to which ventures of these sorts augmented the clergyman's income.

In the case of the *Accounts* the situation is different. Here all the evidence suggests that the income deriving from their publication must have been substantial. Usually sold for 3*d.* or 6*d.* and run off in printings of thousands, they enjoyed one of the widest markets that printed prose narratives could obtain in the eighteenth century. In July 1729, in the context of a wider investigation of prison administration in London, the Court of Aldermen appointed a committee 'to inquire into the profits belonging to the Ordinary of Newgate', but unfortunately the committee's report is lost and we must rely on unofficial estimates.[20] When Charles Brown, born in 'Antigua' and schooled in Philadelphia, refused to confess his crimes to the Ordinary he did so on the grounds that the Ordinary would profit by their publication. Brown understood, and the Ordinary did not deny the suggestion, that every number of the *Account* brought the Ordinary £25.[21] When we consider that between four and six *Accounts* were published annually, we can begin to understand why they were of such material importance to the Ordinary. At the same time we can appreciate the intense competition among printers and 'Grub Street biographers' (Addison's phrase) for part of this market. The Ordinary held decisive advantages over his competitors and to understand these we must look more closely at his work in Newgate.

In the eighteenth century three rituals guided the passage out of this world of the condemned malefactor: first, the judge's sentence of death; second, the condemned sermon; and third, the hanging itself.[22] Between the judge and the hangman stood the Ordinary of Newgate, whose unenviable task was to justify the decisions of the former and to lend Christian sanction to the dark work of the latter. 'It is no idle station to be posted at the gloomy avenue of death', wrote Stephen Roe in the introduction to his first *Account*, 'there to receive the unwilling traveller and conduct him in a path, the reverse of what he had chosen to lead through the course of his former life'.[23] Vigilance at every step was required at that station against the ignorance, insolence and outright opposition of those unwilling passengers at 'the brink of eternity's boundless ocean'. In practice, the most important of the Ordinary's duties was attendance upon the prisoners condemned to die. Special arrangements were made to give them the sacrament, and the Ordinary delivered to them (and to the curious who could pay) the extraordinary condemned sermon. He also rode with them across London to their hanging at Tyburn where he led the condemned and the crowd in the singing of hymns. At each of these steps along 'the gloomy avenue' appearance and reality, duty and actuality, clashed, resulting sometimes in a mockery of the ritual, sometimes in disorders, and often inattention or apathy.

On the Sunday before an execution the Ordinary held what a nineteenth-century observer described as 'a grand ceremony'. The prison chapel, 'plain and neat' Howard called it, contained three pews, the middle one being reserved for the condemned. At the head was the chaplain's seat and table. The whole was surrounded by galleries which were filled by visitors and relatives during the condemned sermon. The 'ceremony' began thus:

> The sheriffs shudder; their inquisitive friends crane forward; the keeper frowns on the excited congregation; the lately smirking footmen close their eyes and forget their liveries; the Ordinary clasps his hands; the turnkeys cry 'hush'; and the old clerk lifts up his cracked voice, saying, 'Let us sing to the praise and glory of God'.

This is a description from the 1820s.[24] The available evidence suggests that we should view the scene in quite a different way for most of the eighteenth century. Thomas Purney, in a letter of 1721 to Sir William Steward, the Lord Mayor, asked,

> whether it be proper that the chapel of Newgate should be crowded sometimes with 100 or more strangers though there is no part of the chapel but what is allotted for those who belong to the prison; which strangers as they come purposely to gaze at the condemned men, stand up over each others backs, and often hang on the posts and beams, pointing and whispering, to the confusion of the wretched men to die, and to the preventing of the serious attention: several boards in the chapel being also broken down by the crowding and boisterous behaviour. Besides which there is at the door of the chapel (which is a small place) a continued noise and swearing and rattling of money, the under-turnkeys sometimes not giving strangers the full change, thinking they will not make a noise to

disturb the service, and the strangers also sometimes refusing to pay, having paid 6*d*. or a shilling at the first gate, and being there promised that for that payment they should go into the chapel.[25]

The hanging from 'posts and beams', the 'pointing and whispering' and the 'rattling of money' suggests that the condemned may have played to a different audience from that which the Ordinary wished to set for them.

The disorders and petty acts of individual rebelliousness at sermon and prayer time are well illustrated by the evidence of the Ordinary himself. James Guthrie, who appears to have had a particularly difficult time, often quoted prisoners in order to show 'the stupidity and hardness of these unthinking and miserable creatures'. Christopher Freeman 'behaved very undecently, laughed and seemed to make a mock of everything that was serious and regular' whenever the Ordinary exhorted him to attend to his soul. Cocky Wager 'in time of worship ... fell a laughing'. When Guthrie reproved him 'he begged a thousand pardons, and promised better behaviour in the future; yet at two or three other times he behaved indecently and disturbed all the rest'. Ann Mudd 'used to sing obscene songs, and talked very indecently. For this I reproved her sharply, showing the great danger her soul was in ...'. Joseph Golding 'was a very profane, unthinking hearer, for he could not abstain from laughing'. William Udall was reproved for smiling in chapel and defended himself by saying that he 'had a smiling countenance'.[26] A song, a laugh, 'a smiling countenance', these were not the means to obtain what Guthrie would call an 'interest in the Kingdom of Heaven'. Perhaps not. But in these gestures we might detect a Blakean note:

> And Priests in black gowns were walking their rounds
> And binding with briars my joys and desires.

The Ordinary also faced other infractions of chapel-time solemnities: vandalism, threats and disregard of property. Christopher Rawlings in the days before he was hanged busied himself in chapel by cutting off the tassels of the pulpit cushion. John Cooper spat on the pulpit. Joseph Parker openly insulted Guthrie during the sermon. Thomas Beck threatened to shoot the Ordinary. John Riggleton made a practice of sneaking up to the Ordinary when his eyes were fast shut in prayer and shouting out loud in his ear.[27] Whether these conflicts are seen in the terms that the Ordinary offers us (insolent stupidity against religious attention) or other terms more sympathetic to the condemned men and women, it would be misleading to regard the Newgate chapel as exclusively the setting of two types of theatre: an official theatre of the Church and the courts versus a counter-theatre of the damned. To be sure, those who paid for their seats in the galleries must have encouraged this, and flashes of resentment and defiance may have taken sustenance from an audience. But, if a dark religiosity could not dominate the atmosphere, neither should we imagine in it only the bold, reckless tones produced by rebellious prisoners. An observer in 1741, writing one of the few descriptions we have of conditions in the prison chapel, introduces another important element.

> I was lately induced by a friend to go and see the condemned felons at chapel: I was averse to his proposal, as I knew the sight of so many unhappy wretches would fill my mind with too many melancholy reflections. It is impossible to describe the shock I felt when I viewed the number of miserable creatures, most of them labouring under all the tortures of hunger, nakedness and chains; but I was still more moved to observe the greatest part of them were so hardened by habitual vice, that they showed little concern at their approaching death, or the grief their families poured out at their fatal destiny.[28]

The passivity of the sick and dying, men with their limbs raw from iron shackles, their spirit drained by fever, 'miserably poor and naked', in the Ordinary's frequent phrase, must remind us that in Newgate both the Ordinary's attempts to impose solemnity, silence and order and the condemned prisoners' often successful efforts to resist pale beside the quite and effective work of *pediculus humanus*.

This, the body louse that carries typhus, thrived upon hosts who enjoyed neither bedclothes, running water nor toilet facilities.[29] Epidemic typhus or 'gaol fever' with its symptoms of fever, headache and back and chest rashes was common in eighteenth-century prisons. In April 1725 the prisoners were so weakened by the distemper that they were unable to leave their cells for chapel. This was the period during which Purney was often absent from Newgate, suffering from sickness and seeking recuperation in the country. Although we do not know the cause of death of the other Ordinaries who died in office, we do know that they took precautions — absenteeism was the main one, the carrying of garlands of camphor as they made their rounds of the cells was another.[30] The judges too did what they could to protect themselves, strewing the dock with sweet-smelling herbs and strong vinegar. We know that at the 1750 'Black Sessions' four of six judges (including the Lord Mayor and an alderman) died of typhus contracted in court. Two or three counsel, an under-sheriff and several jurors also died.[31] Sixty-two prisoners died in Newgate that year.

For many, it is true, Newgate was only a station on the way to death three miles away at Tyburn, but for many more it was in Newgate itself that death struck first. In 1726 twenty-one persons were hanged at Tyburn; in the same year sixty-five men and eighteen women, eighty-three altogether, died in

Newgate of the distemper.[32] In the following year fifty-seven died in gaol and fifteen were hanged at Tyburn. In 1729 ninety-two people died in prison. The number of men and women who 'went West' up Holborn Hill across London to Tyburn, there to be 'launched into eternity' amid crowds of hundreds was small in comparison to the number of those who met a lingering, feverish death in the gaol and were silently carried out at night by the sexton and gravediggers of the parish of Christ Church, Newgate.

The fever's deadly presence in the prison must be recalled as essential background to the Ordinary's business of the salvation of souls and to those close negotiations that he conducted with the condemned for their life stories and confessions. From the point of view of the condemned, it may in part explain why the ride west to the 'nubbing cheat' had advantages over the slow expiration that weeks in the stone-cold gaol all but made certain. Light and air, drink and crowds, friends and relatives seen again, friendly and sympathetic words: none of these was to be had with the Newgate typhus when one's only visitor was likely to be the 'dull gownsman' offering a prayer one minute and interrogations the next. The Ordinary's conduct was not without its critics both within and without the prison confines.

The Ordinary of Newgate, and his *Account* in particular, were attacked from four main quarters in the eighteenth century. The most dangerous of these was the Court of Aldermen. Prisoners had for some time petitioned against John Allen, the Ordinary at the turn of the century. In May 1700 their complaints resulted in the Lord Mayor asking the Court of Aldermen to dismiss Allen for his 'undue practices'. Allen was charged with

> extorting sums of money from several convicts ... under pretence of pro-
> curing them reprieves or pardons or else for his pretended solicitation in
> getting prisoners committed for crimes to be bailed out, as also for his
> frequent prevarications in the printing and publishing the pretended
> confessions of the respective criminals that are executed at Tyburn,
> contrary to the duty of his place and function.

Of these charges, we can learn about only the first in more detail. On 30 May 1700 the City Solicitor prepared a brief for an indictment of libel against the publisher of a pamphlet defending Allen. The brief accused Allen of accepting money from a condemned criminal, John Davis, who wished that his name not appear in the *Account* because this would, Davis feared, embarrass his family. In addition, it appears that Allen ran a small business in funeral accoutrements, selling to the families of condemned prisoners. Allen was dismissed as a result of these charges.[33] No other eighteenth-century Ordinary was thus dismissed, though most of the others at one time or another faced charges that they manipulated the position to extract confessions and 'lives' from the condemned.

Sometimes these charges were based upon religious objections. 'Phila-lethes' described the *Account* under Lorraine as 'the very *Index Expurgatorious* of the whole art and mystery of extorting confessions', an art that violated 'the usage of the Primitive Church'.[34] In January 1730 Dr Bedford, the minister at Hoxton, complained to viscount Percival about the scandal of the playhouses and

> also of the scandalous practice of the Ordinaries of Newgate ... in obliging the prisoners to auricular confession, or declaring them damned if they refuse, which is only to extort from them an account of their lives, that they may afterwards publish the same to fill their printed papers and get a penny.[35]

Patrick Demsey, an Irish sailor and a Catholic, would not talk to the Ordinary for religious reasons: 'auricular confession being sacred among these people', John Taylor wrote, 'no discovery of whatever villainies he may have committed is to be come at'. Earlier Taylor had prevented priests from receiving confession from condemned Catholics, and in April 1749 the Secretary of State ordered the sheriffs of London to direct the Ordinary to allow the 'assistance of a person of their communion' in the last days of their lives.[36]

The third quarter from which the Ordinary and his *Account* were attacked was the noisiest, the most insistent and the most dubious. Competing writers of criminal 'lives' could rarely forego firing off shots at the Ordinary. In 1717 one such author accused Paul Lorraine of extracting confessions from the condemned 'for the lucre that is obtained for so doing'.[37] The author of *A Collection of Dying Speeches* in the following year stated that 'by the iniquity of custom it has come to pass that many of those papers called *The Dying Speeches* are not genuine'.[38] Thomas Purney was often accused of fabricating the 'last dying speeches' of the condemned. One of his critics who believed that he had 'studied the chaplain's performances more than any man living' produced a compendium of criminal biographies parallel to the Ordinary's *Accounts* in which the rendition of the crimes and lives of the malefactors was often neglected in favour of blustering attacks upon Purney's literary incompetence.[39]

'I have made many a good meal on a monster; a rape has often afforded me great satisfaction; but a murder, well-timed, was my never-failing resource'. Thus the distressed poet, incarcerated in the Marshalsea for debt, explained to Roderick Random how he made a living. Already by the 1740s such authors had become stock figures. Their deadlines set by hawkers clamouring for copy, forced to curry favours from minor court and Newgate officials, working fifteen hours a day during quarter sessions or hanging weeks, their work consigned them to obscurity with little prospect of moving to politer branches of literature, though their productions soon formed a permanent but anonymous part of a trans-Atlantic plebian culture. Some who took to this work, like Daniel Defoe or George Borrow, would use the experience in their other writings. Others never ascended to more respectable literary heights. Thomas Gent, an Irish apprentice, used to attend the Old Bailey during the 1720s taking notes on the trials and later working up threepenny pamphlets. One of his employers got into some trouble for printing a malefactor's speech attesting to his innocence and reflecting upon the cruelty of his country's laws. Thomas St Legar, 'being a gentleman without wealth', tried to hustle a penny in every way he could without compromising his social pretensions. A footman, a book-keeper and for a time responsible for getting up 'dying speeches' and 'criminal lives' for *The Penny Post*, he later took to smuggling and was hanged in 1745.[40]

Often imitated, occasionally parodied by more talented pens and constantly threatened by those wishing to get a piece of a lucrative market, the Ordinary's *Account* nevertheless held its own amid the burgeoning forms of 'low' literature of the first three decades of the eighteenth century.

In the face of such attacks, the Ordinary frequently published his own defences or counter-attacks in the pages of the *Account*. Paul Lorraine on half-a-dozen different occasions published in the *Account* a pretended-legal, heavily italicized notice of authenticity.[41] James Guthrie, normally not given to publishing his sermons, did so on one occasion, and for a characteristic reason:

> It is not out of any desire to appear in public that this discourse is published; but because many fictitious accounts and pretended sermons, in name of the Ordinary of Newgate, containing nothing but incoherent stuff and jargon, and done by unskilful, ignorant imposters, are impudently carried about the streets.[42]

Less than a year later Guthrie found it necessary to include among the advertisements in the *Account* the following disclaimer:

> There was, two or three weeks ago, in a paper called Parker's Weekly Journal, a paragraph inserted by way of derision calling the chaplain of Newgate a Great B...p of the Cells; and that on a day about that time there was a great stir and confusion in the chapel.[43]

Derided by the men under his charge in Newgate, laughed at by street-sellers and satirized by Swift, Pope, Defoe, Fielding, Gay and Goldsmith, the Ordinary doubtless found all of this hard to bear in a position that offered ways of getting a penny but little food for vanity. In the twilight world of eighteenth-century crime-writing it is impossible to cast a clear light upon the truths, half-truths and fabrications levelled by hack writers against one another and against the Ordinary. But objections of a different order against the Ordinary's insistent questioning arose within the corridors of the prison itself, and to these we must pay closer attention.

From the Ordinary's point of view, the confessions and short biographies of the condemned served two main purposes. Samuel Rossell explained them in 1746. 'The public may therefore depend upon having a plain, concise and ingenuous narrative of these unhappy objects, and almost in their own words, with such discoveries as may be useful to particular persons, or of general use to mankind'.[44] At a time when the administration of justice depended for its effectiveness on either private prosecutions or the betrayals of those caught in its nets, it is necessary to stress that whenever possible the Ordinary sought to transform these confessions into judicial discoveries. It was a nasty possibility, but one that seems hardly ever to have been successful, a dying person having nothing to gain from it. James Hacket, a ship's carpenter hanged for burglary, received a letter from the Revd Woodward of Poplar in the days before he was to hang. 'I shall only add one thing more, which is that it is necessary to true repentence that you discover your partners in your sins'. Hacket refused. Charles Moor, hanged for stealing Sir John Buckworth's books, said that had he known when he was tried 'that he should have died, he would have had one or two [others] with him for fancy, for then he would have made some discovery of persons concerned with him, but now he was resolved to make none', and at the Tree he still remained firm in this resolve: 'What good would it do me to hang three or four men and ruin their families as mine?'. William Elby, alias 'Dun', 'would not come to particulars; and that in general he was willing to confess that he had been very wicked, and that he had committed all manner of sins whatsoever, and that he would confess them to God alone, and ask His pardon for them'. He planned 'to die in charity with the world; which he could not do if he brought any into trouble'. John Crafts, alias 'Rutt', a Holborn butcher, hoped that he could purchase a reprieve by discovering his accomplices, but when he learned otherwise he changed his mind: 'there were some persons concerned therein [his crimes] whom he was desirous to spare'. James Leonard refused to talk to the Ordinary except insofar as he could provide evidence of the innocence of other prisoners in Newgate.[45]

A second purpose to the confession, its 'general use to mankind', was meant to provide legitimacy to the court's decision and justification for the hanging. Here the Ordinary not only liked to have positive statements of guilt to the particular crime, but assent to a general range of immoral conduct. A story was told about Lorraine and a young pickpocket about to be hanged. The Ordinary, expecting to hear the lad explain his sinful life in terms of Sabbath-breaking, lewd women or drink, was surprised when the boy insisted that he was innocent of them all, particularly the first since as a pickpocket he could never afford to miss a Sunday. 'Sirrah', exclaimed Lorraine, 'you must be one of these three, that you must; therefore recollect yourself, set all your faculties of remembrance at work, or I shall be at a loss to say anything of you in my paper. Such case hardened rogues as you would ruin the sale of my paper'.[46] It was true that most of the Ordinaries tagged these biographies with such homilectic commonplaces. Thomas Ellis, for instance, was willing to confess to his indictment and to other crimes but refused to accept the Ordinary's characterization of his life, that it had been for seven years one of fornication and uncleanliness.[47]

Often, as the Ordinary went from cell to cell in the weeks between sentencing and hanging asking for copy for his 'penny scribble', he met silence. Agatha Ashbrook, condemned for the murder of her bastard infant, 'would not give any particular account of her life'. Peregrine Hudley refused to talk to the Ordinary about anything at all. Thomas Sharp 'would not be persuaded to confess the fact for which he was condemned to die'. Terry Gerrard admitted that he was a great thief but refused to offer any particulars. James Falconer 'would not come to any ingenuous acknowledgement of his errors'. John Barnet told Guthrie that 'he had done enough that way, for confess or not confess, they would hang him on Wednesday', and he had nothing more to say. There were others who might perhaps have been willing to talk or even to confess to the Ordinary had they had assurance that he would not publish their words. Mary Allen, for example, 'resolved to give no account of herself, she said, because she would have no speeches made about her when she was dead'. John Edwards, a sailor and sawyer, also would not talk for fear of having his character 'blasted in London'. Nor could Peter Oldfield, a Southwark hatter, accept such violence to his memory; he 'chose not to have his name blasted in papers after he was dead'. These men and women remind us that getting a living by the publication of other people's misfortunes was inherent in the Ordinary's office.[48]

Many cooperated with the Ordinary, and some in doing so sought some small advantage. Several were willing to confess but only if the Ordinary promised to publish their 'lives' before they were turned off. Richard Eades read his 'dying speech' two days before he was hanged. Thomas Osborn used to doodle on the dungeon wall and with the other condemned men 'laughed all the time at each other, while the person was writing what they said'. His 'life' was made available to him a couple of days before he was hanged in 1732. Advance publication was a favour that Guthrie sometimes chose not to grant. Matthew Mooney, for example, 'was very desirous of having the account of his dying behaviour published before his execution, and being answered that it was impossible, replied it was very common in

Dublin, which is plain demonstration that he was a downright Teague-lander'.[49] At a time when just about everything in gaol had to be paid for, and when the arrangements for burial often occupied what resources the condemned had remaining to them, the stories that circulated of the condemned selling their 'lives' should not be dismissed out of hand. An observer in Newgate in the 1730s 'perceived a slender gentleman address himself to one of the criminals in a low tone to this effect, that he would tip him as handsome a coffin as a man need desire to set his a...se in, if he would come down but half a dozen pages of confession'.[50] At the trial of Joseph Parker in May 1740 a Newgate turnkey admitted accepting bribes from prospective authors who wished to gain knowledge of this sharper and coiner.[51] Money was to be had from the words of the condemned; to lay hold of it was grubby work.

From the behaviour of at least some of the condemned it seems clear that the Ordinary was no more to be trusted in the faithful rendition of 'confessions' than the other literary parasites who loitered about the gates and yards of the dungeon waiting the chance to record the 'lives' of these dying men and women. Some prisoners took careful pains to see that nobody should hear (or read) anything about them until after their hanging by withholding information (or manuscripts) until they were actually at the gallows, and then delivering it to trusted friends or to the printer of the *Account*, who between 1720 and 1744 was John Applebee. Francis Woodmarsh gave his paper to Applebee at the gallows. Joseph Cole and Edward Blastock gave their written confessions to friends. James Hall, a failed mealman and Queenhithe barge factor, delivered a sealed confession to Applebee two days before he was hanged in order to correct the errors that had already been published anonymously about his case in the pamphlet, *Matchless Villany*. John Simmott, a Methodist, wrote to Richard Lee, alias 'Country Dick', while he was waiting his hanging day for stealing a wig, a hat and some buttons:

> As many things will undoubtedly be offered to the public relating to your unhappy affair, and which in all likelihood may be mere invention, I give this caution, as one that wishes your soul well. Let no one have anything from you, except the person who prints the dying speeches, or myself; then I am sure you will have justice done you, as well as the public.

The point was stressed in a postscript: 'I must press you to let nobody have anything from you, but the person whose property it is, or myself; because I know the ill usage of some particular persons to men in your unhappy misfortunes'.[52]

If the condemned chose not to confess to the Ordinary there was little that he could do to make them, though the evidence suggests that this little he tried. We recall that John Allen pretended to obtain reprieves or pardons for the condemned in exchange for money and cooperation. There is no evidence that other Ordinaries went to quite that length to obtain confessions. Thomas Farr, a soap-maker and tallow-chandler, was hanged for forging a will. He had heard Wesley preach in Bristol and London and he used to attend the Moravian chapel in Fetter Lane. The Ordinary offered him the sacrament on condition that he confess. Farr called the Ordinary a 'wicked man', and confessed only after the sheriff's officers kept him from sleeping by banging all night on his cell door. Paul Lewis refused to confess. 'When he was moved to Newgate to take his trial, he now and then came up to the latter part of divine service, strutting and rattling his irons, as if proud of the cause in which he wore them. His voice was now and then exalted in a response, or an amen, in a loud and ludicrous tone'. He said of the Ordinary, 'D...n him, I shall lick him before I have done with him, if he don't give me the sacrament'. No sacrament and no confession: Lewis sold his 'life' to another printer. Matthias Brinsden, hanged for murder in 1723, barely lasted out the ten weeks between the date of his sentence and that of his hanging, spending the time insensible with the 'prison distemper'.[53] The Ordinary was accused of letting this man lie in peace only after he cooperated in providing a confession.

Occasionally then the Ordinary had nothing to report. This was not often: it happened in a dozen or so cases in a thousand. More frequently, difficulties arose when he attempted to obtain a full confession and description of particular crimes and cohorts. In assessing the value of the *Account* it is necessary to treat separately its different parts: as a source of historical knowledge it can neither be accepted nor rejected as a whole. The condemned men and women on whom the *Account* depended might cooperate in some questions but not in others. The attempt to find external corroboration for the *Account* is made simpler by examining its three central parts: the description of the trial, the short biographies and the longer narratives.

The Ordinary's recapitulation of the trial is the simplest of the sections to verify from collateral sources. The Ordinary tells us the nature of the offence, its date and the verdict and sentence of the court. In cases of theft, robbery and burglary the Ordinary further specifies the goods stolen and their value. All of this information is contained in the printed *Proceedings* of the Old Bailey and some of it in the indictments filed against each offender and preserved in the Middlesex or City record offices.[54] As one searches through the City sessions files, the Middlesex sessions rolls and the *Proceedings*, the Ordinary's description of the trial and indictment in all their particulars is confirmed. Once caught in the judicial process, a criminal's name found its way into a number of books, calendars, registers, papers and rolls, and half-a-dozen manuscript sources authenticate the

Ordinary's account of the condemned malefactor's trial. The Ordinary tells us that James Ryan was hanged on 3 March 1737 for a highway robbery committed in December 1736. The *Proceedings* for 14-17 January 1737 confirms the date of the offence, the articles stolen and their value. The gaol delivery roll contains the same information on the indictment and on the parchment calendar in which the files are rolled. The gaol delivery book contains his name, the charge against him and the court's verdict. A calendar of indictments will contain his name in an alphabetical listing of all those appearing at the January sessions. His name again appears in the calendar of commitments and in the calendar of prisoners. One might have pursued his name further into the orders of court book and the sessions papers, but as it happens none of the surviving materials in them bear on James Ryan.[55]

In the second main section of the *Account*, that containing the short biographies of the hanged, the problem of verification is considerably more complicated and one cannot expect to establish an absolutely clear case. These biographies are invariably presented in two parts. The first part is short, a dozen or so lines, containing vital information: the condemned's birthplace, his age, his education, his family and a description of his apprenticeship training and work history. The second part appears to be a summary of the Ordinary's conversations with the malefactor. This section was often thin indeed: the condemned refusing to have any truck with the 'great B...p of the Cells' or being 'too miserably poor and naked' to engage in his extended interrogations. Though we do not regard these reports as fabrications, they were (as we have seen) subject to controversy and contention and it may therefore be best to leave them aside and to turn to the more interesting first section, where we can find a wide variety of sources providing external verification.

The Ordinary tells us first where the condemned was born. We have not attempted to verify this information in all of the 1187 cases. We have looked at approximately 150 cases and have found in each some corroborating evidence.[56] This is of two sorts: it may confirm the fact or it may confirm the Ordinary's faithfulness in reporting what he believed to be fact. Thus, in sixty-one cases the *Proceedings* confirm the Ordinary's statement about the place of birth. This does not, of course, prove that John Wigley, for example, was born in Islington as the Ordinary reports. It only shows that either the Ordinary cribbed from the *Proceedings* or that what John Wigley told the clerk of the court he also told the Ordinary.[57] In half-a-dozen cases we have been able to find not only evidence of the Ordinary's faithfulness to what he was told, but evidence of the fact as established in parochial records of baptisms. Thus both the Ordinary and the *Proceedings* state that John Fairbrother was born in Holborn, and the parish registers confirm this fact.[58] Parish records, the most decisive, are hard to use for this purpose because the Ordinary often mistook the age of the condemned by a year or so. Then we have external evidence that falls between these two stools. Where the origin of the malefactor was of some importance to the newspapers, they reported it and have confirmed the Ordinary's *Account* in five cases. In four cases apprenticeship records have confirmed the place of birth. In sixteen cases the parish of residence as identified in the *Account* is confirmed by that inserted in the indictment. In seven cases the birthplace of the condemned has been verified by incidental remarks made in judicial examinations, depositions and confessions. In fifty-one cases the malefactor was buried, as confirmed by parochial burial registers, in the parish in which according to the Ordinary he had been born, though in these cases the possibility clearly exists that the people were buried where they had lived, not where they were born, despite what the Ordinary said. On the whole, then, the external evidence does not contradict what the Ordinary asserts; there is some independent verification of the facts he reports; and what he reports he does so in good faith, and this is more likely to be true than not.

The margin of error in the Ordinary's report of the age of the condemned can be calculated with some precision. In thirty-nine cases we have found external sources — burial records in the main — with which to compare his reports. In thirteen instances the Ordinary's report is accurate to the year; in nineteen cases it is wrong; and in seven cases it is vague. The magnitude of error is small. In twelve of the nineteen cases it is only a year. In three instances the Ordinary's report is out by two years; in one case it is out by three; in two cases by four; and in one case, the only really large error, it is out by seven years. Vagueness or doubt arises from several sources. In the burial books of St Luke's, Old Street, John Riley, James Taylor and Richard Lane are described as 'youths', which compares favourably but imprecisely with the ages supplied by the Ordinary — seventeen, twenty and seventeen.[59] Where confirmation is obtained from apprenticeship indentures some vagueness is inherent in the source, which does not supply the age of the apprentice at the signing of the indenture. For example, John Rogers was nineteen when he was hanged in 1731. His indenture was signed in 1726, making his age then fourteen, which is plausible enough.[60] Jonathan Thomas, an Irish Quaker, was hanged in 1738 at the age of forty-two according to the Ordinary. The birth records of the Friends Historical Library in Dublin record the birth of a Jonathan Thomas in 1698, although the name was common and they may have been different men.[61] Confirmation of the Ordinary's report of the age of the condemned obtained from those burial records reporting the age of the dead does not prove the Ordinary exactly right in every case, but on the whole the records do establish a rough accuracy and another indication that the Ordinary probably reported what he was told rather than inventing his reports.

In seventy-nine cases we have confirmed from sources external to the Ordinary's *Account* his description of the working experience, or an aspect of it, of the condemned men and women. In about two-thirds of these cases the testimony of witnesses as reproduced in the *Proceedings* was the source of corroboration. In some of these the testimony was precise referring, for example, to the regiment in which a veteran fought. In other cases corroboration is vague — 'country work' being one such imprecise designation that appears from time to time. In eleven cases newspapers provide some confirmation. James Hanns, an innkeeper according to the Ordinary, was hanged in 1743. *The London Magazine* referred to him as the former keeper of 'The Rose & Crown' in Paddington.[62] In six cases parochial records bear out the Ordinary's description. John Drinkwater, hanged in 1731, was described by the Ordinary as a glass-sander. The St George in the East burial book listed his occupation as an hourglass-maker.[63] Examinations before the committing magistrate confirm the Ordinary's report in five cases. A customs officer's diary confirmed an occupation in one case.[64] A Surrey apprenticeship list confirmed it in four.

It must be stressed that the problems of verifying the Ordinary's description of the apprenticeship background and work experience of the condemned are not merely technical. Eighteenth-century work relations, apprenticeship, job mobility and job descriptions are difficult topics. Each underwent fundamental changes, and it should be no surprise that surviving evidence on each of them should be patchy, old sources no longer satisfactory and new ones not yet formed. A man might be a butcher, or a woman a needle-worker, and many other things besides. When so much work was casual, seasonal or conducted outside of traditional juridical standards, we may not expect to find written documents attesting to a transaction that in its nature was either fleeting or concealed from the older corporate and guild organizations of work. This makes it all but impossible to verify the Ordinary's occupational history of single malefactors except in such extraordinary and well-publicized instances as, for example, Bosavern Penlez or James Vaux.[65] Nevertheless, it is safe to conclude that the Ordinary did not actually fabricate these brief descriptions of the felon's previous work experience, that the evidence does not seem to controvert the malefactor's own account of his working life and, finally, that where we have been able to find external evidence it confirms the felon's account.

In addition to corroborating the Ordinary's account of the birthplace, age and work experience of the hanged, we have been able to gather some evidence confirming other miscellaneous facts that he reports. In eleven cases the Ordinary's statement about the religion of the condemned has been corroborated by external sources. In fourteen cases the felon's alias has been confirmed, and in six instances the felon's reputation as a particular type of criminal has been verified by external sources. In all of these categories, particularly the last, further instances could be found in the *Proceedings* and the judicial records. Further exemplification of what by now should be clear may perhaps become tedious. In this part of the *Account* the Ordinary reported what he was told (if he was told nothing he said so) and what was reported to him was probably accurate. This, after all, was a section of the *Account* that found no detractors among the Ordinary's critics, either inside or outside the prison.

Turning to the third section of the *Account*, the part that purported to contain extended narratives often from the pen of individual felons, the picture is far murkier. As short prose narratives they share some common characteristics. They minimize the repenting tone that appears elsewhere in the *Accounts*. When they mention formula apologies at all, they are separated in the form of a prologue from the body of the narrative and are sharply distinct from it in style. They provide a chronological account of the crimes committed, catalogued as discrete episodes without an exterior framework of life or work that might place them in a causal order. They are characterized by a great crowding of local detail about each theft: the time of day, the place, the dangers, the others involved (though, unlike pre-trial depositions, without naming the others) and, perhaps with most care, an itemization of the goods stolen with their value. The narratives share with all types of eighteenth-century 'criminal lives' some common rhetorical devices. Thus they are embroidered with canting terms and embellished with short digressions explaining the technique or 'lays' of particular types of thieving.

Despite the appearance that these narratives are identical in form to some fictional accounts of the careers of thieves, total scepticism about them is unwarranted. To invent them would presuppose an imaginative power quite inconsistent with the moralistic blindness displayed by the Ordinary in other parts of the *Account*. The care for detail, the enjoyment in exposing techniques and the absence of a repentant tone all point to a different author than the Ordinary. Fortunately, we need not rely only upon conjectures based on internal inconsistencies in style to reject the claim that these narrative sections were fabricated. Enough external evidence exists for us to conclude that (at least) each narrative must be carefully assessed upon its merits. Where exaggeration, error or embellishment exist, we can attribute these less to the creative talents of the Ordinary than to the bluster or self-deceptions of men and women speaking their last words.

Though probably not typical of the narratives, it was certainly possible that some of them at any rate may have been written by the felons themselves. In 1753 when John Taylor published a pamphlet about Captain

James Lowrey, hanged for killing some of his crew on a Jamaica run, he found it necessary to attest to the authenticity of the account by inviting readers to inspect the author's manuscript that he had received on the morning of the execution.[66] In 1723 Humphrey Angier, a highwayman and keeper of a Charing Cross alehouse, surprised the judges at the Old Bailey by referring in his testimony to a written journal.

> Being asked by the court what was his design for keeping a journal, whether it was upon the perusal of his robberies he might the more particularly repent of them, he replied, no, but it was for his own safety, that he might be more exact when he would have the opportunity to save himself by becoming an evidence.[67]

There were then some very good reasons for keeping such journals, and though none for the eighteenth century has so far come to light, the evidence suggests that they were written, and that we should therefore carefully examine those printed narratives when they purport to be of the malefactor's hand.

Between pages 5 and 13 of the Ordinary's *Account* of 18 March 1741 there is transcribed 'A Particular Account of the Transactions of Mary Young, alias Jenny Diver'. Longer than most 'Transactions' included in other *Accounts* and describing an especially well-known malefactor, it still poses problems of independent verification common to most narratives of the sort. Beginning in an autobiographical voice expressing remorse ('But oh! that they felt the racks and tortures that I now do!'), the narrative voice shifts as the actual transactions are recorded to someone who, apparently, based the story upon conversations with Mary Young. Some external evidence corroborates the story. The crime (and events leading to it) that brought about her final conviction are verified by the *Proceedings*. Three years earlier, according to the 'Transactions', Mary Young was tried under an alias, 'Jane Webb', for pocket-picking and was sentenced to seven years transportation, a fact the *Proceedings* of April 1738 confirms.[68]

According to the 'Transactions', Mary Young put a heavy emphasis upon 'the cant language' or the 'cant tongue' insofar as it was a satisfactory way of assessing the trustworthiness of those she worked with. Cant terms are frequently employed in the 'Transactions'. Cant is born in spoken speech and is used for the purpose of concealment and mutual recognition. There will always therefore be something self-conscious about its appearance in writing. Nevertheless, when it is used in patently literary contexts as in Shadwell's drama, *The Squire of Alsatia*, or in Fielding's story, *Mr. Jonathan Wild*, a reader can recognize particular purposes and conventions at work. For Shadwell, cant is a conventional type of low wit and it is manipulated through the play as a verbal analogue to the moral degeneration of the leading character. In the inverted moral world of *Mr. Jonathan Wild* it becomes a means of conveying the criminality of Walpole's regime and the obscurity of official corruption.[69] When cant is employed at trials or in depositions or in Mary Young's 'Transactions' such purposes are not at play and its users are quick to explain cant terms in these 'foreign' settings. We need not rely on intuition in finding it likely that the cant terms of the 'Transactions' were genuine. Of the eighteen different cant terms found in the 'Transactions', eleven were published for the first time, not having appeared in the three most recent glossaries of cant, viz., B.E., *The Canting Crew* (1698), Charles Hitchin, *The Regulator* (1718), or the anonymous *A New Canting Dictionary* (1725).[70] Of the others, 'tip'd' (gave) and 'smoak'd' (caught) were more than a century old and were probably already slang; 'feme' (hand) had appeared before under another spelling, and 'muns' (a beau) in a different meaning. To note these neologisms does not of course prove that Mary Young wrote her own 'Transactions', but their existence does make it likely that whoever did compose the narrative did so in close association with her, and that a reader would be over-hasty to dismiss the narrative as a fiction or fabrication.

We may examine a second example of the sort of narrative the Ordinary included in the third part of the *Account*. The narrative published in the *Account* of 9 July 1745 of the robberies of John Jeffs and Joseph Lucas, in its extravagance and braggadocio, cries out for scepticism, if not rejection. And yet much of it can be corroborated. On 23 May 1745 James Bye allowed a City magistrate, John Hankey, to compose a 6000-word examination of his confession to some twenty-odd crimes that he had committed with Jeffs and Lucas during March, April and May 1745.[71] A comparison between the two documents leads to two important conclusions. First, both agree not only in the number, form and types of crime that the group had committed, but also in many other incidental details of the group's internal dynamics. Second, the substantial differences in tone and attitude may be ascribed to the different circumstances producing each document. One is the product of a snitch seeking to save his own skin by implicating as many others as he could. The other is the record of men waiting to be hanged and highly conscious of the picaresque and elegiac possibilities of reporting their 'life and crimes' to an external narrator.

Let us note the similarities. First, each confirms that a loosely associated group of about ten men worked in various combinations during the spring in conducting robberies and burglaries. Second, this group had a number of well-established meeting places, the most frequently used of which was in Thatched Alley near Chick Lane. Third, each of the documents stresses that 'they were in no particular specie of thieving, all being fish that came to net', as the Ordinary put it. Further, each suggests that Lucas in particular had developed a novel technique for robbing western coaches as they arrived at Piccadilly: waiting until the passengers were discharged, diverting the coachmen ('always a-dry') with drink, before they then carried off the moveables and portmanteaux. Fourth, each describes the receiving network of the gang with some attention. Their receivers, nine in all, were women with either a matrimonial or conjugal relation to one of the men. The documents agree on the fact that on the whole they could expect no more from their receivers than one-quarter of the value of the stolen goods. Fifth, each document illustrates various types of mutuality practised by the thieves. A cut of their money was sent to any of their friends, or relatives of their friends, who was confined in Newgate.

The contradictions between the two narratives are differences of tone. Joseph Lucas, the Ordinary reports,

> rose to this dignity [Captain General of Thieves] by his merit and success, and pursued his preferment with great skill and address, having a very particular ambition to equal at least the two famous captains of the north-west and south, to wit, Captain Poney, who rules all the north-west part of the bills of mortality, and whose headquarters are near St Giles's. And Gentleman Harry, whose government includes all the south side of the Thames up to Norwood, and from thence by an imaginary line east and west many miles: his headquarters are in the 'Mint, Southwark. Captain Lucas assumed to himself the sovereignty of the City of London, and all the outparts of the same up to Highgate, and so by an imaginary line west about one mile, and eastwards without limit. His headquarters was in the vicinage of Chick Lane. Jeffs, Horton, Greenaway, Rush and about seven thousand more were his obedient slaves.

We know that in the eighteenth century (and earlier) there was nothing particularly exceptional in the practice of thieves taking on military styles of address. Both the 'Minters' and the Waltham Blacks did this.[72] On the other hand, Bye describes the leadership and social relations of the gang quite differently, showing that it was usually Jeffs who pushed open the window sashes, lifted parlour-door latches and organized scouting, stake-out duties and receivers. However, the jurisdiction that Lucas claimed to have been his corresponds to the areas of the crimes that Bye described. These were along the northern roads leading to Smithfield market, places in Holborn and Soho, with only occasional excursions to the west and none to the east.

In assessing such passages, our problem is not the Ordinary's imaginative powers, but his credulity or (even) sensitivity to the fantasies of the malefactors sentenced to die. 'During the triumphant part of his life', the Ordinary tells us of Lucas, 'the ambition and a desire of universal monarchy reigned in his breast'. Lucas often used to 'pleasantly say that there were but three princes fit to reign, viz., himself, Lewis XV and the king of P...a'. The Ordinary comes out rather well in such passages, having the decency at least to repeat the stories of the condemned without making unnecessary intrusions of his own. He had the grace to say of Lucas's hanging, 'dying so well, I may say so heroically good'. To be sure, there is in this some knowing winking between the Ordinary and his reader as they recognize an established convention, but is there not too some respect, even generosity?

Precisely such passages infuriated Francis Place who grew up in the London of the 1780s when the *Account* was not yet only a memory. In the 1820s when he began to put his personal archive in order he commented on the *Accounts* with a bitterness that suggested that at one time he may have quite enjoyed them. 'What must have been the character of the times when an Ordinary of Newgate could authorize the publication of such tales as merry adventures?'. He had no doubt: the remaining *Accounts* still in his possession together with his commentaries were included in his volume entitled 'Grossness'.[73] Unlike the earlier criticisms of the *Account* that were concerned with the possible cruelties of the Ordinary or with his misrepresentations of the condemned, those of Place were qualitatively different, outraged that criminals had even the opportunity to present their crimes as triumphs, jokes or 'merry adventures'. In the first part of the century the Ordinary's platitudes were accepted or considered only pretentious; to Place (and others) they were sufficiently unconvincing as to be thought ironically intended. In a way Place was right. It *is* possible to read the *Accounts* in a 'Satanic light' and to reconstruct the worlds of London crime from them without the moral reference points that the Ordinary posted on all sides. It is even possible to examine statistically much of the information contained in them, finding out about the mobility, ages, family structure, apprenticeship and work histories of a significant portion of the eighteenth-century London working class. We need read them neither as 'awful examples' nor as 'merry adventures' in order to learn from them.

In conclusion, perhaps we may be permitted a comment of our own on the men who made so much of their living by judging and commenting on others. No doubt the Ordinaries of Newgate were pretentious, full of sham and humbug, and that the depictions of them in *Moll Flanders* or *Mr. Jonathan Wild* are substantially correct. Had they been anything else, it would be very difficult to explain the swift success that George Whitefield, Charles Wesley and other, lesser known, London Methodists enjoyed among Newgate prisoners after they began preaching there in 1737.[74] Although the evidence we have found cannot bear out Place's charge that 'the Ordinary used to torture the persons under sentence of death for confessions', it is clear that in order to get up his copy the Ordinary (perhaps with his printer or others) harried and worried, sometimes unconscionably, the men and women waiting to be hanged. Matters that outside prison are trivial can take on great significance in the barren scene and eventless hours of confinement, becoming even a matter of honour over which men will fight. The Ordinary was probably expert at the manipulations made possible by this situation — denying the sacrament to some, interrupting the feverish rest of others, or messing about with what they wanted the world to remember them by in their 'last words'. The Ordinaries belong in both an ecclesiastical and literary oblivion. However, having said all this, one still remembers that the Ordinary was *of* the prison, that none of the English ruling class knew it and the outcasts and victims it contained any better. In the *Social Contract* Rousseau, in justifying the infliction of the death penalty upon a malefactor, remarked, 'such an enemy is not a moral person, but merely a man'. It was merely men and women the Ordinary wrote of. Corrupted, cynical and unable convincingly to establish much of a moral distance in his hours with the condemned, the Ordinary too was but a mere man, very much part of that crowd at Tyburn, and, as Hogarth showed, closer to the ragged ballad-monger than his stiff collar suggested.

Crime and Criminal Justice:
A Critical Bibliography

L. A. KNAFLA

The main problem confronting those who approach this subject is to judge the literature and the available sources, and to assess the former on the basis of the latter. The purpose of this bibliography is to bring to the reader's attention the principal kinds of secondary literature and source materials, and to provide guidelines for their use. While the selection includes more works than is usual in a select bibliography, it is not designed to be definitive. Its origins have been strictly practical, the guiding principles for inclusion being the degree to which the books are used, and the extent to which the author and his students have found particular works useful in both general reading and specialized research in the history of English crime and criminal justice.

I GENERAL WORKS

The more general works relevant to the history of crime and criminal justice are categorized below. They include the most noteworthy of the legal histories, of histories of the criminal law and justice systems, and of prisons and punishments. Works which significantly overlap these divisions are cross-referenced to their first citation: this occurs mainly in categories B-D. Finally, books in this section which contain the equivalent of specialized research on particular periods are also noted in the appropriate parts of Section II.

A The contextual background

The 'context' of crime and criminal justice is a subject that has no beginning, and it certainly has no conclusion. It is defined here as the social and economic theories of crime, the structure of the criminal justice system, the sources for its examination, and the work of allied disciplines apart from law and history that have been, and will undoubtedly continue to be concerned with crime and criminal justice — namely, sociology, psychology and criminology. Since so much has been written in these fields, it is beyond my capabilities to survey the literature in its entirety. My purpose instead has been simply to list, and to discuss critically those works which my students and I have found to be both relevant and useful to the historical study of crime and criminal justice in the early-modern era.

Allen, C.K., *Aspects of Justice* (London 1958). pp.ix + 310; table of cases; index. Chapters 1-3 contain some provocative analyses of the concepts of criminal justice, criminal law and mercy. The concepts are presented in an historical context ranging from ancient times to the 19th century, with considerable emphasis on the 17th and 18th centuries. A useful work for the philosophical and historical thought of criminal justice.

Baker, J.H., 'The Dark Age of English Legal History', in *Legal History Studies 1972*, ed D. Jenkins (Cardiff 1975), pp.1-27. A perceptive essay exploring the problems which have inhibited research into the legal history of the 16th and 17th centuries. The author also assesses the importance of particular manuscript and printed sources, especially reports of cases. Essential reading for advanced research.

Black, H.K. and Brown, D.J.L., *An Outline of English Law* (London 1966). pp.xvi + 274; index. The authors present definitions and explanations of legal terms and subjects for the uninitiated reader. Although the book is superficial it is concise and generally accurate. The relevant sections are those concerned with criminal procedure (pp.21-31), evidence and trial by jury (36-47), the principles of liability (92-100) and the criminal law — crimes against the State, persons and property (101-58). It should be noted that the categories of the criminal law are structured in their modern context, which differs from that of the early-modern period.

Bonger, W.A., *Criminality and Economic Conditions* (Boston 1916; repr. New York 1967). pp.xxiii + 706; biblio.; index. A heavy-handed critique of authors who have written on criminality, and economic and sexual crimes from basically the 16th to the 20th century. The abstracts of their views and interpretations are concisely and accurately drawn. There is a detailed table of contents, but the index is poor.

Cockburn, J.S., 'Early-Modern Assize Records as Historical Evidence', *Jnl of the Society of Archivists*, V (1975), pp.215-31. Maitland, in *The Shallows and Silences of Real Life*, listed among the sins of legal historians their failure to do justice to the original legal record. Dr Cockburn, writing more than sixty years later, conveys a similar message. After surveying the classes of assize records, he assesses the efficiency of the police and justice systems, the problems in interpreting the records systematically and the difficulties of using indictments as evidence. Along the way he explodes some myths about trial procedure and qualifies the use of the assize indictments which he himself is editing (see p.280). Not for the weak-hearted.

Cross, R., *Precedent in English Law* (Oxford 1961), pp.268; table of cases; subject index. A wide-ranging discussion of the case law approach. The sections relevant to the criminal law comprise the definition and analysis of precedent, *ratio decidendi, obiter dictum* and *stare decisis* (chs 1-3). A classic work.

Geis, G. and Bloch, H.A., *Man, Crime, and Society* (New York 1962; 2nd edn 1970). pp.xx + 552; biblio.; index. The authors are interested in crime as an indicator of social change, adapting to changes in man's political and administrative institutions as well as to his own behaviour. A work of criminology that cuts across the boundaries of law, history and sociology, and that is conceived and written in a clear and elegant style. It includes discussions in historical terms of crime and delinquency, social control, criminal law, of the classes of offences (capital and non-capital, rural and urban), criminal justice and capital punishment. The bibliography is excellent.

Hart, H.A.L., *The Concept of Law* (Oxford 1961). pp.x + 261; index. Chs 2-3 contain an analysis of the sources and sanctions of legal authority. Ch. 4 discusses the responsibilities of the citizen to the legal system, chs 5-7 the foundations and basis of its rules and decisions and chs 8-9 the principles, ideals and validity of common law justice. A perceptive general analysis.

Holdsworth, W.S., *Sources and Literature of English Law* (Oxford 1925). pp.247; index. A discussion of the law reports and abridgments of the early-modern period (pp.89-111), and the contemporary literature on pleading, evidence and precedents for criminal actions at common law (116-22, 125-30), in addition to those in Star Chamber (165-75). This remains a useful guide to contemporary legal literature, including that portion which bears on the criminal law.

Maxwell, W.H. and Maxwell, L.F., eds, *A Legal Bibliography of the British Commonwealth of Nations*, vol. I: *English Law to 1800* (London 1955). pp.xvi + 687. Students and instructors regard this as the best working, annotated bibliography for the printed tracts, reports and abridgments, and important specialized histories and monographs published to the early 1950s. The appropriate sections cover the criminal law and procedure (ch. 9), the central courts (ch. 11) and local jurisdictions (ch. 14). This work is not, however, complete.

Quinney, R., *The Social Reality of Crime* (Boston 1970). pp.x + 339; indices of names, subjects. A study of contemporary crime that has historical relevance. This is a cogent and far-ranging exposition of how criminal definitions are formulated and applied, and how individuals and group behaviour patterns develop in response to those definitions. Considerable historical perspective is given.

Radzinowicz, L., *Ideology and Crime: A Study of Crime in its Social and Historical Context* (New York 1966). pp.xii + 152; biblio.; index. The most succinct statement of the school of 'scientific criminology', written by the founder of the Cambridge Institute of Criminology.

Schoolbred, C.F., *The Administration of Criminal Justice in England and Wales* (Oxford 1966). pp.xxii + 158; tables, appendices, index. An elemental sketch, useful to introductory students, of the structure of the criminal courts and the criminal justice system. Appendix II is a brief glossary of legal terms in criminal law.

Silver, A., 'The Demand for Order in Civil Society: A Review of Some Themes in the History of Urban Crime, Police and Riot', in *The Police: Six Sociological Essays*, ed D.J. Bordua (New York 1967), pp.1-24. An assessment of rioters, professional criminals, the police and the problem of law and order in their historical and sociological perspectives. An intriguing article.

Winfield, P.H., *The Chief Sources of English Legal History* (Cambridge, Mass 1925; repr. New York n.d.). pp.xvii + 374; index. This work contains helpful descriptions of contemporary reports and abridgments of the period (pp.183-251), and of contemporary textbooks and books of practice on the criminal law (324-40). It overlaps with Holdsworth (above p.271), but discusses critically some additional treatises and reports.

B Legal Histories

A considerable number of legal histories, and even more 'legal and constitutional' histories of England, have been written since the late 19th century. Generally speaking, most legal histories are weak in the field of criminal law. Nonetheless, they have been used, and will undoubtedly continue to be consulted by students, and experts in other fields, for information on the criminal justice system. My purpose here is to list the major legal (and not the legal-constitutional) histories, and to discuss their accounts of the criminal justice system. The general reader should be aware of the fact that only a limited amount of information can be garnered on this subject from works such as these. However, there are some important exceptions that have been duly noted, exceptions which relate to the history of particular legal institutions prominent in the history of the criminal law.

Allen, C.K., *Law in the Making* (Oxford 1927; 7th edn 1964). pp.xl + 649; index. Contains thought-provoking discussions of legal principles in their historical development. Particularly relevant are those chapters concerning custom (2), precedent (3-4) and legislation (6). The book is well liked by students.

Baker, J.H., *An Introduction to English Legal History* (London 1972). pp.xxi + 330; tables of statutes, cases; index. The most recent survey of English legal history, it includes a concise statement of the concepts of crime and tort, of the substantive law of crimes (ch. 22), and of the forms of action, and science of pleading in civil and criminal causes (chs 9-10). This is a useful teaching aid. The index, however, is confusing.

Beard, C.A., *The Office of Justice of the Peace in England in its Origin and Development* (New York 1904; repr. 1967). pp.184; appendices. The book includes an account of the Tudor legislation on the J.P.s (pp.74-113), their relations with the central courts and the Privy Council in the 16th and 17th centuries (114-38), the reform of the office in the 1590s (139-57) and the state of legal process in the courts of quarter sessions in the 17th century (158-64). Based on a fragmentary knowledge of the sources, extremely biased in the powers and authority alleged to the J.P.s and inadequate in its knowledge of crime and criminal justice.

Cockburn, J.S., *A History of English Assizes 1558-1714* (Cambridge 1971). pp.xviii + 357; appendices; biblio.; index. The first full-length study of assizes in the early-modern period. Relevant chapters cover the structure of the assize circuits (2), preliminary proceedings (4) and the trial of criminal actions (6). Also important is the account of the role of assizes in local government (8). The work is based on the assize records, a wide range of other manuscript sources and the relevant printed literature. While many of its views are tentative, it is excellent on the structure of assizes, and the relationship of the court and its judges to the Privy Council, the central courts, and local courts and officials in their historical development.

Dawson, J.P., *A History of Lay Judges* (Cambridge, Mass 1960). pp.viii + 310; index. Apart from some cogent, though undisciplined, analysis of trial procedures, officials and the courts in the medieval period, the book's original contribution is Part IV, an account of civil and criminal litigation in the manor of Redgrave, Suffolk, 1461-1711. The account is based on the court rolls, contemporary treatises and law reports.

Harding, A., *A Social History of English Law* (London 1966). pp.503; biblio.; table of cases and statutes; index. The work is better on the medieval and modern periods than on the early-modern. The account of crime, criminal process, criminal law and punishment is largely disjointed and ahistorical (chs 3, 11). However, it contains some excellent stories, interestingly written, and is generally well-liked by students. The scholarship is up to date.

Holdsworth, W., *A History of English Law* (London 1903; 7th edn 1956). Vol. I, pp.lxviii + 77 + 706; lists of cases, statutes; appendices; index. This introductory volume has long been the single most used text on English legal history. The account is clear and concise. But it is also superficial, and many of the interpretations are inaccurate. There are fairly slight discussions of the criminal law of the local courts (pp.142-8), the J.P.s (292-8), King's Bench (212-18) and the ecclesiastical courts (614-21), with a more substantial analysis of Star Chamber (495-516) and trial by jury (321-50). The special introduction to this edition by S.B. Chrimes is an excellent guide as to how more recent research has affected Holdsworth's interpretations.

_____, vol. IV (London 1924; 3rd edn 1945). pp.xxxviii + 600; lists of cases, statutes; appendices; index. This first book of his multi-volume history on the early-modern period concentrates on the development of the public law from late medieval times to the early 17th century. The account of the 16th and early 17th centuries covers the criminal justice system of the local courts (pp.137-66), and that of the central courts, divided into the subjects of treason, felonies, misdemeanours and trial procedure (492-532). Based almost exclusively on statutes, a few treatises and Stephen's history of the criminal law. Both the legal and historical details must be read with some reservations.

_____, vol. V (London 1924; 3rd edn 1945). pp.xxxvi + 529; lists of cases, statutes; appendices; index. Concerned with the non-public law for the same centuries as volume IV, this book has an excellent section illustrating the criminal business adjudicated before the court of Star Chamber from the 16th century to its abolition in 1641. Based on statutes, printed cases and contemporary treatises. The account, however, is lacking in its discussion of court procedure, and of the political and administrative background.

_____, vol. VI (London 1924; 2nd edn 1937). pp.xxxii + 719; lists of cases, statutes; appendix; index. Discusses the statute of frauds, crime and tort in the 17th century (pp.379-407, 673-7), the law reports and legal treatises of the 17th century (551-613) and the legal literature of the Restoration period (683-99). Useful as a guide to the more specialized contemporary legal literature of the era.

_____, vol. VIII (London 1925; 2nd edn 1937). pp.xxxiv + 500; lists of cases, statutes; index. This volume contains general discussions of a number of topics in the history of the criminal law. These include the history of the law of treason *c.*1540-1800 (pp.309-33), defamation before the common law and prerogative courts *c.*1600-1825 (333-78), conspiracy, malicious prosecution and maintenance *c.*1500-1714 (378-402), crimes against persons and crimes against property in the 16th and 17th centuries (421-33) and the principles of criminal liability in the 17th and 18th centuries (433-46). Based on a fair reading and understanding of statutes and secondary works.

_____, vol. IX (London 1926; 2nd edn 1938). pp.xxxiv + 457; lists of cases, statutes; appendices; index. The problem of evidence in the early-modern period (pp.127-44, 163-81, 203-21), and of procedure and pleading in criminal actions (222-46), form the relevant sections in this book. There are serious interpretive problems, however, in the discussion of these topics.

_____, vol. XI (London 1938). pp.xli + 658; lists of cases, statutes; index. This volume centres on the evolution of statute law. It includes relatively good analyses of the statutes relating to the development of criminal procedure in the 18th century (pp.550-56, 580-86), and statutes and writings on punishment in the 18th and early 19th centuries (556-80).

_____, vol. XII (London 1938). pp.xxxviii + 784; lists of cases, statutes; appendices; index. There is a useful study of the law reports, abridgments, dictionaries and legal treatises of the 18th century (pp.101-78), and the sources for the study of criminal law procedure (350-61). The materials are, however, poorly organized.

Holmes, O.W., *The Common Law* [1881], ed M.D. Howe (Cambridge, Mass 1963). pp.xxvii + 337; glossary; tables of cases, sources; index. These lectures erect a theoretical framework for the evolution of the common law that is based on the case method of analysis. The lectures on the theory of torts, criminal law, trespass, negligence, fraud, malice and intent (chs 2-4) are among the best in the book. The conceptual categories and patterns which Holmes developed marked the height of 'scientific jurisprudence'. Throughout his interpretation of cases he searches for the 'external' factors — social, metaphysical and psychological — which lay behind the law.

Milsom, S.F.C., *Historical Foundations of the Common Law* (London 1969). pp.xiv + 466; tables of cases and statutes; index. A monumental though difficult study of the history of the common law. Unfortunately, the section on the criminal law (ch. 14) is the weakest in the book. Relevant are his analyses of the pattern of litigation and trial by jury in the 16th and 17th centuries (pp.51-73), the development of trespass from the 16th to the 19th centuries (259-70) and of the law of tort (316-52).

Osborne, B., *Justices of the Peace 1361-1848* (Shaftesbury 1960). pp.254; index. The book centres on the 16th, 17th and 18th centuries (pp.27-215). The J.P.s are discussed topically within chronological periods. The work, while remarkably lucid, is completely uncritical. It can serve, however, to introduce the student to the topics of crime and criminal justice at the local level. Based on widely chosen examples from printed quarter sessions records.

Plucknett, T.F.T., *A Concise History of the Common Law* (London 1929, 5th edn 1956). pp.xxvi + 802; tables of cases and statutes; index. A good survey of the central courts, common law and prerogative (bk I, pt 1, chs 7-10). The latter section, which is substantial, is one of the best sections of the work. The book, however, is badly disjointed, and several of the generalizations are now questionable. It has been written for this period largely from secondary works.

Radcliffe, G.R.Y. and Cross, G., *The English Legal System* (London 1937; 3rd edn 1954). pp.viii + 440; index. Ch. 12 contains sketches of criminal prosecution, the trial process and criminal justice. While students find these useful as introductions to the subjects, both material and treatment are now out of date.

C The criminal law and justice system

The distinction between crime as part of the history of the behaviour of individuals in society, and criminal justice as the way in which those individuals are treated by law enforcement agencies and the courts, is a distinction that is more apparent in theory than it is in literature. Whether one is reading about state trials or about local and central courts, both subjects are intertwined. The same 'corporate' feature occurs with histories of crime on the one hand, and histories of the criminal law on the other. The purpose of this section is to list and comment upon the major works on the history of crime, criminal law enforcement and the criminal courts — their law both procedural and substantive. An attempt has also been made to assess the degree to which these studies are drawn from the original record.

Chambliss, W.J., ed, *Crime and the Legal Process* (New York 1969). pp.xii + 447; biblio.; index. A very uneven collection of essays. Those of interest are by Jeffrey on the historical development of crime (ch. 1), Chambliss and Foote on vagrancy (3, 17) and Seidman on *mens rea* (20). The section of the bibliography on the administration of the criminal law, though it leans to the modern period, is useful.

Critchley, T.A., *A History of Police in England and Wales 900-1966* (London 1967). pp.xx + 347; biblio. of printed sources; index. This work has in fact little to offer prior to the 19th century, and the period 1550-1800 is covered in only 32 pages (10-42). The sources are largely 19th-century secondary works, and the account is vague, disjointed and inaccurate. The index is also poor.

Du Cann, C.G.L., *English Treason Trials* (London 1964). pp.272; index. A vague and impressionistic series of accounts ranging from Roger Mortimer's trial in 1330 to the Cato Street Conspiracy of 1816. The work seems to be based on pamphlets and unverifiable contemporary accounts. The historical background of the majority of cases is poor and inaccurate, and there is absolutely no documentation.

Edwards, G.J., ed, *The Grand Jury* (Philadelphia 1906; repr. New York 1973). pp.xciii + 219; tables of texts, cases; index. The introductory chapter (pp.1-44) contains an essay on the history of the grand jury in criminal causes from the 11th century down to the 19th. The interpretation, while out of date, has points of interest on the composition and function of the jury in trial process. The writing, however, is disjointed, and historical continuity is lacking.

Hall, J., *Theft, Law and Society* (Indianapolis 1935; 2nd edn 1952). pp.xxiv + 398; appendices; table of cases; indices of names, subjects. Pt I explores the history of the law of theft in the context of the relationship between theft and property, economic and legal institutions, and social and legal thought. Ch. I centres on the Carrier's Case (1473), its precedents and antecedents to the 17th century. Ch. II assesses fully a number of cases and statutes of the 18th century. The topics discussed include law and fact, legal sanctions and social and economic conditions. This is a useful work in the historical and legal thought on theft, but lacking in its knowledge of social and economic history. There is a useful appendix of statutes on benefit of clergy, non-clergyable offences and transportation (pp.356-63).

Howell, T.B., ed, *A Complete Collection of State Trials*, Vols I-XXXI (London 1816-31). This is the fifth and best edition of the state trials series which began with four volumes in 1719. When the cases are taken from contemporary sources and printed verbatim this is an excellent work. But often the cases are compiled from old histories and printed tracts, incorporating all the biases and distortions of the earlier compilers. This can be a good source if used cautiously.

Melling, E., ed, *Kentish Sources*, Vol. VI: *Crime and Punishment* (Maidstone 1969). pp.xii + 294; illus; biblio. Documents from the records of petty and quarter sessions *c.*1590-*c.*1820. The material is organized under the subjects of preliminary inquiries, the presentment and trial of minor and major offences, summary jurisdiction and punishment — execution, transportation, branding, whipping, the stocks, fines, gaols and imprisonment. The book is weak on trial procedure, but strong on punishment. The general introduction and special introductions to each section are good, as is the editing of the records.

Moir, E., *The Justice of the Peace* (London 1969). pp.205; biblio.; index. A brief, lucid account of the history of the office of J.P. and of the court of quarter sessions. The relevant sections for these centuries are at pp.26-130. This is based largely on secondary works, except for the 18th century which is written closer to the sources. Students find this a useful introduction.

Pike, L.O., *A History of Crime in England* (London 1873-6; repr. New Jersey 1968). Two vols, pp.xxix + 539, xx + 719; appendices and index to each vol. The

16th, 17th and 18th centuries occupy vol. II to page 407. This is a very absorbing and readable compendium on the history of crime, focussing on the politically and religiously oriented crimes against local communities and the State. The account is unique, original and uneven. It is based on the Hale and Petyt manuscripts at the inns of court, the *Baga de Secretis* at the PRO, statutes, state papers and state trials and some contemporary printed collections of source materials. The references are presented in a narrative of their own and worth reading separately (pp.603-34). Despite the poor state of legal, social and economic history at that time, there is a wealth of discursive material here that is worth the effort to find.

Rumbelow, D., *I Spy Blue: The Police and Crime in the City of London from Elizabeth I to Victoria* (London 1971). pp.250; appendices; biblio.; index. A brief and entertaining history of the London City police from the 16th century down to 1800 (pp.25-114), compiled from contemporary pamphlets, surveys and secondary works with a few manuscripts. The book is well written and contains some attractive line drawings. It includes appendices of City watchmen and police, with their allowances and profits, *c.*1663-1762 (pp.223-7).

Spooner, L., *An Essay on the Trial by Jury* (London 1852; repr. New York 1971). pp.ii + 224. The thesis of this work is the revival of trial by jury in modern times as opposed to trial by 'government' (judges). It attempts to assert from historical precedents that jurors in the old courts — leet, hundred and county — were judges judging the law, and hence that common law juries became courts of conscience. An interesting, suggestive, but in too many places untenable account of the historical development of trial by jury.

Stephen, J.F., *A History of the Criminal Law of England* (New York 1883); repr. 1973). Three vols, pp.xv + 576, 497, 592; tables of cases and statutes; index. A strange mélange of historical anecdotes, of the discussion of social, political, religious and constitutional issues, and of the history of crime and criminal justice. The author completely eschews concepts, generalizations, historical continuity and development, and legal sources. The result is a history of the criminal law that is non-history. Sections of the work are organized artificially into the courts, procedure, trial by jury, punishment (vol. I), the substantive law by criminal offence (vols II-III) and 19th-century cases (vol. III). The only sections containing substantially coherent discussions are those on trial by jury 1554-1760 (I, pp.319-427), offences against religion *c.*1530-1714 (II, 396-497) and the history of the law of homicide *c.*1500-1800 (III, 44-77).

Thomas, D., ed, *State Trials*, vols I-II (London 1972). pp.236, 247. Commentaries and extracts from trials for treason, libel, witchcraft and murder, 1535-1817. Only those for the 18th century include a relatively full transcript of the record. Unfortunately, there are no footnotes or references to the material quoted or used.

Walker, N., *Crime and Insanity in England*, vol. I: *The Historical Perspective* (Edinburgh 1968). pp.302; tables of statutes, cases; appendices; biblio.; index. The historical account from *c.*1550-1800 is at pp.35-83, and it centres on the Hadfield Case of 1800. There is surprisingly more on the medieval period than on the early-modern. This brief survey is based on the printed reports and legal treatises. Interesting tables and appendices include lists of Old Bailey trials from 1740 (pp.67, 69), and documents from the Bellingham, Milesent and Broadric cases (270-77).

Webb, S. and B., *English Poor Law History, Part One: The Old Poor Law. English Local Government*, VII (London 1927; repr. 1963). pp.xxvi + 447; indices of persons, places, subjects. A comprehensive history of poor relief, the poor law and its administration from the 1590s to 1835. It includes a discussion of vagrancy and several other misdemeanours, and provides an institutional context for an important part of local government and the law in the period. Based broadly on contemporary local records, printed pamphlets and special studies. This is perhaps their best work in the series.

————, *The Story of the King's Highway. English Local Government*, V (London 1913; repr. 1963). pp.279; appendices; index. A cumbersome study of the economic life and administration of the highways from *c*.1500 to 1835. Chapter II (pp.14-26) contains a rather weak discussion of the 16th- and 17th-century background, but is useful for the study of theft, larceny and murder.

D Histories of prisons and punishment

Punishment has always been an attractive topic in English historical literature, but seldom has it been researched with the methodology and sophistication that has dominated the best kind of research and writing in the field of legal history. Too often studies of prisons, imprisonment and capital punishment have been based on the exceptional institution or the overly zealous narrative reporter, rather than the multitude of records upon which such history should rest. My purpose is to appraise the most often used histories of these subjects — the works which one tends to find in the published literature, either general or specialized, that treat of these matters. In many instances it is either the social and economic background, or the records of the institutions, which are most lacking in the histories of punishment.

Andrews, A., *Old Time Punishments* (Hull 1890; repr. London n.d.). pp.251; index. Contemporary descriptions, without documentation, of methods of punishment from the later Middle Ages to the 19th century. The only adequate discussions are those of the brank (pp.38-64), the pillory (65-89) and gibbet lore (188-246). The material seems to be derived largely from contemporary ballads, broadsheets and local antiquarian writings.

Hibbert, C., *The Roots of Evil: A Social History of Crime and Punishment* (Boston 1963). pp.524; biblio.; index. Really not much of a history at all. The period *c*.1500-1815 is covered on pp.20-66. The book is concerned largely with the 19th and 20th centuries. Based on older secondary works, and of little historical value.

Ives, G., *A History of Penal Methods: Criminals, Witches, Lunatics* (London 1914; repr. New Jersey 1970). pp.xi + 409; indices of authors and subjects. An attempt to demonstrate that criminal laws and methods of punishment were severe and in ignorance of the conditions of society. Covers a multitude of unrelated topics such as witch trials, the insane, banishment, prisons, retaliation, classes of crimes and reform, with little on the early-modern era. The work is based, however, on an incredible array of primary legal scources, and legal and historical monographs. Difficult to judge and use.

Lawrence, J., *A History of Capital Punishment* (New York 1960). pp.xxvi + 230; illust. Chapter 1 contains an almost useless historical survey from the Middle Ages to the present. The rest of the book is useful: a factual presentation of the full details, historically, of hanging and beheading, their places and forms. These chapters concentrate on the 17th and 18th centuries, and are based on newspapers, printed correspondence, state papers and statutes. Unfortunately, its use is made difficult by the lack of adequate documentation and the absence of an index.

Mayhew, M. and Binny, J., *The Criminal Prisons of London and Scenes of Prison Life* (London 1862; repr. New York 1968). pp.xii + 634; illust; tables of diet. A fairly interesting, though convoluted study of the prisons of the metropolitan area. In each instance the history of the particular prison is given prior to a description and assessment of the contemporary Victorian conditions. Includes histories of Pentonville (pp.112-21), Brixton female prison (172-82), the Woolwich hulks (197-202), Millbank (232-40), the Middlesex house of correction (277-89), the Surrey house of correction (487-500), the Holloway house of correction (533-9) and Newgate gaol (586-93). Based on local records and including considerable detail; unfortunately there are no citations to the sources or indications of their provenance.

Melling, *Kentish Crime and Punishment*. See above p.276.

Walker, N., *Crime and Punishment in Britain* (Edinburgh 1965), pp.xiii + 367; biblio.; index. A sophisticated and elegant exposition of the systems for defining, accounting for and disposing of offenders, written from a sound and unemotional position. Political, constitutional, legal, economic, social and philosophical perspectives to the problem of penal measures are drawn upon in this complex and engaging book. It includes a measure of historical perspective from the 17th to the 19th centuries.

Webb, S. and B., *English Prisons Under Local Government. English Local Government*, VI (London 1922; repr. 1963). pp. lxxiii + 261; index. The history of prisons and prison reform from the 16th century to 1835, concentrating on the 18th century (chs 2-6). Coherently organized and written, and based on original local records. This is one of the better volumes in the series, and it includes an interesting introduction by G.B. Shaw.

II SPECIALIZED STUDIES AND SOURCE COLLECTIONS

A The sixteenth century, c.1520-1603

The 16th century serves as a battleground for a number of historical controversies — king versus parliament, despotism versus democracy, the bureaucratic state, old and new learning, the old and new religion, and the agricultural, industrial and commercial revolutions. Furthermore, the years between 1520 and 1590 have been viewed by most modern scholars as a crucial era of historical change. Since this is also the period when the historical records begin to loom large, multiplying and recording in a more consistent fashion the history of men and their institutions, it is the first to which systematic techniques can be applied. This development too impinges directly upon the history of crime and the criminal justice system.

The purpose of this section is to list and discuss more extensively those works which bear directly upon an understanding of crime and criminal justice c.1520-1603. Since opinions vary widely I have attempted to assess them within the context of the historical record as it has come down to us. In terms of published records we now have a good sample of most legal jurisdictions in the reign of Elizabeth. These include essentially accurate editions of manorial and assize records which comprise a reasonable full range of these classes.[1] The problem, however, is that with the exception of the assizes, for which we will eventually have a full calendar for the South-Eastern Circuit,[2] these editions are each in themselves isolated records. We lack a range of published records or even a good sample of them for any one area of the country and for any specific period of time. There has been an attempt to provide this for Essex, but the work of Emmison, Samaha and others has not been able to stand the test of handling and interpreting the sources critically.[3] Hence the relationship of the courts and their officials, the working of legal processes and the substance of the criminal law are fields ripe for further research.

The older sketches by Pike and Holdsworth of crime and criminal justice in this era — while they are generally the fullest — simply will not stand up to critical scrutiny. Dr Baker's attempt in this volume to write an analysis of the system that bears a relationship to its sources is the first one for the early-modern era. It follows his earlier essay on 'The Dark Age of Legal History' which should be required reading for those considering advanced work in this field.[4] Some topics in this area, however, are being adequately developed. These include treason, witchcraft, crimes against morality, vagrancy and the 'criminous class' of Elizabethan society.[5] Here also are topics for fruitful undergraduate essays. Nevertheless, the reader is in the enviable position of being able to interpret the field outside the shadow of a definitive work, let alone a complete collection of sources or a large corpus of literature on a specific subject. He should also enjoy following the review literature on recent editions of these source materials and controversial special studies.

Aydelotte, F., *Elizabethan Rogues and Vagabonds* (Oxford 1913; repr. London 1967). pp.xii + 187; appendix; index. A descriptive account of rogues and vagabonds, including their criminal adventures, that is based on contemporary pamphlets, plays and memoirs. The material is well presented and the illustrations are excellent. This is a useful background work, capturing the details of the Elizabethan underworld as it was envisaged by the ruling class. The documents in the appendices (pp.140-74) contain some helpful sources.

Barnes, T.G., 'Due Process and Slow Process in the late Elizabethan-Early Stuart Star Chamber', *American Journal of Legal History*, VI (1962), pp.221-49. A concise discussion of Star Chamber procedure from the 1580s to the 1630s. The sources are manuscript tracts, deposition, interrogatories, orders, precedent and process books, centring on Ellesmere's presidency, 1596-1617.

Beier, A.L., 'Vagrants and the Social Order in Elizabethan England', *Past & Present*, LXIV (1974), pp.3-29. A study of the vagrant class apart from the views which their betters have left behind them for the historical record. The author uses search and examination records from the state papers, and the quarter sessions rolls of Essex, Warwickshire and Middlesex to compile an analysis of 752 cases. He also consults contemporary pamphlets and treatises.

Brinkworth, E.R., ed, *The Archdeacon's Court*, Oxford Hist. Soc. XXIII-IV (Oxford 1942). Vols I-II, pp.xxiii + 127, xxxi + 265. A calendar in Latin of the act book for 1584. The offences are social, moral and sexual. The introduction to vol.II discusses the records and their problems, such as framing presentments for moral charges and disturbances.

Charles, B.D., ed, *Calendar of the Records of the Borough of Haverfordwest 1539-1660* (Cardiff 1967). PP.viii + 274; index. The best printed record of a Welsh town in the 16th and 17th centuries. The full calendar includes the records of the great sessions, with more detail for the 17th century than for the 16th. Crimes include nuisances, vagrancy, theft, burglary and slander.

Cockburn, J.S., ed, *Calendar of Assize Records: Sussex Indictments, Elizabeth I; Sussex Indictments, James I; Hertfordshire Indictments, Elizabeth I; Hertfordshire Indictments, James I*. Four vols (HMSO 1975). pp.viii + 587, vii

+ 215, vii + 268, vii + 385; indices of persons, places, subjects to each volume. The first four of ten calendar volumes of assize records from the South-Eastern Circuit in the reigns of Elizabeth and James I. Each volume contains assize commissions, lists of J.P.s and other officials, prisoners, grand and trial jurors, and notes of cases including judgments. The indices are full and meticulously prepared. These volumes are major sources for research into the criminal law and justice system of the 16th and early 17th centuries.

Edwards, I.O., ed, *A Catalogue of Star Chamber Proceedings relating to Wales* (Cardiff 1929). pp.viii + 225. A collection of Star Chamber records centring on the reigns of Elizabeth (pp.18-146) and James I (147-223), compiled from the Star Chamber proceedings in the PRO. The work is organized by Welsh county within each reign, alphabetical by the surname of the complainant. It provides the manuscript reference and date together with the names of the parties, and summarizes the cause. No judgments are given. Includes references to other manuscript material bearing on the causes from the British Library and the National Library of Wales.

Elton, G.R., *Policy and Police; the Enforcement of the Reformation in the Age of Thomas Cromwell* (Cambridge 1972). pp.xi + 447; index. An examination of the treason trials of the 1530s based chiefly on the statutes, state papers and the records of the Exchequer, King's Bench and Star Chamber. This is a seminal work on the enforcement of the treason statutes in the 16th century, the techniques of which can be used for the study of treason trials in the Elizabethan period.

_____, *Star Chamber Stories* (London 1958). pp.244; index. Six stories of the middle Henrician period illustrating the criminal activities of university students, informers, treasury men, monks and clerics. The Star Chamber records are used largely to fill in gaps in the accounts provided by the state papers and allied sources. Entertaining reading.

_____, ed, *The Tudor Constitution; Documents and Commentary* (Cambridge 1960). pp.xvi + 496; table of docs; biblio.; index. An excellent definition and discussion of the law of treason (pp.59-86), the origins and development of Star Chamber (158-84), and statutes and orders concerning the expansion in the responsibilities of the J.P.s (452-70). The discussion is clear and lucid, and the extracts cogent and well documented. Students find this book very useful.

Emmison, F.G., *Elizabethan Life: Disorder* (Chelmsford 1970). pp.xvi + 364; illust; appendices; indices of subjects, persons, places. Includes selected extracts in story form from the Elizabethan quarter sessions rolls, assize indictment files and Queen's Bench plea rolls relating to Essex. The records relevant to the criminal law include a fairly representative number among crimes against the peace, persons and property. The stories told from these records are generally interesting, although in many instances there is not sufficient material from other sources to make them complete. The essential problem of the collection, however, is that the evidence is not presented verbatim or calendared, and there is no attempt to evaluate it.

_____, *Elizabethan Life: Morals and the Church Courts* (Chelmsford 1973), pp.xvi + 348; indices of subjects, persons and places. This volume contains extracts from the act, visitation, deposition and excommunication books of the archdeacons of Essex and Colchester, and the act book of the Commissary of the bishop of London, c.1561-1603. These include extracts illustrative of personal crimes (largely sexual offences) in chs 1-2, and of the trial process and punishment in ch. 9. Unfortunately, the extracts are taken out of context and are printed without references. This book must be used with extreme caution.

Ewen, C.L., *Witchcraft and Demonianism* (London 1933; repr. 1970). pp.495; appendices; index. An inquiry into these practices taken from printed trials and pamphlet accounts. Includes useful material on evidence and court procedure (pp.111-30), a full calendar of selected confessions and depositions 1566-1701 (142-390) and an appendix containing a brief calendar of indictments from assize circuits other than the South-Eastern *c.*1580-1690.

————, *Witch Hunting and Witch Trials* (London 1929; repr. 1971). pp.xiii + 345; illust; appendices; index of names. The development of the laws, legal procedures and punishments for witchcraft from the assize indictment files of the South-Eastern Circuit *c.*1560-1701. Includes transcripts and translations of the indictment records (pp.77-79), and tables noting the accused, offence, sentence and judge 1564-1663 (98-112). The chief selection comprises an abstract of indictments 1560-1701. Although this is not an exhaustive search of every indictment file, the work includes the great majority of cases before the assizes. Proceedings from other courts are included as examples in the appendices.

Finch, H., *Law, or A Discourse Thereof in Foure Books* (London 1613; repr. New York 1969 based on the 1759 edn). Finch was one of the few original common law writers of the early 17th century. Bk 3 contains cogent definitions of what constitutes an actionable offence, giving equal treatment to misdemeanours and felonies. The work is based on both statutes and common law precedents.

Glazebrook, P.R., 'Misprision of Felony — Shadow or Phantom?', *American Journal of Legal History*, VIII (1964), pp.189-208, 283-302. An analysis of the origins of misprision of treason in the 16th century from contemporary printed treatises and law reports.

Gleason, J.H., *The Justices of the Peace in England 1558 to 1640* (Oxford 1969). pp.xvi + 285; appendices; indices. Contains brief chapters on the commissions, education, religion and politics of selected J.P.s in six counties: Kent, Norfolk, Northamptonshire, Somerset, Worcestershire and the North Riding. Since the author is not interested in the law or the court system, there is nothing relevant to criminal justice. Another section of the book is its appendices (pp.123-64) which comprise incomplete lists of J.P.s and biographical information on selected ones.

Hair, P., *Before the Bawdy Court* (New York 1972). pp.271; illust; biblio.; indices of places, dates. Ostensibly a collection of cases with comments from 'church court and other records relating to the correction of moral offences in England, Scotland and New England, 1300-1800'. The book, however, is to be avoided. The materials are selected second-hand, condensed beyond recognition, and too scattered in time and place to provide any meaningful knowledge. The commentary (pp.232-58) is completely ahistorical and un-legal. There is a useful list of printed sources (262-66) for research into the subject.

Holdsworth, *History of English Law*, vols IV, V, VIII. See above. p.274.

Hughes, P.L. and Larkin, J.F., eds, *Tudor Royal Proclamations* (New Haven 1969), vols II-III. pp.xxxiii + 584, xiii + 439; glossary of terms; biblio.; index of subjects. Tudor proclamations, like Tudor statutes, are an invaluable source for the study of the interpretation and enforcement of the criminal law. Like vol. I for the early Tudor era, these two volumes comprise a nearly exhaustive edition of the extant proclamations 1553-1603, both printed and manuscript. The texts are meticulously and fully edited. Each proclamation is accompanied by an explanatory headnote, and is copiously referenced. The subjects include vagrancy, piracy and sedition, and jurors, judges and local governors. There is a lengthy glossary of terms, and the bibliography is an excellent guide to the printed sources and historical studies for the second half of the 16th century.

Hunnisett, R.F., ed, *Calendar of Nottinghamshire Coroners' Inquests 1485-1558*, Thoroton Soc. Rec. Ser. XXV (Nottingham 1969). pp.xxxi + 242; indices of persons and places, subjects. A full and impeccable calendar of the coroners' inquisitions returned, and of the further entries and proceedings in the King's Bench and assize records. Gives the name and occupation of the deceased, date and place of inquest, jurors and an account of the cause of death. From the mid 1530s this comprises a nearly complete record of all inquests held. There is an excellent introduction on the coroners, their duties and the classes of relevant records.

Johnson, H.C., ed, *Wiltshire County Records: Minutes of Proceedings in Sessions 1563 and 1574 to 1592*, Wilts. Rec. Soc. IV (Devizes 1949), pp.xxviii + 246; indices of persons and places, subjects. A transcript of the minute book which is prefaced by a register of badgers' recognizances 1574-89 (pp.3-14). The textual notes are useful and the indices excellent. But since only the minute book survives there is little criminal activity recorded.

Judges, A.V., ed, *The Elizabethan Underworld* (London 1930; repr. 1965). pp.lxiv + 543; glossary; illust; index. An interesting collection of contemporary tracts and writings on the 'Elizabethan underworld'. Copious extracts are edited from the sources. There is, however, little examination of the provenance of these materials, and they are discussed uncritically. The index is slight.

Kaye, J.M., 'The Early History of Murder and Manslaughter', *Law Quarterly Review*, LXXXIII (1967), pp.365-95, 569-601. Pt II comprises an analysis of the history of murder and manslaughter in the 16th century, especially in Elizabeth's reign. The focus is on how the distinction between murder and manslaughter became drawn in the 16th century. Based largely on printed reports and treatises.

Kirbus, A.M., ed, *The Records of the Commissioners of Sewers in the Parts of Holland 1547-1603*, vol. I; and A.E.B Owen, ed, vol. II. Lincoln Rec. Soc. LIV, LXIII (Lincoln 1959, 1968). Two vols, pp.ci + 168 + biblio.; ix + 187; indices of subjects, persons and places to each volume. A full transcript of the accounts, joyce and acre books, orders, and verdict and law books. The courts of sewers heard a wide range of nuisance suits which are peripheral to but nonetheless part of crime and criminal law. Volume I contains an excellent introduction to the court, its records and officials. Volume II includes a calendar of court meetings (pp.xxxviii-xlix) and biographies of judges (l-lxxxv).

Lambard, W., *Archeion or, a Discourse upon the High Courts of Justice in England* [1591] (London 1635; ed C.H. McIlwain and P.L. Ward, Cambridge, Mass 1957). pp.ix + 176; appendix. A good contemporary definition of the authority and jurisdiction of the courts. The most substantial section of the book is that on the Star Chamber and the offences adjudicated before it (pp.48-116) based on contemporary precedent books. The changes made by Lambard in his two editions are assessed soundly by the editors in the appendix (145-76).

―――――, *Eirenarcha, or of the Office of the Justices of Peace* (London 1581; 12th edn 1619). A renowned handbook for J.P.s penned by the famous Kent lawyer and antiquarian. The book contains verbatim transcripts of charges to grand juries at quarter and special sessions. It must be noted that this work was composed prior to Lambard's experience as a magistrate and that it was based largely on late-medieval sources. Hence it is a better source for the late 15th and early 16th centuries than it is for later periods. Since Lambard was also extremely conscientious, it can not be assumed that the duties of the J.P.s which he describes were universally discharged.

Langbein, J.H., *Prosecuting Crime in the Renaissance: England, Germany, France* (Cambridge, Mass 1974). pp.ix + 321; appendices; index. Pt I is an analysis of the Marian bail and committal statutes of 1554-55, the historical background of preliminary examinations by the J.P.s, the role of these statutes in consolidating and making more effective the pre-trial process, and the structure of the criminal courts and juries in the succeeding half-century. The author has opened up a number of serious questions pertaining to the conduct of criminal trials. However, the analysis of pre-trial procedures, and the alleged crucial role played by the J.P.s in criminal causes before the assizes, is suspect. Our knowledge of legal procedures must come more substantially from the assize and King's Bench records and ancillary documents rather than from statutes, sketchy treatises and popular pamphlets.

Leonard, E.M., *The Early History of English Poor Relief* (Cambridge 1900; repr. London 1965). pp.xviii + 397; appendices; index. Despite the date of its composition, this is a fair account of the history of poor relief in the era: its economic foundations, the machinery of the new institutions, and the criminal offences which resulted from the failure to cope successfully with social and economic problems. Based on statutes, state papers and printed local records. The book is inaccurate in its discussion of legal matters, but it is useful nonetheless. Chs 3-4 cover the decades 1514-1644, and the bulk of the material stems from the period 1597-1644. The appendices (pp.305-97) contain a considerable amount of source material relating to the J.P.s.

Macfarlane, A.D.J., *Witchcraft in Tudor and Stuart England* (London 1970). pp.xvi + 334; lists of plates, maps, tables; appendices; index. Pt I comprises a study of the legal and literary sources for witchcraft trials in Essex, *c*.1560-1680. The judicial sources cover the assizes, quarter sessions, ecclesiastical and borough court records. An appendix (pp.254-312) includes brief abstracts of the witchcraft cases; fuller abstracts are contained in Ewen, *Witch Hunting and Witch Trials*. There is a bibliography of manuscript and printed sources. The approach and structure of the book is thought by some to inhibit its use.

McPeck, J.A.S., *The Black Book of Knaves and Unthrifts* (Storrs 1969). pp.xiii + 298; illust; index. An account of the fraternity of beggars, paupers, vagabonds and 'knaves' in the late 16th and early 17th centuries, taken from the dramatic literature of the period. Following in the footsteps of Aydelotte and Judges, this socio-literary history is interesting and well documented. Useful for contemporary, literary, upper-class depictions of this 'criminous class'.

[Manchester], *The Court Leet Records of the Manor of Manchester* (Manchester 1884-89). Vols I-VI, 1552-1730, pp.xxiv + 295, vii + 370, ix + 382, ix + 364, ix + 288, ix + 322. Vols VII-X (1731-1820), pp.vii + 292, viii + 279, viii + 274. This court heard all minor crimes from trial to judgment, and held presentments for major crimes to be prosecuted at quarter sessions or assizes. The first set of volumes above is a complete and verbatim transcript of these records to 1730. The second set is a brief calendar, not nearly as complete as the first and not as useful for the study of crime and criminal justice.

Marshburn, J.H., *Murder and Witchcraft in England 1550-1640* (Norman 1971). pp.xxvii + 287; illust; aux. entries; indices of plays, persons and topics. An attempt to capture the 'progress of murder' through the narrative discussion of plots from the planning and committing of the crime to trial, judgment and conviction. Based entirely on literary sources, contemporary artistic, and non-legal views of murder and witchcraft. The auxiliary items (pp.234-73) comprise a bibliography of the literary sources for such cases in chronological order. The substance of these sources is usually slight; their use is negligible.

Pike, *History of Crime in England*, vol. II. See above. p.276.

Read, C., ed, *William Lambarde and Local Government: His 'Ephemeris' and Twenty-nine Charges to Juries and Commissions* (Ithaca 1962). pp.xi + 189. The *Ephemeris* was Lambard's calendar of his work as a J.P. in the western division of Kent, 1580-88 (pp.15-52). It provides an interesting catalogue, lacking, however, in substantive comments. His 'charges' to quarter and special sessions, largely at Maidstone 1582-1601 (67-189), comprise a unique legal record for the period. These exhortations are useful chiefly for the attitude of the landed gentry towards crime and law enforcement, and the regulation of life in the localities. Unfortunately there is no index, which makes the book difficult to use.

Richardson, H., ed, *Court Rolls of the Manor of Acomb*, Yorks. Arch. Soc. CXXXI (York 1969). pp.vii + 252. An excellent calendar of the court rolls of this township in the city of York c.1544-1760. There is material for all periods; nuisances, trespasses, theft and assault comprise the criminal business of the court.

Rye, W., ed, *Depositions taken before the Mayor and Aldermen of Norwich, 1549-1567* (Norwich 1905). pp.205; indices of persons, places. A revealing collection of depositions civil and criminal, including many on the same crime which rebut or corroborate the other evidence. Unfortunately, there is no adequate introduction to the context of these documents.

Salgado, G., ed, *Cony-Catchers and Bawdy Baskets* (Harmondsworth 1972). pp.391. An anthology of ten contemporary tracts printed c.1552-92 which were designed to expose the rogues, vagabonds and 'anti-society' of Elizabethan England. The introduction includes a slight account of their professional organization and activities (pp.13-22).

Samaha, J., *Law and Order in Historical Perspective: The Case of Elizabethan Essex* (New York 1974). pp.xvi + 176; appendices; biblio.; index of subjects. A provocative study of crime, criminals and punishment in Elizabethan Essex. The study is largely statistical, an attempt to elucidate the system by revealing the details which have been left in its records. There are 56 tables (pp.114-71) providing statistical accounts of violent crime and punishment, social status and crime, social status and judgments, court officials and meetings. The work, however, poses some major dilemmas. First, it is based in part on an inadequate calendar of the Essex assize records, and thus has many omissions and errors. Second, it omits all misdemeanours, thereby treating only one side of the criminal justice system. Third, none of the Queen's Bench records are consulted, making it a study of only part of the common law jurisdiction. Fourth, the critical apparatus — which is nowhere adequate — does not make clear the sources from which the statistical data, which do not always tally, are drawn.

Smith, T., *De Republica Anglorum* (London 1583; repr. Menston 1970). Contains a concise and lucid description of the theoretical workings of the judicial system. In

Book II, chs 8-12, 15 he discusses trial by jury, in chs 19-22 pre-trial process in criminal causes and in chs 23-25 the trial process. Judgment and criminal justice are discussed all too incompletely in Book III, chs 1-3. This treatise should be used with caution, as it was composed not from actual judicial experience but while Smith was serving as ambassador to France.

The Statutes of the Realm (London 1819-22; repr. 1963). Vols IV-IX, pp.lxxvii + 1275, xix + 942, xiii + 615, xxix + 750, lxi + 852, xxxiii + 1005. Each volume has a chronological table of statutes and an index of major topics. Vol. X comprises an alphabetical index of topics, while vol. XI is a chronological index of statutes. The series covers the period 1547-1714. The original statutes of the realm can be said to be one of the most important legal histories in existence and their coverage of the criminal law and its administration is no exception. To be used always instead of one of the various collections of the 'Statutes at Large'.

Staunford, W., *Les Plees del Coron* (London 1557; repr. 1975). Ff. 198. The contemporary text on pleas of the Crown for the 16th and 17th centuries. Written in the form of a compendium, based on earlier authorities, statutes and law reports, the work is frankly a mess. It is, nonetheless, indispensable for the criminal law of the period. Book I covers treason and felonies. Book II the criminal courts and legal process, and Book III trial by jury, judgment and punishment.

Tanner, J.R., ed, *Tudor Constitutional Documents a.d. 1485-1603 with an historical commentary* (Cambridge 1922; 2nd edn 1930). pp.xiv + 636; list of docs; biblio.; index. Useful for its documents, but not for its commentary which in most places is no longer tenable. The interesting collections of documents published in nearly complete form and fully annotated include the Elizabethan penal laws (pp.143-63); cases and orders from the records of Star Chamber and extracts from legal treatises (265-98); criminal cases in the ecclesiastical courts and commissions (362-73); the treason statutes (381-421); the statutes relating to the jurisdiction and procedures of the J.P.s (464-510).

Thomas, K., *Religion and the Decline of Magic* (London 1971). pp.xviii + 716; index. A seminal study of religion, magic, astrology, prophesy and other beliefs in the 16th and 17th centuries. Of relevance are the chapters on the crime of witchcraft and its religious and social backgrounds (14-18). These are based on contemporary literature and tracts, and various printed and manuscript archidiaconal, episcopal and quarter sessions records. The notes are a rich source of information for further research.

Wiener, C.Z., 'Sex Roles and Crime in Late Elizabethan Hertfordshire', *Jnl of Social History*, VIII (1975), pp.38-60. An interesting examination of female crimes of political, financial and interpersonal natures based on samples from quarter sessions and assize records, and archdeacon act books and depositions. The notes include useful comments on contemporary literature and secondary studies.

B The Seventeenth Century, 1603-1714

Historians of the 17th century, even more than those of the 16th, have been concerned with critical 'national' issues of State, and these concerns to some extent explain the existence of a greater number of published sources than exist for the 16th century. For the law, however, this has been a mixed blessing. To take the courts of quarter sessions as an example, no fewer than five counties have published quarter sessions records in a way that makes them useless for the study of crime and criminal justice, or in fact for legal history itself.[6] Some of the published borough court records are equally of little use, such as those for Leicester and Nottingham.[7] Editions such as these comprise extracts from 'select' records which simply make it impossible to judge, or to study either the working of the courts or the presentments and indictments that came before them for litigation. Such works are excluded from this bibliography.

There are, however, a fair number of good record publications that shed light on the problem of crime in the 17th century. The courts which have the best edited records for comparative study are the courts leet and baron, and the assizes.[8] The assize calendar series discussed above (p.280) also includes the reign of James I. This series, together with the assize orders for the Western Circuit (1629-59), provides an important link between local and central institutions in the criminal justice system and a rich source for historical examination.[9] With regard to the other local jurisdictions, there are four good series of borough court records but none of them overlap for comparative study.[10] A similar situation exists for the records of quarter sessions. Five counties have full calendars or transcripts of the nearly complete record, but all except one are in the south-eastern area, and none of them overlap.[11] However, the manorial, borough, quarter sessions and assize materials comprise at least a fair representation of the judicial records relevant to the study of crime and criminal justice in the 17th century.

Some significant secondary literature has also appeared during the last decade. This includes useful works on local government,[12] and interpretive studies of crime and criminal prosecution.[13] Again, the best studies attack the problem from the local perspective, just as Ewen, Macfarlane and Thomas have examined the topic of witchcraft, or Beier and Slack the problem of vagrancy.[14] Nonetheless, we will still be somewhat limited in our understanding of both crime and the criminal justice system until we have more published materials and studies of the central courts, and contiguous or comparative works for the local ones. The central courts did decline in influence in the 17th century. But what they declined to will not be known until they have been examined, and it should be noted that contemporary writers on the criminal law in that century, such as Pulton, Coke and Hale, still considered the criminal law and its administration a topic existing on a national, as opposed to a local or regional basis.[15] Thus the student, as well as the expert, has a wide field to play on.

Barnes, 'Slow Process ... Star Chamber'. See above, p.280.

Barnes, T.G., *Somerset 1625-1640* (London 1961). pp.xiii + 369; biblio.; index. Contains an excellent account of the judicial activities of the J.P.s, including the innovations in criminal procedure brought about by their attempts to come to grips with misdemeanours and lesser felonies at the local level (ch 3). There is also a full discussion of the 'Book of Orders' of 1631, and the impact of its enforcement on the county judicial system. The bibliography of manuscript and printed sources is excellent.

_____, ed, *Somerset Assize Orders 1629-1640*, Somerset Rec. Soc. LXV (Frome 1959). pp.xxxvi + 88; index. The assize order books are an important source for the interpretation of procedure in criminal causes. In this edition the orders for Somerset are transcribed in full and annotated. The introduction discusses the courts of assize and quarter sessions, and the relationships of their officials.

Beattie, J.M., 'The Pattern of Crime in England 1660-1800', *Past & Present*, LXII (1974), pp.47-95; graphs. An analytical treatment based on data from the assize and quarter sessions records for Surrey and Sussex. A pioneer survey of the subject, and of the problems for future research. Crimes against persons and property are linked in rural and urban settings to population mobility, prices and wars.

Beloff, M., *Public Order and Popular Disturbances 1660-1714* (Oxford 1938; repr. London 1963). pp.viii + 168; appendices; index. Only ch. 7 and the conclusion (pp.129-58) are concerned directly with the corn riots and other popular disturbances of the period, and prosecutions by the authorities. Good on the political, economic and social background, but altogether too brief on apprehension and trial. The notes contain references to the printed sources for such a study.

Charles, *Records of Haverfordwest 1539-1660.* See above p.280

Chinnery, G.A. and Newman, A.N., ed, *Records of the Borough of Leicester*, vol. VII (Leicester 1974), pp.xl + 591; indices of persons, places, subjects. A calendar of all the judicial classes of borough records 1689-1835 including transcripts of cases heard and concluded before the mayor, borough, quarter sessions and common law courts. The introduction is a superb critical analysis of the borough records. Crimes before the borough's courts are largely theft, assault and slander. A previous volume in the series under the same title (IV, Cambridge 1923) contains only isolated and poorly abridged extracts from the judicial records for the years 1603-88 and should be avoided.

Cockburn, *Calendar of Assize Records.* See above p.280.

Cockburn, *Assizes.* See above p.273.

Cockburn, J.S., ed, *Somerset Assize Orders 1640-1659*, Somerset Rec. Soc. LXXI (Frome 1971). pp.xxvi + 89; appendices; index. A full transcript of Somerset assize orders of the Civil War and Interregnum. The introduction discusses the organization and membership of the Western Circuit and the role of assizes in the political history of the period. An appendix (pp.57-80) contains the memorandum book of a Somerset sheriff 1654-56.

———, ed, *Western Circuit Assize Orders 1629-1648*, Camden Soc. 4th Ser., XVII (London 1976), pp.xiv + 352; index. A full annotated calendar of all the assize orders for the Western Circuit's six counties — Cornwall, Devon, Dorset, Hampshire, Somerset and Wiltshire — to the death of Charles I. Includes the orders transcribed in full in the two Somerset volumes (above).

Coke, E., *The Third Part of the Institutes of the Lawes of England* (London 1644; best later edns are 1669-70, 1809, 1817). pp.ix + 243; table of matters. An excellent collection of common law and statute crimes organized by offence. The work is noteworthy for its classification and analysis of the criminal law, and for its historical perspective. It is, however, a personal interpretation. It supersedes Staunford but only partially replaces Pulton.

Dawson, *Law Judges* [Redgrave Manor]. See above. p.273.

Edwards, *Star Chamber Proceedings ... Wales.* See above, p.281.

Ewen, *Witchcraft.* See above p.282.

Ewen, *Witch Hunting.* See above. p.282.

Forster, G.C.F., *The East Riding Justices of the Peace in the Seventeenth Century*, E. Yorks. Local Hist. Ser. no.30 (Guisborough 1973). pp.72. A succinct account of the personnel and work of the E. Riding bench. Ch. 5 (pp.36-67) includes an admirable and concise account of the judicial business of quarter sessions in this period.

Hale, M., *Historia Placitorum Coronae* [1676], ed S. Emlyn (London 1736). Two vols, pp.4 + xix + 8 + 710, 6 + 414 + 148; index. The first history of the criminal law. Never completed in the author's lifetime, it was published posthumously. Volume I traces the history of capital crimes, and vol. II criminal procedure in capital crimes. His work on misdemeanours was never finished. Written as a genuine monograph, it is well organized and thoughtful but lacking in consistent technical details. His *Pleas of the Crown* (1678; corr. edn 1682) was merely a faulty outline for the *Historia*.

Harrison, G.B., ed, *The Trial of the Lancaster Witches A.D. MDCXII* (London 1929; repr. New York 1971). pp.xlvi + 188. Publishes contemporary printed examinations of the Lancaster witches tried in 1612. The introduction traces the background of the cases to the early 1590s.

Havinghurst, A.F., 'James II and the Twelve Men in Scarlet', *Law Quarterly Review*, LXIX (1953), pp.522-46. A balanced assessment of the judges of James II: the criminal charges laid against them and their trial for treason 1685-9.

Holdsworth, *History*, vols V-VI, VIII-IX. See above p.274.

Howell, *State Trials*, vols II-XV. See above p.276.

Kenyon, J.P., ed, *The Stuart Constitution; Documents and Commentary* (Cambridge 1966). pp.xvi + 523; tables of docs; biblio.; index. Contains little relating to the law, crime or criminal justice. The account of the judiciary (pp.420-26) is poor, as is that of the local courts (492-7). However, there are some brief extracts relating to the J.P.s in the reign of Charles I (497-503), and to treason and desertion in the Restoration period (432-41).

Larkin, L.F. and Hughes, P.L., *Stuart Royal Proclamation: Royal Proclamations of King James I 1603-25* (Oxford 1973), pp.xxxiv + 679; index. See above p.282.

Lawrence, *Capital Punishment*. See above p.278.

Le Hardy, W., ed, *Calendar to the Buckinghamshire Sessions Records* (Aylesbury 1933-39). Vols I-III, 1678-1712, pp.xxiv + 622, xxxv + 554, xxvii + 427; appendices; indices to each vol. A brief calendar of the quarter sessions order books to 1701, and order books and rolls 1701-12. The more complete record from 1701 presents a full range of criminal presentments and prosecutions even though the rolls are not completely extant. The introduction discusses the records uncritically, but there is a useful schedule of offences (pp.xxii-iv).

———, ed, *Calendar to the Middlesex Sessions Records* (London 1935-41). Vols I-IV pp.xxvi + 591, xxii + 447, xxvi + 423, xv + 463; index to each vol. A calendar of the indictment book, sessions rolls and register, and gaol delivery register 1612-18. The most complete published record for an urban area in the early 17th century and an important source for the history of crime and criminal justice in this period. The introductions are of little value.

Leonard, *Early History of Poor Relief*. See above p.284.

Lister, J., ed, *West Riding Sessions Records*, Yorks. Archaeol. Soc. LIV (Wakefield 1915). pp.lv + 446; indices of names, places, subjects. A full transcript of indictments 1637-42, and the orders of the court 1611-42. The major crimes include arson, burglary, extortion, larceny, murderous intent, nuisances, rape, riot and robbery. The introduction discusses the records briefly but does not seem aware of their significance.

Macfarlane, *Witchcraft*. See above p.284.

[Manchester], *Court Leet*. See above p.284.

Marcham, W.M. and Marcham, F., ed, *Court Rolls of the Bishop of London's Manor of Hornsey 1603-1701* (London 1929). pp.xliv + 301; list of court sittings, index; map. A complete transcript of the court rolls of this Middlesex manor owned by the bishop of London to mid-century and by the Wollaston family of London goldsmiths afterwards. No capital crimes were within its jurisdiction but misdemeanours were. The material is excellently produced.

Melling, *Kentish Crime and Punishment*. See above p.276.

Nott, H.N., ed, *The Deposition Books of Bristol*, Bristol Rec. Soc. VI, XIII (Bristol 1935, 1948). Vol. I, *1643-47*; vol. II, *1650-54*. pp.xii + 307, ix + 234; indices to each vol. of persons and places, select subjects. A full transcript of depositions before the mayor and aldermen of Bristol. These include evidences on theft and riot at sea, and theft, quarrels and other misdemeanours in the city. The indices are not trustworthy.

Peyton, S.A., ed, *Minutes of Proceedings in Quarter Sessions held for the Parts of Kesteven in the County of Lincoln 1674-95*, Lincoln Rec. Soc. XXV-VI (Lincoln 1931-2). pp.cxliv + 546; biblio.; appendices; indices of persons, places, subjects. A full transcript of the minute books, including files of indictments and recognizances. Due to the limited nature of the evidence, the only crimes included are those of bastardy, vagrancy and various moral offences. The introduction contains a good history of the local courts and officials, and a cogent analysis of the remaining judicial records. An appendix has a unique table of population by parish (pp.cxxxi-viii).

Pike, *History of Crime*. See above p.276.

Pulton, F., *De Pace Regis et Regni* (London 1609; repr. 1973). ff. 258; general index. A useful study of the criminal actions at common law by a contemporary lawyer and antiquarian. It is largely based on statutes, treatises and a few printed reports. The index is a detailed table of contents. The work is difficult to use and not necessarily authoritative. Nonetheless, it is an important book.

Redwood, B.C., ed, *Quarter Sessions Order Book 1642-1649*, Sussex Rec. Soc. LIV (Lewes 1954). pp.xxxvi + 248; glossary; indices of names and places, subjects. A transcript of the order book of the east and west sessions with matters added from the sessions rolls. The crimes include assault, drunkenness, riot, slander and trespass. The introduction contains a good discussion of court procedure, and there are appendices of writs of *certiorari* and other documents relating to court procedure.

Ratcliff, S.C. and Johnson, H.C., ed, *Warwick County Records* (Warwick 1935-39). Five vols, pp.xxxv + 300, xxxv + 314, li + 421, lxii + 371, lxxiv + 275; indices of persons, places, subjects. A full transcript of the quarter sessions order books 1625-74. This is the most complete published series of 17th-century order books, and the county of Warwick is an attractive one for the study of the administration of the local criminal justice system. Each volume has a valuable introduction listing the J.P.s and county officials, describing the records and giving biographical sketches of the mayors and J.P.s.

Richardson, *Manor of Acomb*. See above p.285.

Singleton, R.R., 'English Criminal Biography, 1651-1722', *Harvard Library Bulletin*, XVII (1970), pp.63-83; biblio. A summary assessment of the 58 criminal biographies published in the period 1651-1722. Written largely for comic relief, they comprise the sequel to the ballads, broadsides and jestbooks of the previous era.

Slack, P.A., 'Vagrants and Vagrancy in England 1598-1664', *Economic Hist. Review*, 2nd ser., XXVII (1974), pp.360-79; tables; maps; appendix. An examination of the problem and characteristics of vagrancy from passport lists, J.P. returns and mayoral court books relating chiefly to the towns of Colchester, Norwich and Salisbury. The essay centres on the vagrants' status groups and patterns of mobility. The notes contain a wide series of references to extremely useful local records and specialized studies.

Statutes of the Realm, vols V-IX. See above. p.286.

Thomas, *Religion and Magic*. See above. p.286.

Wake, J. and Peyton, S.A., eds, *Quarter Sessions Records of the County of Northampton*, Northants Rec. Soc. I (Hereford 1924). pp.lvi + 311; indices of persons, places, subjects. The only calendar of all classes of quarter sessions records published for the period. Covering the years 1630, 1657-58, all kinds of crimes except major felonies are represented in these records. The introduction contains a classic discussion of the history of the J.P. in the 16th and 17th centuries.

Willcox, W.B., *Gloucestershire: A Study in Local Government 1590-1640* (New Haven 1940). pp.xvi + 348; biblio.; map; index. An admirable study of the institutions of county government — administrative, fiscal and judicial. Chs 2-3 cover the work of the central and county institutions, and chs 7-10 those of the town, parish, manor and forest. In legal matters the author is concerned with the court structures, functions and questions of jurisdiction rather than with the procedural or substantive law itself. Based on a rich array of original sources, the notes are a study in themselves. The criticisms in the bibliographical essay are as relevant today as they were in 1940.

Willis, A.J., ed, *Borough Sessions Papers 1653-1688*, Portsmouth Rec. Ser. (Chichester 1971). pp.xxxiv + 212; appendices; glossary; index. A calendar of all the sessions files, including recognizances, presentments, examinations and informations. The fullest catalogue of borough court papers published for the 17th century. The major crimes are adultery, arson, assault, bastardy, embezzlement, fornication, riot, slander, theft, treason and wife-beating. The introduction has an excellent analysis of the court and its officials, and the appendices provide transcripts of sample documents and lists of court officials.

————, ed, *A Hampshire Miscellany* (Folkestone 1963). pp.vii + 79; index. A group list of actions from the court book of the archdeacon of Winchester 1607-8. Sexual offences comprise the largest class of cases before the court. The brief entries provide names of the parties, the charge and the judgment.

C The Eighteenth Century, 1714-c.1815

The publication of sources virtually ceases with the accession of George I. But there are two full calendars of the nearly complete record of quarter sessions for the mid 18th century.[16] Equally useful are calendars of the court records of several boroughs and manors.[17] In addition, the 18th century is well served with treatises on the criminal law. In fact, those of Hawkins, Foster, Eden, Blackstone and East give us contemporary analyses for almost each quarter-century.[18] To these treatises may be added a good edition of the statutes. Also useful are the parliamentary commissions of the 19th century (not listed here) which provide considerable evidence and testimony on the legal system and the crime problem in the 18th century.

Secondary works have developed some traditional subjects to a much greater extent in the 18th century than in earlier periods. The lead has been taken by social, economic and political historians rather than by legal historians themselves, and this has had both positive and negative results. Prisons, prison theory, convicts and transportation have received considerable attention.[19] Another popular topic, also beginning at about mid century, has been the origins of a semi-professional system of police and magistrates.[20] Much of this writing, however, has centred on the Fieldings of Bow Street, Covent Garden, an important area of commercial London. Coupled to the increased interest in urban crime in the literature of the 18th century has been the continuing study of social disorder and public disturbances.[21] In addition, there are the topics of libel, general warrants, and freedom of the press and liberty which came to dominate the political and constitutional history of the last quarter of the century.[22] Some of this literature also throws light on seventeenth-century problems. Taken together, these subjects provide considerable scope for the student and general reader. The rich variety of source materials available should allow the history of the crime problem to develop in all its dimensions, rather than in the disjointed and limited perspective it receives in some of the standard texts.[23]

Babington, A., *A House in Bow Street; crime and the magistracy in London, 1740-1881* (London 1969). pp.252; illust; biblio.; index. A popular history of crime and justice in Covent Garden, London, centring on the years 1740-1815 (pp.11-209). The work is structured on the careers of P. Colquhoun, Col T. DeVeil, H. and J. Fielding and S. Welch. While interesting for the general reader, the book has no documentation and makes no scholarly pretensions.

Beattie, 'Pattern of Crime'. See above p.288.

Beattie, J.M., 'Towards a Study of Crime in 18th-Century England: A Note on Indictments', in *The Triumph of Culture: Eighteenth-Century Perspectives*, ed D Williams and P. Fritz (Toronto 1972), pp.299-314. A pioneer work on the possibilities and limitations of indictments as a source for the study of crime. Although dealing specifically with the 18th century, the comments apply equally to work in earlier periods.

_____, 'The Criminality of Women in Eighteenth-Century England', *Jnl of Social Hist*. VIII (1975), pp.80-116. An intriguing conception of the patterns of offences charged against women, derived from the quarter sessions records and assize indictments for Surrey and Sussex 1663-1802. The focus is on the differences in the pattern of female crimes in rural and urban areas. The notes include a fine survey of published records and literature on crime, women and life in these local communities.

Bentham, J., *An Introduction to the Principles of Morals and Legislation* (London 1789; repr. New York 1948). pp.xxx + 378; index. Chs 7-27 contain an admirable contemporary analysis of the principles of criminal behaviour and the law: human actions, motives and intentions, the classes of criminal offences, the structure of punishment and a science of penal jurisprudence.

Blackstone, W., *Commentaries* (London 1768-9; repr. New York 1969, from the Philadelphia edn 1803). Vols IV-V, pp.iv + 455 + xxvii + 74, iii + 442 + vii +

60; appendices; indices. A very confusing work with an inflated reputation. There is no clear concept of crime or criminal law, no consistent use of the records and no adherence to technical accuracy. Wrongs of a personal and property nature are discussed in Bk 3 (vol. IV), chs 7-10); and crimes in Bk 4 (vol. V). There is more on substantive than on procedural law, and more research in textbooks and books of practice than in printed reports. Statutes are discussed as if they were implemented without exception, and there is no use of the original court records. The work gives considerable attention to historical background and context but is altogether too disjointed. Blackstone writes, however, in a convincing manner and students find his work attractive for general reading. The index is excellent.

Burn, R., *Justice of the Peace and Parish Officer* (London 1755; 19 edns to 1800). Two vols. This was the standard manual and text for J.P.s in the second half of the 18th century. Organized into topical sections of writs, actions and subjects, the discussions are unusually distinct. Since the law changed significantly in this half century one must be careful to note that Burn was up-dated each time he was republished.

Chinnery, *Borough of Leicester*. See above. p.288.

Cobley, J., *The Convicts 1788-92* (Surry Hills 1965). pp.104; appendices; biblio. A statistical biography of 248 of the 4973 convicts who were transported from England and Ireland to New South Wales 1787-92. The information includes age, sex, marital status, occupation, county, offence, sentence, time in transit and later activities. The latter contain numerous amusing incidents (pp.24-44).

————, *The Crimes of the First Fleet Convicts* (Sydney 1970). pp.xv + 324; appendices. A calendar of the prosecutions of 733 persons convicted and transported to Australia 1782-87. Presented in alphabetical order, the evidence consists of the place and date of trial, a description of the crime, the sentence and references. Based on the records of the courts of quarter sessions and assizes in 34 counties and the Old Bailey sessions papers, Middlesex. Two appendices comprise a bibliography of source material (pp.303-11).

Cockburn, J.S., 'The North Riding Justices 1690-1750', *Yorks Archaeol. Jnl*, XLI (1965), pp.481-515. Includes an examination of morality, crime and punishment, and the poor law (pp.485-97) from the quarter sessions books and rolls. The works of the J.P.s is placed within the context of the common law and local courts.

Darvall, F., *Popular Disturbances and Public Order in Regency England* (Oxford 1934; repr. London 1969). pp.xix + 363; biblio.; index. A history of the Luddite uprisings in northern England and the west midlands 1811-37. The study goes back into the 18th century to inquire into the origins of industrial sabotage and rioting, the police machinery established to discover and apprehend the leaders and their prosecution. Based on a wide range of social, economic and legal sources, the new imprint has a historiographical essay and bibliographical note by A. Macintyre.

Dinwiddy, J.R., Baxter, J.L. and Connelly, F.K., 'Debate', *Past & Present*, LXIV (1974), pp.113-35. A debate over the extent of an underground, revolutionary movement that worked towards the destruction of society in the West Riding of Yorkshire 1796-1802. Includes contemporary correspondence and court records (especially examinations).

Dowdell, E.G., *A Hundred Years of Quarter Sessions; The Government of Middlesex from 1660-1760* (Cambridge 1932). pp.lxxv + 215; table of statutes;

appendices; index. Only Pt II (pp.16-43) is concerned with the criminal law and it is one of the poorest sections of the book. The historical introduction to the office of J.P. by W. Holdsworth is, however, an interesting and wide-ranging piece of literature.

East, E.H., *Pleas of the Crown* (London 1803; repr. 1972). Two vols, pp.lxiv + 1126; index of subjects; tables of statutes, cases. One of the first professional treatises on offences triable at assizes, the work summarizes cogently the criminal law practised before the circuit courts. It is organized according to the subjects of morality, treason, bullion, murder, homicide, mayhem, rape, burglary, larceny, robbery, piracy, forgery, fraud and slander. Includes cases from manuscript reports.

Eden, W., *Principles of Penal Law* (London 1771; 3rd edn 1775). pp.xxvii + 331. The first attempt to formulate a plan for reforming English penal law, this work should be reprinted. Based on Beccaria's *Dei Delitte e Delle Pene* (1764). Eden first discusses the theoretical doctrines of English penal law and then presents a plan for its total reform. A large number of local tracts on this subject were afterwards written in various countries.

Foster, M., *Discourse upon a Few Branches of the Crown Law*, Part Two of *A Report of Some Proceedings* (Oxford 1762; repr. 1809); tables of cases, matters. A well researched and reasoned analysis at mid century of the law of high treason, homicide and other capital offences by a distinguished King's Bench judge. This is particularly useful for a contemporary view of the principles of the criminal law. Based on a voluminous analysis of reported cases.

Fowle, J.P.M., ed, *Wiltshire Quarter Sessions and Assizes, 1736,* Wilts. Archaeol. and Nat. Hist. Soc. XI (Devizes 1955). pp.lxv + 213; appendices; indices of subjects, persons and places. A full calendar of the quarter sessions minute and order books, estreats of fines and rolls, and the assize indictment file and gaol delivery roll. This is the only complete quarter sessions and assize collection published for a year in the 18th century. The introduction is an excellent account of the classes of judicial records in the county from the 16th to the 18th centuries, and of the local judicial system.

Halévy, E., *England in 1815*; Vol. I of *A History of the English People in the Nineteenth Century* (London 1924). pp.xv + 655; annotated biblio.; index. Perhaps the most poignant sketch of England's institutions (pt I) and its social and economic conditions (pt II) at the end of the 18th century.

Hall, *Theft, Law and Society*. See above. p.276.

Hawkins, W., *A Treatise of the Pleas of the Crown* (London 1716; 7th edn by T. Leach 1795). Two vols, pp.xxix + 576, xiv + 661; index of subjects to each vol. The best treatise on the subject in the early 18th century. Bk I covers crimes and Bk II legal processes and punishment. The treatise is especially well researched, organized and written. It is critical of the law and its writers and offers some challenging views. The historical aspects, however, contain errors and some misunderstandings.

Hay, D., Linebaugh, P. and Thompson, E.P., eds, *Albion's Fatal Tree: Crime and Society in Eighteenth-Century England* (London 1975). pp.352; illust; appendices; indices of persons and places, subjects. Essays by D. Hay on 'Property, Authority and Criminal Law' and 'Poaching and the Game Laws on Cannock Chase'; P.

Linebaugh, 'The Tyburn Riot Against the Surgeons; C. Winslow, 'Sussex Smugglers'; J.G. Rule, 'Wrecking and Coastal Plunder'; and E.P. Thompson, 'The Crime of Anonymity'. The appendix to the latter essay contains an interesting edition of threatening letters illustrating public protest and private grievances from rural and urban areas. A good volume of essays, distinguished by a common political stance. Hay's initial paper should be noted for its critique of Radzinowicz.

Heath, J., *Eighteenth Century Penal Theory* (Oxford 1963), pp.viii + 288; appendices; index. The introductory section contains interesting though discursive chapters on ethics, police, trials and punishments in 18th-century Europe (pp.3-65). The remainder consists of useful extracts from the published writings of 18th-century theorists.

Hibbert, C., *The Road to Tyburn: the story of Jack Sheppard and the 18th Century Underworld* (London 1957). pp.163; biblio.; glossary; index. The book is a caricature of Sheppard's world of Newgate and the environs of greater London in the year 1724. More a novel than history, the book has a number of memorable scenes and passages.

Holdsworth, *History*, vols VIII-IX, XI-XIII. See above. p.274.

Howard, J., *The State of the Prisons in England and Wales* (London 1778; 1929 edn). pp.xxii + 306; index. A collection of contemporary evidence on the state of European prisons in the late 18th century by the most prominent prison reformer of the era. The section on Britain, based on records and personal observations, is at pp.162-432 of the original edition and is organized by county. Tables III-XI comprise some interesting 'select' statistics on crimes and prisoners in English counties *c.*1749-78.

Howell, *State Trials*. See above p.276.

Howson, G., *Thief-Taker General: The Rise and Fall of Jonathan Wild* (London 1970). pp.xiv + 338; biblio.; index. A popular account of Wild's career 1712-25, including the rise of gang-style 'hooliganism', of Wild's 'reformers' who destroyed those gangs in southern England and established their own underworld syndicate, and of their swift prosecution and demise. An entertaining and well-writted account based on the original administrative and judicial records, and contemporary pamphlets and newsletters.

Ives, *Penal Methods*. See above. p.278.

Lawrence, *Capital Punishment*. See above. p.278.

McCloskey, R.E., ed, *The Works of James Wilson* (Cambridge, Mass 1967), vol. II, pp.441-875. The law lectures of James Wilson, Associate Justice of the U.S. Supreme Court 1790-91, contain a fascinating account of criminal justice in the late 18th century (pp.611-707). Heavily steeped in Scots, English and American law, his analysis of crimes against the person ranks as one of the most interesting of the period. Based largely on English sources. Wilson, a student of 'The Enlightenment', is critical of English legislation and judicial practices.

[Manchester], *Court Leet*. See above p.284.

Mandeville, B., *An Inquiry into the Causes of the Frequent Executions at Tyburn* (London 1725; repr. Los Angeles 1964). pp.vii + 55. A contemporary attack on the laws pertaining to theft and theftbote (compounding felonies) and on the useless ceremonies of hanging, drawing and quartering. It advocates stiffer prison terms and conditions, and transportation. There is an introduction by M.R. Zirker Jr.

Melling, *Kentish Crime and Punishment*. See above p.276.

Moir , E.A.L., 'Sir George Onesiphorus Paul', in *Gloucestershire Studies*, ed. H.P.R. Finberg (Leicester 1957), pp.195-224. A cogent discussion of the prison reformers of the late 18th century, including G.O. Paul of Gloucester.

[Nottingham], *Records of the Borough of Nottingham*, vol. VII, *1760-1800* (Nottingham 1947), pp.xv + 534; index. A calendar of the common council, chamberlains, constables and quarter sessions records combined on a yearly basis and fully annotated. This is one of the best compilations of borough records for the century and useful for criminal administration. The previous volume for the 18th century (VI, *1702-1760*) contains only extracts from some of the records and thus is not useful for the study of crime or the judiciary.

Pike, *History of Crime*, vol. II. See above p.276.

Pringle, P., *Hue and Cry; The Birth of the British Police* (London 1955). pp.230; biblio.; index. A popular narrative history of the London metropolitan police under the direction of J. Fielding 1758-80. This provides some insight into the prosecution of gang warfare and industrial riots, and police reform. The writer, however, is biased in his assessment of the success of the police system, and the work is completely undocumented. The index is also faulty.

Radzinowicz, L., *A History of English Criminal Law and its administration from 1750* (London 1948-68). Four vols, pp.xxiv + 853, xv + 751, xv + 688, ix + 492; biblio.; tables of cases, statutes; index to each vol. Vol. I is concerned largely with the 18th century. It has sections on capital punishment, its statutes and contemporary views, and reform ideas to 1819 (pts I—IV). Vol. II discusses punishment and police in the 17th and 18th centuries (pts I-III). Vol. III includes a section on the Bow Street magistracy in the 18th century (pp.29-62). This is not a history of criminal law or its administration. The work is largely a compilation of statutes, pamphlets and printed tracts on police and punishment together with a commentary. The bibliographies are excellent guides to these materials.

Richardson, *Manor of Acomb*. See above. p.285.

Rose, R.B., 'Eighteenth-Century Price Riots and Public Policy in England', *International Review of Social Hist.*, VI (1961), pp.277-92. An analysis of popular riots and their role as a reaction to, and correction of the government's protectionist policies in the 18th century. There is also information on the shopkeepers and merchants who were victimized.

Rudé G., *Wilkes and Liberty; A Social Study of 1763 to 1774* (Oxford 1962). pp.xvi + 240; appendices; biblio.; index. Chs 2-4 describe and assess the trials of Wilkes and others for seditious libel and riot 1763-9. The discussion of the social disorder of the time, politics and the law, and the general warrant issue is excellent. The trials, however, are not in themselves discussed for their law.

Shaw, A.G.L., *Convicts and the Colonies: a study of penal transportation from Great Britain and Ireland to Australia and other parts of the British Empire* (London 1966). pp.399; tables, appendices; biblio.; index. An important scholarly study of the transportation in the 18th and 19th centuries (pp.17-131, 146-83). It is based on a nearly exhaustive examination of the original records but is difficult to read. The notes are a book in themselves and the appendices contain useful material for further research. The bibliography is excellent.

Shelton, W.J., *English Hunger and Industrial Disorders; A Study of social conflicts during the first decade of George III's reign* (London 1973). pp.ix + 225; select biblio.; index. An excellent analysis of the rural and metropolitan riots of the 1760s, the social tensions which underlay them, and the interaction of the poor, landowners and industrialists with the institutions of local and central government. Based on a critical examination of the manuscript and printed sources, legal and non-legal.

Sparks, S., ed, *Libel: Four Tracts 1770* (New York 1974). pp. item 1-68, item 2-198, item 3-46, item 4-65. The work contains the full text (item 1) of the record of the trial before the King's Bench in June 1770 of J. Almon, bookseller, for libel in selling the Junius letters. Also of general interest is item 2, a treatise on the history of the prerogative courts since the early 17th century, including an analysis of the doctrines of Coke, Ellesmere, Holt and Vaughan, and the libel cases of the 1640s.

_____, ed, *Libels, Warrants and Seizures: Three Tracts 1764-1771* (New York 1974). pp.135 + 164 + 48. Three letters which discuss in treatise form the history of general warrants and the prerogative writs from the late 17th century down through the Wilkes case.

_____, ed, *The Prosecution of Thomas Paine: Seven Tracts 1793-1798* (New York 1974). pp. item 1-196, item 2-25, item 3-31, item 4-16, item 5-23, item 6-31, item 7-33. The first tract is a transcript of the trial of Paine for libel in the King's Bench in December 1792. The fourth is the indictment against T. Spence for selling Paine's 'Rights of Man'. Items 5-6 comprise the indictments against his publisher T. Williams. The trial of Daniel Eaton for the publication of the second part of Paine's work is edited separately as *Daniel Isaac Eaton and Thomas Paine: Five Tracts 1793-1812* (New York 1974), pp.50 + 65 + 15 + 62 + 80.

_____, ed, *Three Trials: John Peter Zenger, H.S. Woodfall and John Lambert 1765-1794* (New York 1974). pp. item 1-54, item 2-x, item 3-67, item 4-34, item 5-32, item 6-68. Includes some interesting contemporary evidence and writing on the law of libel and trial by jury. Item 3 is an articulate letter from a barrister on the development of trial by jury since the late 17th century, and the different forms of proceeding between Westminster and the counties. Item 4 has several letters from another lawyer on the development of the law of libel in the same period. Item 5 is a verbatim account of the original records of *R. v John Lambert* (KB 1793-94) together with contemporary comment.

The Statutes at Large, vols V-XVIII (London 1768-1800). A good edition of the text of the parliamentary statutes 1714-1800. It includes all Acts both private and public. There is a topical index at the end of each volume. However, there is no table of contents and the marginal notes are often given irregularly.

Thompson, E.P., *Whigs and Hunters: The Origins of the Black Act* (London 1975). pp.313; illust; appendices; indices of persons and places, subjects. The Black Act of 1723 introduced the death penalty for a wide range of social and economic crimes against property. This is an analysis of the class interests behind the Act, and of the role and activities of Walpole's politicians in the parks of Surrey, Hampshire and Berkshire. A challenging and controversial work. Based on an extremely wide range of public records.

Walker, *Crime and Insanity*. See above p.277.

Webbs, *English Prisons*. See above p.279.

Webb, S. and B., *The History of Liquor Licensing. English Local Government* XI (London 1903; repr. 1963). pp. ix + 176; appendix; index. A short and sketchy history from 1700 to 1830, including an account of the different court procedures used by rural and urban J.P.s in liquor related offences. This is based on little research, and few sources are cited.

_____, *The Manor and the Borough. English Local Government* II-III (London 1908; repr. 1963). pp.xiii + vi + 858; indices of subjects, persons, places. The work concentrates on the borough corporations 1689-1835. The structure of their institutions and courts are given in Bk II, ch. 6, a number of 'closed' and 'democratic' corporations are discussed in chs 8-9, and the City of London in ch. 11. The book can be said to provide a foundation from which one can turn to the study of crime and criminal justice in the boroughs.

_____, *The Parish and the County. English Local Government* I (London 1906; repr. 1963). pp.xxxiv + 664; indices of subjects, persons, places. This contains a good account of the court of quarter sessions as an administrative and legislative body *c.*1689-1832 from a wide range of local sources. However, there is little generalization or interpretation of judicial procedures. The legal officers are defined in Bk II, chs 1 and 5, and the J.P.s and quarter sessions in chs 3-4. There is some reference to criminal jurisdiction in ch. 6.

Webbs, *Poor Law History*. See above p.277.

Webbs, *Story of the King's Highway*. See above p.278.

Williams, E.N., ed, *The Eighteenth-Century Constitution 1688-1815* (Cambridge 1968). pp.xvi + 464; biblio.; index. Ch. 7 has a collection of documents illustrating the authority and powers of local officials and of judicial process at quarter sessions. Ch. 6 contains statutes, petitions and cases concerning arrest, riot, rebellion and treason before the central courts.

Williams-Jones, K., ed, *A Calendar of the Merioneth Quarter Sessions Rolls*, vol. I, *1733-1765* (Aberystwyth 1965). pp.xc + 376; illust; appendices; indices of persons and places, subjects. An excellent calendar of the sessions rolls with a transcript of the notes on cases. The records comprise a full range of local criminal prosecutions. The introduction has a good analysis of the manuscripts, but there is no discussion of the procedure or substance of the law. One of the useful appendices contains a list of causes removed to King's Bench (pp.284-6).

Notes

Introduction:

1 E.g. J.S. Cockburn, *A History of English Assizes 1558-1714* (Cambridge 1972); J. Samaha, *Law and Order in Historical Perspective: The Case of Elizabethan Essex* (New York 1974); *Albion's Fatal Tree: Crime and Society in Eighteenth-Century England*, ed D. Hay, P. Linebaugh and E.P. Thompson (1975).

2 Cf. *House of Commons Sessional Papers of the Eighteenth Century*, ed S. Lambert (Wilmington 1975-), introduction, I, p.*35*.

3 Ingram (p.113 below) includes these.

4 E.g. B. Woodcock, *Medieval Ecclesiastical Courts in the Diocese of Canterbury* (Oxford 1952); *An Episcopal Court Book for the Diocese of Lincoln 1514-1520*, ed M. Bowker (Lincs. Rec. Soc., LXI, 1967), introduction.

5 The history and purposes of the Act are very inadequately handled by Radzinowicz whose erroneous interpretation distorts parts of E.P. Thompson's *Whigs and Hunters: the Origins of the Black Act* (1975). Cf. *House of Commons Sessional Papers*, ed Lambert, pp.*37-8*.

6 G.R. Elton, *Policy and Police: the enforcement of the Reformation in the Age of Thomas Cromwell* (Cambridge 1972); J.H. Langbein, *Prosecuting Crime in the Renaissance* (Cambridge, Mass 1974).

7 See e.g. Cockburn, *Assizes*, especially the revealing bibliography of manuscript sources.

8 See especially Cockburn (pp.50-51 below); Dr Ingram's essay, too, is pervaded by a recognition of these problems.

9 J.S. Cockburn, 'Early-Modern Assize Records as Historical Evidence'. *Jnl of the Society of Archivists*, V (1975), pp.215-31.

10 Also by Douglas Hay whose remarkable essay on 'Property, Authority and the Criminal Law' (*Albion's Fatal Tree*, pp.17ff.) at times falls into the error of relying on assumptions taken to be axiomatic.

Chapter 1:

1 To save space, no references are given in the notes to sources of elementary propositions which may readily be found in the principal textbooks. Law reports are cited by the abbreviations in general use among lawyers. A list of the latter may be found in *A Manual of Legal Citations* (Institute of Advanced Legal Studies 1959), I, pp.39-75; or in C.W. Ringrose, *Where to Look for Your Law* (1962), pp.187-237. References to state trials are to vols I-XXVII of *State Trials* (1809-20), ed F. Hargrave, W. Cobbett, T.B. Howell and T.J. Howell.

2 T.F.T. Plucknett, *Concise History of the Common Law* (5th edn 1956), p.432.

3 Langbein, *Prosecuting Crime*, p.35.

4 J.S. Cockburn, 'Trial by the Book? Fact and Theory in the Criminal Process 1558-1625': paper delivered at the Cambridge Legal History Conference, 8 July 1975.

5 Z. Babington, *Advice to Grand Jurors in Cases of Blood* (1677), p.6.

6 A judge could, however, direct others to initiate proceedings, or advise on the settling of an indictment: e.g. *R.* v *Page* (1633), Cro. Car. 332; Hale, *Pleas*, II, pp.159-61; Baker, 'Newgate Reports', pp.317-18. He probably had no judicial authority to do so, and could not enforce his direction.

7 The only important exception was impeachment: see below p.26.

8 These involve no prosecutor, no indictment and no jury: see Blackstone, *Commentaries* (1765), IV, pp.287-8 ('not agreeable to the genius of the common law'); J.C. Fox, *History of Contempt of Court* (Oxford 1927). For a well-known example see Cockburn, *Assizes*, p.110. For contempt out of the view see *R.* v *Alman* (1765), Wilm. 243.

9 21 Hen. VIII, c. 11.

10 Babington, *Advice to Grand Jurors*, pp.90-91.

11 3 Hen. VII, c.1. For the prior position see A. Fitzherbert, *La Graunde Abridgement* (1577 edn), tit. 'Corone', pl.44.

12 *Egerton* v *Morgan* (1610), 1 Bulst. 69-88.

13 *Stout* v *Cowper* (1699), 12 Mod. 375.

14 The latest are *Bigby* v *Kennedy* (1770), 5 Burr. 2643; *Smith* v *Taylor* (1771), ibid., 2793. In 1771 Eden described appeals as 'an old branch of the law, which by possibility may become an essential safeguard of the rights of the people': *Principles*, p.184. See also n.42 below.

15 If an appeal was discontinued, the Crown could arraign the appellee on the declaration (without indictment): Staunford, *Plees*, ff. 147*v*-48; Hale, *Pleas*, II, pp.149*-50*; *Reade* v *Rochforth* (1556), Dy. 120, 131.

16 Coke, *Institutes*, III, p.136.

17 Quoted by Nicholas Fuller in *Omer's Case* (1608), HLS, MS 118, f. 187 (translated).

18 11 Hen. VII, c.3 (repealed by 1 Hen. VIII, c.6); An Act for establishing an High Court of Justice, 26 Mar. 1650: *Acts and Ordinances of the Interregnum*, ed C.H. Firth and R.S. Rait (1911), II, pp.364-7.

19 All indictments were presentments, but usage reserved the latter term for those made from the jurors' own knowledge (i.e. without bills): Lambard, *Eirenarcha* (1581), p.383; Blackstone, *Commentaries*, IV, p.301. The latter were made in the form of a note which the clerk drew into an indictment: *A Guide to Juries* (1703 edn), p.39; J. Gonson, *Charge to the Grand Jury of Westminster* (1729), p.25. But not all presentments were indictments: e.g. presentments of suicide by a coroner's jury: Hale, *Pleas*, II, pp.152-3. •

20 *Cobat's Case* (1368), cited in Hale, *Pleas*, II, pp.60-1.

21 See below nn.89-90.

22 [J. Somers], *The Security of English-men's Lives* (1766 edn), p.11, says 23 or 25; *Form and Method*, p.12, says 17, 19 or 21.

23 Somers, *Security*, pp.83-107; [J. Hawles], *The English-man's Right* (1680), pp.47-8; *Guide to Juries*, pp.40-81, 105-108.

24 Babington, *Advice to Grand Jurors*, pp.119, 124-5.

25 Hale, *Pleas*, II, p.157; *R.* v *Earl of Shaftesbury* (1681), *State Trials*, VIII, at col. 770, *per* Pemberton C.J. ('probable cause'); J. Hawkins, *Charge to the Grand Jury of Middlesex* (1770), pp.24-8; Blackstone, *Commentaries*, IV, p.303; Eden, *Principles*, p.322n.

26 Hale, *Pleas*, II, p.61; *R.* v *Culliford* (1704), 1 Salk. 382.

27 *Guide to Juries*, p.41.

28 Radzinowicz, *History*, I, p.92; F.W. Maitland, *Justice and Police* (1885), p.139.

29 Hale founded it on a case of 1291: *Pleas*, II, pp.156-149*.
30 See M.W. Beresford, 'The Common Informer, Penal Statutes, and Economic Regulation', *Economic History Review*, 2nd ser., X (1957), pp.221-37; G.R. Elton, 'Informing for Profit' in *Star Chamber Stories* (1958), pp.78-113; T.G. Barnes, *Somerset 1625-1640* (Cambridge, Mass 1961), pp.54-6.
31 *R. v Berchet* (1690), 5 Mod. 459, 1 Show. K.B. 106.
32 4 & 5 Wm & Mary, c.18; Blackstone, *Commentaries*, IV, p.309.
33 For summary procedure see below p.24.
34 A. Esmein, *History of Continental Criminal Procedure*, transl. J. Simpson (1914); Holdsworth, *History*, III, pp.620-23; V, pp.170-78; Langbein, *Prosecuting Crime*, pp.129-251.
35 J. Fortescue, *De Laudibus Legum Anglie*, ed S.B. Chrimes (Cambridge 1949), pp.69-73; Lambard, *Eirenarcha*, pp.436-7; Blackstone, *Commentaries*, IV, p.350.
36 Stephen, *History*, I, p.426.
37 28 Hen. VIII, c.15; Blackstone, *Commentaries*, IV, p.269.
38 See J.H. Wigmore, 'The Privilege against Self-Crimination: its History', *Harvard Law Review*, XV (1902), pp.610-23; R.G. Usher, *The Rise and Fall of the High Commission* (1913).
39 16 Chas I, c.10. See also *Lilburne's Case* (1637), *State Trials*, III, col.1315.
40 Smith, *De Republica*, p.44; Coke, *Institutes*, III, p.52; Hale, *Pleas*, I, p.499; L. Boynton, 'Martial Law and the Petition of Right', *English Historical Review*, LXXIX (1964), pp.255-84.
41 Hale, *Pleas*, II, p.71. The last instance of such a trial for theft was at Halifax in 1650: Stephen, *History*, I, pp.265-70.
42 Staunford, *Plees*, f.177 (translated); Smith, *De Republica*, pp.49, 93; *Lord Rea v Ramsey* (1631), *State Trials*, III, col. 483; *Ashford v Thornton* (1818), 1 B. & Ald. 405; 59 Geo. III, c.46; G. Neilson, *Trial by Combat* (Glasgow 1890), pp.322-34.
43 Langbein, *Prosecuting Crime*, pp.63-4.
44 See L.O. Pike, *Constitutional History of the House of Lords* (1894), pp.209-28. See also 7 Wm III, c.3, ss 10-11.
45 2 Hen. V, c.3; 19 Hen. VII, c.13; 23 Hen. VIII, c.13. The old rule that some jurors should be 'of the hundred' was obsolete by Hale's time.
46 *R. v Thomas* (1554), Dy. 99. An alien, however, could by statute claim trial by a jury *de medietate linguae* (that is, one-half foreigners): see *R. v Sherleys* (1557), Dy. 144.
47 Hawles, *English-man's Right*, pp.10-18; *Guide to Juries, passim*. Horne Tooke's acquittal in 1794 was commemorated by medals inscribed: 'Not guilty say the jury, equal judges of law and fact'.
48 P. 10 Hen. IV, Fitzherbert, *Abridgement*, tit. 'Attaint', pl.60, 64; 12 Rep. 23. The reason was that two juries (24 in all) had already passed on him.
49 Smith, *De Republica*, pp.87-8; BL, Harl. MS 5141(a) (hereafter cited as Dalison, Reports), f.27.
50 *R. v Bushell* (1670), Vaugh. 146. Cf. *R. v Leach* (1664), T. Ray. 98; *R. v Hood* (1666), Kel. 50; *R. v Windham* (1667), 2 Keb. 180.
51 R. Crompton, *Loffice et auctoritie de Justices de Peace* (1617 edn), p.114, pl.6 (c.1572); *R. v Mansell* (1584), 1 And. 103, 104; *R. v Chichester* (1671), Aleyn 12.
52 BL, Add. MS 25228, f.41, pl.850 (1620).
53 Hawles, *English-man's Right*, pp.36, 9-10. See also *Guide to Juries*, pp.20-22.
54 15 Ric. II, c.2; 13 Hen. IV, c.7; J.C. Fox, *History of Contempt of Court* (Oxford 1927), pp. 70-83; Langbein, *Prosecuting Crime*, pp.64-75.

55 Blackstone, *Commentaries*, IV, p.281.
56 *Gardner's Case* (1592 or 1601), 5 Rep. 72, Cro. Eliz. 822.
57 *R.* v *Chandler* (1702), 1 Ld. Raym. 581.
58 *R.* v *Dyer* (1703), 1 Salk. 181, 6 Mod. 41. For all the law on the subject see W. Boscawen, *Convictions on Penal Statutes* (1792); W. Paley, *Law and Practice of Summary Convictions* (1814).
59 For a judicial retaliation see *R.* v *Moreley* (1760), 2 Burr. 1040.
60 Game Act 1670, 22 & 23 Chas II, c.25.
61 11 & 12 Vict., c.43; Stephen, *History*, I, pp.122-6.
62 12 Edw. III, *Liber Assisarum*, pl.5; Coke, *Institutes*, IV, pp.163-4; Hawkins, *Pleas*, II, ch. 1, ss 7-8; Stephen, *History*, I, pp.109-10.
63 Blackstone, *Commentaries*, IV, p.259. Cf. *R.* v *Blair* (1689), *State Trials*, XII, col. 207, which broke the rule.
64 See C.G.C. Tite, *Impeachment and Parliamentary Judicature in Early Stuart England* (1974); P.J. Marshall, *The Impeachment of Warren Hastings* (Oxford 1965).
65 *R.* v *Edgerley* (1641), March N.C. 131; *R.* v *Johnson* (1686), Comb. 36, *per* Herbert C.J.; *R.* v *Abraham* (1689), Comb. 141, *per* Holt C.J.; Hawkins, *Pleas*, II, ch. 3, s.4.
66 E.g. *R.* v *Taverner* (1616), 3 Bulst. 171; *R.* v *Gibbons* (1651), *State Trials*, V, col. 366.
67 Courts Act 1971, c.23, s.1. From about 1916 until 1971 a composite short-form commission had been used. The 1971 Act restrains only commissions of assize, not gaol delivery or oyer and terminer; but the three types had long been inseparable.
68 The Home, Midland, Norfolk, Oxford, Northern and Western. See Cockburn, *Assizes*, pp.23-48, and Map I. There were also two Welsh circuits (North and South).
69 Statute of Northampton, 2 Edw. III, c.2; 4 Edw. III, c.2.
70 There were also special commissions (limited by person, place or subject-matter): e.g. those for the Lord High Steward (trial of peers), state trials of commoners, the Court of the Verge (offences within 12 miles of the royal household), Justice Seats of the Forests, University Courts and Admiralty Sessions.
71 Bro. N.C. 37 (1555); *Anon.* (1584), 1 And. 111; *R.* v *Pursell* (1590), Cro. Eliz. 179; Hale, *Pleas,* II, pp.34-5. It was once argued that the jurisdiction extended only to those in gaol at the time of the commission: 1 And. 111. The distinction between the commissions is discussed in Dalison, Reports, f.27*v* (where Staunford J. opposes the orthodox view) and f.29*v*; 'Justice Jones his opinion touching the commissions by which the Justices sit at Newgate' (*c.*1635): CUL, MS Ll.3.11, ff.208-11. The forms of the commissions will be found in Coke, *Institutes*, IV, pp.162-3, 168; Holdsworth, *History*, I, pp.669-70.
72 Lambard, *Eirenarcha* (1588 edn), p.549; Dalton, *Countrey Justice* (1630 edn), p.49; F. Bacon, *Use of the Law* (1639 edn), p.12. Langbein, *Prosecuting Crime*, p.105, traced the passage to the 1588 edition of Lambard.
73 Barnes, *Somerset*, pp.50-4; Cockburn, *Assizes*, pp.90-9.
74 1 & 2 P. & M., c.13; 2 & 3 P. & M., c.10; Hale, *Pleas*, II, p.46; Blackstone, *Commentaries*, IV, p.268; Barnes, *Somerset*, p.53; Cockburn, *Assizes*, pp.90, 91; Langbein, *Prosecuting Crime*, pp.104-18.
75 Cockburn, *Assizes*, pp.97-8, and Table I.
76 J.S. Cockburn, *A History of English Assizes 1558-1714* (Cambridge 1972).
77 A. Fitzherbert, *The newe Boke of Justices of the peas* (1538), f.21; Crompton,

Justice, p.19; *R.* v *Buckler* (1551), Dy. 69. Fitzherbert's view was expressly denied by Hales and Portman JJ. in 1553: Dalison, *Reports*, f.10v.

78 2 Hen. V, c.4.

79 12 Ric. II, c.10. These statutory provisions were often ignored: Lambard, *Eirenarcha*, pp.482-91.

80 Blackstone, *Commentaries*, I, p.340; J.H. Gleason, *The Justices of the Peace in England 1558-1640* (Oxford 1969), pp.48-51, 104-8, 137-8; Langbein, *Prosecuting Crime*, pp.112-18.

81 For the quarter sessions' functions in general see E.G. Dowdall, *A Hundred Years of Quarter Sessions* (Cambridge 1932); Barnes, *Somerset*, ch. 3, esp. pp.68-81; E. Moir, *Local Government in Gloucestershire 1775-1800* (Bristol 1969), pp.85-107; F.G. Emmison, *Elizabethan Life: Disorder* (Chelmsford 1970); A.H. Smith, *County and Court: Government and Politics in Norfolk 1558-1603* (Oxford 1974), esp. pp.47-138.

82 S. and B. Webb, *English Local Government: Parish and County* (1906), pp.421-79.

83 'Henry Townshend's "Notes on the Office of a Justice of Peace" 1661-63', ed R.D. Hunt, *Worcs. Hist. Soc. Misc.*, II (1967), pp.113-14.

84 27 Hen. VIII, c.24.

85 Lambard, *Eirenarcha*, pp.500-503. See also Hawkins, *Pleas*, II, ch. 8, s.47.

86 Hicks' Hall was built in 1612, the new Clerkenwell Sessions Court in 1779. For much information about the sessions in the 18th century see B.H. Davis, *A Proof of Eminence: The Life of Sir John Hawkins* (Bloomington 1973), pp.175-299.

87 Hale, *Pleas*, II, pp.69-71; Hawkins, *Pleas*, II, chs 10-11; Blackstone, *Commentaries*, IV, p.273; S. and B. Webb, *Manor and Borough*, I (1908), pp.21-30; Holdsworth, *History*, I, pp.134-8; Barnes, *Somerset*, pp.48-9.

88 M. 22 Edw. IV, 22, pl.2; M.1 Ric. III, 1, pl.1; T. 6 Hen. VII, 4, pl.4; P.11 Hen. VII, 22, pl.11.

89 1 Edw. III, c.17 (leet); 1 Edw. IV, c.2 (tourn).

90 P.27 Hen. VIII, 2, pl. 6.

91 H. 21 Edw. III, Fitzherbert, *Abridgement*, tit. 'Barre', pl.271; P.8 Edw. IV, 5, pl.17; M. 2 Ric. III, 11, pl.25; T. 20 Hen. VII, Keil. 66, pl.8; Dy. 13; Hale, *Pleas*, II, p.155; Hawkins, *Pleas*, II, ch. 10, s.76. See also J. Ritson, *The Jurisdiction of the Court Leet* (1809).

92 *R.* v *Roupell* (1776), 1 Cowp. 458.

93 12 Rep. 93; Holdsworth, *History*, I, p.618. Abolished by 29 Chas II, c.9.

94 Holdsworth, *History*, I, pp.616-21; R.A. Marchant, *The Church Under the Law 1560-1640* (Cambridge 1969); P. Hair, *Before the Bawdy Court 1300-1800* (1972); F.G. Emmison, *Elizabethan Life: Morals and the Church Courts* (Chelmsford 1973). See also Usher, *High Commission*.

95 The following section draws heavily on a series of formularies showing how clerks were to order proceedings at criminal sessions. The oldest is: (i) *Hic sequuntur regule atque ordines nonnulle observande tam in sessionibus pacis quam in sessionibus gaole deliberacionis (c.*1550): Bodleian Lib., MS *e Museo* 57, ff.87v-89. The remainder distinguish sessions of the peace from sessions of gaol delivery. For gaol delivery or assizes: (ii) 'The manner and form of proceedings at the Assizes and General Gaol Delivery holden by his Majesty's Justices according to the Law and Custom of England' (temp. Jas I): BL, Lansd. MS 569, ff.5-20; Bodleian Lib., Rawl. MS C.271, f.3; (iii) 'Here follows the Order of the Gaol Delivery' (*c.*1610): BL, Harl. MS 1603, ff.75-78; (iv) T.W., *Clerk of*

Assize; (v) *Form and Method*; (vi) *Crown Circuit Companion*. For quarter sessions: (vii) 'Instructions for Proceedings at the Sessions of the Peace' (temp. Jas I): BL, Lansd. MS 569, ff.1-5; (viii) Richard Bragge, *Regule per Clericum ad Generalem Sessionem Pacis Observande* (temp. Chas II): in *Quarter Sessions Order Book 1642-49*, ed B.C. Redwood, *Sussex Rec. Soc.*, LIV (1954), pp.210-14; (ix) 'Directions to hold a Sessions for a Port' (*c*.1690): in M. Reed, 'The Keeping of Sessions of the Peace in Hastings', *Sussex Archaeological Collections*, C (1962), pp.55-59; (x) *Crown Circuit Companion*, pp.29-86. Other forms for use at sessions, not consulted by the writer: Bodleian Lib., Rawl. MS B. 257, f.77 (Kent, temp. Jas I or Chas I); Rawl. MS D. 1136 (temp. Chas II); 'The form and manner how to hold a General Sessions' in J.W., *Officium Clerici Pacis* (1686 edn), pp.2-11.

96 H. 14 Hen. VIII, 16, pl.3; Coke, *Institutes*, IV, pp. 177-8; Hale, *Pleas*, II, pp.79-80, 107; Hawkins, *Pleas*, II, ch. 13, ss 11, 18-20; Blackstone, *Commentaries*, IV, p.290.

97 *Scavage* v *Tateham* (1601), Cro. Eliz. 829; *Morgan* v *Lloyd* (1649), HLS, MS 106, pp.528-32; Hale, *Pleas*, II, pp.120-21; Hawkins, *Pleas*, II, ch. 16, ss 3, 12.

98 1 & 2 P. & M., c.13; 2 & 3 P. & M., c.10; Smith, *De Republica*, p.72; Dalton, *Countrey Justice*, pp.295-304. For the power to release see Langbein, *Prosecuting Crime*, pp.7-8; Hawkins, *Pleas*, II, ch. 16, s.22.

99 Statute of Westminster I, c.15; 3 Hen. VII, c.3; Staunford, *Plees*, ff.71-77*v*; Crompton, *Justice*, pp.152-3; Dalton, *Countrey Justice*, pp.304-26; Hale, *Pleas*, II, pp.136-40; Hawkins, *Pleas*, II, ch. 15, ss 54-64. Blackstone said that bail in capital cases was exceptional: *Commentaries*, IV, p.296. It was argued in 1552 that a sheriff or constable acting alone could bail suspects at common law: Dalison, Reports, f.6.

100 Hale, *Pleas*, II, p.159; *R.* v *Earl of Shaftesbury* (1681), *State Trials*, VIII, col. 771. The latter case was attacked in Somers, *Security*, pp.31-50. It was the last instance: E. Christian at Blackstone, *Commentaries*, IV, p.302n.

101 [J. Hawles], *Remarks upon the Tryals of Fitzharris* [*and others*] (1689), pp.20-21; *State Trials*, V, col. 972n; ibid., VIII, col. 773n.

102 *R.* v *Lilburne* (1653), *State Trials*, V, at col. 416; *R.* v *Harrison* (1660), ibid., at col. 996; Hale, *Pleas*, II, p.219; Blackstone, *Commentaries*, IV, p.323; Eden, *Principles*, pp.186-7.

103 37 Edw. III, c.15 (as interpreted); *R.* v *Humfrey* (1607), Exeter Coll. Oxford, MS 93, f.110; *Anon.* (1618), HLS, MS 2072, f.91; Hale, *Pleas*, II, p.169. English was introduced by 4 Geo. II, c.26.

104 *R.* v *Vane* (1661), *State Trials*, VI, col. 132.

105 Hale, *Pleas*, II, p.236; *R.* v *Rosewell* (1684), *State Trials*, X, at cols 266-8; *R.* v *Charnock* (1696), ibid., XII, at cols 1381-83; M. Foster, *Crown Law* (Oxford 1762), p.228. But he could have it repeated, and by indulgence might copy it from dictation: *R.* v *Gibbons* (1651), *State Trials*, V, at col. 268; *R.* v *Ratcliffe* (1746), Fost. 40.

106 Hale, *Pleas*, II, pp.219, 258; *Form and Method*, p.23; Blackstone, *Commentaries*, IV, p.339; Stephen, *History*, I, p.297n. Doubters: D. Barrington, *Observations on the Ancient Statutes* (1775 edn), p.419n; Christian's note to Blackstone (1800 edn), at p.340.

107 *R.v. Abington* (1586), *State Trials*, I, col. 1143; *R.* v. *Harrison* (1660), ibid., V, col. 999; *R.* v *Axtel* (1660), ibid., col. 1008. Axtel's objection was that God was not 'locally present'. Other prisoners would only put themselves on God: e.g. *R.* v *Peters* (1660), ibid., col. 1007; *R.* v *James* (1661), ibid., VI, col. 75. See also Baker, 'Newgate Reports', p.315; 9 Rep. 32.

108 P. 4 Edw. IV, 11, pl.18; T. 14 Edw. IV, 7, pl.10; Hale, *Pleas*, II, p.258.

109 Babington, *Advice to Grand Jurors*, p.192; *R.* v *Thorely* (1672), Kel. 27; Barrington, *Observations*, pp. 82-8.

110 Barrington, *Observations*, p.86 (instance at Cambridge, 1741); 12 Geo. III, c.20; 1 Lea. 83; E. Christian at Blackstone, *Commentaries*, IV, p.328n.

111 As to clergy see below p.41.

112 Staunford, *Plees*, f.150v; Hale, *Pleas*, II, p.257; Hawkins, *Pleas*, II, ch.31, s.5; Blackstone, *Commentaries*, IV, p.334.

113 Staunford, *Plees*, f.142; Hale, *Pleas*, II, p.225; Blackstone, *Commentaries*, IV, p.329.

114 Lambard, *Eirenarcha*, pp.522-3; Hawkins, *Pleas*, II, ch.31, s.3. Cf. the plea *non vult contendere*: *R.* v *Templeman* (1702), 7 Mod. 40.

115 Staunford, *Plees*, f.78; Coke, *Institutes*, II, p.315; III, p.34; Hale, *Pleas*, II, p.219; Kel. 9, 10; *State Trials*, V, at cols 979-81(f); *R.* v *Waite* (1743), 1 Lea. 28, 36; Eden, *Principles*, pp.187-8.

116 Smith, *De Republica*, p.79; R. Bernard, *The Legall Proceeding in Man-Shire against Sinne* (1630), p.233. In many accounts '*countez*' is corrupted to 'count these'; as to which see also Blackstone, *Commentaries*, IV, p.340n.

117 22 Hen. VIII, c.14; 32 Hen. VIII, c.3; 33 Hen. VIII, c. 23; 1 & 2 P. & M., c.10. At common law the prisoner was treated as mute of malice after challenging 36; but after these statutes, challenges over 20 were disregarded and the jury sworn: Hale, *Pleas*, II, pp.269-70.

118 *R.* v *Harman* (1619), HLS, MS 106, f.38; *R.* v *Vane* (1661), *State Trials*, VI, col. 132.

119 T. 9 Edw. IV, 27, pl.40; *R.* v *Salisbury* (1554), Plowd. 100; *R.* v *Dennis and May* (1557), Dalison, Reports, f.42v; *Trial of the Regicides* (1660), Kel. 9, resoln 8; *Form and Method*, p.29; Foster, *Crown Law*, pp.106-7.

120 *St Germain's Doctor and Student*, ed T.F.T. Plucknett & J.L. Barton, Selden Soc. XCI (1974), pp.284-6; Staunford, *Plees*, f.151v; *R.* v *Boothe* (1602), BL, Add. MS 25203, ff.569v-70 (translated); Coke, *Institutes*, III, p.137; *R.* v *Thomas* (1613), 2 Bulst. 147, *per* Coke C.J.; F. Pulton, *De Pace Regni* (1609), pp.184-5. Smith (*De Republica*, p.51) wrote as if it were somehow disloyal to argue against the Crown.

121 See, e.g., Baker, 'Newgate Reports', pp.311, 313, 314, 316; *R.* v *Mason* (1756), Fost. 132.

122 7 & 8 Wm III, c.3. Extended to impeachment by 20 Geo. III, c.30. As to questioning the prisoner, see Wigmore, 'The Privilege against Self-Crimination', at pp.629, 633-4.

123 Foster, *Crown Law*, p.231; Blackstone, *Commentaries*, IV, pp.354-6; Eden, *Principles*, pp.156-61; Stephen, *History*, I, p.424. There are numerous instances in Leach's reports. It did not become a right until 1836: 6 & 7 Wm IV, c.114.

124 Smith, *De Republica*, p.80; *R.* v *Abington* (1586), *State Trials*, I, col. 1143; *R.* v *Udall* (1590), ibid., col. 1278; Holdsworth, *History*, IX, pp.226-8.

125 *R.* v *Rosewell* (1684), *State Trials*, X, at col. 190, *per* Jeffreys C.J.; *R.* v *Hardy* (1794), ibid., XXIV, at cols 659-60, 754-6.

126 For the course see *R.* v *Raleigh* (1603), *State Trials*, II, at col. 4, *per* Popham C.J.; *R.* v *Axtell* (1660), ibid., V, at col. 1149, *per* Bridgman C.B.; *R.* v *Wakeman* (1679), ibid., VII, at col. 609, *per* North C.J. Cf. W. Sheppard, *Epitome of the Laws of this Nation* (1656), p.1051, who says that the prisoner spoke first and then the Crown witnesses were called.

127 *R.* v *Throckmorton* (1554), *State Trials*, I, at cols 887-8 (but he was not allowed to call witnesses); *R.* v *Udall* (1590), ibid., at cols 1281, 1304; Holdsworth, *History*, V, pp.192-4. The exclusionary rule was of Civil Law origin: Stephen, *History*, I, pp.350-4.

128 Coke, *Institutes*, III, p. 79; Crompton, *Justice*, p.110, pl.12; Dalton, *Countrey Justice*, pp.300-301; *R.* v *Moseley* (1647), *The Harleian Miscellany*, ed W. Oldys and T. Park, III, pp.499-502; *R.* v *Harvey* (1660), *State Trials*, V, col. 1197; *R.* v *Hurdman* (1661), *Worcs. Hist. Soc. Misc.*, II, p.95; Hale, *Pleas*, II, p.283; G. Duncomb, *Trials per Pais* (1766 edn), II, ch. 16; 7 & 8 Wm III, c.3, s.1; 1 Anne, st.2, c.9, s.3.

129 *R.* v *Tindal* (1633), Cro. Car. 291.

130 Dalton, *Countrey Justice*, p.301, citing a case before Popham C.J. at Cambridge.

131 Cockburn, *Assizes*, pp.110-11. After-dinner sittings were sometimes disgraced by drunkenness, somnolence and noise; at the Old Bailey they continued into the middle of the 19th century.

132 E. Christian at Blackstone, *Commentaries*, IV, p.360n; *R.* v *Tooke* (1795), *State Trials*, XXV, at cols 128-32 (12-hour sitting). In 1798 an Irish state trial lasted for 24 hours without a break: ibid., XXVII, col. 364.

133 Staunford, *Plees*, f.163 (translated).

134 Holdsworth, *History*, I, p.333.

135 *R.* v *Thomas* (1554), Dy. 99; *R.* v *Udall* (1590), *State Trials*, I, at col. 1282 ('There was much said, to prove that the testimony of a man absent was sufficient, if it were proved to be his upon the oaths of others').

136 *R.* v *Throckmorton* (1554), *State Trials*, I, at col. 875; *Anon.* (1556), Dalison, Reports, f.37 (Serjeants' Inn); *R.* v *Duke of Norfolk* (1571), *State Trials*, I, at col. 992; *R.* v *Udall* (1590), ibid., at cols 1279-81, 1283, 1302-3; *R.* v *Raleigh* (1603), ibid., II, at cols 15-16; *R.* v *Harman* (1619), HLS, MS 106, f.38. A reaction against the practice may be discerned in 5 & 6 Edw. VI, c.11; 1 & 2 P. & M., c.10, s.11 (discussed in Dalison, Reports, f.37); Smith, *De Republica*, pp.79-80. It is difficult to know which school of thought prevailed in ordinary cases. In state trials the judges openly admitted the fear that a deponent might retract his accusation if called: see, e.g., *State Trials*, II, at col. 16, *per* Popham C.J.

137 BL, Add. MS 25228, f.12v, pl.225. See also *R.* v *Raleigh* (1603), *State Trials*, II, at col. 18, *per* Warburton J. ('so many horse-stealers may escape, if they may not be condemned without witnesses'). Cf., to the contrary, Smith, *De Republica*, p.76; *Guide to Juries*, pp.22-3, 81.

138 *R.* v *Lord Morley* (1666), Kel. 55, resolns 4-6; *R.* v *Bromwich* (1666), 1 Lev. 180, 2 Keb. 19; *R.* v *Thatcher* (1676), T. Jo. 53; Hale, *Pleas*, I, p.305; II, pp.52, 284; Duncomb, *Trials per Pais*, II, ch. 16. By the 1690s it was thought that depositions were evidence only by virtue of the Marian legislation: see *R.* v *Paine* (1695), 5 Mod. 163, Comb. 281; *R.* v *Kirk* (1699), 12 Mod. 304. For the civil rule, see *Fortescue* v *Coake* (1616), Godb. 193.

139 J.H. Wigmore, 'History of the Hearsay Rule', *Harvard Law Rev.* XVII (1904), at p.445; Hawkins, *Pleas*, II, ch. 46, s.14. Some earlier hints of the rule: *R.* v *Love* (1651), *State Trials*, V, at cols 77-81; *R.* v *Moders* (1663), ibid., VI, at col. 276 ('hearsays must condemn no man'); *R.* v *Langhorn* (1679), ibid., VII, at col. 441, *per* Atkins J. ('that is no evidence against the prisoner, because it is by hear-say') and Scroggs C.J. ('the jury ought to take notice, that what another man said is no evidence against the prisoner'); *R.* v *Lord Russell* (1683), ibid., IX, at col. 613.

140 *Anon.* (1775), cited by Cowper at 1 Lea. 130.

141 *R.* v *Tong* (1662), Kel. 18; Hale, *Pleas*, I, p.304.

142 *R.* v *Rudd* (1775), 1 Lea. 115, 119, Cowp. 331; Blackstone, *Commentaries*, IV, p.331.

143 T. Leach at Hawkins, *Pleas* (1787 edn), ch. 46, s.18; Barrington, *Observations*, p.181. Cf. Hale, *Pleas*, I, p.305 ('considerable circumstances').

144 Stephen, *History*, I, pp.400-401.

145 *R.* v *James* (1661), *State Trials*, VI, at col. 84. Langbein, *Prosecuting Crime*, p.50, cites a still shorter address used where a jury had even asked for advice.

146 Fees on acquittal seem to have ranged from about 8*s.* to £1: W. Stubbs and G. Talmash, *The Crown Circuit Companion* (6th edn 1790), pp. 43, 718, 743; F.D. MacKinnon, *On Circuit* (1940), pp.90-91.

147 M. Madan, *Thoughts on Executive Justice* (1785), pp.82-4.

148 *R.* v *Geary* (1688), 2 Salk. 630, 1 Show. K.B. 131. The *allocutus* was quietly abandoned in 1967 on the assumption that it did not survive the abolition of the distinction between felony and misdemeanour.

149 By the 18th century a speech in mitigation was allowed in non-capital cases after a plea of guilty: *Crown Circuit Companion*, p.45. Ironically, there was no *allocutus* in such a case.

150 Psalm LI, v.1. It is alluded to as the neck-verse in *The Sermons of Master Samuel Hieron* (1620), pp.222-3; Eden, *Principles*, p.192. But in *R.* v *Thomas* (1613), 2 Bulst. 147, verse 14 was used: *Libera me a sanguinibus, Domine.* Smith (*De Republica*, p.83) says: 'the judge commonly giveth him a psalter, and turneth to what place he will'.

151 *Anon.* (1666), Kel. 51; Cockburn, *Assizes*, pp.125, 129; Baker, 'Newgate Reports', p.315.

152 E.g. *Anon.* (1561), Dy. 205, pl.6.

153 Hob. 288; 5 Anne, c.6; Blackstone, *Commentaries*, IV, p.370.

154 4 Hen. VII, c.13; *R.* v *Scott* (1785), 1 Lea. 401; E. Christian at Blackstone, *Commentaries*, IV, p.371n; Cockburn, *Assizes*, pp.128-9.

155 1 Edw. VI, c.12, s.14; *R.* v *Harman* (1620), HLS, MS 106, ff.38, 55; Babington, *Advice to Grand Jurors*, p.93.

156 Foster, *Crown Law*, p.372. Eden, *Principles*, pp.59-60, gives the impression that it could still be a real stigma. Between 1717 and 1779 it was possible to order transportation instead of branding: 4 Geo. I, c.11. The statute 19 Geo. III, c.74, s.3, did not abolish branding but made its continued use unnecessary.

157 In King's Bench, however, it was (throughout the period) the secondary justice's duty to pronounce judgment.

158 30 Geo. III, c.48. Convictions of women for *high* treason were rare; perhaps Alice Lisle and Elizabeth Gaunt (1685) were the last.

159 *Historical Collections of Private Passages of State 1618-29*, ed J. Rushworth (1659), pp.652-3; Anon. reports, CUL, MS Ee.5.17, f.254.

160 Smith, *De Republica*, p.84; *R.* v *Hale* (1741), 1 Lea. 21; *R.* v *Doyle* (1769), 1 Lea. 67; Blackstone, *Commentaries*, IV, p.201; Eden, *Principles*, pp.79-80.

161 Hale, *Pleas*, I, p.501; II, p.411; Foster, *Crown Law*, p.268; Radzinowicz, *History*, I, pp.209-13. The last instance of burning at the stake in England occurred in 1789.

162 *R.* v *Walcot* (1695), 4 Mod. 395. See also Smith, *De Republica*, p.84.

163 Blackstone, *Commentaries*, IV, p.4; Eden, *Principles*, pp.317-21; Madan, *Thoughts, passim.*

164 Radzinowicz, *History*, I, pp.140-51; Cockburn, *Assizes*, p.131.

165 *R.* v *Harrison* (1638), Cro. Car. 504, *per* Keeling Cl. Cor.

166 *R.* v *Edgerley* (1641), March N.C. 131.

167 *R.* v *Oates* (1688), *State Trials*, X, col. 1325. See also *R.* v *Duke of Devonshire* (1687), ibid., XI, col. 1353 (judges censured for fine of £30,000).

168 Blackstone, *Commentaries*, IV, p.372; Stephen, *History*, I, p.490; A.F. Granucci, '"Nor Cruel and Unusual Punishments Inflicted": The Original Meaning', *California Law Review*, LVII (1969), pp.839-65.

169 Staunford, *Plees*, f.198v; Dalison, Reports, f.30 (1555); Hale, *Pleas*, II, p.413; *Form and Method*, pp.40-42; Baker, 'Newgate Reports', pp.314-15.

170 Coke, *Institutes*, III, p.6; Blackstone, *Commentaries*, IV, p.24.

171 *Les Reportes del Cases in Camera Stellata 1593 to 1609*, ed W.P. Baildon (1894), p.113; *R.* v *Compton* (1625), BL, Lansd. MS 1098, f.126 (under-sheriff spared execution for £100 bribe, contrary to express direction of assize judge); Cockburn, *Assizes*, p.130.

172 Mentioned in 39 Eliz. I, c.4. Craies attributed the idea to Sir Thomas Dale (1611): *Law Quarterly Review*, VI, p.398. In 1614 and 1615 transportations to Penguin Island were ordered at the Old Bailey: P. della Valle, *Travels into East-India* (1665 edn), pp.333-6, who relates that the 1615 contingent heard such frightening tales of the fate of their precursors that they begged to be hanged. In *R.* v *Strickland* (1617), HLS, MS 114, f.141, a convict reprieved to be sent to Virginia took fright and escaped. See further A.E. Smith, 'The Transportation of Convicts to the American Colonies in the 17th Century', *American Hist. Review*, XXXIX (1934), pp.232-49.

173 Eden, *Principles*, pp.34-7; *R.* v *P. Madan* (1780), 1 Lea. 223; Madan, *Thoughts*, pp.76-7, 94. The two Madans seem not to have been related: F. Madan, *The Madan Family* (1933), p.220.

174 Barrington, *Observations*, pp.445-6; Eden, *Principles*, pp.32-3. As alternatives, Barrington suggested the Falkland Islands, while Eden suggested the sale of convicts to redeem slaves.

175 Eden, *Principles*, pp.80-82; Madan, *Thoughts*, pp.111-15; Cockburn, *Assizes*, p.129.

176 Blackstone, *Commentaries*, IV, p.371; 19 Geo. III, c.74.

177 *Winchcomb* v *Goddard* (1601), Cro. Eliz. 837, *per* Popham C.J.; *R.* v *Rice* (1616), Cro. Jac. 404; *Anon.* (1661), 1 Keb. 195, pl.186; *R.* v *Porter* (1703), 1 Salk. 149, 2 Ld Raym. 937.

178 Hale, *Pleas*, II, p.210; *R.* v *Foxby* (1704), 6 Mod. 178.

179 *R.* v *Long* (1596), Cro. Eliz. 489. Technically, a 'conviction' was a verdict of guilty, whereas the 'judgment' was the sentence of the court following a verdict or upon a point of law.

180 *R.* v [*Saunders*] (1669), 1 Vent. 33; *R.* v *Phorbes* (1681), T. Raym. 433; *R.* v *Lomas* (1694), Comb. 297; *R.* v *Leighton* (1708), Fort. 173. For the practice in detail see W. Hands, *The Solicitor's Practice on the Crown Side of the King's Bench* (1803), pp.27-44.

181 Maitland, *Justice and Police*, p.163.

182 *R.* v *Wye* (1595), HLS, MS 110, f.103v.

183 *R.* v *Gargrave* (1615), 1 Rolle Rep. 175; *R.* v *Allen* (1662), 1 Sid. 69; Hale MS cited in 1 Vern. 175; *R.* v *Wilkes* (1770), 4 Burr. at p.2550, *per* Ld Mansfield C.J.; Blackstone, *Commentaries*, IV, p.390.

184 Baker, 'Newgate Reports', pp.307-8, n.3.

185 Barrington, *Observations*, p.248; Hale, *Pleas*, II, p.193; Eden, *Principles*, p.181.

186 *R.* v *Vane* (1661), *State Trials*, VI, at col. 193, 1 Sid. 85, Kel. 15, resoln 5; *The Rioters' Case* (1681), 1 Vern. 175.

187 Foster, *Crown Law*, p.76; Hale, *Pleas*, II, pp.295-6.

188 Coke, *Institutes*, I, f.227v; III, p.110; Hale, *Pleas*, II, pp.295-7; *Anon.* (1698), Carth. 465; *R.* v *Kinloch* (1746), Fost. 16, 22-39.

189 Hale, *Pleas*, II, pp.294-5; *R.* v *Gardiner* (1665), Kel. 47; *R.* v *Jones and Bever* (1665), Kel. 52; Hawles, *English-man's Right*, p.93.

190 *Noys* v *Downing* (1663), 1 Keb. 484; *Primate* v *Jackson* (1664), 1 Lev. 10n, 1 Keb. 568, 638; *R.* v *Latham* (1673), 3 Keb. 143; *R.* v *Smith* (1681), T. Jo. 163, 2 Show. K.B. 165. New trials were never granted after acquittal.

191 This expression was used for meetings of the justices of the King's Bench and Common Pleas and barons of the Exchequer, though the total number of them was not always twelve. In the 16th century the body seems rather to have included all the assize commissioners, and therefore some serjeants-at-law attended.

192 See *R.* v *Hodgson* (*c.*1700), 1 Lea. 6.

193 E.g. *R.* v *Dunn* (1765), 1 Lea. 57, 61; *R.* v *Shaw* (1785), ibid., 360.

194 See Baker, 'Newgate Reports', pp.308-9.

Chapter 2:

1 In order to provide what is perhaps best regarded as a companion piece to J.M. Beattie, 'The Pattern of Crime in England 1660-1800', *Past & Present*, LXII (1974), pp.47-95, I have followed, in so far as the data allow, the approach pioneered by Dr Beattie in that article. I am also grateful to him for commenting upon an earlier draft of this essay and to R.F. Hunnisett and J.B. Post for several useful suggestions.

2 J.J. Tobias, *Crime and Industrial Society in the Nineteenth Century* (1967), p.44.

3 Beattie, 'Pattern of Crime', pp.47-9.

4 Bellamy, *Crime in the Later Middle Ages*, pp.3-10.

5 *William Lambarde and Local Government*, ed C. Read (Ithaca 1962), p.68.

6 *A Relation of the Island of England*, ed C.A. Sneyd (Camden Soc. XXXVII, 1847), p.34. Cf. the complaint in 1597 of the Jesuit Robert Parsons: *The Jesuit's Memorial for the Intended Reformation of England under their First Popish Prince*, ed E. Gee (1690), pp.210-11, 252-4.

7 Huntington Lib., Ellesmere MS 2468 (unfoliated). Such comparisons were not new. In the late 15th century Chief Justice Fortescue boasted that 'there be more men hanged in England in a year for robbery and manslaughter than there be hanged in France for such cause of crime in seven years': J. Fortescue, *The Governance of England*, ed C. Plummer (Oxford 1926), pp.141-2.

8 Lambeth MSS 9, ff.62-62v, 77; 15, ff.22, 114 (Chaloner to Anthony Bacon, from Florence, 1596-7).

9 González de Cellorigo, cited in I.A.A. Thompson, 'A Map of Crime in Sixteenth-Century Spain', *Economic History Review*, 2nd ser., XXI (1968), pp.244-68.

10 F. Braudel, *La Méditerranée et le monde méditerranée à l'époque de Philippe II* (Paris 1949), p.658.

11 Shakespeare's concern with law and order, most clearly evident in the four 'Roman' plays, is most uncompromisingly treated in *Troilus and Cressida*, published in 1609. The 'degree' speeches from *Troilus* were apparently providing material for judicial charges at least as late as 1620: Cockburn, *Assizes*, pp.68, 308-11.

12 For recent restatements of the violence and delinquency of 16th-century England see A.L. Rowse, *The England of Elizabeth* (New York 1966), p.344; L. Stone, *The Crisis of the Aristocracy 1558-1641* (Oxford 1965), pp.223-34; F.G. Emmison, *Elizabethan Life: Disorder* (Chelmsford 1970), p.148.

13 G.R. Elton, *The Sources of History: England 1200-1640* (1969), p.62.

14 Seventeen counties are represented in assize records surviving from the period 1559-1625: Home Circuit (series begins 1559); Norfolk Circuit (1606); Northern Circuit (1607). Quarter sessions records survive for 18 counties, although only 6 — Essex (1558), Hants (1559), Midd (1558), Norf (1558), Som (1561), Wilts (1563) — have records earlier than 1570.

15 Preserved in the Public Record Office (ASSI 35). There are no Hertfordshire files before 1573.

16 For the jurisdictional division between assizes and quarter sessions in this period see Cockburn, *Assizes*, pp.88-97. Quarter sessions confined themselves largely to misdemeanours and such minor crimes as assault and petty larceny. Since both assaults and some petty larcenies were also tried at assizes, totals of these crimes drawn exclusively from the records of one court, as mine are, are to some extent defective. I have further narrowed the data by excluding from consideration all indictments for recusancy.

17 For a full discussion of this see J.S. Cockburn, 'Early-Modern Assize Records as Historical Evidence', *Jnl of the Soc. of Archivists*, V (1975), pp.215-31.

18 See Beattie, 'Pattern of Crime', pp.52-8; J.M. Beattie, 'Towards a Study of Crime in Eighteenth-Century England: a note on Indictments', in *The Triumph of Culture: Eighteenth-Century Perspectives*, ed P. Fritz and D. Williams (Toronto 1972), pp.299-314.

19 BL, Lansd. MS 81, f.161.

20 T. Sellin and M.E. Wolfgang, *The Measurement of Delinquency* (New York 1964), pp.36-40.

21 39 Eliz. I, c.15.

22 5 Eliz. I, c.11; 5 Eliz. I, c.17.

23 *Les Reportes del Cases in Camera Stellata 1593-1609*, ed W.P. Baildon (1894), p.166.

24 For a contrary view see J. Samaha, *Law and Order in Historical Perspective: The Case of Elizabethan Essex* (New York 1974), esp. pp.81-3. Although the number of J.P.s in the peace commissions for Kent (59 to 96) and Essex (47 to 71) almost doubled between 1559 and 1603, the proportion actually committing suspects to assizes remained constant at about 43 per cent.

25 Beattie, 'Pattern of Crime', pp.57-8.

26 The Elizabethan assize files for the counties of the Home Circuit are unique; Jacobean files survive from the Norfolk and Northern circuits but both series are very fragmentary. The contents of all the surviving Home Circuit files for the reigns of Elizabeth I and James I are being published in calendar form by Her Majesty's Stationery Office. There will be two volumes of text for each of the circuit's five counties — Essex, Hertfordshire, Kent, Surrey and Sussex — and a general introductory volume will follow. The first volume in this series, containing Sussex material for the reign of Elizabeth, appeared in 1975; it is here referred to as *Sussex*, I. A further four volumes forthcoming are referred to as *Sussex*, II, *Herts*, I, *Herts*, II and *Essex*, I, respectively. The references — which are to entries not pages — are given in square brackets after the PRO call numbers.

27 The following is based upon F. Hull, 'Agriculture and Rural Society in Essex 1540-1640' (London Univ. Ph.D. thesis 1950).

28 See below p.61.

29 E. Straker, *Wealden Iron* (1931). For a useful description of Elizabethan Sussex see R.B. Manning, *Religion and Society in Elizabethan Sussex* (Leicester 1969), pp.3-8.

30 A survey in 1582 revealed that in two Hertford parishes alone 1,028 beds were occupied by 'strangers': PRO, SP 12/155/103 (Burghley to Walsingham). In 1624 a Hertfordshire grand jury claimed that there were more than 540 alehouses in the county: PRO, ASSI 35/66/1/44 [*Herts*, II, 1369].

31 E.g. *APC 1577-78*, pp.146-7; *1598-99*, pp.128-30, 140-42. For a contemporary description of London low life see G. Whetstones, *A Touchstone for the Time: Containing many perillous Mischiefes bred in the Bowels of the Citie of London* (1584).

32 Years for which one or both of the assize files are missing have been excluded from these calculations.

33 See below p.67.

34 Printed in E.E. Rich, 'The Population of Elizabethan England', *Economic Hist. Rev.* 2nd ser., II (1949), p.254. There are no reliable estimates of the rate of population growth in the late 16th and early 17th centuries and it is therefore not possible to correct for changes over time.

35 F.H. McClintock and N.H. Avison, *Crime in England and Wales* (1968), pp.23-4.

36 But see below p.72.

37 See below pp.83-8; Thomas, *Witchcraft and Magic*, pp.534-8.

38 See below p.60. The homicide figures are also considerably higher than those adduced for Sussex and Surrey in the late 17th and 18th centuries: Beattie, 'Pattern of Crime', p.61.

39 E.g. *Two Unnatural Murders* (1605) [basis for the anonymous play *A Yorkshire Tragedy* (1608)]; *The crying Murther: Contayning the cruell and most horrible Butchery of Mr Trat, curate of olde Cleave; who was first murthered as he travailed upon the highway, then was brought home to his house and there was quartered and imboweld; his quarters and bowels being afterwards perboyld and salted up, in a most strange and fearefull manner* ... (1624).

40 PRO, ASSI 35/32/8/34 [*Sussex*, I, 1212].

41 Ibid., 35/3/2/33 [*Essex*, I, 131].

42 Ibid., 35/24/7/50-52, 55, 57 [*Sussex*, I, 856].

43 E.g. ibid., 35/34/1/30; 35/43/1/1; 35/43/2/2 [*Essex*, I, 2271, 3057, 3107].

44 Ibid., 35/48/2/11 [*Herts*, II, 163].

45 *The Horrible Murther of a young Boy of three yeres of age, whose sister had her tongue cut out: and how it pleased God to reveale the offendors by giving speech to the tongueles Childe* (1606); *The most cruell and bloody murther committed by an Inkeepers Wife, called Annis Dell* ... (1606). The two accounts vary on some points of detail; in particular whether the Dells themselves murdered the boy or merely assisted three of the vagrants to do so.

46 Cf. *A Most horrible & detestable Murther committed by a bloudie minded man upon his owne Wife* (1595) with the laconic indictment upon which he was convicted: PRO, ASSI 35/37/7/23 [*Sussex*, I, 1537].

47 PRO, ASSI 35/59/4/2, 5 [*Herts*, II, 890].

48 A similar pattern has been noted in modern homicide statistics: T. Morris and L. Blom-Cooper, *A Calendar of Murder* (1964), p.379. I owe this reference to J.B. Post.

49 *The Lamentable and True Tragedie of M. Arden of Feversham in Kent* (1592); PRO, ASSI 35/40/2/38, 47 [*Herts*, I, 871]; 35/30/2/39 [*Essex*, I, 1919].

50 E.g. *A True Relation of the most Inhumane & bloody Murther of Master James, Minister & Preacher of the word of God at Rockland in Norfolk. Committed by one Lowe his Curate, and consented unto by his wife* ... (1609); Baker, 'Newgate Reports', pp.317-18 [Hertford assizes *c.*1616]; PRO, ASSI 35/14/6/5 [*Sussex*, I, 412]; 35/31/2/48, 49 [*Essex*; I, 2016], 35/43/2/65 [*Essex*, I, 3149]; 35/35/7/53, 72 [*Sussex*, I, 1403].

51 e.g. PRO, ASSI 35/10/2/13; 35/12/6/5; 35/28/1/11; 35/31/2/38; 35/43/2/2 [*Essex*, I, 349, 442, 1638, 2011, 3107].

52 See above p.54.

53 PRO, ASSI 35/37/2/11 [*Essex*, I, 2670] augmented by *Two notorious Murders. One committed by a Tanner on his wives sonne, nere Hornechurch in Essex* ... (1595). Cf. ASSI 35/22/1/36 [*Essex*, I, 1188] for another murder related to a property dispute.

54 PRO, ASSI 35/22/9/40 [*Sussex*, I, 800]; 35/49/4/22 [*Herts*, II, 200]. In Table I these two cases are included in the figures for buggery.

55 5 Eliz. I. c.17.

56 But cf. Beattie, 'Pattern of Crime', pp.61-2 for the 18th century.

57 33 Hen. VIII., c.6.

58 E.g. 2 Edw. VI, c.4; 4 & 5 P. & M. c.2; *APC 1559*, p.101; *1579*, pp.295-6; *A Bibliography of Royal Proclamations of the Tudor and Stuart Sovereigns ... 1485-1714*, ed R. Steele (Oxford 1910), nos 511, 701, 739, 871, 910, 1124, 1184.

59 HMC, *Marquess of Salisbury*, II, p.123.

60 E.g. Steele, *Proclamations*, nos 1142, 1184.

61 Ibid., no. 739. For an example see the accidental shooting of Henry Cooper, an E. Grinstead tailor, during 'the skirmish' while 200 locals were being 'trained with calivers' in June 1588: PRO, ASSI 35/30/8/28 [*Sussex*, I, 1110].

62 PRO, SP 12/154/10.

63 Steele, *Proclamations*, nos 804, 818, 840.

64 *The Lamentable and True Tragedie of M. Arden of Feversham* (1592), sc.2.

65 PRO, SP 12/261/70. For the theft in 1593 of guns and other weapons from the constables of Feering see ibid., ASSI 35/35/2/9 [*Essex*, I, 2443].

66 PRO, ASSI 35/19/3/36, 37 [*Herts*, I, 119]. Cf. another Hertfordshire highway robbery in which the assailants broke their victim's neck: 35/43/4/8 [*Herts*, I, 1028].

67 Ibid., 35/34/1/30 [*Essex*, I, 2271]; 35/27/1/50 [*Essex*, I, 1537].

68 Several of the metropolitan crimes described in pamphlet accounts involved the use of handguns: e.g. *Two notorious Murders* ... (1595); *A True Relation of a most desperate Murder, committed upon the Body of Sir John Tindall, knight, one of the Maisters of the Chancery* ... (1617).

69 e.g. PRO, ASSI 35/21/9/26, 27 [*Herts*, I, 175, 176].

70 Ibid., 35/9/2/28 [*Essex*, I, 309]; F.G. Emmison, *Elizabethan Life: Disorder* (Chelmsford 1970), pp.103-4.

71 E.g. PRO, ASSI 35/39/3/40 [*Herts*, I, 834]; 35/23/2/12 [*Essex*, I, 1257].

72 E.g. *Two notorious Murders* ... (1595).

73 J. Jones, *The Arte and Science of preserving Bodie and Soule in al Health, Wisdome, and Catholike Religion: Phisically, Philosophically, and Divinely* (1579), pp.61-2.

74 E.g. *APC 1559*, p.116; *1613-14*, pp.597-8; *1615-16*, pp.210-12; *1616-17*, pp.193-4 (orders for prosecution of rogues, vagrants, idle persons and other criminally-inclined elements in and about London); Steele, *Proclamations*, nos 1188, 1538.

75 Huntington Lib., Ellesmere MSS 2525, 2526, 6297 (orders for the control or suppression of alehouses); PRO, ASSI 35/42/2/46 [*Essex*, I, 3048]; SP 12/19/43 (Wm Tyldsley to Cecil, 1561).
76 *Two notorious Murders* ... (1595). For a dramatic expression of the same view see *Eastward Hoe* (1605), Act IV, sc.2.
77 Huntington Lib., Ellesmere MSS 2468 (Chaloner's 'The Usurer Reformed ...'); 7922 (memorandum, *c.*1621, claiming that organized crime was the exclusive monopoly of corporate towns, where it was encouraged by corrupt civic officials); W. Harrison, *The Description of England* (Ithaca 1968), pp.193-4; *Lambarde and Local Government*, pp. 96, 114.
78 *A True Relation of a most desperate Murder ... upon ... Sir John Tindall ...* (1617). For a similar sentiment in 1596 see *Lambarde and Local Government*, p.129.
79 For illustrations and some discussion of the problem see Cockburn, 'Assize Records as Historical Evidence', pp.222-5.
80 PRO, ASSI 35/9/2/8, 9 [*Essex*, I, 289, 290].
81 *Lambarde and Local Government*, pp.183-4.
82 Steele, *Proclamations*, nos 818, 840, 849.
83 39 Eliz. I, c.17.
84 Kent RO, QM/SB/145.
85 PRO, ASSI 35/39/7/42 [*Sussex*, I, 1703, 1715].
86 E.g. ibid., 35/42/2/40, 46 [*Essex*, I, 3036, 3048]; 35/44/4/3, 4 [*Herts*, I, 1077].
87 Herts RO, HAT/SR3/88; SR5/29.
88 Kent RO, QM/SB/635.
89 Most notably in *The Elizabethan Underworld*, ed A.V. Judges (repr. 1965); see also the more recent collection *Cony-Catchers and Bawdy Baskets*, ed G. Salgado (Harmondsworth 1972).
90 P.A. Slack, 'Vagrants and Vagrancy in England 1598-1664', *Economic Hist. Rev.*, 2nd ser., XXVII (1974), pp.360-79; A.L. Beier, 'Vagrants and the Social Order in Elizabethan England', *Past & Present*, LXIV (1974), pp.1-29. Cf. Cockburn, 'Assize Records as Historical Evidence', p.224, n.59. For some suggestive comments on vagrant crime in early-seventeenth-century Wiltshire see below pp.130-3.
91 The legislation is summarized in F. Aydelotte, *Elizabethan Rogues and Vagabonds* (1913), pp.62-75.
92 T. Harman, *A Caveat or Warning for Common Cursitors* (1566). A case discussed in Sergeants' Inn in 1583 provides dramatic confirmation of vagrant expertise. Hookers using 'engines' inserted through an open window had successfully removed bed linen and other articles from the house of Chief Justice Edmund Anderson: Yale University Beinecke Lib., Law Deposit GR 29.5, case no. 14. I owe this reference to J.H. Baker.
93 BL, Lansd. MS 81, ff.161-62*v*.
94 *Lambarde and Local Government*, p.181.
95 14 Eliz. I, c.5.
96 See above, p.000. According to the pamphlet account, a band of nine vagrants had attacked the house and murdered its occupants.
97 Cockburn, 'Assize Records as Historical Evidence', pp.223-4.
98 Ibid., pp.224-5.
99 PRO, ASSI 35/36/8/2, 52 [*Sussex*, I, 1471].
100 Ibid., 35/63/2/21, 70 [*Herts*; II, 1143].
101 Herts RO, HAT/SR2/128; cf. BL, Lansd. MS 81, f.162*v*.

102 Herts RO, HAT/SR5/168-71.

103 Ibid., HAT/SR1/46, 47; SR2/10. See also Kent RO, QM/SB/335 (London woman caught shoplifting in Gravesend).

104 As does the Act of 1601 which provided for the summary punishment of those cutting growing corn and robbing orchards and gardens: 43 Eliz. I, c.7.

105 PRO, ASSI 35/24/7/50-52, 55, 57 [*Sussex*, I, 856]; 35/52/8/8 [*Sussex*, II, 164]. See also ibid., 35/58/4/13, 14 [*Herts*, II, 810]; Kent RO, QM/SB/874.

106 8 Eliz. I, c.4.

107 Kent RO, QM/SB/65.

108 E.g. PRO, ASSI 35/23/3/7; 35/42/3/8, 30 [*Herts*, I, 220, 934, 946]; 35/45/3/20; 35/62/4/6, 22 [*Herts*, II, 19, 1100]. Such gangs frequently included one or more females.

109 PRO, SP 12/155/103 (Burghley to Walsingham).

110 *The Jesuit's Memorial*, pp.210-11.

111 E.g. PRO, ASSI 35/58/4/29, 60; 35/63/2/8, 9, 41 [*Herts*, II, 823, 1132].

112 Ibid., 35/32/3/14, 32, 33 [*Herts*, I, 464-66]. Cf. another robbery yielding £200 in cash: 35/48/2/17 [*Herts*, II, 169].

113 The following is based on W.G. Hoskins, 'Harvest Fluctuations and English Economic History, 1480-1619', *Agricultural History Review*, XII (1964), pp.28-46, and 'Harvest Fluctuations and English Economic History, 1620-1759', ibid., XVI (1968), 15-31.

114 The deputy lieutenants of Hertfordshire reported in Oct. 1595 on the small yield of the recent harvest, 'which succeeding a dear year, wherein all former stores were spent, upheld the high prices. Wheat is better in quality this year, but the quantity is small, whereby barley, which was but thin, carries a higher price, as the poor who were wont to feed upon wheat and rye are driven to it. These things being dear, all other victuals bear higher prices. White meats are high, through the great loss last year of milch beasts, and those which escaped were so poor as to yield little profit, whereby the store of butter and cheese failed': *CSPD 1595-97*, p.107, quoted in Hoskins, 'Harvest Fluctuations 1480-1619', p.38, n.2. Further hardship in Hertfordshire attributed to the high price of corn was reported in Nov. 1595: *CSPD 1595-97*, p.126.

115 PRO, ASSI 35/36/2/39, 40 [*Essex*, I, 2579, 2580].

116 E.g. *CSPD 1595-97*, pp.316-20, 401.

117 See above pp.65-6.

118 Work now in progress on the much fuller data from Kent and Surrey may make this possible and, in addition, clarify the trend in subsequent years.

119 B.R. Mitchell, *Abstract of British Historical Statistics* (Cambridge 1962), p.497. There are no price data for 1616.

Chapter 3:

1 This essay is based on my *Witchcraft in Tudor and Stuart England* (1970), here-after cited as Macfarlane, *Witchcraft*. Fuller accounts and references for most of the topics mentioned below will be found there. The second part of the essay owes much to an article printed in *Witchcraft, Confessions and Accusations*, ed M. Douglas (Assoc. of Social Anthropologists Monograph 9, 1970). I am grateful to Tavistock Publications for permission to quote from that article and to Routledge and Kegan Paul Ltd, London, for permission to include the graph of accused persons (Figure 1). I am also grateful to the Essex Record Office, Chelmsford, and the Public Record Office, London, for permission to quote from their archives. My other acknowledgments are as stated at the front of

Witchcraft, but I would like to stress again my intellectual debt to Keith Thomas of St John's College, Oxford.

2 W. Notestein, *A History of Witchcraft in England from 1558 to 1718* (1911).

3 C.L. Ewen, *Witch Hunting and Witch Trials* (1929). Further documents are contained in the same author's *Witchcraft and Demonianism* (1933).

4 Cockburn, *Assizes*, pp.ix-x.

5 The cases are abstracted, with full references, in Macfarlane, *Witchcraft*, App.1. The three main classes of documents used for the study are as follows: PRO, Home Circuit Assize Indictments (ASSI 35); ERO, Quarter Sessions Rolls, 1556-1680 (Q/SR/1-441) and the Archdeaconry Act Books, for Essex (D/AEA/1-44) and Colchester (D/ACA/1-55).

6 A more detailed account of the legal background and the sources for its study is given in Macfarlane, *Witchcraft*, ch. 2.

7 A 'familiar' was a small animal, often a rat, mouse, toad or small bird, but infrequently a cat at this time, which was believed to be a devil or the Devil in disguise and which was sent by the witch to harm people and rewarded by sucking her blood.

8 The procedure and injunctions of the ecclesiastical courts are described in Macfarlane, *Witchcraft*, pp.66-74.

9 The contemporary views of the supernatural and natural world forming the background to witchcraft accusations have been fully described in Thomas, *Religion and Magic*.

10 There is a more detailed comparison of Essex records with those for other English counties in Macfarlane, *Witchcraft*, pp.62, 74, 78, 86, 91.

11 For a fuller discussion, with graphs of the distribution by place and time, see Macfarlane, *Witchcraft*, ch. 3.

12 There is a brief description of the procedure at assizes in Macfarlane, *Witchcraft*, ch. 3 and a much fuller account in Cockburn, *Assizes*, pt two.

13 Cockburn, *Assizes*, p.131.

14 For a description of the various ecclesiastical jurisdictions in Essex and the detailed figures upon which this is based see Macfarlane, *Witchcraft*, pp.66-9.

15 These villages and the sources for studying them, as well as the witches residing in them, are described in Macfarlane, *Witchcraft*, ch. 6.

16 *A Detection of damnable driftes, practized by three Witches arraigned at Chelmisforde in Essex …* (1579). There is an original copy in the British Library and the pamphlet is reprinted in *Witchcraft*, ed B. Rosen (New York 1972), pp.92-9.

17 *An Historicall Description of the Island of Britayne*, first published in Raphael Holinshed, *Chronicles* (1577), vol. I.

18 'Victim' includes the owner of betwitched property. The four 'pamphlets' are those for 1566, 1579, 1589 and a set of ecclesiastical depositions summarized in Macfarlane, *Witchcraft*, App. 1, case 861. The 1582 Essex pamphlet is not included since that trial seems to have been exceptional in several ways. The title of the 1579 pamphlet is given in n.16 above. That for 1566 is *The examination and confession of certaine Wytches at Chensforde in the Countie of Essex before the Quenes maiesties Judges, the xxvi daye of July Anno 1566* (1566; the only surviving copy is in the Lambeth Palace Lib., but there is a full transcript in *Witchcraft*, ed Rosen, pp.73-82). The 1589 pamphlet is *The Apprehension and Confession of three notorious Witches …* (1589; the only copy is in the Lambeth Palace Lib.; abstracts are printed in Ewen, *Witchcraft and Demonianism*, pp.167-8).

19 Detailed maps and graphs illustrating the following arguments more fully are printed in Macfarlane, *Witchcraft*, ch. 3.

20 Ascriptions of occupation and status in court records are not really trustworthy. Comparison with other local records shows that they were often incorrect. These findings can, therefore, be given only a little weight.

21 J. Stearne, *A Confirmation and Discovery of Witchcraft* (1648), p.39.

22 R. Scot, *The Discoverie of Witchcraft* (1584; repr. 1964), p.25.

23 *A True and Exact Relation of the Several Informations, Examinations, and Confessions of the late Witches, arraigned and executed in the county of Essex* (1645), p.23. Abstracts are printed in Ewen, *Witchcraft and Demonianism*, pp.262-77.

24 This is based on the well-known distinction first elaborated in E.E. Evans-Pritchard, *Witchcraft, Oracles, and Magic among the Azande* (Oxford 1937).

25 *A True and Just Recorde of the Information, Examination and Confession of all the Witches, taken at S. Oses in the countie of Essex, by W.W.* (1582). A full transcript of the pamphlet is printed in *Witchcraft*, ed Rosen, pp.104-57.

26 G. Gifford, *A Discourse of the Subtill Practises by Devilles by Witches and Sorcerers* (1587), sigs G4-G4v.

27 J.O. Haweis, *Sketches of the Reformation and Elizabethan Age* (1844), p.244.

28 T. Ady, *A Candle in the Dark: or, A Treatise Concerning the Nature of Witches and Witchcraft* (1656), p.130.

29 T. Cooper, *The Mystery of Witchcraft* (1617), p.288.

30 *The examination and confession of certaine Wytches at Chensforde ...* (1566).

31 This is being undertaken by Dr C. Larner of the Dept of Sociology, Glasgow University.

32 H.C. Erik Midelfort, *Witch Hunting in Southwestern Germany 1562-1684* (Stanford 1972).

33 G. Henningsen, 'The Papers of Alonso de Salazar Frias, A Spanish Witchcraft Polemic 1610-1614', *Temenos*, 5 (1969). A monograph of Frias, de Lancre and the Basque witches by the above author is due to be published shortly.

34 *Europe's Inner Demons. An Enquiry Inspired by the Great Witch-Hunt* (1975).

35 *Religion and Magic.*

36 P. Boyer and S. Nissenbaum, *Salem Possessed, The Social Origins of Witchcraft* (Cambridge, Mass 1974). Many of the documents upon which their study is based are printed by the same authors in *Salem-Village Witchcraft* (California 1972).

37 Work on the Earls Colne records has been made possible by generous support from the Social Science Research Council and the Research Centre, King's College, Cambridge.

Chapter 4:

1 An introduction to this type of approach is provided by Beattie, 'Pattern of Crime', and J. Samaha, *Law and Order in Historical Perspective: The Case of Elizabethan Essex* (New York 1974). For an early analysis of a county's quarter sessions records see A.H.A. Hamilton, *Quarter Sessions from Queen Elizabeth to Queen Anne* (1878).

2 Especially Cockburn, *Assizes*, and the very useful introduction to *Somerset Assize Orders 1629-1640*, ed T.G. Barnes (Somerset Rec. Soc. LXV, 1959).

3 ERO, Q/SBa/2/91.

4 ERO, Q/SR/332/107.

5 ERO, Q/SBa/2/102.

6 E.g. ERO, Q/SBa/2/45, 91, 99; Q/SR/367/90.

7 The best introduction to the work of the ecclesiastical court whose records have been most used in the present study, the court of the archdeacon, remains E.R. Brinkworth, 'The Study and Use of Archdeacons' Court Records: Illustrated from the Oxford Records (1556-1759)', *Transactions of the Royal Historical Soc.* 4th ser., XXV (1943), pp.93-120. R.A. Marchant, *The Church Under the Law: Justice, Administration and Discipline in the Diocese of York 1560-1640* (Cambridge 1969) is the fullest account yet printed of the ecclesiastical courts in action.

8 This conclusion is tentative, and will remain so until further research is carried out. One obvious problem lies in the development of regular petty sessions, which may well have provided the same cheap and local remedy against certain types of minor offender that was obtained in the archdeacons' courts. It is the impression of the present writer that the business of the archdeaconry courts after the Restoration, when the ecclesiastical courts returned after ceasing to sit during the Civil Wars and Interregnum, was smaller in volume and narrower in scope than it had been before 1642. Since evidence of the work of Essex petty sessions during this period is extremely fragmentary it is impossible to test the suspicion that this trend was matched by an increase in the work of these latter institutions.

9 S. and B. Webb, *English Local Government from the Revolution to the Municipal Corporations Act: The Manor and Borough*, pt 1 (1924), pp.13-30, is still the most useful introduction to the state of the manorial courts in the 17th century.

10 Perhaps the most advanced of these studies is currently being conducted by a team headed by Alan Macfarlane of King's College, Cambridge.

11 The Essex files in the Home Circuit assize records for the period 1600-1640 (PRO, ASSI 35/42-82) were searched for references to Kelvedon inhabitants, as were quarter sessions rolls for the same period (ERO, Q/SR/148-311). Quarter sessions bundles, commencing in 1621 (Q/SBa/2/1-40), were also used. The most important source from the archdeaconry of Colchester archives was the act books for the period (ERO, D/ACA/24-54). The deposition books for 1612-41 (D/ACD/2-7) and visitation books for 1601-1603, 1604-12 and 1633 (D/ACV/3-5) were also consulted. The surviving records of Felix Hall and Little Coggeshall manors are in private hands. Church Hall manor documents are mainly deposited at the Guildhall Lib., the most important for this study being court rolls and a copy of a rental of 1618 (Guildhall MSS 10470A, 10129). Rolls survive for Kelvedon Hall manor during this period (ERO, D/DU/19/31-33) but apparently the leet was not active. Background on inhabitants of the parish was derived from the manorial records listed above and from taxation returns, namely the subsidies of the period (the most useful of which were PRO, E 179/112/509, 588, 607, 638) and the ship money assessment of 1636 (ERO, T/A/42). Further information was drawn from the parish registers, which are almost full for this period (ERO, T/Z/12). Additional background was provided by a sample of some sixty wills. These are listed in F.G. Emmison, *Wills at Chelmsford 1400-1619* (The Index Library, LXXVIII, 1958), and *Wills at Chelmsford 1620-1720* (The Index Library, LXXIX, 1961).

12 No satisfactory history of Kelvedon exists. B.L. Kentish, *Kelvedon and its Antiquities* (Chichester 1974) has, as its title suggests, a largely antiquarian approach, but provides some useful information.

13 The economic life of the county during this period is described in F. Hull,

'Agriculture and Rural Society in Essex 1560-1640' (London Univ. Ph.D. thesis, 1950).

14 E.g. ERO, D/ABR/8/99; D/ACW/3/30.

15 This account is based on P. Morant, *The History and Antiquities of the County of Essex*, 2 vols (1816), II, pp.150-4.

16 I should like to thank Mr G. Houghton Brown for his kindness in allowing me to consult the records of Felix Hall manor in his possession.

17 I should like to express similar thanks to Mr Anthony Bonner for his kindness in allowing me to consult the records of Little Coggeshall manor in his possession.

18 Details of these presentments are set out in the appendix.

19 Aylett's career and importance are described in B.W. Quintrell, 'The Government of the County of Essex 1603-1642' (London Univ. Ph.D. thesis 1965), p.149.

20 H. Smith, *The Ecclesiastical History of Essex under the Long Parliament and the Commonwealth* (Colchester n.d.), pp.52-3.

21 No recent comprehensive work exists covering this group in its economic, social and cultural contexts. M. Campbell, *The English Yeoman Under Elizabeth and the Early Stuarts* (New Haven 1942) is dated but at least attempts a comprehensive approach. A.D.J. Macfarlane, *The Family Life of Ralph Josselin* (Cambridge 1970) is an imaginative study of the experiences and attitudes of an Essex clergyman living in a style similar to that of a yeoman farmer, but is stronger in its suggestions than its conclusions.

22 This account is based upon most of the sources listed in n.11.

23 Felix Hall court roll, 30 Apr. 1639. For further details of the Aylett family see Morant, *History of Essex*, I, pp.142, 245, 380, 420; II, pp.144, 148, 154, 161, 177, 257, 393.

24 Felix Hall court rolls, 21 Apr. 1629, 22 Apr. 1636; PRO, E 179/112/607, 638; ERO, T/A/42; D/ACA/43, f.99v.

25 Felix Hall court roll, 22 Apr. 1636; ERO, D/ACV/5, f.37v.

26 Felix Hall court roll, 21 Apr. 1623; PRO, E 179/112/588, 607, 638; ERO, T/A/42; D/ACA/46, f.134v; 53, f.219v.

27 Guildhall MS 10470A; ERO, D/ACV/5, f.37.

28 Blackbourne was a copyhold tenant of the manor: Guildhall MS 10129. Numerous references can be found to members of the family in this period, notably in the parish registers.

29 Guildhall MS 10470A; John Clench's will, made in 1672, reveals that the family was well established in the parish by that date: ERO, D/ABR/9/227.

30 Guildhall MS 10470A; ERO, D/ACA/32, ff.21, 72; 34, f.15; 40, ff.130v, 203v; 43, f.140v; 49, f.112; Q/SR/246/48.

31 Guildhall MS 10470A; ERO, D/ACA/40, ff.173v, 203v; Q/SR/273/15.

32 See the views of J.J. Tobias, *Crime and Industrial Society in the Nineteenth Century* (1967), especially p.52.

33 For a lively critique of the implications of the acceptance of this 'conventional wisdom' see D. Chapman, *Sociology and the Stereotype of the Criminal* (1968).

34 Examples of the aristocratic and gentry violence of the period are provided in L. Stone, *The Crisis of the Aristocracy 1558-1641* (Oxford 1965), pp.223-34.

35 Guildhall MS 10470A.

36 ERO, D/ACA/34, ff. 53, 184; 40, ff. 115, 186v.

37 Ibid., 48, f. 240.

38 ERO, D/B3/3/198.

39 ERO, D/ACA/47, f. 107; 49, f. 112.

40 PRO, E 179/112/509; ERO, D/ACA/32, ff. 22v, 202v; 34, f. 9v; 37, ff. 54, 87v; 40, ff. 85, 137v, 158v, 186, 204v; 43, f. 28v; Q/SR/216/64, 226/36, 228/10, 231/11.

41 ERO, D/ACA/37, f. 54.

42 Ibid., 34, ff. 184v, 185, 214, 230v; 37, ff. 37v, 54v, 97; 40, f. 147v; 43, f. 140v; 44, f. 49v; 45, ff. 52v, 95, 313; 46, f. 83v; 47, ff. 12, 46, 127v; 48, f. 14v; 49, f. 81; 50, ff. 136v, 194; Q/SR/251/80; Felix Hall court rolls, 23 May 1621, 12 Apr. 1631.

43 Mainly through an uncritical acceptance of the popular literature of the period, examples of which can be found in *The Elizabethan Underworld*, ed A.V. Judges (1930), whose introduction is more useful than that of the more recent collection *Cony-Catchers and Bawdy Baskets*, ed G. Salgado (Harmondsworth 1972). The image of the vagrant presented by this literature has recently been challenged by historians working on primary sources, notably P.A. Slack, 'Vagrants and Vagrancy in England 1598-1664', *Economic History Review*, 2nd ser., XXVII (1974), pp.360-79. A.L. Beier, 'Vagrants and the Social Order in Elizabethan England', *Past & Present*, LXIV (1974), pp.1-29, also offers some perceptive comments.

44 ERO, D/ACA/32, f. 12.

45 Ibid., f.91.

46 Ibid., f. 123v.

47 Ibid., 34, f. 9v.

48 Ibid., ff. 15, 83v.

49 Ibid., f. 83v.

50 Ibid., 37, f. 54.

51 Ibid., 40, f. 204; 47, f. 12; 48, f. 14v; 51, f. 249; Colchester Borough archives, Sessions Book 1630-63 (unfoliated), 20 June 1636.

52 ERO, Q/SR/160/194.

53 PRO, ASSI 35/64/1/41.

54 Ibid., 35/72/2/71.

55 See, for example, the conclusions reached by Beattie, 'Pattern of Crime'.

56 John Selfscall, hanged for theft in 1600: PRO, ASSI 35/42/2/14. Even in this case the accused was indicted with a Thomas Selfscall of Feering, the next village to Kelvedon, almost certainly a relative of the accused.

57 PRO, ASSI 35/62/1/25-27, 61-4.

58 Ibid., 35/50/1/48; ERO, D/ACA/25, f. 136v; 30, f. 252v; D/ACV/3, f. 52; Q/SR/186/90.

59 ERO, Q/SR/219/22.

60 Ibid., 160/176-81; 150/37; 151/17.

61 PRO, ASSI 35/59/2/41, 69, 70.

62 Ibid., 35/59/2/41, 69, 70; 35/60/1/45; ERO, D/ACA/37, f. 141.

63 PRO, ASSI 35/60/1/78; ERO, D/ACA/30, f. 87. Spradborough's wife was later presented before the archdeacon as a common scold: D/ACA/35, f. 137v.

64 PRO, ASSI 35/60/1/83.

65 Examples of such recognizances involving Kelvedon inhabitants include ERO, Q/SR/171/77; 175/93, 94; 177/126; 179/86; 183/82.

66 See, for example, the preamble to the statute 1 Jas I, c.9.

67 ERO, D/ACA/34, f.185.

68 Ibid., 40, f.147v.

69 ERO, Q/SR/247/43.

70 ERO, D/ACA/45, f.313.

71 ERO, Q/SR/265/28.
72 Felix Hall court roll, 21 Apr. 1626.
73 ERO, D/ACA/43, f.140.
74 Ibid., 44, f.116v.
75 ERO, Q/SR/231/11.
76 Ibid., 247/41.
77 Guildhall MS 10470A.
78 ERO, D/ACA/43, f. 140v.
79 Ibid., 34, f. 57. The incident apparently occurred during a period of friction between the two men. Hilderslye had already once presented Armin for taking his cart to Maldon on a Sunday, and two months later he was excommunicated on the vicar's presentment for failing to return his churchwarden's accounts: ibid., ff.52, 159.
80 ERO, D/ACD/6, surviving fragment of book, dated 30 June 1631.
81 ERO, D/ACA/44, f.99v.
82 Ibid., 49, f.81.
83 Ibid., 47, f.56v.
84 Ibid., 50, f.136v.
85 Ibid., 52, f.58v.
86 Ibid., f.84v.
87 Ibid., 37, f.37.
88 Ibid., 34, f.137.
89 Ibid., 37. f.5.
90 Ibid., f.10.
91 Ibid., 48, ff.120v, 165, 194; 51, ff.138v, 220, 230v, 246v. Cudmore stood excommunicate and apparently never attended church throughout the decade.
92 A sensitive discussion of this topic, and of others related to it, can be found in Thomas, *Religion and Magic*, ch. 6.
93 ERO, Q/SR/311/46.
94 The younger Ayly's misdeeds included absence from church, failing to pay church fees, not rendering an account of his parents' goods after their decease, fornication and standing excommunicate. On one occasion he achieved the unusual distinction of being presented jointly with his father for adultery with the same woman: ERO, D/ACA/49, ff.32v, 102, 228; 50, ff.18, 137; 51, f.8; 52, f.140; 53, f.37; 54, f.4v.
95 Ibid., 51, f.106.
96 Ibid., 54, f.73v.
97 Ibid., 53, ff.271-71v.
98 Ibid., 34, f.99; 54, f.108v; T/A/42.
99 Guildhall MSS 10129, 10470A; ERO, D/ACA/46, f.127v; 54, f.4v.
100 Guildhall MS 10470A.
101 ERO, D/ACA/48, f.121.
102 ERO, D/ABW/56/240.
103 PRO, ASSI 35/50/1/48.
104 These and those of her husband are recorded in ERO, D/ACA/50, ff.72v, 176; 51, f.34; 53, ff.196v, 197, 220; 54, f.108v.
105 ERO, Q/SR/313/32, 38.
106 ERO, D/ACA/54, f.155v.
107 This is one of the underlying themes of the most recent survey of the subject, C. Hill, *The World Turned Upside Down* (1972), especially ch. 2.
108 ERO, D/ACA/40, f.173.

109 The existence of such a group is postulated by A.M. Everitt in *The Agrarian History of England and Wales*, IV (1500-1640), ed J. Thirsk (Cambridge 1967), pp.462-4. On the evidence of Kelvedon, this group and the problems it caused were by no means restricted to the forest areas that were the preoccupation of Professor Everitt.

110 The classic work dealing with this type of criminal is E.H. Sutherland, *White Collar Crime* (New York 1949).

111 PRO, C 3/419/83.

112 ERO, T/A/42.

Chapter 5:

1 C. Hill, *Puritanism and Revolution* (1958), pp.67-87.

2 G. Norburie, 'The Abuses and Remedies of Chancery', in *A Collection of Tracts relative to the Law of England*, ed F. Hargrave (Dublin 1787), I, pp.433-4; J. Aubrey, *The Natural History of Wiltshire*, ed J. Britton (1847), pp.11, 118; M. Hale, *The History of the Common Law of England*, ed C.M. Gray (Chicago 1971), p.112.

3 Lambard, *Eirenarcha* (1619), p.10; Thomas, *Religion and Magic*, p.154 and the references there cited.

4 B.S. Capp, *The Fifth Monarchy Men* (1972), pp.161, 164 and the references there cited.

5 B. Willis, *A Survey of the Cathedrals ...* (1742), III, p.123. The materials for the study of population in Wiltshire are very inadequate, and the figure quoted here is no more than a very rough estimate.

6 The most important forms of prosecution thus omitted were the *detecta* of churchwardens certified at ecclesiastical visitations, and the presentments of constables and hundred juries at quarter sessions and assizes.

7 *Wiltshire Quarter Sessions and Assizes, 1736*, ed J.P.M. Fowle (Wilts. Archaeol. and Nat. Hist. Soc. Records Branch, XI, 1955), pp.xiv-xv, xxix. Salisbury, Marlborough and possibly Devizes had separate courts of quarter sessions, but their surviving records are fragmentary: M.G. Rathbone, *List of Borough Records earlier in date than 1836* (Wilts. Archaeol. and Nat. Hist. Soc. Records Branch, V, 1951), pp.11, 14, 36, 46, 66, 74-5.

8 A comparison between the numbers of offenders dealt with by quarter sessions and assizes in Devon in this period is provided by Cockburn, *Assizes*, pp.94-6.

9 Cf. *Wilts. QS & Assizes, 1736*, ed Fowle, pp.xxxi-xxxiii.

10 See below p.127.

11 *Tradesmen in Early-Stuart Wiltshire*, ed N.J. Williams (Wilts. Archaeol. and Nat. Hist. Soc. Records Branch, XV, 1960), pp. xvi-xvii, 82-98.

12 G.R. Elton, *The Tudor Constitution* (Cambridge 1960), pp.170-1. Cf. below p.119.

13 The relevant cases are listed in T.G. Barnes, *List and Index to the Proceedings in Star Chamber ... (1603-1625)* (Chicago 1975), III, pp.132-6.

14 Salisbury alone had a population of about 7,000 at the end of the 16th century: P. Slack, 'Poverty and Politics in Salisbury 1597-1666', in *Crisis and Order in English Towns 1500-1700*, ed P. Clark and P. Slack (1972), p.195 n7.

15 Rathbone, *List of Borough Records*, pp.10-11, 13-14, 36, 40, 51, 66, 81, 87, 91-2.

16 Blackstone, *Commentaries*, (5th edn 1773), III, pp.33-4.

17 WRO, 288/1 (unfoliated volume).

18 E. Kerridge, 'Agriculture c.1500-c.1793', in *VCH Wiltshire*, IV (1953), pp.58-9.

19 The surviving fragments are listed in M.G. Rathbone, *Guide to the Records*

in the Custody of the Clerk of the Peace for Wiltshire (Wilts. County Council, 1959), p.28.

20 E.g. WRO, QS/GR/H 1625/136; QS/GR/M 1628/138, 142; QS/GR/T 1629/122, 137. Virtually all the surviving pre-civil war records of the court refer to pleas of debt.

21 *Summary Guide to Private Records in the Wiltshire County Record Office* (Wilts. County Council, 1969), pp. 4, 6, 9; Rathbone, *List of Borough Records*, p.xi; WRO, QS/GR/E 1620/201.

22 The 17th-century records of the court are included in PRO, SC 2/209/32-41. The year 1619-1620 is included in SC 2/209/37.

23 W.J. Jones, 'The Crown and the Courts in England 1603-1625', in *The Reign of James VI and I*, ed A.G.R. Smith (1973), pp.180-82.

24 No Wiltshire cases were discovered in the record for Michaelmas Term 1618, located in PRO, E 13/489; but the records of this court are known to be defective: M.S. Guiseppi, *Guide to the Contents of the Public Record Office* (revised edn 1963-8), I, pp.92, 94.

25 M. Blatcher, 'Touching the Writ of Latitat: an Act "of no great moment"', in *Elizabethan Government and Society*, ed S.T. Bindoff, J. Hurstfield and C.H. Williams (1961), pp.192-4.

26 T. Powell, *The Attourney's Academy* (1630), p.167.

27 PRO, KB 27/1469-77. The total includes a few entries relating to writs of *scire facias* and to prohibition and writ of error proceedings; in addition, actions laid in localities other than Wiltshire have been omitted even when one or more of the parties resided in the county. A fuller picture of the business of the court might be obtained from a study of the writ files, but these are at present not available for search.

28 PRO, CP 40/2022-27. The total excludes common recoveries, to be found in CP 43/143, and actions involving Wiltshire people laid in other counties.

29 For the location of the records on which these figures are based see nn.22, 27 and 28 above. The various types of suit available at common law are described in F.W. Maitland, *The Forms of Action at Common Law*, ed A.H. Chaytor and W.J. Whittaker (Cambridge 1971).

30 But the equity side of the Exchequer was also important; for an indication of the volume of business in this court in the early 17th century see W.H. Bryson, *The Equity Side of the Exchequer* (Cambridge 1975), pp.16, 168-9.

31 W.J. Jones, *The Elizabethan Court of Chancery* (Oxford 1967), p.305; Jones, 'The Crown and the Courts', p.180.

32 R.G. Usher, *The Rise and Fall of the High Commission* (Oxford 1913), pp.256, 257 n1, 279.

33 P. Stewart, *Guide to the Records of the Bishop, the Archdeacons of Salisbury and Wiltshire, and other Archidiaconal and Peculiar Jurisdictions* (Wilts. County Council, 1973), pp.xiii-xiv.

34 The business for these years is registered in Salisbury D(iocesan) R(ecord) O(ffice), B/ABI 41, 42, 50, 51.

35 These statements are based on a study of Salisbury DRO, B/DB 18-57; B/CP Libels, etc., bundles 1-4; B/CP Citations, bundles 1-5.

36 The records on which these generalizations are based are listed in Stewart, *Guide*, pp.57-60, 63-4, 68-70, 75, 78-83, 95-100, 105-12, 115-17, 119-21.

37 In the first place, it is common for records to provide more detail about defendants than plaintiffs. Second, there is the question of accuracy. The 'styles' noted on felony indictments are notoriously misleading: see below pp.129-32. As

regards other types of legal material, however, collation of court records with parochial, manorial, fiscal and probate records for the parishes of Keevil and Wylye suggests that the 'styles' ascribed to the parties were roughly appropriate.

38 These figures lean heavily on Barnes, *List and Index to Proceedings in Star Chamber*, III, pp.132-6.

39 For the location of the records on which these figures are based see n.28 above.

40 This conclusion is based on a detailed study of some sociological aspects of the working of the church courts in Wiltshire in the early 17th century, in which I have used a variety of legal, fiscal, parochial, manorial and probate material to supplement the evidence of the court records themselves. I hope to present the fruits of this study in detail on another occasion.

41 See below pp.129-32.

42 Of males indicted for misdemeanours at quarter sessions in 1616 and 1623, for example, over 80 per cent were designated as yeomen, husbandmen, craftsmen or tradesmen. Of males bound over but not indicted in 1615, over 90 per cent of those for whom information is available were designated as belonging to these ranks. There is less information available about the status of complainants than of defendants; but of those males who sued out recognizances of the peace in 1615 and whose status was recorded, all were designated as being members of these middling ranks.

43 See, for example, G.H[akewill], *An Apologie of the Power and Providence of God* (Oxford 1627), pp.432-3; L. Stone, *The Crisis of the Aristocracy 1558-1641* (Oxford 1965), pp.240-42.

44 See below pp.128-34.

45 Salisbury DRO, D/DB 33, ff. 35 sqq, 106v, 161.

46 Ibid., B/DB 30, ff. 130-31.

47 Ibid., B/DB 31, ff. 80v sqq; B/DB 32, ff. 63v sqq.

48 *Records of the County of Wilts*, ed B.H. Cunnington (Devizes 1932), p.188; WRO, QS/GR/H 1615/183; QS/GR/M 1627/221.

49 The sample comprised: 200 debt suits and 139 actions of trespass (including 38 cases of assault) before the Common Pleas in Michaelmas Term 1618; 94 Wiltshire suits before King's Bench in 1618 (for the composition of this total, see p.114 above), 100 ecclesiastical court suits of the most important types, viz. tithe, testamentary and defamation; 90 quarter sessions indictments for the year 1616. Less than 5 per cent connections emerged, and of those some could be explained by circumstances other than those whose presence the test was designed to reveal. Further evidence of allegations of violence would no doubt have emerged from collation with recognizances on writs of *supplicavit*, but unfortunately this operation was not feasible; cf. Giuseppi, *Guide to the PRO*, I, p.12.

50 In the 5 years 1616-20, for example, 12 indictments were preferred at the Wiltshire quarter sessions for assaults on officers in the execution of their duty: WRO, QS/GR/H 1616/122; QS/GR/E 1616/141; QS/GR/T 1616/111; QS/GR/H 1617/121; QS/GR/E 1617/119; QS/GR/T 1617/97, 104; QS/GR/M 1618/132; QS/GR/H 1620/122; QS/GR/E 1620/201; QS/GR/T 1620/112; QS/GR/M 1620/155. Offenders were usually punished strictly.

51 See below pp.125ff.

52 Cf. Stone, *Crisis of the Aristocracy*, pp.241-2.

53 See below pp.122-3.

54 M.G. Davies, *The Enforcement of English Apprenticeship, 1563-1642* (Cambridge, Mass 1956), pp.17, 20, 22; *Tradesmen in Early-Stuart Wilts.*, ed Williams, pp.xviii-xix.

55 T.G. Barnes, 'Due Process and Slow Process in the Late Elizabethan-Early Stuart Star Chamber', *American Jnl of Legal History*, VI (1962), p.226.

56 To those noted by Barnes, *List and Index to Proceedings in Star Chamber*, III, pp.132-6, should be added the following: PRO, STAC 8/59/11; 8/94/18; 8/123/16; 8/186/2; 8/226/2; 8/159/27.

57 Barnes, 'Due Process and Slow Process', pp.315-40.

58 Jones, *Chancery*, pp.196-9.

59 There are brief comments in W.B. Willcox, 'Lawyers and Litigants in Stuart England: A County Sample', *Cornell Law Quarterly*, XXIV (1938-39), p.538.

60 WRO, QS/GR/T 1616/143; cf. QS/GR/M 1619/152; QS/GR/M 1627/210. In PRO, STAC 8/54/10 there is a reference to an allegedly malicious charge of felony which actually led to an indictment.

61 See above pp.114-15.

62 E.g. PRO, STAC 8/307/25; *Records of Wilts*, ed Cunnington, p.188; Jones, *Chancery*, pp.425-6.

63 One way of exploiting debt suits vexatiously, of which contemporaries sometimes complained, was to bring actions in the name of other persons, or indeed of fictitious people: Blatcher, 'Touching the Writ of Latitat', pp.189, 201. The only Wiltshire reference to this practice in actual operation that I have noticed is in PRO, STAC 8/23/8.

64 Dalton, *Countrey Justice* (1622), p.177. Cf. Maitland, *Forms of Action*, ed Chaytor and Whittaker, p.59. The records of prosecutions are sometimes a very uncertain guide to the nature of the behaviour which underlay them. In 1618, for example, James Jey of Compton Chamberlayne was indicted for a trespass of breaking a close and trampling crops; his actual offence, as a deposition reveals, was carrying around a bucket of dung to smear on stiles: WRO, QS/GR/H 1618/127, 174.

65 W. Hawkins, *Pleas of the Crown* (1724-6), I, pp.133-4.

66 See above p.114 and Table I. I make the assumption that only a few assault and trespass cases would have been found in the assize records had they survived; cf. Cockburn, *Assizes*, p.98.

67 In legal theory, indictment and action were simply alternative ways of proceeding in cases of assault and other forms of trespass: Blackstone, *Comentaries*, III, pp.120-22. In most cases prosecuted by indictment, however, the specifically criminal offence of affray was also included; but it is very doubtful whether this was more than common form: cf. Lambard, *Eirenarcha*, pp.125-6.

68 Cf. above p.119. On quarter sessions indictments for trespass, charges of riot were sometimes added as interlineations, apparently as an afterthought.

69 WRO, QS/GR/H 1617/117, 119, 124, 125; QS/GR/H 1618/126; cf. PRO, STAC 8/271/8; 8/284/27; C 2/Jas I, bundle B 18/59; CP 40/2026, rot 2921; Salisbury DRO, B/ABI 43, f. 219; B/ABI 44, f. 35ν. WRO, QS/GR/M 1615/104, 105; cf. PRO, STAC 8/265/24. WRO, QS/GR/T 1618/105, 107-109; cf. PRO, CP 40/2022, rot 172. WRO, QS/GR/E 1619/138-41; QS/GR/E 1620/185. Ibid., QS/GR/H 1620/126-28. Ibid., QS/GR/E 1620/196, 198, 199. Ibid., QS/GR/M 1620/156, 158. Ibid., QS/GR/M 1623/129-32; cf. PRO, STAC 8/159/27. WRO, QS/GR/H 1624/86, 87; cf. PRO, C 3/252/31; C 2/Jas I, bundle S 9/24. WRO, QS/GR/T 1624/101, 109, 110; QS/GR/M 1624/136.

70 See above p.120.

71 To the references in note 69, add WRO, QS/GR/E 1621/119; cf. PRO, STAC 8/52/20; 8/307/25.

72 WRO, QS/GR/H 1619/119, 174; PRO, CP 40/2026, rot 2797. Cf. WRO,

QS/GR/E 1619/148; QS/GR/T 1619/189; PRO, CP 40/2022, rot 169; WRO, QS/GR/H 1619/197; PRO, CP 40/2026, rot 2781; CP 40/2022, rot 165*v*.

73 This conclusion is based on a study of 157 slanders alleged in defamation causes in the period 1615-1629; they are included in Salisbury DRO, B/DB 29-43; B/ABI 41-51; B/CP Libels, etc., bundles 1-3.

74 For a particularly blatant example see Salisbury DRO, B/DB 37, f.52.

75 E.g. Salisbury DRO, B/DB 37, ff. 87*v*-88; B/DB 39, ff. 9*v*-10; cf.WRO, QS/GR/M 1621/164; QS/GR/E 1624/141. Salisbury DRO, B/DB 34, ff. 105*v* sqq to B/DB 35, f. 13.

76 E.g. Salisbury DRO, B/DB 30, ff. 130-31; B/ABI 42, f. 78*v*; B/DB 38, f. 121*v*; B/DB 43, ff. 5*v*-6*v*.

77 E.g. ibid., B/DB 34, ff. 104, 129; B/DB 36, f. 10.

78 Dalton, *Countrey Justice*, pp.31-2.

79 For an example of a barratry indictment that was probably vexatious see WRO, QS/GR/E 1619/143; cf. PRO, STAC 8/59/11. For examples of barratry indictments against informers see WRO, QS/GR/H 1620/118, 121, 135.

80 See below pp.125-7.

81 *Tradesmen in Early-Stuart Wilts.*, ed Williams, pp.xv-xx.

82 E.g. WRO, QS/GR/E 1617/186; QS/GR/T 1618/103, 144; QS/GR/E 1623/153; PRO, STAC 8/54/10.

83 T.E. Hartley, 'Under-sheriffs and Bailiffs in some English Shrievalties, *c*.1580 to *c*.1625', *Bulletin of the Institute of Historical Research*, XLVII (1974), pp.168-9.

84 M. Dalton, *Officium Vicecomitum. The Office and Authoritie of Sherifs* (1623), ff. 176-8, 193*v*-4*v*.

85 Cf. T.G. Barnes, *Somerset 1625-1640* (Cambridge, Mass 1961), pp.139-41; A.H. Smith, *County and Court: Government and Politics in Norfolk, 1558-1603* (Oxford 1974), p.145; Hartley, 'Under-sheriffs and Bailiffs', p.171.

86 WRO, QS/GR/M 1620/188; QS/GR/E 1627/172; PRO, STAC 8/287/7.

87 Under-bailiffs were subordinates employed on a regular basis to help the head bailiff perform his work; they were sometimes his sons or other relatives: see, for example, WRO, QS/GR/T 1617/149; and cf. Hartley, 'Under-sheriffs and Bailiffs', p.169. Special bailiffs were men sworn in for particular tasks; their employment was theoretically illegal, but Dalton thought they often had to be used because individuals on whom writs were to be served tended to make themselves scarce if they recognized a bailiff: *Officium Vicecomitum*, f.178.

88 For the nature and condition of returns of bailiffs see *Wilts. QS & Assizes, 1736*, ed Fowle, p.xx.

89 E.g. WRO, QS/GR/E 1624/127, 120; cf. QS/GR/H 1624/118 (barratry). QS/GR/T 1622/100; QS/GR/E 1623/226 (forgery, falsification). Extortion often incidentally involved forgery and falsification.

90 E.g. WRO, QS/GR/H 1615/100-104; QS/GR/M 1617/108, 109, 111-14; QS/GR/T 1616/149; QS/GR/M 1624/146; PRO, STAC 8/296/16; 8/145/17; 8/23/8.

91 WRO, QS/GR/T 1617/167; cf. QS/GR/M 1617/108, 109, 111-14.

92 PRO, STAC 8/23/8; cf. STAC 8/59/11, m.1.

93 WRO, QS/GR/T 1617/167.

94 E.g. ibid., QS/GR/E 1617/123, 136; QS/GR/T 1617/98; QS/GR/H 1624/85 (assault). QS/GR/T 1622/99; QS/GR/M 1617/110 (taking goods and animals). QS/GR/H 1621/133; QS/GR/M 1624/132 (false imprisonment, etc.). QS/GR/E 1617/149; QS/GR/M 1617/122 (drunkenness, etc.).

95 E.g. ibid., QS/GR/M 1617/108-13. The justices sometimes complained that writs of *certiorari* limited their powers: *APC 1619-1621*, p.42.

96 In 1618, for example, the county gaoler allowed Elididas Clifford, in trouble for extortion, to go free: WRO, QS/GR/E 1618/130.

97 Dalton, *Officium Vicecomitum*, ff. 169v-71, 174. Cf. Barnes, *Somerset*, p.141; Hartley, 'Under-sheriffs and Bailiffs', pp.164-5.

98 Jones, *Chancery*, pp.269-80; J.P. Dawson, *A History of Lay Judges* (Cambridge, Mass 1960), pp.163-70.

99 Cf. R.H. Helmholz, *Marriage Litigation in Medieval England* (Cambridge 1974), pp.101, 137. It is common to find act book references indicating that certain suits were *sub spe concordie, in tractatu pacis* or *concordata* (e.g. Salisbury DRO, B/ABI 41, 24/1/1615, *Maurice* v *Walker*; B/ABI 41, 14/3/1615, *Randall* v *Randall*; B/ABI 43, 9/11/1616, *Hacker* v *Selman*); unfortunately, the entry of such notes was too sporadic to permit an estimate of the proportion of suits dealt with in this way.

100 E.g. PRO, STAC 8/23/8, answer (debt suits); C 2/Jas I, bundle B 18/59, m. 2 (actions of battery, etc.); Salisbury DRO, B/DB 39, f. 14 (action of defamation); B/DB 39, f. 112 (action of trespass); B/DB 41, f. 94; B/DB 43, f. 20 (nature of actions unspecified). Again, it is unfortunately not possible to estimate what proportion of actions were settled by such means.

101 E.g. WRO, QS/GR/M 1626/115; *Records of Wilts*, ed Cunnington, p.96; and see above p.121. The Act 43 Eliz. I, c.7, though potentially severe towards poor trespassers, enabled justices to deal with certain trespasses relatively informally: see, for example, WRO, QS/GR/H 1619/197.

102 Salisbury DRO, B/DB 41, ff. 14v-15.

103 One of the best sources of information about arbitration procedures are church court deposition books; they do not refer only to the settlement of ecclesiastical causes. The features noted in the text are illustrated in Salisbury DRO, B/DB 28, f. 67; B/DB 30, ff. 54v-55; B/DB 32, ff. 155v-56; B/DB 33, ff. 20v-21, 178v; B/DB 34, ff. 40v-43; B/DB 39, ff. 61v-62, 64, 111v; B/DB 41, ff. 94-5, 99; B/DB 43, ff. 10, 20 sqq. Cf. PRO, STAC 8/156/4, mm. 9, 10.

104 E.g. Salisbury DRO, B/DB 33, f. 180; B/DB 34, f. 17; B/DB 36, ff. 84v, 140v, 142v, 144.

105 E.g. WRO, QS/GR/H 1617/186; QS/GR/H 1628/144. Cf. J. Samaha, *Law and Order in Historical Perspective: the Case of Elizabethan Essex* (New York 1974), pp.46-7.

106 Salisbury DRO, D/AB 39, f. 52; WRO, QS/GR/E 1619/173; QS/GR/E 1613/208; QS/GR/E 1617/142; QS/GR/T 1650, examinations, etc., contemporary number 2; QS/GR/H 1632/94. Cf. QS/GR/M 1624/167; QS/GR/M 1628/149.

107 E.g. WRO, QS/GR/M 1624/111, 177; QS/GR/M 1628/95, 148.

108 E.g. WRO, QS/GR/M 1616/156; QS/GR/E 1624/173.

109 E.g. Salisbury DRO, B/DB 32, f. 72; WRO, QS/GR/T 1628/145; and see below p.134.

110 WRO, QS/GR/H 1622/94, 153; QS/GR/M 1616/145.

111 The quarter sessions indictments for the year 1616, for example, show a virtually 100 per cent correspondence.

112 Samaha, *Law and Order*, p.46.

113 J.S. Cockburn, 'Early-Modern Assize Records as Historical Evidence', *Jnl of the Soc. of Archivists*, V (1975), pp.220-28. Though Cockburn is writing specifically about assize indictments, much of what he has to say is relevant to the records of the Wiltshire quarter sessions.

114 These documents are described and their origin discussed in *Wilts. QS & Assizes, 1736*, ed Fowle, pp.xxxi-xxxii, xxxv.

115 The quarter sessions roll for Hilary 1623, including the depositions, is missing. On the files for the other 11 sample sessions are 33 larceny indictments for which no depositions are available and which are ignored in the following pages.

116 Accessories, who in fact appeared on indictments only rarely, are for the sake of brevity ignored.

117 The relevant indictments and depositions are: WRO, QS/GR/M 1616/135, 143; QS/GR/E 1619/120, 121, 175; QS/GR/M 1619/144, 158; QS/GR/E 1623/142, 208; QS/GR/ T 1623/97, 149; QS/GR/M 1623/124, 180, 111, 189, 121, 192.

118 WRO, QS/GR/H 1616/117, 135; QS/GR/E 1616/131, 196, 121-4, 173-8, 133, 180, 134, 171, 128, 190, 192-4; QS/GR/T 1616/102, 151, 103, 104, 152, 106, 140; QS/GR/M 1616/133, 156, 131, 132, 154 (cf. QS/GR/H 1622/163; Salisbury DRO, B/DB 34, ff. 172-3; B/DB 36, f.77); QS/GR/H 1619/115, 166; QS/GR/E 1619/122, 174, 129, 130, 176, 133, 134, 173; QS/GR/T 1619/120, 192, 119, 202; QS/GR/E 1623/124-6, 196, 197, 127, 213, 128, 211, 129, 195, 130, 194, 132, 202, 133, 216, 138, 200, 139, 193, 140, 204, 142, 208, 143, 144, 201; QS/GR/T 1623/99, 151; QS/GR/M 1623/115, 179, 122, 173.

119 Cf. A.D.J. Macfarlane, *Witchcraft in Tudor and Stuart England* (1970), p.168. Virtually nothing is at present known in detail about the geographical patterning of social relationships in early-modern England, but it would be facile to assume that the parish boundary, which historians have frequently treated as a definer of 'community', was an impassable barrier to neighbourly relations: cf. P. Laslett, *The World We Have Lost* (2nd edn 1971), pp.82-3; D.G. Hey, *An English Rural Community: Myddle under the Tudors and Stuarts* (Leicester 1974), pp.190-91. On the basis of a microscopic study of a group of well-documented parishes, it may ultimately be possible to plot social networks.

120 WRO, QS/GR/H 1616/100, 142, 103-5, 136, 107, 140, 108, 109, 137, 110, 111, 138, 112-15, 132; QS/GR/E 1616/125-7, 170, 129, 188, 128, 130, 190, 192-4, 135, 172; QS/GR/T 1616/97, 148, 101, 146, (cf. QS/GR/H 1620/105, 196); QS/GR/T 1616/100, 147, 105, 149; QS/GR/M 1616/125, 126, 146, 127, 128, 144, 130, 157; QS/GR/H 1619/111, 175, 112, 171, 113, 163, 164, 114, 172; QS/GR/M 1619/145, 157; QS/GR/E 1623/131, 198, 135, 217, 136, 191, 154, 203; QS/GR/T 1623/94, 95, 147, 96, 143, 98, 153, 113, 145; QS/GR/M 1623/ 104, 196, 200, 105, 194, 106, 107, 196, 108, 188, 113, 172, 114, 186, 116, 193, 117, 195, 120, 185, 124, 180.

121 Ibid., QS/GR/H 1616/132.

122 Ibid., QS/GR/H 1616/116, 133; QS/GR/E 1616/121-4, 173-8, 134, 171, 136, 181, 132, 182-4; QS/GR/T 1616/103, 104, 145; QS/GR/M 1616/129, 152; QS/GR/H 1619/100-105, 169; QS/GR/E 1619/120, 121, 175, 123-5, 169, 171, 145, 172; QS/GR/T 1619/121, 193; QS/GR/M 1619/142, 143, 156; QS/GR/E 1623/125, 196, 134, 199, 140, 204; QS/GR/M 1623/118, 176-8. The evidence of indictments is probably an exceedingly uncertain guide to the incidence of thefts by servants. The law relating to larceny committed against a master or mistress was very complex (see Dalton, *Countrey Justice*, pp.239-40); in any case, since masters had power of correction over servants, many minor thefts were probably treated as matters of household discipline.

123 WRO, QS/GR/E 1616/171.

124 On the institution of service see Laslett, *The World We Have Lost*, p.15; A.D.J. Macfarlane, *The Family Life of Ralph Josselin* (Cambridge 1970), pp.205-10.

125 As to what follows, it is recognized that a variety of agencies — prosecutors and witnesses, individual justices and the bench as a whole, grand jurymen, petty jurymen, possibly the clerk of the peace, sometimes people who knew the alleged criminal and felt moved to send in petitions or certificates of good or bad character — influenced the fate of any individual before the court, and clamour for investigation. The suggestion here is simply that a rough parallel can be drawn between the treatment of accused people in court and attitudes in the parishes.

126 Two of the local group were hanged; none of the servants; and seven of the outsiders, though one other member of this group suffered *peine forte et dure* for refusing to plead. The proportion of servants and outsiders indicted for capital offences was roughly the same; the proportion of locals was rather smaller — but this may reflect a deliberate undervaluing of goods.

127 WRO, QS/GR/H 1619/171, 205; cf. QS/GR/T 1619/206; QS/GR/E 1623/215, 245.

128 Ibid., QS/GR/H 1619/165; QS/GR/E 1619/181; QS/GR/M 1619/153; QS/GR/E 1623/214.

129 Ibid., QS/GR/H 1616/134, 203; QS/GR/E 1616/191, 197; QS/GR/T 1616/143, 144, 150, 142; cf. QS/GR/M 1620/196; QS/GR/M 1616/145; QS/GR/E 1619/170; QS/GR/T 1619/197, 204; QS/GR/M 1619/152; QS/GR/E 1623/192, 207, 212; QS/GR/T 1623/148, 154 (locals). QS/GR/H 1616/139; QS/GR/E 1619/167, 168, 170, 182; QS/GR/T 1623/144 (servants). QS/GR/E 1616/186, 187, 195; QS/GR/T 1619/196, 217; QS/GR/T 1623/150; QS/GR/M 1623/174 (outsiders).

130 At least a further two of the outsiders, though they escaped indictment, were sent to the house of correction: ibid., QS/GR/E 1616/187; QS/GR/T 1619/196, 217.

131 G.D. Ramsay, *The Wiltshire Woollen Industry in the sixteenth and seventeenth Centuries* (Oxford 1943), ch. 5, *passim*.

132 WRO, 653/1, 18/5/1583; QS/GR/T 1606/43; QS/GR/H 1621/129, 176; QS/GR/T 1623/106; Salisbury DRO, B/ABO 6, f. 4v.

133 WRO, QS/GR/E 1623/138, 200.

134 Ibid., QS/GR/M 1620/153, 201; QS/GR/E 1616/121-4, 173-8. Because depositions did not necessarily record previous offences or suspected offences, it is not possible to say to what proportion of prosecutions these ideas are relevant.

135 Macfarlane, *Witchcraft*, pp.168-76, 205-6.

136 WRO, 288/1 (unfoliated volume), court baron, 8 Oct. 14 Jas I; view of frankpledge, 29 Sept. 21 Jas. I. In 1625 it was said that 'a great company of poor impotent people' had to dwell in barns and outhouses in the parish: WRO, QS/GR/E 1625/139.

137 Cf. J. Walter and K. Wrightson, 'Dearth and the Social Order in early-modern England', *Past & Present*, LXXI (1976), p.25.

Chapter 6:

1 Unless otherwise stated, the primary sources upon which this essay is based are housed in the Castle, Chester. I am grateful to Mr K.V. Thomas for pointing me towards this kind of study and to Peter Hall for his careful reading of earlier drafts. Errors are mine.

2 E.g. J. Bond, *A complete guide for Justices of Peace* (1685); R. Chamberlain, *The Complete Justice* (1681); and, better known, Dalton, *Countrey Justice* (5th edn 1697) and Lambard, *Eirenarcha* (2nd edn 1591).

3 Dalton, *Countrey Justice*, pp.205, 385.

4 E.g. ibid., pp.413-14; W. Nelson, *The Office and Authority of a Justice of Peace* (5th edn 1715), p.594.

5 W. Lambard, *The duties of Constables, Borsholders, Tythingmen, and such other low and lay Ministers of the Peace* (2nd edn 1619), pp.28-9.

6 E.g. QS files, Oct. 1618, no. 40.

7 For a brief, but reasoned, discussion of travelling criminals in general see the introduction to *The Elizabethan Underworld*, ed A.V. Judges (repr. 1965).

8 For a statistical picture of Cheshire crime in selected 17th-century periods see T.C. Curtis, 'Some Aspects of the History of Crime in Seventeenth-Century England' (Manchester University Ph.D. thesis, 1973), pp.56-70.

9 QS files, Apr. 1680, no. 62. For other very similar cases see ibid., Oct. 1684, no. 77; Oct. 1680, no. 86.

10 Ibid., Jan. 1610, no. 25.

11 Ibid., Jan. 1682, no. 80. For other cases in which economic tension played a part see ibid., Apr. 1680, no. 43; Oct. 1610, no. 4; Jan. 1680, no. 69.

12 Ibid., Jan. 1682, no. 93.

13 Ibid., no. 116.

14 Cf. R.C. Cobb, *Reactions to the French Revolution* (Oxford 1972), p.172: 'Fairs were, of course, further occasions for violence arising out of drunkenness, as well as for crimes of every description'.

15 QS files, July 1680, no. 79.

16 Ibid., Oct. 1684, no. 63. For further discussion of the case see ibid., no. 117.

17 Ibid., Jan. 1611, no. 22.

18 Ibid., Jan. 1682, no. 53.

19 E.g. R. Baxter, *The Autobiography of Richard Baxter* (Everyman edn 1931), pp.2-6. Baxter's own family was the object of control, of course.

20 E.g. M. Campbell, *The English Yeoman under Elizabeth and the Early Stuarts* (2nd edn 1960), pp.253-4, 282.

21 QS files, Jan. 1610, no. 25.

22 Ibid., Jan. 1682, no. 93.

23 Ibid., Oct. 1610, no. 4.

24 Ibid., Oct. 1680, no. 11.

25 Ibid., Jan. 1684, no. 93.

26 Ibid., Oct. 1684, no. 116.

27 Ibid., Jan. 1610, no. 24.

28 Ibid., Jan. 1611, nos 3-13. The parish constable was present at the fracas as a Calverly supporter.

29 E.g. ibid., Apr. 1610, no. 3; Jan. 1611, no. 28.

30 Ibid., July 1610, no. 13; Oct. 1610, no. 6.

31 QS Book, 5a, pp.35, 36; 3a, pp.127-8.

32 For a similar case see QS files, Apr. 1610, no. 9. See also ibid., Oct. 1680, no. 43.

33 E.g. QS files, Jan. 1611, no. 28.

34 Ibid., Oct. 1610, no. 2.

35 Ibid., Jan. 1611, no. 32.

36 Ibid., Jan. 1610, nos 30, 35.

37 Ibid., nos 36-38.

38 See, for example, Bellamy, *Crime in the Later Middle Ages*, pp.117-19.

39 Thomas, *Religion and Magic*, p.154.

40 QS files, Apr. 1680, no. 98.

41 Ibid., Oct. 1682, no. 58.

42 Ibid., July 1680, no. 24. There are further references to a wiseman in ibid., Oct. 1681, no. 78, but he is not identified. Again he seems to have been providing much the same kind of service.

43 QS Book, 13a, Jan. 1682 (unpaginated); QS files, Jan. 1682, no. 97.
44 QS files, Jan. 1610, no. 42; QS Book, 5a, p.22.
45 QS Book, 13a, Oct. 1684; QS files, Oct. 1684, no. 138.
46 QS files, Jan. 1682, no. 3.
47 Chesh. Friends Sufferings, E.F.C. 1/10/1 (unpaginated).
48 QS Book, 13a, Jan. 1682. They regarded Sir Robt Leicester as their other chief opponent (Chesh. Friends Sufferings, E.F.C. 1/10/1) and it seems likely that it was a Quaker who was involved in abusing him on the occasion of his death: QS files, Oct. 1684, no. 1.
49 E.g. E.G. Dowdell, *A Hundred Years of Quarter Sessions. The Government of Middlesex from 1660 to 1760* (Cambridge 1932), pp.31-2.
50 Ches. Society of Friends, Copies of Epistles, E.F.C. 1/30, p.48.
51 W.L.M. Lee, *A History of Police in England* (1901), p.84; more recently, Radzinowicz, *History*, I, p.28 and Cockburn, *Assizes*, pp. 102-7.
52 Chesh. Friends Sufferings, E.F.C. 1/10/1.
53 QS files, Jan. 1682, nos 3, 4.
54 Ches. Soc. of Friends, Quarterly Men's Meeting, E.F.C. 1/1/1, 2 Jan. 1685 (unpaginated).
55 Curtis, 'Crime in Seventeenth-Century England', pp.38, 65. It should be pointed out that the onslaught on the Quakers was paralleled by an attack on Catholic recusants and thus a number of the constables were probably suspected of Catholic sympathies. This does not, of course, alter the argument in substance.
56 Ches. Soc. of Friends, Quarterly Men's Meeting, E.F.C. 1/1/1, 1 Mar. 1680.
57 QS files, July 1682, no. 116. See also ibid., Oct. 1680, no. 43. Cf. Bellamy, *Crime in the Later Middle Ages*, p.69.
58 QS files, July 1614, no. 65.
59 See ibid., Apr. 1684, no. 83 for another similar case.
60 See above p.138.
61 QS files, Jan. 1610, no. 25.
62 See above p.136.
63 QS files, Jan. 1682, no. 93.
64 This paragraph is based on four depositions collected in QS files, Oct. 1680, no. 86.
65 E.g. QS files, Oct. 1614, no. 47; Oct. 1648, nos 126-8; Apr. 1684, no.108.
66 Ibid., July 1684, no. 141.
67 On the question of violence against the authorities in the late medieval period see Bellamy, *Crime in the Later Middle Ages*, pp.18ff.
68 QS files, Oct. 1682, no. 61.
69 E.g. ibid., Apr. 1680, no. 43; Apr. 1684, no. 87.
70 Ibid., Oct. 1682, no. 109. This occasion was actually the second on which Hamlet had found Turner in Venables's warren and warned him off.
71 See Curtis, 'Crime in Seventeenth-Century England', p.61 for a statistical picture.
72 See above p.139.
73 QS files, Oct. 1614, no. 15.
74 *Minutes of Proceedings in Quarter Sessions held for the Parts of Kesteven in the County of Lincoln 1674-95*, ed S.A. Peyton (Lincs. Rec. Soc., XXV, 1928), p.lxxiii.
75 Dalton, *Countrey Justice*, p.414.
76 Cockburn, *Assizes*, pp.158-72. Cheshire, however, occupied an exceptional position within the assize system: ibid., p.23, n.1.

77 QS files, Jan. 1610, no. 1.
78 Cf. G.V. Portus, *Caritas Anglicana* (1912), p.63.
79 QS files, Apr. 1610, no. 9.
80 K.R. Wark, *Elizabethan Recusancy in Cheshire* (Chetham Soc. 3rd ser., XIX, 1971), p.28.
81 QS Book, 13a, Oct. 1682 (unpaginated).
82 QS files, Oct. 1682, no. 93.
83 Ibid., Jan. 1682, no. 92.
84 For another similar case see ibid., Jan. 1682, no. 37. The man, Daniel Siddon, involved in this case was certainly a Quaker (Ches. Friends Sufferings, E.F.C. 1/10/1, Frandly Meeting); it seems likely that Hudson was also.
85 J.H. Gleason, *The Justices of the Peace in England 1558-1640* (Oxford 1969), p.4.
86 For an impression of similar type of work, albeit at a higher level, in the late medieval period see Bellamy, *Crime in Later Middle Ages*, pp.84-8.
87 QS Book, 13a, p.45.
88 QS files, Apr. 1680, nos 57, 137.
89 Ibid., Jan. 1610, no. 17. From internal evidence it seems likely that the writer was a J.P., although the signature is indecipherable.
90 Ibid., July 1615, no. 16. This is the first reference that I had located to the embryonic petty sessions, but Dr J.S. Morrill has kindly told me that these meetings actually began as early as the late 16th century.
91 See above pp.139-40.
92 See above p.145.
93 Chesh. Soc. of Friends, copies of Epistles, E.F.C. 1/30 (1681), pp. 41, 43.
94 Ches. Soc. of Friends, Quarterly Men's Meeting, E.F.C. 1/1/1, meeting of 6 Apr. 1682.
95 Ches. Soc. of Friends, copies of Epistles, E.F.C. 1/30, p.48.
96 Ches. Soc. of Friends, Quarterly Men's Meeting, E.F.C. 1/1/1, Apr. 1681.
97 See above p.147.
98 Dowdell, *Quarter Sessions*, pp.31-2.
99 QS files, Jan. 1610, nos 2, 101-11. The approximation is due to damage to some of the documents.
100 Ibid., Apr. 1680, no. 91.
101 W. Parry-Jones, *The Trade in Lunacy* (1971), pp. 6-7.
102 QS files, Apr. 1684, no. 46.
103 E.g. ibid., Jan. 1682, no. 53 (the case of Richard Rylands referred to above); Oct. 1684, no. 59.
104 Ibid., July 1684, nos 39, 94, 111. He was eventually found guilty: QS Book, 14a, p.236. It has been suggested that 17th-century assize judges used their capital powers in much the same way that the J.P.s used their full powers 'only if the felony was particularly heinous or after all possibilities for mitigation had been exhausted': Cockburn, *Assizes*, p.132.
105 QS files, Oct. 1610, no. 13. For a similar case see ibid., July 1614, no. 59; Oct. 1614, no. 53. For a third case see ibid., Jan. 1610, no. 4.
106 Ibid., Apr. 1611, no. 21.
107 For an illuminating account of one such struggle at an earlier date see G.R. Elton, *Policy and Police* (Cambridge 1972). Cf. Cobb, *French Revolution*, p.7.
108 W.R. Prest, *The Inns of Court 1590-1640* (1972), p.142.
109 For a discussion of this question in terms of assize trials see Cockburn, *Assizes*, pp.124-8.

Chapter 7:

1   I would like to express my thanks to the staff of the Surrey County Record Office for their kind help and to the Canada Council and the University of Toronto for financial support. I am grateful to Douglas Hay, Peter Munsche and Nicholas Rogers for their helpful comments on an earlier draft of this essay.

2   H. Fielding, *An Enquiry into the Causes of the Late Increase of Robbers*, in *The Works of Henry Fielding*, 10 vols (1806), X, p.347.

3   *House of Commons Jnls*, XXVI (1750-54), p.27.

4   Ibid., pp.159-60, 190; Radzinowicz, *History*, I, pp.399-424; H. Amory, 'Henry Fielding and the Criminal Legislation of 1751-2', *Philological Quarterly*, L (1971), pp.175-92.

5   Accounts of assize trials in Surrey were published from the late 17th century on but, unlike the reports of trials at the Old Bailey which are complete after 1729, they do not appear to have been regularly published in the 18th century. I have found accounts of 36 sessions altogether, including a complete run for the years 1738-42. They were published under a variety of titles ('The Proceedings at the Assizes for ... Surrey ...'; 'The Proceedings at the Sessions of Oyer and Terminer and General Gaol Delivery ...', etc). I have referred to them all simply as *Surrey Assize proceedings*.

6   For benefit of clergy see above pp.41-2.

7   Radzinowicz, *History*, I, pp.3-8.

8   5 Anne, c.6.

9   4 Geo. 1, c.11.

10 A.E. Smith, *Colonists in Bondage: White Servitude and Convict Labor in America, 1607-1776* (Chapel Hill 1947), pp.96-7; A.G.L. Shaw, *Convicts and the Colonies* (1966), pp.23-5.

11 The heart of the Surrey urban population was in the Borough of Southwark, which fanned out around the southern entrance to the City across London Bridge. Though the connection was frequently disputed, Southwark was tied administratively to the City and its Borough quarter sessions were presided over by the Lord Mayor. But Southwark was also part of the county of Surrey and it always contributed heavily to the criminal business of the assizes and the county quarter sessions. The Borough was noted for its inns, long established along the main roads that led from London into Kent and the southern coast. It was also, however, a centre of industry, particularly tanning and brewing, and it was flanked by several other parishes along the Thames that were by the mid century becoming heavily populated and increasingly linked by buildings and commercial and industrial development. Rotherhithe, Lambeth, Bermondsey and Newington, along with Southwark, formed the core of the area I have designated as 'urban'. But it also seems reasonable to think that by the mid century the ring of parishes just beyond this built-up area were also within the orbit of the metropolis and I have also included the parishes of Camberwell and Clapham to the south and Wandsworth and Putney to the west within the 'urban' area. Of course, beyond that there were parishes in which crime might well have been heavily influenced by the closeness of London, especially the parishes dotted with the houses of city merchants and crossed by well-travelled roads.

12 I hope to deal with this question of seasonal variation in property crime in future work.

13 T. Firmin, *Some Proposals for the Employing of the Poor especially in and about the City of London* (1678) reprinted in *A Collection of Pamphlets Concerning the Poor* (1787), p.1.

14 See, for example, Sir Stephen Theodore Jannssen, 'Tables of Death Sentences, 1749-1771', published as a broadside in 1772 and subsequently reprinted by Howard; and *Gentleman's Magazine*, XVIII (1748), p.293.

15 Two men complained, for example, that it was impossible to make money at the summer fairs in Surrey in 1740 because 'the country people had none to spare': *Surrey Assize Proceedings*, July 1740, p.9; and more than one man in these years claimed 'extreme want' as the reason for his committing a crime. William Rogers, sentenced to transportation to America for a theft in Kent in 1741, pleaded the size of his family — 6 children 'and his wife ready to lie in' — and the fact that 'lately provisions had been very dear' in asking for a pardon: PRO, SP 36/56, f.210.

16 *House of Commons Jnls*, XXIII (1737-41), pp.572, 585-6, 690.

17 See above p.27; Cockburn, *Assizes*, pp.90-97.

18 The J.P.s in quarter sessions dealt with an unusually large number of criminal cases in 1750 and 1751; beginning in Jan. 1752 they began to hold an adjourned session at Southwark several weeks after the general sessions to deal specifically with crimes against property.

19 At the winter assizes in 1745, for example, 3 of the men tried had been in the county gaol for 32 weeks and a third of the accused had been held for more than 4 months. The average period at this session and at the winter assizes in 1747 was 14 weeks: PRO, ASSI 35/185/7; 35/187/7 (gaol calendars).

20 *Surrey Assize Proceedings*, Mar. 1749, p.4.

21 Ibid., Mar. 1739, p.19.

22 PRO, ASSI 35/182/7 (gaol calendar: case of John Kelly). Some prosecutors managed similarly to plead successfully for a delay on the grounds that an important witness was ill or simply had not appeared: ASSI 35/184/7 (gaol calendar: case of Charles Massingham); 35/191/8 (gaol calendar: case of Charles Cosins).

23 PRO, ASSI 35/191/12 (grand jury presentment).

24 See below p.166.

25 See above p.19.

26 See above p.23.

27 Information from the jury panels in the assize files; occupations are listed for perhaps half of the jurymen.

28 As late as the reign of Charles II it was thought that they should be drawn from 'the neighbourhood ... where the offence was committed: for [they] are presumed to know something experimentally (besides what they have in testimony) both of the quality of the person, truth and nature of the offence, with all its circumstances, and happily the credit of the accuser and his witnesses': Z. Babington, *Advice to Grand Jurors in Cases of Blood* (2nd edn 1692), pp.3-4. In the 18th century, jurors were clearly not expected to know the prosecutor or the prisoner, but the modern concept of the jury had not emerged either, for if a juryman did happen to know one of the principals involved in a trial he was encouraged by the court as a valuable witness, not disbarred as partial. In a tangled case in 1739, for example, in which a man and two women were accused of enticing Stephen Freeman into some low drinking place in Southwark late at night and robbing him, the judge became very interested in the prosecutor himself, for the defence claimed that he had been brought into the room by a woman he had picked up and that he was very drunk. The judge was obviously inclined not to take the prosecutor's story too seriously. 'Where do you live, and can you bring any body to your character?', he asked Freeman. At that point a member

of the jury spoke up. 'I know him, my Lord. I have known him several years; he's an honest man'. The prisoners had nothing further to say and they were convicted of robbery and sentenced to death. It seems very clear indeed that that juryman's testimony supplied crucial support for the very shaky evidence actually present in court: *Surrey Assize Proceedings*, Aug. 1739, p.15.

29 The assize court met at Kingston at least once and sometimes twice a year in this period: 25 of the 36 sessions held between 1736 and 1753 were there. The other sessions were divided between Croydon and Guildford. When the court met at Kingston, the jurors were drawn overwhelmingly from the town of Kingston itself or from neighbouring parishes like Richmond and Thames Ditton. Some came from further afield — often one or two lived in Southwark, for example — but the vast majority of jurors appear to have lived within a 5-mile radius of the assize town.

30 See above p.35.

31 PRO, ASSI 31/2, pp.136-42 (Home Circuit Agenda Book).

32 The number of felons dealt with in a day at the Old Bailey was reported in the newspapers; the following examples were collected at random from the *London Evening Post* for 1738: 13-15 Apr. — 26 and 27 per day; Jan. 14-17 — 22 and 16; June 29-July 1 — 19 and 22; 7-9 Dec. — 29, 21 and 5.

33 For an excellent analysis of trials in an earlier period see Cockburn, *Assizes*, esp. pp.120-33.

34 *Surrey Assize Proceedings*, Aug. 1739, pp.2, 17; July 1740, pp.7, 10.

35 Ibid., Aug. 1738, pp.6, 10, 19.

36 Ibid., Mar. 1738, p.19; Mar. 1740, pp.7, 10, 11. Henry Fielding, for one, thought that the rules restricting the use of uncorroborated evidence of accomplices were 'too tender': *Causes of the Late Increase of Robbers*, pp.451-7.

37 *Surrey Assize Proceedings*, Mar. 1738, pp.3-4.

38 On the rewards system see Radzinowicz, *History*, II, pp.57-137.

39 *Gentleman's Magazine*, II (1732), p.1029; III (1733), p.493.

40 Hawkins, *Pleas of the Crown* (3rd edn 1739), p.432.

41 See above p.37; the role of defence counsel was outlined by a judge at the trial of a highwayman in 1752: he told the prisoner that his counsel could 'speak for you in any matter of law that may arise on your trial, but cannot as to matter of fact, so you must manage your defence in the best manner you can yourself': *Surrey Assize Proceedings*, Mar. 1752, p.11. In practice, however, they were allowed rather more latitude than this suggests, for defence counsel often cross-examined on behalf of prisoners.

42 *Surrey Assize Proceedings*, Mar. 1726, p.2.

43 Ibid., Mar. 1738, pp.18, 20, 22.

44 Ibid., p.17.

45 Ibid., Aug. 1739, pp.9-10.

46 Ibid., Aug. 1738, p.6. In a similar case, Carter inquired whether a man's confession had been 'voluntary, without threats or promises': ibid., Mar. 1738, p.18.

47 Ibid., Aug. 1738, p.14.

48 Ibid., pp.7-10.

49 For this, and more generally for an important analysis of the administration of the criminal law in the 18th century, see D. Hay, 'Property, Authority and the Criminal Law', in *Albion's Fatal Tree: Crime and Society in Eighteenth-Century England* (1975), ed D. Hay, P. Linebaugh and E.P. Thompson, pp.17-63.

50 *Surrey Assize Proceedings*, Aug. 1742, p.13.

51 Ibid., Aug. 1739, p.17.

52 Ibid., July 1740, p.11.

53 See below p.179.

54 PRO, SP 36/116, ff. 105-6.

55 *Surrey Assize Proceedings*, Aug. 1738, pp.8, 17.

56 Ibid., p.15.

57 Ibid., Mar. 1740, pp.5-6.

58 See above p.35.

59 *London Evening Post*, 5-7 Dec. 1738; and see *Gentleman's Magazine*, VIII (1738), p.659.

60 *London Evening Post*, 5-7 Dec. 1738.

61 *Surrey Assize Proceedings*, July 1740, pp.4-8.

62 Normally an acquitted prisoner was discharged (paying his gaol fees) though judges had the power to bind over even an acquitted man to good behaviour, which meant in effect condemning him to another term in gaol. Francis Thompson and William Bull were found not guilty of highway robbery at the winter assizes in 1737, for example, but the judge declared them to be 'of bad reputation' and ordered them to be returned to gaol until they could find sureties for their good behaviour. They obviously could find no one to guarantee their future conduct, for they were not discharged until the following assize in August. They had been in gaol the best part of a year.

63 Guildford Muniment Room, Losely MSS 1067/2.

64 The remainder were probably too old or infirm to work in America. Two men sentenced to be transported in 1727 were recommended by the judge for free pardons, there being, he said, 'by reason of their old age no likelihood of their being transported': PRO, SP 36/2, f. 22; and another man was recommended for a free pardon in 1753 because he was lame and unwell and not fit for 'service' in the colonies: SP 36/124, f.52. On the other hand, as we have seen, some were perhaps saved from transportation by persuasive and influential character witnesses. Those not transported were granted benefit of clergy, branded on the thumb (now largely symbolic) and discharged.

65 Radzinowicz, *History*, I, pp.83-7. It was Foster's opinion that 'exact proof of sheepstealing' was needed 'upon so penal a statute' and that in the case of theft from a warehouse 'The safer construction of so penal a statute will be to confine it to goods ... exposed to sale': PRO, SP 36/113, f. 107; M. Foster, *Crown Law* (Oxford 1762), p.79.

66 It is possible that some of the pardons granted by the king to those who had not been reprieved by the trial judge may not have been subsequently recorded by the clerks of assize and the records on which my figures are based may be a little deficient in this respect. But it is extremely unlikely that a large number were missed, certainly not enough to change the general picture.

67 PRO, SP 35/56, f. 96; 36/137, f. 232.

68 George Rudé, '"Mother Gin" and the London Riots of 1736', *The Guildhall Miscellany*, no. 10, 1959; reprinted in *Paris and London in the 18th Century* (1970).

69 See J.M. Beattie, 'The Criminality of Women in Eighteenth-century England', *Jnl of Social History*, VIII (1975), pp.80-116.

70 W. Hooper, *The Englishwoman's Legal Guide* (1713) pp.93-4.

71 Elizabeth Hood, for example, was indicted with her husband for stealing from a warehouse but whereas he was found guilty, she 'was acquitted as acting under the direction of her husband': *Surrey Assize Proceedings*, Mar. 1745, pp.13-14. For another case, ibid., Aug. 1738, p.17.

72 PRO, SP 35/52, f. 57.
73 A similar infrequency of hanging was commented on during the Seven Years' War: *Gentleman's Magazine*, XXVII (1757), p.43; XXVIII (1758), p.240.
74 Of course it is likely that a sentence of transportation was more difficult to carry out during the war because of the interruptions to trade. Convicts so sentenced may have had to wait in gaol longer, a burden to the gaoler and the county. It is possible, then, that judges were under some local pressure to curtail transportation, though I have as yet no evidence of that.
75 J. Fitzsimmons, *Free and Candid Disquisitions on the Nature and Execution of the Laws of England* (1751), pp.38-9.
76 Mr Justice Foster in explaining to a secretary of state in 1751 why he had not reprieved Paul Tierney, an Irishman convicted at the Kent assizes of persuading John May to join the French army and sentenced to death: Foster was uneasy about the verdict because the only evidence he could 'according to the established rules of law, admit against [Tierney] was John May himself' and because he was in any case not satisfied with the evidence he gave. The jury, however, brought in a guilty verdict and he had to sentence him to death. He did not reprieve him because the crime was of 'national concern' and, presumably, he thought that leaving the man to hang provided a necessary public demonstration of its seriousness. Now, however, in private, he wanted Tierney reprieved until he could report more fully on the case at the conclusion of the circuit: PRO, SP 36/116, f. 107.
77 I am indebted in this and the following paragraph to the suggestive discussion of this theme in Hay, 'Property, Authority and the Criminal Law'.

Chapter 8:
1 A number of people have generously assisted me in the preparation of this essay. Mr Ernst Loeb and Mr Roger MacGregor helped me with some sources in German; two members of the Faculty of Medicine at Queen's University, Dr Michael Partington and Dr Hugh Smart, took the trouble to read an earlier version of the paper; and several historians have offered helpful comments and criticisms, notably Mr James Cockburn, the editor of this volume, Mr John Beattie, Mr Douglas Hay, Mrs Patricia Malcolmson, and Mr Edward Thompson. I am especially grateful to Miss Kathy Grier for her very competent work as a research assistant during the summer of 1972. Financial assistance has been provided by the Canada Council and the Advisory Research Committee of Queen's University.
2 *Northampton Mercury*, 6 Oct. 1729, 24 Nov. 1729, 1 Mar. 1731, 13 Apr. 1761.
3 *Gentleman's Magazine*, XIII (1743), p.387.
4 See, for instance, A.J. Krailsheimer, *Rabelais and the Franciscans* (Oxford 1963), p.56.
5 *Encyclopaedia of the Social Sciences*, VII, p.579.
6 See especially O.H. Werner, *The Unmarried Mother in German Literature, With Special Reference to the Period 1770-1800* (New York 1917; repr. 1966); J.M. Rameckers, *Der Kindesmord in der Literatur der Sturm-und-Drang-Periode* (Rotterdam 1927). I am indebted to Mr Roger MacGregor for an English summary of this work.
7 *Guardian*, no. 105, 11 July 1713; I. Maddox, *The Wisdom and Duty of preserving destitute Infants. A Sermon Preached ... on Monday, April 16, 1753* (London n.d.), p.15.
8 *The Rev. Oliver Heywood, B.A., 1630-1702; His Autobiography, Diaries,*

Anecdote and Event Books, ed J.H. Turner (Brighouse & Bingley 1881-85), II, pp.258, 267, 268, 273, 285; IV, pp.49-50.

9 J. Bunyan, *The Pilgrim's Progress and the Life and Death of Mr Badman*, ed G.B. Harrison (Nonesuch Press 1928), p.265.

10 D. Defoe, *Augusta Triumphans: Or, the Way to Make London the most flourishing City in the Universe* (1728), p.9; *Salisbury Jnl*, 16 May 1737; *Nothampton Mercury*, 3 July 1738.

11 *Northampton Mercury*, 25 Apr. 1737.

12 *An Account of the Hospital for the Maintenance and Education of Exposed and Deserted Young Children* (1749), p.iii.

13 See especially P.A.O. Mahon, *An Essay on the Signs of Murder in New Born Children*, trans. C. Johnson (Lancaster 1813); G.E. Male, *Elements of Judicial or Forensic Medicine* (2nd edn 1818), pp.128-52; W. Hutchinson, *A Dissertation on Infanticide, In Its Relations to Physiology and Jurisprudence* (2nd edn 1821); C. Severn, *First Lines of the Practice of Midwifery: To Which are Added Remarks on the Forensic Evidence requisite in Cases of Foeticide and Infanticide* (1831), pp.133-43; W. Cummin, *The Proofs of Infanticide Considered* (1836).

14 *The Proceedings at the Sessions of the Peace, and Oyer and Terminer, for the City of London, and County of Middlesex ...*, hereafter referred to as *Old Bailey Proceedings*. I have used the set of *Proceedings* in the Library of the Faculty of Law, Harvard University.

15 Mr J.S. Cockburn has kindly provided me with photocopies of the depositions relating to 19 infanticide cases from the Northern Circuit in the 1670s and 1680s (PRO, ASSI 45/11-14; for detailed references see below n. 40).

16 'Select Committee On Infant Life', *Parliamentary Papers*, 1871, VII, p.774, evidence of Dr E. Lankester.

17 My statement on Staffordshire is entirely dependent on evidence given to me by Mr Douglas Hay; I am indebted to him for this helpful information.

18 Beattie, 'Pattern of Crime', pp.60-62.

19 *Jackson's Oxford Jnl*, 28 Dec. 1754.

20 George Eliot, *Adam Bede*, ch. 35.

21 W. Hunter, *On the Uncertainty of the Signs of Murder in the Case of Bastard Children* (1812), p.10, a paper first read in 1783.

22 Ibid., p.10.

23 *Old Bailey Proceedings* (1737), no. I, pt ii, p.26, Dec. sessions, 1736.

24 *Purefoy Letters 1735-1753*, ed G. Eland (1931), I, p.138.

25 *Salisbury Jnl*, 1 Aug. 1757.

26 *Weekly Worcester Jnl*, 31 Aug. 1733.

27 Blackstone, *Commentaries* (Philadelphia 1897), IV, p.198.

28 See especially Hunter, *Uncertainty of Signs of Murder*, a work which appears to have been fairly widely read in the late 18th and early 19th centuries. A more sympathetic expression of French opinion may be found in *Moyens Proposés Pour Prévenir l'Infanticide* (n.p. 1781), held in the Academy of Medicine, Toronto; on Germany see Werner, *Unmarried Mother in German Literature*, especially ch. 2.

29 *Parliamentary History*, XVII (1771-74), cols 451-3, 699-700; Radzinowicz, *History*, I, pp.430-36.

30 See, for instance, P. Willughby, *Observations in Midwifery*, ed H. Blenkinsop (East Ardsley 1972), pp.11-12, 270, 273-5; N. Walker, *Crime and Insanity in England, Volume one: The Historical Perspective* (Edinburgh 1968), p.126-7; K. Wrightson, 'Infanticide in Earlier Seventeenth-Century England', *Local*

Population Studies, no. 15 (Autumn 1975), p.15. Eleven of the 23 infanticide cases tried at Essex assizes in the period 1684-1714 resulted in convictions (ERO, 'Calendar of Essex Assize Files in the Public Record Office', citing PRO, ASSI 35/126-54); the rates of convictions in other areas during the middle and later years of the 18th century were very much lower. Cf. Beattie, 'Pattern of Crime', p.61.

31 *Old Bailey Proceedings* (1734), no. IV, pp.108-109, Apr. sessions, 1734.

32 Ibid. (1743), no. VIII, p.277n, Oct. sessions, 1743.

33 Four other acquittals from this period are reported in *The Genuine Proceedings at the Assizes on the Home Circuit, Held in March, 1739* (London n.d.), pp.9-10; and *The Proceedings at the Session of Oyer and Terminer ... for the County of Surry ... March 1759* (1759), pp.11, 13-14, 16-17. I am grateful to Mr John Beattie for referring me to this latter source.

34 I am indebted to Mr Douglas Hay for this information.

35 Blackstone, *Commentaries*, IV, p.198.

36 *Parliamentary History*, XVII (1771-4), cols 699-700; cf. ibid., XXXVI (1801-1803), col. 1246.

37 W. Scott, *The Heart of Midlothian* (Rinehart edn, 1969), pp.133-4. Defoe alludes to the perjury of certain midwives in *Augusta Triumphans*, p.9.

38 *The Diary of Richard Kay, 1716-1751, of Baldingstone, near Bury: A Lancashire Doctor*, ed W. Brockbank and F. Kenworthy (Chetham Soc. 3rd ser., XVI, 1968), pp.122, 125.

39 *Cambridge Jnl*, 31 Mar. 1750.

40 For exampe, 10 of 19 infanticide cases from the Northern Circuit in the 1670s and 1680s included a claim by the suspected woman that the baby was still-born: PRO, ASSI 45/11/1, nos 8, 82-5; 11/2, nos 2-4; 11/3, no. 53; 12/1, no. 61; 12/4, nos 88, 89, 139; 13/2, nos 3-5, 14-16, 27-32, 67, 96-103; 13/3, no. 105; 14/1, nos 32, 33, 83-6, 94; 14/2, nos 44-8; 14/3, nos 125, 134.

41 *Norwich Mercury*, 12 Apr. 1755.

42 For an estimate of the incidence of still-births in relation to all births in one 17th-century Essex parish see Wrightson, 'Infanticide', p.18.

43 Defoe, *Augusta Triumphans*, pp.9-10.

44 *Old Bailey Proceedings* (1734) no. IV, pp.108-109, Apr. sessions, 1734. For an apparent attempt to bribe a midwife, see ibid. (1745), no. VIII, p.247, Oct. sessions, 1745.

45 Ibid. (1737), no. IV, p.91, Apr. sessions, 1737; (1744), no. V, pp.115-16, May sessions, 1744; (1755), no. VI, p.239, July sessions, 1755; (1768), no. III, pt ii, p.107, Feb.-Mar. sessions, 1768.

46 Ibid. (1771), no. IV, pt iii, p.201, Apr. sessions, 1771.

47 *Salisbury and Winchester Jnl*, 3 Apr. 1775. For a detailed account from 1665 of an alleged infanticide involving several women, including the mother and two sisters of the pregnant girl, see *Depositions from York Castle*, pp.131-3.

48 *Cambridge Jnl*, 24 Feb. 1753; cf. Beds. RO, H.S.A. 1683S, 31.

49 *Weekly Worcester Jnl*, 20 July 1733.

50 *Northampton Mercury*, 2 Apr. 1759; cf. ibid., 30 Sept. 1734, 11 Aug. 1735, 2 Apr. 1739, 28 July 1760.

51 *Weekly Worcester Jnl*, 9 Nov. 1733. The trial of the daughter is reported in *Old Bailey Proceedings* (1733), no. I, pp.10-11, Dec. sessions, 1733.

52 *Northampton Mercury*, 5 May 1766; cf. ibid., 10 Feb. 1729, 18 May 1752.

53 Beds. RO, H.S.A. 1683S, 31; *Northampton Mercury*, 18 May 1752, 23 July 1764; *Depositions from York Castle*, pp.131-3; Ipswich & E. Suff. RO, B 104/1/35/67, 68 (1669).

54 *Northampton Mercury*, 2 July 1764.

55 Ibid., 20 Aug. 1759.

56 Ibid., 2 May 1768.

57 R. Mayo, *A Present for Servants, From their Ministers, Masters, or Other Friends, Especially in Country Parishes* (1693), pp.39-40.

58 *A Present for a Servant-Maid: or, The Sure Means of Gaining Love and Esteem* (1743), pp.35, 43-9.

59 S. Richardson, *Pamela*, letter XXVII (Everyman edn 1962), I, p.57.

60 Hunter, *Uncertainty of Signs of Murder*, p.13.

61 *Old Bailey Proceedings* (1737), no. IV, p.89.

62 B. Mandeville, *The Fable of the Bees*, ed P. Harth (Penguin edn 1970), pp.107-8.

63 Scott, *Heart of Midlothian*, p.250.

64 Mandeville, *Fable of the Bees*, pp.108-9.

65 There are also some cases of older children being killed by one of their parents, and the circumstances of these deaths often seem to be similar to those observed in contemporary instances of battered children.

66 *Northampton Mercury*, 6 May 1751.

67 A reasonable proportion of the abandoned babies were, in all probability, the legitimate offspring of poor parents. 'Sometimes indeed', thought a writer in 1740, 'the deep poverty of the parents overcomes the fond dictates of nature, and rather than their children shall remain with them as a continual burden, and be subject to the misery of daily starving with themselves, they will throw them on the mercy of providence, and the uncertain compassion of others, and venture to expose and desert them, with the hope that some will be found to receive and cherish them': *Some Considerations on the Necessity and Usefulness of the Royal Charter, Establishing an Hospital for the Maintenance and Education of Exposed and Deserted young Children* (1740), p.3.

68 See, for instance, M.D. George, *London Life in the Eighteenth Century* (Harper Torchbook edn 1965), pp.43, 56, 217; I. Pinchbeck and M. Hewitt, *Children in English Society, Volume I: From Tudor Times to the Eighteenth Century* (London and Toronto 1969), pp.176-8. One of the best literary representations of the implications of baby-farming may be found in the late-19th-century novel by George Moore, *Esther Waters* (1894), chs 18, 19.

69 See, however, Wrightson, 'Infanticide', pp.16-18 for some evidence on infanticidal nursing in 17th-century Lancashire.

70 J.D. Chambers, *Population, Economy, and Society in Pre-Industrial England* (1972), pp.79-80.

71 *Salisbury Jnl*, 6 June 1757. Mary Mussen's trial is reported in the *Old Bailey Proceedings* (1757), no. V, pt ii, pp.221-7, May sessions, 1757.

72 See, for instance, C. Darwin, *The Descent of Man, and Selection in Relation to Sex* (2nd edn 1896), pp.46, 591-3; E. Westermarck, *The Origin and Development of the Moral Ideas* (1906), I, pp.394-413; A.M. Carr-Saunders, *The Population Problem, A Study in Human Evolution* (Oxford 1922), pp.146-9, 169, 179-80, 190-91, 214-23, 257-62; S.X. Radbill, 'A History of Child Abuse and Infanticide', in *The Battered Child*, ed R.E. Helfer and C.H. Kempe (Chicago and London 1968); W.L. Langer, 'Infanticide: A Historical Survey', *History of Childhood Quarterly*, I, no. 3 (Winter 1974), pp.353-5.

73 For some brief observations on medieval infanticide, see R.H. Helmholz, 'Infanticide in the Province of Canterbury During the Fifteenth Century', *History of Childhood Quarterly*, II, no. 3 (Winter 1975), especially pp.386-7.

Chapter 9:

1 I wish to thank J.M. Beattie, R.W. Malcolmson, G.E. Mingay and E.P. Thompson for reading and commenting on an earlier version of this article.

2 J. Addison, Sir R. Steele *et al.*, *The Spectator* (Everyman edn 1945), I, p.7 (no. 2: 2 Mar. 1711). For examples of the confusion caused, see J. Chitty, *A Treatise on the Game Laws and on Fisheries* (1812), II, pp.1125-30, 1183-92.

3 At various times, the term 'game' encompassed different animals. In the 17th century, conies (rabbits) and sometimes deer came under this classification; in the 18th century, they generally did not, but grouse, 'black game' and bustards did. The vast majority of game cases, however, concerned partridges, pheasants and hares; it is to these animals that 'game' in this paper refers.

4 13 Ric. II, st. 1, c.13; 1 Jas I, c.27; 22 & 23 Chas II, c.25. See also C. and E. Kirby, 'The Stuart Game Prerogative', *English Historical Review*, XLVI (1931), pp.239-54.

5 22 & 23 Chas II, c.9, s.136. The limitation was dropped in 1697 (by 8 & 9 Wm & Mary, c.11), but it was still necessary to prove that prior notice to stay off the land had been given, a requirement which greatly inhibited suits against sportsmen.

6 5 Anne, c.14, s.4. Imprisonment could be extended to 4 months if the offender had a previous conviction.

7 22 & 23 Chas II, c.25, s.2; 4 & 5 Wm & Mary, c.23, s.3; 5 Anne, c.14, s.4. Guns might also be seized, but the unqualified possessor of them was not liable to any penalty.

8 9 Anne, c.25, s.2.

9 22 & 23 Chas II, c.25, s.2; 5 Anne, c.14, s.4; 9 Anne, c.25, s.1. On searches without warrant, cf. E. Christian, *A Treatise on the Game Laws* (1817), pp.143-4.

10 1 Jas I, c.27, s.2; 22 & 23 Chas II, c.25, s.7.

11 Beattie, 'Pattern of Crime', pp.78-9.

12 8 Geo. I, c.19, and see alterations in 26 Geo. II, c.2 and 2 Geo. III, c.19, s.5, the latter of which assigned the whole fine to the plaintiff.

13 5 Anne, c.14, s.2; 28 Geo. II, c.12. Unlike the Act of 1707, however, the latter did not prohibit the purchase of game; this was not outlawed until 1818 (by 58 Geo. III, c.75).

14 23 Eliz. I, c.10; 9 Anne, c.25, s.3.

15 10 Geo. III, c.19. The prison term could be doubled if there was a previous conviction.

16 13 Geo. III, c.80. The penalty also applied to those who hunted on Sundays and Christmas Day.

17 Actually, the Act of 1784 applied only to qualified sportsmen, but in the following year it was altered to include any person who hunted game. 24 Geo. III, sess. 2, c.43; 25 Geo. III, c.50; see also 26 Geo. III, c.82, ss 7-8. In 1791 the duty was increased to 3 guineas (by 31 Geo. III, c.21); there was a lower duty for gamekeepers.

18 WRO, Savernake MSS, Bill to Ailesbury, 30 Nov. 1777.

19 *VCH Wilts.*, IV, pp.160-67.

20 Ibid., pp.43-64.

21 Ibid., pp.63, 167; E.C.K. Gonner, *Common Land and Enclosure* (2nd edn 1966), p.448.

22 P. Deane and W.A. Cole, *British Economic Growth 1688-1959* (Cambridge 1969), p.103; *VCH Wilts.*, IV, p.49; Gonner, *Common Land*, pp.448-9.

23 *VCH Wilts.*, IV, pp.62-3.

24 J. Aubrey, *The Natural History of Wiltshire*, ed J. Britton (1847), p.60.

25 *Salisbury Journal*, 4 Dec. 1780, 10 Dec. 1781, 15 Dec. 1783.

26 WRO, Savernake MSS, Bill to Bruce, 24 Dec. 1770.

27 W.B. Daniel, *Rural Sports* (1801-2), II, p.388. The preferred method in Wiltshire seems to have been breeding birds in a 'pheasantry' until they were ready to face the sportsman's gun.

28 E.g. WRO, Longleat MSS, Account Book, 1774: payment of £4 16s. for killing 222 rats, 4 kites, 5 hawks, 10 grey owls, 35 crows, 32 magpies, 30 jays and 1 pole-cat. Foxes were also deemed by many game preservers to be 'vermin' (as indeed they were, under common law) and this naturally led to some acrimony with the hunting fraternity; see *Pembroke Papers 1780-1794*, ed Sidney lord Herbert (1950), pp.327-8, 331.

29 WRO, QS/Roll of Gamekeepers' Deputations; 3 Geo. I, c.11.

30 WRO, QS/Roll of Gamekeepers' Deputations, 1773, 1782.

31 Estimates of the number and type of gamekeepers are difficult to make. By law (9 Anne, c.25, s.1), all deputations after 1711 were supposed to be registered with the clerk of the peace, but lords of manors do not appear to have done this conscientiously. In 1784, when keepers were required to take out certificates, there was a rather unseemly rush to register previously unrecorded deputations. A comparison of the Savernake and Longleat MSS with the deputations roll confirms that many gamekeepers, particularly non-honorary ones, were not registered with the clerk before 1784. The best lists of working gamekeepers can be found in the autumn numbers of the *Salisbury Jnl* after 1785, although these too can be misleading since some keepers worked for more than one lord and therefore took out more than one certificate.

32 J. Mordant, *The Complete Steward* (1761), I, pp.252-3. See also *Gentleman's Magazine*, V (1735), pp.195-6, and E.W. Bovill, *English Country Life 1780-1830* (Oxford 1962), p.178.

33 WRO, Longleat MSS, Account Books, 1786-1800.

34 At Longleat, reimbursement for such expenses could be delayed for as long as three years: e.g. ibid., 1794.

35 WRO, Savernake MSS, Bill to Ailesbury, 31 Oct. 1779; see also 16 Nov. 1765.

36 *Salisbury Jnl*, 7 Feb. 1757. The writer said that this 'evil' had been going on for the past ten years and was the reason for the high price of corn. See also WRO, Savernake MSS, Bill to Ailesbury, 25 Dec. 1779.

37 *Salisbury Jnl*, 9 Feb., 27 July, 30 Nov. 1778; 25 Oct. 1779. The season for part-ridge and pheasant shooting was set by law; see 7 Jas I, c.11. s.2; 2 Geo. III, c.19; 36 Geo. III, c.39; 39 Geo. III, c.34.

38 *Gentleman's Magazine*, V (1735), pp.195-6.

39 Based on lists of holders of game licences in autumn numbers of the *Salisbury Jnl*, 1785-1799 and Deane and Cole, *British Economic Growth*, p.103. The average number of licence holders (excluding gamekeepers) was 507. This does not, of course, include Wiltshire sportsmen who took out their licences in another county or those who did not take out a licence at all, but it seems doubtful that this would affect the percentage more than marginally.

40 WRO, Savernake MSS, Bill to Bruce, 20 Jan. 1770.

41 Ibid., Bill to Neate, 10 Jan. 1770 (copy).

42 Ibid., Bill to Ailesbury, 10 Nov. 1779.

43 Ibid., Bill to Bruce, 9 Feb. 1765.

44 WRO, Longleat MSS, Account Books, 1751-1800. This sum included the cost of

beer given to the men during their vigils; in the winter of 1787-8, for example, they consumed £4 17s. 10d. worth.

45 Such engines were not totally unknown in Wiltshire; see *Salisbury Jnl*, 19 Sept. 1763, 26 Sept. 1791. But I have found no evidence that they were placed in game preserves; if they had been, the fact would have been publicized.

46 *Wilts. Archaeol. & Natural History Magazine*, XXI (1884), p.200n.

47 E.g. *Salisbury Jnl*, 8 Jan. 1770, 6 Jan. 1772; see also 5 Anne, c.14. s.3.

48 WRO, Longleat MSS, Account Book, 1782. The prosecution was successful and Price was further rewarded with a present of clothes worth three guineas.

49 *Salisbury Jnl*, 22 Sept. 1783; *Northampton Mercury*, 19 Nov. 1753. For the latter reference, I am indebted to R.W. Malcolmson.

50 WRO, Savernake MSS, Bill to Bruce, 23 Jan. 1767, 18 Jan. 1768. See also 9 Nov. 1777.

51 Ibid., Bill to Ailesbury, 25 Oct. 1776, 21 Oct. 1778; *Salisbury Jnl*, 14 Nov. 1791.

52 WRO, Savernake MSS, Bill to Ailesbury, 14 Jan. 1777.

53 WRO, 283/248; see also 383/957.

54 WRO, Longleat MSS, Account Book, 1756; *Salisbury Jnl*, 6 Sept. 1779.

55 WRO, Savernake MSS, Bill to Bruce, 28 Dec., 30 Dec. 1767; 3 Jan., 4 Jan., 9 Jan., 11 Jan. 1768.

56 WRO, QS/Order Book, 1737-55: H 1755 (table of clerk's fees); Longleat MSS, Account Books, 1780, 1787.

57 *Some Considerations on the Game Laws and the Present Practice in Executing Them* (1753), p.14.

58 C. Kirby, 'The English Game Law System', *American Historical Review*, XXXVIII (1933), pp.253-6.

59 *Salisbury Jnl*, 18 Aug. 1755. The newspaper was not always so enthusiastic: ibid., 14 Feb. 1757.

60 WRO, Longleat MSS, Account Book, 1764-65; *Salisbury Jnl*, 4 Mar., 9 Sept. 1782.

61 WRO, 332/277; *Salisbury Jnl*, 24 Sept., 19 Nov. 1787; WRO, 383/957: 26 Nov. 1787. The association seems to have been inspired by the example of game preservers in the neighbourhood of Newbury and Hungerford; see *Salisbury Jnl*, 10 Sept. 1787.

62 Most civil prosecutions of this kind were tried at the assizes under the *nisi prius* system. Records of these are too vague to allow one to identify a game case, let alone one initiated by an association. There are, however, occasional reports of cases in the press; see, for example, *Norwich Mercury*, 4 Aug. 1781.

63 In 1786, one-sixth of the J.P.s were clergymen: *VCH Wilts.*, V, p.177.

64 WRO, QS/Summary Convictions: Game; A2/4/73-342; QS/Great Rolls, 1782-1800. The set of gaol calendars is reasonably complete: 85 per cent for the half century, and 95 per cent from 1763 to the end of the century.

65 A projection based on the gaol calendars, which suggest that only 30 per cent of his conviction certificates are missing.

66 The ability to pay the fine was not limited to Webb's district. Three-quarters of all those convicted of game offences in the county between 1750 and 1800, for whom conviction certificates survive, were able to pay the fine and escape imprisonment. It is possible that the money in some of these cases was raised by 'distress' (the forced sale of goods and chattels which was customary when the convicted person was unable to pay the fine) but it seems unlikely that this could account for more than a small percentage of these cases.

67 WRO, Savernake MSS, Bill to Bruce, 23 Jan. 1767; 332/277 (resolution of the Wiltshire game association).

68 The activities of poachers, like those of legal sportsmen, were concentrated in the months between August and March; thus, a presentation of game committals by calendar year would give a distorted picture. I have therefore arranged the data by 'season', i.e. from Michaelmas through Trinity.

69 Based on the 34.5 per cent of the committals in these decades for which there is information about the original fine.

70 Webb, for example did this in at least four cases, three of which resulted in the imprisonment of the offender.

71 See n.69 above.

72 See Beattie, 'Pattern of Crime', pp.53-8.

73 WRO, Longleat MSS, Account Books, 1770-1800.

74 Based on the monthly averages reported for Wiltshire in the *Gentleman's Magazine*, 1780-1800.

75 *Salisbury Jnl*, 31 Aug. 1789.

76 See C. Kirby, 'English Game Law Reform', in *Essays in Modern English History in Honor of Wilbur Cortez Abbott* (Cambridge, Mass 1941), pp.345-80, and N.H. Pollock, 'The English Game Laws in the Nineteenth Century' (Johns Hopkins Univ. Ph.D. thesis, 1968).

Chapter 10:

1 B.L. of Twickenham, *An Accurate Description of Newgate* (1724), p.14; *History of the Press Yard* (1717), pp.1-2; J. Hall, *The Memoirs of the Villainous John Hall* (1714), pp.7-9. Newgate had served as a criminal prison since the 12th century. For the gaol's early history see M. Bassett, 'Newgate Prison in the Middle Ages', *Speculum*, XVIII (1943), pp.233-46; R.B. Pugh, *Imprisonment in Medieval England* (Cambridge 1968), pp.103-7; C. Dobb, 'Life and Conditions in the London Prisons, 1543-1643', (Univ. of Oxford B.Litt. thesis, 1953), pp.129-39.

2 CLRO, Misc. MS 185.2, pp.10-11; Rep. 205, ff.158-62.

3 CLRO, Rep. 161, ff. 173-74; MRO, Sessions Papers (Apr. 1765), Acc. 275/188, pp. 43-44; J. Lind, *An Essay on the Health of Seamen* (1774), p.331; CLRO, Reps 77, f. 149; 80, ff. 208-9; 201, ff. 314-15.

4 CLRO, Misc. MS 54.8; C. Gordon, *The Old Bailey and Newgate* (1902), pp.168-73; A. Babington, *The English Bastille* (1971), pp.97-100.

5 The best discussion of the popular demand for Newgate's demise is S.T. Janssen, *A Letter to the Lord Mayor ... and the Gentlemen of the Committee Appointed for Rebuilding the Jail of Newgate* (1767); H.D. Kalman, 'Rebuilding Newgate Prison', *Architectural History*, XII (1969), pp.50-61. The City began tearing down Newgate in 1767 to make way for a new gaol; this structure was almost complete in 1780 when it was burned by the Gordon rioters. Eventually the new prison was completed in 1785 and continued in use until 1902 when it was razed to make room for the present Central Criminal Court building.

6 PRO, SP 35/14, f. 55; CLRO, Sessions Papers, Dec. 1724; Rep. 133, ff. 459-64; Small MSS Box 11, no. 8.

7 CLRO, Jnl 57, f. 71; MRO, Sessions Papers (Apr. 1765), Acc. 275/188, pp.84-85; For the pattern of Newgate deaths see *The Registers of Christchurch, Newgate, 1538-1754*, ed W.A. Littledale, Harleian Soc. Publications, XXI (1895).

8 *Parliamentary Papers*, XXXV (1779), pp.6-7; CLRO, Rep. 200, ff. 150-52.

9 For the rebuilding of Newgate see CLRO, Misc. MS 172.4. The most detailed account of the prison's exterior is J. Earle, *The World Dismayed* (1742), pp.200-203; also useful is E. Hatton, *A New View of London* (1708), I,

pp.801-802. A complete set of plans for the gaol, dating from about 1755, may be found in CLRO, Surveyors' Justice Plans, Portfolio 1, nos 1-4.

10 B. Ralph, *A Critical View of the Public Buildings ... of London* (1734), p.16.

11 For Newgate's interior see B.L. of Twickenham, *Newgate, passim*; Hall, *Memoirs*, pp.7-25; *History of the Press Yard*, pp.3-34. For the background on fees in Newgate see Pugh, *Imprisonment*, pp.154-5, 167-70.

12 CLRO, Sessions Min. Bk 97, 1729; Rep. 149, ff. 100-108. The Newgate fees were completely revised by the City authorities in 1729 and, except for minor revisions in 1744, remained in effect until the 19th century.

13 Hall, *Memoirs*, p.15.

14 CLRO, Rep. 135, f. 171. On the Newgate chapel see Rep. 36, ff. 31-32, 214-15.

15 CLRO, Rep. 42, ff. 86-87; Guildhall MS 98, p.54; MRO, Sessions Papers (Apr. 1765), Acc. 275/188, pp.12-13, 35-6; CLRO, Rep. 50, ff. 114-15, 216-17.

16 MRO, Sessions Papers (Apr. 1765), Acc. 275/188, pp.31-2, 38-9; *Secret History of the Rebels in Newgate* (1717), pp.5-6; Middlesex Quarter Sessions, *Excerpts from the Middlesex Quarter Sessions Regarding Newgate Prison*, (1832), pp.29-30.

17 *Rebels in Newgate*, p.7. In September 1717 several prisoners recounted that they had paid 30 guineas each to enter the Press Yard and 10s. for each following week: PRO, SP 35/14, f. 55.

18 CLRO, Comptrollers' Deeds 28, no. 33; CLC Jnl 54, ff. 140, 170-73; Reps 129, f. 363; 130, f. 351; 132, ff. 362-5.

19 CLRO, Misc. MS 185.2, pp. 5-8; Dobb, 'London Prisons', pp.297-8; Society for the Improvement of Prison Discipline, *Remarks on the Form and Construction of Prisons* (1826), pp.11-12, 40.

20 CLRO, Sessions Papers, Misc. 1735; Misc. MS 185.2, pp.2-3.

21 PRO, PCOM, 2/166-81. These records are the commitment books for the years 1770-97.

22 PRO, SP 36/19, f. 199; J. Besse, *A Collection of the Sufferings of the Quakers* (1753), I, pp.479-82; A. Griffiths, *Chronicles of Newgate* (1884), I, pp.226-9; J. Bernardi, *A Short History of the Life of Major John Bernardi* (1729). Bernardi's autobiography shows that he was a prisoner by command in Newgate for a quarter of a century without trial.

23 CLRO, Rep. 136, f. 454; MRO, MA/G/Gen., 1150-53; Sessions Papers (Apr. 1765), Acc. 275/188, pp.3, 68-69; For abuses of this procedure see R. Phillips, *A Letter to the Livery of London* (1808), pp.28-38, 55-74.

24 B.L. of Twickenham, *Newgate*, pp.10-11; PRO, SP 36/106, ff. 179-80. During harsher weather the gaol opened an hour later and closed earlier: *Prisons*, VIII, p.303. For an interesting account of life in Newgate see CLRO, 33C, 'Diary of Newgate Gaol by Carleton Smith, Temporary Custodian of the Press Yard, 1717'.

25 *Prisons*, VII, p.274.

26 CLRO, Rep. 189, f. 73; Misc. MS 184.4; W. Smith, *The State of the Gaols of London* (1776), p.13; *Transportation*, I, pp.50-51.

27 Hall, *Memoirs*, p.11.

28 Guildhall MS 98, pp.74-75; CLRO, Small MSS Box 23, no. 34; Rep. 18, ff. 208-11; PD. 10.66; Pugh, *Imprisonment*, pp.186-8.

29 CLRO, Rep. 201, ff. 68-69; Ald. Papers, Jan.-Feb. 1797, 'Observations on the Gaol of Newgate by Sheriff Stephen T. Langton', pp.1-2.

30 CLRO, Rep. 218, ff. 598-9.

31 CLRO, Jnl 67, ff. 74-75; Small MSS Box 23, no. 34. On Ludgate see M.

Johnson, *Ludgate: What it is, Not what it was* (1659), reprinted by J. Strype in John Stowe's *Survey of London* (1720), II, bk 6, pp.27-33; Philopolites, *The Present State of Ludgate* (1711), pp.24-36.

32 CLRO, Rep. 47, ff. 183-85. The stewardship at Newgate was an ancient institution which has been traced to the 16th century: Dobb, 'London Prisons', pp.193-4.

33 CLRO, Rep. 133, ff. 429-30; B.L. of Twickenham, *Newgate*, p.38.

34 CLRO, Small MSS Box 19, no. 3; Sessions Papers, Dec. 1724.

35 *Transportation*, I, pp.54-55; *Prisons*, VII, p.277.

36 S. and B. Webb, *English Prisons Under Local Government* (1922), pp.24-34, 65-6; CLRO, Small MSS Box 8, no. 30; Rep. 218, ff. 645-46; *Prisons*, VII, pp.299-300.

37 *House of Commons Jnl*, XLVII (1792), p.652.

38 Of course, the City authorities had made lesser offenders do forced labour in the Bridewell since the 16th century. For background on the Bridewell, or House of Correction, see E.D. Pendrey, 'Elizabethan Prisons and Prison Scenes' (Birmingham Univ. Ph.D. thesis, 1954), pp.40-56.

39 18 & 19 Chas II, c.9.

40 CLRO, Rep. 91, f. 121.

41 Ibid., 199, ff. 457-59; *Transportation*, I, p.51.

42 CLRO, Reps 187, f. 168; 199, ff. 457-9.

43 The origins of the appointment of the Ordinary of Newgate are traced by C. Dobb, 'Henry Goodcole, Visitor To Newgate, 1620-1641', *Guildhall Miscellany* (Feb. 1955), pp.15-21; CLRO, Reps 80, ff. 154-5; 161, f. 357; 200, ff. 122-4. The latter citations detail the duties of the Ordinary. See also below pp.246 ff.

44 CLRO, Rep. 18, ff. 210-11.

45 Ibid., 47, ff. 182-6.

46 Ibid., 112, f. 332; *Prisons*, VII, p.314.

47 CLRO, Rep. 120, f. 361.

48 Ibid., 112, f. 332; H.O. White, *The Works of Thomas Purney*, (Oxford 1933), pp.xx-xxi.

49 CLRO, Rep. 218, ff. 544-45; *Prisons*, VII, pp.313-15.

50 CLRO, CLC Jnl 16, ff. 88-89; Rep. 218, f. 499. The regulations concerning the condemned prisoners' final hours are found in Guildhall MS 98, ff. 94-95; CLRO, Reps 132, ff. 362-65; 139, ff. 228-31.

51 CLRO, Sessions Papers, Dec. 1724.

52 CLRO, Rep. 123, f. 423.

53 Ibid., 139, ff. 228-29; 154, ff. 417-18; 206, f. 19.

54 Quoted by Radzinowicz, *History*, I, p.168.

55 CLRO, Ald. Papers, Dec. 1814, 'An Account of the Salary, Fees and Emoluments ... of the Officers at Newgate'; Rep. 154, ff. 141-4.

56 E. Gayton, *Wil Bagnal's Ghost* (1655), p.41.

57 *Prisons*, VII, p.283.

58 S. Told, *An Account of the Life and Dealings with God of Silas Told* (1786), pp.133-4.

59 CLRO, Rep. 220, ff. 14-19; *Prisons*, VII, p.283.

60 *History of the Press Yard*, p.60.

61 CLRO, Rep. 121, f. 180; CLC Jnl 15, f. 146; PRO, SP 35/8, f. 97.

62 CLRO, Rep. 131, ff. 311-12.

63 *History of the Press Yard*, p.20.

64 R. Andrews, *The Gaol of Newgate Unmasked* (1809), p.22.

65 CLRO, Rep. 147, ff. 286-7.
66 Ibid., f.300.
67 *Transportation*, I, p.50; MRO, Sessions Papers (Apr. 1765), Acc. 275/188, p.52.
68 *House of Commons Jnl*, XLVII (1792), p.659. In 1814 one prison officer noted that 'children have to fend for themselves' and that there were often efforts 'to hide them so they could stay with mothers or with both parents': *Prisons*, VII, p.283.
69 CLRO, 33C, 'Smith Diary', pp.29-30; *Rebels in Newgate*, p.32.
70 CLRO, Misc. MS 249.5.
71 Hall, *Memoirs*, p.10; *History of the Press Yard*, p.43; *Prisons*, VII, pp.280-82.
72 J. Stanley, *Life of John Stanley* (1723), pp.39-40; B. Montague, *An Enquiry into Aspersions Cast on the Late Ordinary of Newgate* (1815), p.1-2.
73 SPCK, Standing Committee Book, 1720-1725, SM/04, pp.48, 100; Abstract Letter Bk 14, p.67.
74 W. Bagwell, *The Distressed Merchant* (1644), pp.18-19.
75 CLRO, Reps 85, f. 127; 86, f. 155.
76 *History of the Press Yard*, pp.22-9.
77 PRO, SP 35/18, f. 141.
78 E. Olivier, *The Eccentric Life of Alexander Cruden* (1934), pp.204-5.
79 Hall, *Memoirs*, pp.10-11; *History of the Press Yard*, p.43.
80 W.C. Hazlitt, 'A Tentative Catalogue of Our Prison Literature', *The Bibliographer*, VI (1884), pp.70-75; Dobb, 'London Prisons', *passim*; K. Hollingsworth, *The Newgate Novel, 1830-1847* (Detroit 1963).
81 For example, Defoe has Moll Flanders born in Newgate and she often returned to the gaol during her ill-fated life.
82 T. Lloyd, *To the Grand Juries ... of the City of London* (1794); D. Eaton, *Extortions and Abuses of Newgate* (1813); on Dr Dodd see G. Howson, *The Macaroni Parson: Life of the Unfortunate Dr. Dodd* (1973), pp.158-72.
83 J. Taylor, *Account ... of Six Malefactors ... Executed at Tyburn* (Dublin 1750), pp.10, 17-18.
84 CLRO, Small MSS Box 41, no. 5.
85 Stanley, *Life*, pp.39-40; *History of the Press Yard*, pp.50-52.
86 CLRO, Rep. 104, f. 340.
87 Ibid., 167, f. 436.
88 The catalogue of the British Library gives a good idea of the way the Ordinaries exploited this appeal. For example, Samuel Smith, Ordinary during the years 1676-1698, is credited with 17 accounts; Paul Lorraine served as Ordinary from 1700-1719 and there are 56 accounts under his name. This practice is discussed by Radzinowicz, *History*, I, pp.178-87, and, more extensively, below pp.246ff.
89 Villette also resorted to the most blatant plagiarism: Howson, *Macaroni Parson*, p.219.
90 CLRO, Rep. 68, f. 92; B.L. of Twickenham, *Newgate*, p.7.
91 CLRO, Rep. 217, f. 497; CLC Jnl 36, f. 74. After 1752 it was impossible for the prisoners to go up on the roof because the City installed a large windmill device in an effort to pump the putrid air out of the gaol: CLRO, Misc. MS 54.8.
92 *History of the Press Yard*, pp.15, 34.
93 CLRO, CLC Jnl 23, ff. 21-2.
94 J.C. Lettsom, *Hints Respecting the Prison of Newgate* (1794), pp.19-20.
95 B. Mandeville, *An Inquiry into the Causes of the Frequent Executions at Tyburn* (1725), p.36. The prisoners' right to strong drink had long been recognized by both Parliament and the City: CLRO, Small MSS Box 23, no. 34; 22 & 23 Chas II, c.20; 32 Geo. II, c.28; Pugh, *Imprisonment*, pp.188-9.

96 *Calendar of Letter Book 'K'* , ed R.R. Sharpe (1912), pp.125-6; CLRO, Rep. 18, f. 209.
97 CLRO, Rep. 133, f. 450; BL, Stowe MS 373, 40-42.
98 J. Hanway, *Solitude in Imprisonment* (1776), pp.108-9; G.O. Paul, *Defects of the Prisons* (Gloucester 1784), pp.35-6.
99 CLRO, Rep. 133, f. 450; Small MSS Box 11, no. 8.
100 CLRO, Misc. MS 182.3 (entry dated 3 Apr. 1787).
101 CLRO, Rep. 193, ff. 151-3.
102 Ibid., 133, f. 419; PRO, SP 35/14, f. 55.
103 CLRO, Sessions Papers, Dec. 1724; Small MSS Box 11, no. 8.
104 J. Ilive, *A Scheme for the Employment of All Prisoners ...* (1759), pp.23-32.
105 CLRO, Reps 141, f. 87; 209, ff. 318-19; *Prisons*, VII, p.300.
106 It seems that the prisoners were even able to yell through the prison windows to the local publicans and have their orders delivered: CLRO, Reps 136, ff. 63-7; 141, f. 87; B.L. of Twickenham, *Newgate*, p.11.
107 *Rebels in Newgate*, pp.9-10.
108 CLRO, Rep. 125, f. 77.
109 CLRO, Ald. Papers, Nov. 1731.
110 CLRO, Rep. 141, f. 87.
111 CLRO, Misc. MS 182.3 (n.d. but probably early March 1788).
112 *History of the Press Yard*, pp.53-4; CLRO, Reps 47, f. 185; 141, f. 87.
113 CLRO, 33C, 'Smith Diary', p.63.
114 CLRO, Rep. 131, f. 295.
115 Ibid., 141, f. 87.
116 *Transportation*, I, p.55; *Prisons*, VII, p.302.
117 CLRO, Rep. 209, ff. 318-19.
118 In May 1717 the prisoners in the Press Yard hired a fiddler to come into the gaol to play 'treasonable ballads': CLRO, 33C, 'Smith Diary', p.29.
119 CLRO, Rep. 209, f. 319.
120 Such parties had been forbidden in 1784 by the sheriffs: B. Turner and T. Skinner, *An Account of Some Alterations and Amendments Attempted in the Duty and Office of Sheriff ... of the City of London* (1784), p.38; *Prisons*, VII, p.339.
121 A. Smith, *A Complete History of the Lives and Robberies of the Most Notorious Highway-Men* (1719), I, p.77; II, p.262.
122 CLRO, Sessions Papers, Jan. 1756.
123 *Rebels in Newgate*, pp.11, 16-18.
124 CLRO, Sessions Papers, Dec. 1724; Reps 133, ff. 423-4; 144, f. 321.
125 CLRO, Rep. 79, f. 216; Hall, *Memoirs*, p.19.
126 CLRO, Rep. 209, f. 318.
127 CLRO, Misc. MS 185.2, pp.10-11.
128 CLRO, PD. 10.66; Rep. 141, f.6.
129 CLRO, Rep. 47, ff. 183-5.
130 25 Geo. II, c.40; 24 Geo. III, sess. 2, c.57.
131 CLRO, Misc. MS 182.3.
132 Janssen, *Rebuilding Newgate*, p.23.
133 N. Ward, *The London Spy* (1700), pp.64-6.
134 B.L. of Twickenham, *Newgate*, p.35.
135 CLRO, CLC Jnl 55, f. 267.
136 Ibid., 50, f. 114; *Gentleman's Magazine*, XXII (Sept. 1762), p.445; CLRO, CLC Jnl 39, f. 45.

137 CLRO, Rep. 218, ff. 539-40.
138 D. Layard, *Directions to Prevent the Contagion ... of Jail Fever* (1772), p.13; Lind, *Health of Seamen*, pp.336-7.
139 CLRO, 33C, 'Smith Diary', p.10.
140 S. Denne, *A Letter to Sir Robert Ladbroke* (1771), p.35.
141 Turner and Skinner, *Duty and Office of Sheriff*, p.36.
142 CLRO, Ald. Papers, Jan. 1797, 'Langton Observations', pp.11-12.
143 *Transportation*, I, p.51.
144 CLRO, PD, 10.66; Small MSS Box 23, no. 34; Bassett, 'Newgate Prison in Middle Ages', p.238. In 1639 the Aldermen had the women's wards sealed off and connected by a single stairway in order to keep them separated: CLRO, Rep. 53, ff. 304-305. The female wards were on the ground, third and fourth floors of the north section. The keeper of Newgate had to swear to keep the sexes separate as part of the conditions of his office: ibid., 37, ff. 154-5.
145 CLRO, PD. 10.66.
146 CLRO, Small MSS Box 23, no. 34.
147 Dobb, 'London Prisons', pp.208-9.
148 BL, Add. MS 38856, f. 132.
149 SPCK, Wanley MSS, pp.26-34. On this practice see R. Burn, *New Law Dictionary* (1792), II, pp.235-6.
150 Told, *Account*, p.150.
151 CLRO, CLC Jnl 16, f. 88; *Prisons*, I, p.314.
152 H.G. Bennett, *A Letter to the Common Council and the Livery of the City of London* (1818), p.14.
153 T. Ellwood, *The Life of Thomas Ellwood* (1714), p.171.
154 This account of the 1702 events is based upon BL, Add. MS 38856, ff. 128-30; CLRO, Small MSS Box 19, no. 3; MRO, Sessions Book 597, July 1702, pp.42-5. The 1702 incident took on a farcical tone when one of the turnkeys mistook the chaplain's wife for a whore and refused to let her enter the gaol until she paid an entry fee.
155 The details surrounding the 1707 episode are found in CLRO, Sessions Papers, Sept. 1707. These records include the sworn testimony of several of the Newgate prisoners who complained of Robinson's activities. The excesses are briefly mentioned in Rep. 111, f. 208.
156 *History of the Press Yard*, p.85; *Rebels in Newgate*, p.7.
157 CLRO, 33C, 'Smith Diary', pp.63-5.
158 BL, Stowe MS 373, ff. 42-3.
159 CLRO, Papers of the Committee of General Purposes, entry dated 16 Feb. 1810.
160 Andrews, *Newgate Unmasked*, p.22; Bennett, *Letter to the Common Council*, p.14. In 1797 a sheriff concluded that 'for those who can pay for it, every indulgence is granted for a free and criminal intercourse between the sexes': CLRO, Ald. Papers, Jan. 1797, 'Langton Observations', pp.2-3.
161 CLRO, Ald. Papers, Jan. 1791, 'Langton Observations', p.2.

Chapter 11:

1 An earlier version of this essay received the comments of E.P. Thompson and J.S. Cockburn. I am grateful to them both. A more complete treatment of the subject may be found in P. Linebaugh, 'Tyburn: A Study of Crime and the Labouring Poor in London During the First Half of the Eighteenth Century' (Warwick Univ. Ph.D. thesis, 1975), pp.166-325.

2 The author expects to publish shortly a list, with full bibliographical information, of the *Accounts* so far located; this will contain acknowledgements of the help received from many librarians and colleagues.

3 F.W. Chandler, *The Literature of Roguery* (New York 1907), I, p.181.

4 W.R. Irwin, *The Making of Jonathan Wild: A Study in the Literary Method of Henry Fielding* (New York 1941), p.81.

5 M.D. George, *London Life in the Eighteenth Century* (revised edn 1965), p.431.

6 Ordinary's *Account*, 14 Feb. 1774.

7 House of Commons, *Municipal Corporations: Section Report* (1837), *London and Southwark*, contains a concise description of the office.

8 CLRO, Rep. 104, f.340 (28 May 1700). H. Bleackley, *The Hangmen of England* (1929), provides a list of the 18th-century Ordinaries together with their dates in office.

9 See his *The Dying Man's Assistant* (1702); his translation of Muret's *Rites of Funerals Ancient and Modern in Use Through the known World* (1702); *The Secret Transactions during the Hundred Days Mr. William Gregg Lay in Newgate under Sentence of Death* (1711); *The Whole Life and Conversation, Birth, Parentage, and Education of John Sutton* (1711); and his *The Memoirs of the right Villainous John Hall* (1707).

10 H.O. White, 'Thomas Purney, A Forgotten Poet and Critic of the Eighteenth Century', *Essays and Studies of the English Association*, XV (1929), pp.67-97.

11 CLRO, Misc. MS 33.9, 'The Petition of James Guthrie, 1734'; Rep. 150, ff. 240-41 (14 May 1746).

12 Ibid.

13 CLRO, Rep. 151, ff.250-52 (12 May 1747).

14 'A Biographical Memoir, supposed to be written by the Ordinary of Newgate', in *The Miscellaneous Works of Oliver Goldsmith*, ed J. Prior (New York 1854), I, pp.368-71. See the Ordinary's *Account*, 5 Oct. 1757, for his attack on the Methodists' 'boast of instantaneous conversion and sudden changes in moral character'.

15 Bleackley, *Hangmen of England*, p.260; CLRO, Reps 168, f.354 (23 Oct. 1764); 170, f.481 (4 Nov. 1766); Ordinary's *Account*, 13 Feb. 1765.

16 CLRO, Rep. 150, ff.240-41 (14 May 1746).

17 The value of different ecclesiastical livings in 18th-century London may be found in the Company of Parish Clerks, *New Remarks of London* (1733).

18 CLRO, Misc. MS 162.3, Chamber Vouchers (19 Feb. 1706); and various complaints by Lorraine reported in the Repertories for 1716 and 1717.

19 CLRO, Misc. MS 162.3, 'Statement of the Salary and Allowances of the late and present Ordinary of Newgate'; J. Howard, *The State of the Prisons* (Everyman edn 1929), p.161.

20 Ibid.

21 Ordinary's *Account*, 23 Nov. 1763.

22 For an important discussion of the ritual of sentencing to death see, in particular, D. Hay, 'Property, Authority and Criminal Law', in *Albion's Fatal Tree: Crime and Society in Eighteenth-Century England*, ed D. Hay, P. Linebaugh and E.P. Thompson (1975), pp.17-64. For the hanging itself see P. Linebaugh, 'The Tyburn Riot Against the Surgeons', in ibid., pp.65-118.

23 Ordinary's *Account*, 5 Oct. 1757.

24 E.G. Wakefield, *Facts Relating to the Punishment of Death in the Metropolis* (2nd edn 1832), p.164. The author survived three years (1826-9) in Newgate.

25 White, 'Thomas Purney'.

26 See Ordinary's *Account*, 24 May 1736, 3 Mar. 1737, 29 June 1737, 26 May 1738, 14 Mar. 1739.
27 Ibid., 20 May 1728, 22 Nov. 1742, 7 May 1740, 22 May 1732, 26 July 1745.
28 *The Universal Spectator*, 7 Mar. 1741; and reprinted in *The London Magazine*, Mar. 1741.
29 *The Parliamentary History of England*, VIII, *1722-1733* (1811), pp.734-5, part of the report of the 1729 Select Committee on the State of the Gaols of the Kingdom.
30 W. Andrews, *The Doctor in History, Literature and Folklore* (1896), p.34.
31 B. O'Donnel, *The Old Bailey and Its Trials* (New York 1951), pp.108-9; Holdsworth, *History*, XI, pp.567-8; B. Williams, *The Whig Supremacy 1714-1760* (2nd edn 1962), p.135; W. Besant, *London in the Eighteenth Century* (1903), p.534.
32 The number hanged in these years is determined from the appropriate Ordinary's *Accounts*. The number of those dying from gaol fever can be determined from *The Registers of Christchurch, Newgate, 1538-1754*, ed W.A. Littledale (Harleian Soc. Publications, XXI, 1895), which notes the cause of death for each burial in the parish graveyard.
33 See CLRO, Rep. 104, f.340 (28 May 1700); Small MSS Box 4, no. 18 (30 May 1700); T. Lucas, *Authentick Memoirs Relating to the Lives and Adventures of the Most Eminent Gamesters and Sharpers* (2nd edn 1744), p.133.
34 *An Answer to a Narrative or the Ordinary of Newgate's Account* (1718).
35 HMC, *MSS of the Earl of Egmont: Diary of viscount Percival afterwards first earl of Egmont*, I, *1730-1733* (1920), p.11.
36 Ordinary's *Account*, 7 Feb. 1750; PRO, SP 44/84/143.
37 *History of the Press Yard* (1717), pp.50-52.
38 *A Collection of Dying Speeches* (1718), pp.4-5.
39 *Select Trials ... at the Sessions-House in the Old Bailey*, 2 vols (1734), *passim*.
40 See T. Smollett, *Roderick Random* (1872), pp.547 ff; *The Life of Mr. Thomas Gent, Printer of York* (1832), pp.19, 59-60, 140; J.R. Moore, *Daniel Defoe, Citizen of the Modern World* (Chicago 1958), p.269; G. Borrow, *Lavengro* (Everyman edn 1961), pp.19 ff; and (for the story of St Legar) Ordinary's *Account*, 26 July 1745. W.D. Miller, 'Thomas Mount and the Flash Language', *Rhode Island Historical Society Collections*, XII, 3 (July 1929), pp.65-9, illustrates the trans-Atlantic character of much of this literature.
41 Ordinary's *Account*, 21 June 1704, 22 Sept. 1704, 25 Oct. 1704, 7 May 1705, 4 May 1705.
42 *A Sermon Preach'd in the Chapel of Newgate Upon the Particular Desire of Robert Hallam under Sentence of Death* (1732).
43 Ordinary's *Account*, 9 Oct. 1732.
44 Ibid., 1 Aug. 1746.
45 Ibid., 6 June 1707, 12 Sept. 1707, 24 Sept. 1708, 14 Mar. 1739.
46 *History of the Press Yard*.
47 Ordinary's *Account*, 3 Mar. 1708.
48 Ibid., 27 Oct, 1708, 14 Mar. 1739, 22 Nov. 1704, 18 Jan. 1738, 3 Mar. 1736, 23 Dec. 1730, 17 June 1747, 18 May 1757, 26 Mar. 1750.
49 Ibid., 31 July 1741, 5 June 1732, 22 Nov. 1742.
50 *A Trip Through the Town* (1735?), p.30.
51 Ordinary's *Account*, 7 May 1740.
52 Ibid., 14 May 1731, 4 Feb. 1736, 26 May 1738, 14 Sept. 1741, 7 Nov. 1744.
53 Ibid., 10 Nov. 1976, 4 May 1763; *Select Trials at the Sessions-House in the Old Bailey* (1742), I, pp.254 ff.

54 *The Whole Proceedings upon the King's Commission of Oyer and Terminer and Gaol Delivery for the City of London and also the Gaol Delivery for the County of Middlesex*, a rough synopsis of Old Bailey trials published periodically throughout the 18th century, is hereafter referred to as *Old Bailey Proceedings*. Good runs exist in Lincoln's Inn and in the Library of the Harvard Law School.

55 MRO, MJ/GSR.2670 (gaol delivery roll, Jan. 1737); MJ/GBB. 315/55-67 (gaol delivery bk, Jan. 1737); MJ/CJ.4/206-7 (calendar of indictments); MJ/CC calendars of commitments, Newgate 1736); MJ/CP. Box 3 (calendar of prisoners, Newgate 1736); MJ/OC.4 (orders of court bks, 1733-43); MJ/SP (sessions papers, Jan. 1737).

56 Detailed substantiation of each of these cases is presented in Linebaugh, 'Tyburn: A Study of Crime in London', n.1.

57 *Old Bailey Proceedings*, 30 Aug.-1 Sept. 1721.

58 Guildhall MS 6673/9 (St Andrew, Holborn, Register of Baptisms 1724-39).

59 Greater London RO, P76/LUK/75 (St Luke, Old Street, Burials 1742-52), pp.281, 323, 207.

60 *Surrey Apprenticeships from the Registers in the Public Record Office 1711-1731*, Surrey Record Soc., X (1929), no. 2202.

61 I am grateful to Malcolm Thomas of Friends House, London, for tracking down this information.

62 *The London Magazine*, Oct. 1743.

63 Tower Hamlets Central Lib., MS S/127 (St George in the East, Day Book of Burials 1729-36).

64 Shoreditch Branch Lib., MS Diary of John Dawson, 1722-68, entry for 31 Aug. 1735.

65 See Linebaugh, 'Tyburn Riot Against the Surgeons', p.90, n.1, for references to some literature on Penlez. See also the exceptional edition by N. McLachlan of *The Memoirs of James Hardy Vaux* (1964), *passim*.

66 *The Only Genuine and Authentic Narrative of the Proceedings of the Late Captain James Lowrey* (1752).

67 *Old Bailey Proceedings*, 28-9 Aug. 1723.

68 See ibid., Jan. 1741, 12-15 Apr. 1738. Although the 'Transactions' assert that Mary Young had begun her career as a pickpocket in 1727 there is no reason to believe that Gay used her as his model for a character in *The Beggar's Opera* (1728). 'Diver' was at least a century old in its cant meaning of 'pickpocket': E. Partridge, A *Dictionary of the Underworld* (3rd edn 1968). Whether she was or not, this should not detract from the skills that have been the basis of her fame in other works. See *The Complete Newgate Calendar*, ed J.L. Raylor and G.T. Cook (1926), III, pp.102-8; W. McAdoo, *The Procession to Tyburn: Crime and Punishment in the Eighteenth Century* (New York 1927), pp.232-45.

69 *The Complete Works of Thomas Shadwell*, ed M. Summers (1927), IV; S. Borgman, *Thomas Shadwell: His Life and Comedies* (New York 1928), p.211; H. Fielding, *Mr. Jonathan Wild*, particularly a New York edn (1962) containing a foreword by J.H. Plumb who regards the novel as 'a straight-forward portrait of London low life'.

70 The new terms are 'cheving the froe', 'Miss Slang all upon the safe', 'glim star', 'bulk the muns forward', 'saweer clearly', 'vid Loge', 'tales', 'biding', 'lower', 'ridge', 'the twant Adam cove' and the 'slang mort lay'. These terms are picked up for a glossary provided in the 1742 edition of *Select Trials* and it is on the basis of that, not the 'Transactions', that they are included in Partridge's dictionary.

71 CLRO, Sessions Papers, 1745: examination of James Bye, 23 May 1745.
72 On the 'Minters' see *House of Commons Jnls*, 26-7 Feb. 1723, pp.154-7, and Ordinary's *Account*, 4 June 1725. On the Waltham Blacks see *The History of the Blacks of Waltham* (1725), *passim*, and E.P. Thompson, *Whigs and Hunters: The Origins of the Black Act* (1975), pp.142-5. Bellamy, *Crime in the Later Middle Ages*, p.75, reports this practice in quite a different context.
73 BL, Add. MSS 27825 (Place Collection), ff.33-4, 79-84; 27826, f.111.
74 C. Wesley, *The Journal* (1849), I, p.96; L. Tyerman, *The Life of Rev. George Whitefield* (1876), I, *passim*.

Bibliography:
1 Namely, the works listed below of Richardson, *Court Rolls of Acomb*; [Manchester], *Court Leet*; Charles, *Court Rolls of Haverfordwest*; Rye, *Depositions of Norwich*; Brinkworth, *Archdeacon's Court*; Kirbus and Owen, *Commissioners of Sewers of Holland*; Johnson, *Wiltshire Sessions Records*; Cockburn, *Assize Indictments, Sussex and Hertfordshire*; and Edwards, *Star Chamber Proceedings, Wales*.
2 The counties of Essex, Kent and Surrey are to follow Hertfordshire and Sussex.
3 The two volumes of Emmison's *Elizabethan Life*, and Samaha's *Law and Order*. The publication of quarter sessions order books does not advance our knowledge of the legal system: *Essex Quarter Sessions Order Book 1652-1661*, ed D.H. Allen (Chelmsford 1974).
4 Baker, 'Dark Age', listed above p.271.
5 The studies below of Elton and Langbein and the various State Trials for treason; Macfarlane, Thomas and Ewen for witchcraft; Aydelotte, Beier, Leonard and Slack on vagrancy; and Aydelotte, Judges, McPeck and Salgado on the criminal class.
6 *Quarter Sessions Records 1605-1750*, ed J.C. Atkinson, North Riding Rec. Soc. I-VIII (York 1884-90); *Records for the County of Somerset 1607-67*, vols I-IV, ed E.H. Bates-Harbin, Somerset Rec. Soc. XXIII-IV, XXVIII, XXXIV (London 1907-8, 1912, 1919); *Notes and Extracts from the Session Rolls*, 1581-1850, ed W.J. Hardy, Herts. Rec. Soc. I-II (Hertford 1905); *Calendar to the Sessions Books*, 1619-1799, ed W.J. Hardy, Herts, Rec. Soc. V-VIII (Hertford 1930-35); *Middlesex County Records*, vols I-IV, ed J.C. Jeaffreson (Middlesex 1888-92; repr. London 1972-5); *Abstract of the Orders of the Shropshire Quarter Sessions*, 1638-1839, vols I-III (n.p., n.d.). There are other less prominent examples.
7 *Records of the Borough of Leicester*, vol. IV, 1603-88, ed H. Stocks and W.H. Stevenson (Cambridge 1923); and *Records of the Borough of Nottingham*, vols IV-VI, 1603-1760 (Nottingham 1910-14). Other edited borough records generally have similar inadequacies.
8 [Manchester], *Court Leet*; Marchams, *Court Rolls of Hornsey*; Richardson, *Manor of Acomb*. Another court whose records will now be more accessible is Star Chamber: T.G. Barnes, *List and Index to the Proceedings in Star Chamber for the Reign of James I (1603-1625)* (Chicago 1975), 3 vols.
9 Barnes, *Somerset Assize Orders 1629-40*; Cockburn, *Somerset Assize Orders 1640-59* and *Western Circuit Assize Orders 1629-48*.
10 The port boroughs edited by Nott, *Bristol*, and Willis, *Borough Sessions* [Portsmouth]; and the market boroughs by Charles, *Haverfordwest*, and Chinney, *Leicester*.
11 Le Hardy, *Bucks. Sessions Recs.* and *Middlesex Sessions Recs.*; Lister, *West*

Riding Sessions Recs.; Wake and Peyton, *Quarter Sessions Northants*; and Redwood, *Quarter Sessions (Sussex)*.

12 Particularly Willcox, *Gloucester*; J.S. Morrill, *Cheshire 1630-1660* (Oxford 1974).

13 Beattie, 'Pattern of Crime', and the works in the following section by D. Hay and E.P. Thompson.

14 Ewen, *Witchcraft* and *Witch Hunting*; Macfarlane, *Witchcraft*; Thomas, *Religion and Magic*; and Beier and Slack on vagrants.

15 Coke, *Third Institute*; Hale, *Historia*; and Pulton, *De Pace*.

16 Fowle, *Wiltshire 1736*; Williams-Jones, *Merioneth 1733-65*.

17 E.g. [Nottingham], *Records of the Borough, 1760-1800*; [Manchester], *Court Leet*.

18 Hawkins, *Pleas of the Crown*; Foster, *Discourses of Crown Law*; Eden, *Principles of Penal Law*; Blackstone, *Commentaries*; East, *Pleas of the Crown*. Several other important treatises have been reprinted in the English Classical Law Texts series by Professional Books, London.

19 The general works of G. Ives, J. Lawrence and L.O. Pike noted above in sections C-D, and those of Radzinowicz and the Webbs below, in addition to the monographs of J. Cobley, J. Heath, J. Howard, E.A.L. Moir and A.G.L. Shaw.

20 E.g. Babington, *House in Bow Street*; Hibbert, *Road to Tyburn*; Pringle, *Hue and Cry*; and Webbs, *Parish and County*.

21 Beattie, 'Criminality of Women'; Darvall, *Popular Disturbances*; Dinwiddie *et al.*, 'Debate'; Howson, *Thief-Taker*; W.J. Shelton, *English Hunger*; and the several works of J. Cobley, G. Rudé and E.P. Thompson, only some of which are noted above.

22 Discussed in many of the works listed above in sections A-B, and below. The source materials edited by S. Sparks are particularly useful.

23 E.g. Holdsworth, *History* (above p.274); Radzinowicz, *Criminal Law* (below p.296); and Stephen, *Criminal Law* (above p.277).

Index

The main subject groupings are courts; criminal and other offences; judges; juries; Justices of the peace; officials; procedure and process; punishments; trades and occupations; and writs.